Women's Spirituality

Resou~~rces for~~ ~~Christian~~ Development

Paulist Press ◆ *New York* ◆ *Mahwah, N.J.*

Cover design by Cindy Dunne.

Book design by Theresa M. Sparacio.

Library of Congress Cataloging-in-Publication Data

Women's spirituality : resources for Christian development / edited by
   Joann Wolski Conn.—2nd ed.
      p.   cm.
   ISBN 0-8091-3656-2 (alk. paper)
   1. Christian women—Religious life.   2. Women—Psychology.
I. Conn, Joann Wolski.
BV4527.W595   1996
248'.082—dc20   96-17621
                                                            CIP

Published by Paulist Press
997 Macarthur Boulevard
Mahwah, New Jersey 07430

Printed and bound in the
United States of America

Contents

iii

Acknowledgments

"Conflict, Leadership and Knowledge Creation" by Robert Kegan is reprinted from *In Over Our Heads: The Mental Demands of Modern Life* by Robert Kegan by permission of Harvard University Press. Copyright © 1994 by the President and Fellows of Harvard College. "Jesuits and the Situation of Women" is reprinted by permission of the Jesuit Conference, Washington, D.C. "Feminist View of Christian Anthropology" from *Transforming Grace*, copyright © 1988 by Anne E. Carr, is reprinted by permission of HarperCollins Publishers, Inc. "The Development of Women's Sense of Self" by Jean Baker Miller is reprinted by permission of *Work in Progress* No. 12 (1984) published by Stone Center for Developmental Studies, Wellesley College, Mass. "On the Open Road to Galilee" from *Jesus: Miriam's Child, Sophia's Prophet* by Elisabeth Schüssler Fiorenza, copyright © 1994 by Elisabeth Schüssler Fiorenza, is reprinted by permission of The Continuum Publishing Company. "The Passion of My God" from *The Wound of Knowledge,* 2nd ed., by Rowan Williams is reprinted by permission of Cowley Publications and Darton, Longman & Todd Ltd. The articles "Desolation of Dark Night: The Tranformative Influence of Wisdom in John of the Cross" by Constance FitzGerald and "Woman-body, Man-body: Knowing God" by Wendy M. Wright are reprinted by permission of The Editors of *The Way*, Journal of Spirituality, Heythrop College, Kensington Square, London W8 5HQ. "A Developmental View of Salesian Spirituality" by Joann Wolski Conn is reprinted by permission of *Review for Religious*. "Cancer in the Body of Christ" by Mary Jo Weaver is reprinted by permission of the author; the meditation it contains is taken from *Healing into Life and Death* by Stephen Levine, copyright © 1987 by Stephen Levine, by permission of Doubleday, a division of Bantam Doubleday Dell Publishing Group. Paulist Press has granted permission to reprint selections from *Women at the Well: Feminist Perspectives*

vii

on *Spiritual Direction,* © 1988 by Kathleen Fischer; *Beyond Patching: Faith and Feminism in the Catholic Church,* © 1991 by Sandra M. Schneiders; *Women, Earth and Creator Spirit* by Elizabeth A. Johnson, © 1993 by Saint Mary's College; *Changing Life Patterns: Adult Development in Spiritual Direction,* © 1992 by Elizabeth Liebert, SNJM; *Francis de Sales and Jane de Chantal: Letters of Spiritual Direction,* translated by Péronne Marie Thibert, VHM, selected and edited by Wendy M. Wright and Joseph F. Power, OSFS; as well as the article "Dancing in the Dark: Women's Spirituality and Ministry" by Joann Wolski Conn from *Handbook of Spirituality for Ministers,* edited by Robert J. Wicks, © 1995 by Robert J. Wicks. "Women and the Spirituality of Hope and Fear" by Rosemary Haughton is reprinted by permission of the author. "In a Different Voice: Visions of Maturity" is reprinted from *In a Different Voice: Psychological Theory and Women's Development* by Carol Gilligan by permission of Harvard University Press, © 1982 by Carol Gilligan. "The Construction of Femininity" is reprinted by permission of Basic Books, Inc., Publishers, from *Understanding Woman: A Feminist Psychoanalytic Approach* by Luise Eichenbaum and Susie Orbach. Copyright 1983 by the authors. ICS Publications has granted permission to reprint a selection from *The Collected Works of St. Teresa of Avila,* translated by Kieran Kavanaugh, O.C.D., and Otilio Rodriguez, O.C.D., © 1976 by the Washington Province of Discalced Carmelites, Inc., and a selection from *The Collected Works of St. John of the Cross,* translated by Kieran Kavanaugh, O.C.D., and Otilio Rodriguez, O.C.D., © 1964 by the Washington Province of Discalced Carmelites, Inc. The selection from *A Commentary on Saint Ignatius' Rules for the Discernment of Spirits,* translated by Jules J. Toner, S.J., © 1982, is reprinted by permission of The Institute of Jesuit Sources. Excerpts from *The Spiritual Exercises of St. Ignatius Loyola. A New Inclusive Language Translation,* 2nd Revised Ed. by Elisabeth M. Tetlow, © 1996, Loyola Press New Orleans, are reprinted with permission. Summaries of the "Stages of Faith," pages 133, 149, 172 and 197 in *Stages of Faith: The Psychology of Human Development and the Quest for Meaning* by James W. Fowler, are reprinted by permission of Harper & Row, Publishers, Inc. © 1981 by James W. Fowler. "Impasse and Dark Night" by Constance FitzGerald is reprinted from *Living with Apocalypse:*

Spiritual Resources for Social Compassion, edited by Tilden H. Edwards, © 1984 by Shalem Institute for Spiritual Formation, Inc., by permission of Harper & Row Publishers, Inc. "Thérèse of Lisieux from a Feminist Perspective" by Joann Wolski Conn first appeared in *Spiritual Life* (Winter 1982): 233–39. "Group Psychotherapy as Spiritual Discipline" by John McDargh with a response by John Carter is reprinted by permission of *The Journal of Psychology and Theology* and of the authors.

Appreciations

For helping me to appreciate the consolation as well as the desolation of women's spirituality I am grateful to my companions for many years in the Sisters, Servants of the Immaculate Heart of Mary (Monroe, Michigan), especially to the women in my Mission Unit and those I work with in the IHM Theological Project. Other friends and colleagues who deserve special thanks are: Eileen Flanagan, Constance FitzGerald, Elizabeth Koenig, Joan Koliss, Kathleen McAlpin, and Mary Jo Weaver.

A generous Neumann College Faculty Development Grant supported the work of this second revised edition. I appreciate the interest and support shown by all the administration, faculty, staff and students in my spirituality courses, especially those in the Neumann Graduate Program in Pastoral Counseling and Spiritual Direction.

I would like to thank my editor, Donald Brophy, for his encouragement and support at every stage of the project.

Most of all, I want to thank my husband, Walt, for suggesting the idea of this book in the first place, and for continuing to be *the* great resource for this woman's spirituality.

In memory of my mother and father
Gladys Strand Wolski and
Joseph Bernard Wolski

Introduction

Joann Wolski Conn

This book would be more accurately titled "(Some) Women's Spirituality." It cannot claim to be a resource for all women's Christian development. Because I am a white, North American, middle-class, academic I can speak only out of this experience, though I have lived briefly in other contexts such as Israel, Europe, New Zealand and Australia. The women who bless me by sharing their spirituality are trying to develop their relationship to God, in Christ-Jesus, through the Spirit, out of a predominantly Anglo-European American Catholic or Episcopal or mainstream Protestant tradition. Although we may love African-American literature and music, practice Zen meditation, study Islamic feminists or appreciate why friends are attracted to goddess worship, we come to all of these perspectives as outsiders. Any integration of these views into our own spirituality will be done from the central focus of our own female Christian culture.

That culture has changed in significant ways since the first edition of this anthology came out ten years ago. First, both feminist concerns and feminist theology have become more widely understood and accepted. Feminist concerns include: (1) exploration and validation of all aspects of women's experience, (2) recovery of women's history, (3) affirmation of women's leadership in church and society, (4) insistence on full collaboration with men in ministry, (5) resistance to the unique ways poverty affects women and children, (6) refusal to deny the fact or the scope of sexual abuse and harassment, (7) vigilance regarding the fear and ignorance that generate a backlash against claims to share equally

1

with men in the transforming work of Jesus. Insofar as these are concerns for justice and mutuality, feminist Christians regard them as gospel values. By using tactics of non-violent resistance and persuasive argument, Catholic feminists have been so influential that even the pope has acknowledged the need to repent and apologize to women for the injustices they have suffered from men in the church and society. Two Catholic bishops have risked speaking publicly about reconsidering the Vatican ban on ordination of women. The Episcopal communion, which in the United States has ordained women for almost twenty years, now has several women bishops.

Today more theology, both professional and personal, has a feminist voice. The past ten years have witnessed feminist theologians becoming officers of professional religious and theological societies, for example president of The Catholic Theological Society of America. Feminist theologians are now recognized by students and peers as some of the best teachers on college and university campuses. Their books are now among the best-sellers of almost all religious publishers and they contribute to the most important theological journals and conferences.

These dramatic changes have, of course, stirred a strong counter-movement which generates passionate discussion, withdrawal of even whole parishes from a communion that ordains women, rigorous study of positions and counter-positions, and confusion among people who rely on second-hand contact with Christian tradition in order to sort out the issues. All of this swirling motion of positive and negative thought and feeling touches women's spirituality. Essays in Section I aim to be resources for this spirituality by clarifying the issues (Sandra Schneiders, Wendy Wright, Joann Wolski Conn), by reminding women of some men's commitment to listen, learn, and act with mutuality (Jesuit Decree), and by speaking directly of strategies for integrating prayer and compassion with resistance to the cancer of sexism in the church (Mary Jo Weaver).

A second shift in our North American Christian female culture also affects our spirituality. In the Catholic community there are now remarkably fewer men in ordained ministry. Catholic women, consequently, have more opportunities for ministry as pastoral associates in parishes where women and men affirm their gifts and wonder aloud, "Why can't these women say mass? They certainly preach as well or better than the priests, and they get out and meet us where we really are." Thus, more Catholics experience God revealed and mediated through women and more women experience themselves as revealing the risen Jesus' healing and forgiving love. While the same revelation of God through women also affects Episcopal and Protestant spirituality, another effect on these women is more painful. That is, ordained women begin to realize how much ordination is only the beginning of the process of equal discipleship in the church. These women priests and ministers are noting how difficult it still is for their male colleagues to relate to them fully as equals, and how much stereotypical expectations of women shape both men's and women's style of relating to them as clergy. Despite notable exceptions, a "glass cathedral ceiling" blocks them from becoming full pastors or rectors of a parish. Essays in Section IV speak to all women whose spirituality continues to include identification with the "dark night" experience (Constance FitzGerald, Rosemary Haughton), and who long for mentoring from women whose theological reflection flows from personal struggle to integrate Christian tradition with affirmation of women's equality (Elizabeth Johnson, Anne Carr, Joann Wolski Conn), and who strive to resist all domination (Elisabeth Schüssler Fiorenza).

Still another change that influences women's spirituality is the fact that so many women are on the other side of fifty years old. For example, in the majority of Catholic religious congregations most members are attending to mid-life issues, to retirement plans, or to declining years. These older women have experienced profound changes in church and society in the last thirty years. Many who were oriented for most of their religious life to a model of spiritual expectations that anticipated a secure, contemplative retirement now feel like novices as they attend to theological and psychological issues associated with the mature autonomy feminists value. Thus many older women are awakening to see themselves as something they previously feared and resisted. That is, they look in the mirror and say, "I can hardly believe it; but, my God, I am becoming a feminist!"

In contrast, relatively younger women (i.e., in their thirties and forties) are so comfortable with autonomy that their spiritual "growing edge" is attending to their experience of the limits of self-directed consciousness. In other words, speaking and praying as a self that is independent and competent, they are learning to explore the strange and uncomfortable implications of the challenge to deeper intimacy that is only possible "on the other side" of finding one's true self. They feel the invitation to create meaning *together*, to exercise leadership and deal with conflict in ways that create and sustain genuine partnership and promote authentic intimacy with God, others and oneself. Fully collaborative ministry remains a deep desire and an area of creative struggle and spiritual growth.

In response to this desire for collaboration, a developmental perspective is the centerpiece of this anthology (Sections II and III). I believe this perspective is an essential resource for approaching diversity, conflicting opinions, and struggles to act in mutuality and communicate among different perspectives. The twofold contribution of a developmental perspective is presented in Section II. First, it identifies *why* communication is such a struggle: different ways of making the meaning of oneself and others result in either inability or ability to comprehend and accurately interpret others' experience (Carol Gilligan, Robert Kegan, Jean Baker Miller). For example, if one's meaning of self is that of *being* relationships with persons who favor only traditional roles for women, rather than *having* these relationships with some differentiated psychic distance, one will be unable to comprehend as legitimate the experience of a Christian feminist. Second, a developmental perspective suggests action. For example, (1) it offers practical ways to promote connection and growth such as developing awareness of how meanings of "femininity" are not natural but socially constructed (Luise Eichenbaum and Susie Orbach), (2) it demonstrates how awareness of the source of one's feelings could result in finding constructive modes of response to them (Kathleen Fischer), and (3) it helps one notice how a characteristic of many women— neglect of one's own needs and feelings—is also characteristic of some men and suggests appropriate ways to heal (John McDargh).

Essays in Section III assume that the pattern offered by developmental psychologists has always been a theme of great Christian spiritual teachers. That is, religious development moves in a pattern of dying and rebirth (Rowan Williams), death of a self that is fused with conformity to external "shoulds" and rebirth to a self directed from within in a relationship of mutuality and friendship with God who supports more expansive life and spiritual freedom (Teresa of Avila, John of the Cross, Ignatius Loyola, Jane de Chantal). For example, one can see direct correlations between the advice of great spiritual directors such as Francis de Sales and Jane de Chantal and the developmental stages described by Robert Kegan (Joann Wolski Conn). Or one could notice how the basic Christian spiritual pattern of losing one's self (i.e., one's restricted self) is mirrored in the changing life patterns examined by developmental psychologists (James Fowler, Elizabeth Liebert).

All the selections in this anthology aim to be resources for women's Christian spirituality by presenting a perspective that integrates spiritual and psychological development. From one angle or another, these essays reinforce a conviction that spiritual maturity invites us to the same pattern of inner freedom for the sake of loving intimacy that psychological maturity involves. While the focus may often seem to be on issues related to individual spiritual and psychological growth, the essays essentially present strategies for bringing into being a community of women and men transformed by the Spirit of expansive life and love.

Section I

Issues in Women's Spirituality

Dancing in the Dark:
Women's Spirituality and Ministry

Joann Wolski Conn

Why single out women? This volume has no chapter about men's spirituality and ministry, though it might. So why have one focused on women? We are not a "specific population," as they say in counseling, like Hispanics or the homeless, though these two include women. Rather, I would guess that we comprise the basic population of persons in ministry; that is, those professionally giving and explicitly receiving ministry today are mostly women. Is that the reason for this chapter? Only indirectly. My reason for looking carefully at women has more to do with the meaning of spirituality.

WOMEN'S SPIRITUALITY

Although the term spirituality has a general meaning, there is no such thing as generic spirituality. Spirituality refers to the totality of human life energized by an inner drive for self-transcendence, that is, for moving beyond self-maintenance to reach out in love, in free commitment to seek truth and goodness. When this basic human capacity for spirituality is believed to be actualized by the holy, there is religious spirituality, and when this capacity is experienced in relation to the divine mystery as Source, and Incarnate Word, and life-giving Spirit there is Christian spirituality. Other experiences of the holy would generate Jewish or Muslim spirituality. However, because this general meaning of the word spirituality refers to *experience,* it cannot be generic Christian or Catholic spirituality. For human experience is always particular to *that* human and is shaped by the richness and complexity of each person's living. This would include a person's gender, race, social class, psychological development, family history, and whatever influences one's reaching out in freedom and love. Thus, one's spirituality is deeply influenced by gender, to take just the one example of our focus for this chapter. Here gender refers not to biological sex (female) but, rather, to the meaning one's culture gives to that sex. Gender refers to the socially constructed meaning of sex that is pervasive in a culture at any historical period.

Until very recently, "female" or "feminine" universally connoted meanings such as passive, emotional, intuitive, more closely related to nature and matter than to spirit and culture, guardian of virtue in the midst of an aggressive world, naturally designed to be the complement to men; that is, by nature made for roles which support the leadership natural to men. Today, female gender identity is ambiguous because the former meanings are not universally accepted. Now that we understand better how all meanings change over time and depend on who has the cultural power to create meaning, we realize this ambiguity has a double effect: freedom to create new meaning and problems of identity and communication when vastly different meanings are possible.

This combination of freedom and problems profoundly affects women's spirituality and ministry, once we accept the inseparability of Christian spiritual development and human development. Let us first consider the problematic consequences of this inseparability for women's spirituality, then notice some effects on ministry, and, finally, indicate some resources to promote women's flourishing in their spirituality and ministry. In all that follows I assume the context is the Christian church, especially the Roman Catholic communion, whenever I refer to spirituality and ministry.

Although many women now regard as common currency the issues I will describe, many more are just beginning to function with this "coin of the realm" as they reflect upon their experience of preparing for ministry or of immersion in it. Therefore, I want to clarify these issues in order to affirm women's judgment that their spirituality is indeed problematic. When the heat of these issues begins to warm one's life, one can begin to wonder how and why so much warmth can be simultaneous with so little light. My goal is light for the way, insofar as that is possible, and energy for the dance of ministry that must be done despite the darkness character-istic of movement over a horizon into territory one can feel but not yet see with more than the blurred vision of a newborn.

Why Women's Spirituality Is Problematic

Women's spirituality is problematic for three central reasons. First, the possibilities for women's mature human spirituality are restricted. Second, Christian teaching and practice, instead of pro-moting women's maturity, has too often supported restriction. Third, prevailing God-images have detrimental effects on women's spirituality.

1. *Women's Humanity/Spirituality Is Restricted.* Most pat-terns of family and education continue to reinforce two roles for women. They are socialized toward being desirable objects who dress, think and act in order to receive acceptance, especially from males. Living for "another" is the second pervasive role expectation set for women. This usually means: submerge your-self in another's needs and interests. Even career-oriented women receive a version of this conditioning. "The other" she serves is the school, or hospital, or parish that needs to have her fit in to policy, or image, or "the bottom line." Evidence is everywhere showing lay women struggling to be supermom because they feel compelled to add work to the traditional role of primary parent, or religious sisters become workaholics because that lifestyle is subtly promoted as holiness, as living for others.

The feminist movement addresses these problems by freeing women from restrictive conformity, promoting mature autonomy, and moving beyond autonomy to relationships of mutuality and collaboration. Most feminist issues are also spirituality issues be-cause they focus on self-transcendence: mutuality rather than domi-nation in female-male relationships, symmetrical family patterns of work and parenting, justice in care for the neglected, convic-tion that women-to-women relationships are as life-sustaining as conjugal relationships. The link with spirituality is deep but needs elaboration.

Christian women need networks of assistance to help them see connections between feminist goals and spiritual development. For example, spiritual direction cannot be fruitful unless one has the ability to heighten awareness of what one *really wants* in life and how one *really feels* in God's presence. Women conditioned to role conformity, to self-doubt, and to dependence find it quite difficult to get in touch with their deepest desires or to be peacefully present to God who calls them friend, not child or servant. Freedom and friendship require significant decisions and taking responsibility for the consequences. Until women become more secure in addressing feminist issues they will be insecure in the very prerequisites for mature spirituality.

2. *Christian Tradition Has Legitimated Women's Restriction.* Christian tradition has functioned as one of the most effective means for legitimating and even promoting women's restriction. Recent research has so carefully documented the sexism that permeates Christian teaching and practice that just a few representative examples are sufficient to focus the issue. Although Jesus' acceptance of women's equal dignity and his calling of women to full discipleship are clear in the gospels, early church practice was too often inconsistent with the gospel vision. Pastoral epistles show how churches began to conform more to the surrounding culture's household codes of male-dominated conduct than to Jesus' example of a discipleship of equals. From patristic times to the present, men have seen women as the image of God only or especially when conformed to male-approved roles which restrict women's possibilities and serve men's interests.

Recent Vatican documents continue to demonstrate the church's severe crisis of credibility regarding women. Margaret O'Brien Steinfels, editor of the journal *Commonweal,* has noted how discussion of gender issues pivots on just two terms: "radical feminism" and "complementarity." Vatican documents speak with horror about a "radical feminism" that is not defined or documented or linked to any particular author. Thus it is a label used to convict without identifying the accused or even arguing the case. Consequently, Steinfels infers, the term could mean whatever is more impatient, aggrieved or egalitarian than an archbishop. "Complementarity" is the other pivotal term used in connection with the fact that women and men differ. The significant issue is not the fact of "difference," but the interpretation, namely "complementarity." What does that mean? For one official, it means that women's naturally "tender hearts" disqualify them from serving on marriage tribunals. Evidence shows this term is so burdened with a history and load of assumptions regarding the link between natural characteristics and women's traditional roles that it has become a language ultimately calculated *not* to name reality but to evade real equality in the church.[1]

3. *Detrimental Effects of Prevailing God-Images.* Women's spirituality is also restricted by absorption of the dominant God-images. Bible translations use masculine pronouns for the Spirit God; lectionaries exclude most of the biblical texts that image God as female; preaching and teaching reinforce the implicit assumption that maleness is closer to divinity. These distortions of biblical revelation prevent a woman from valuing and affirming herself as an authentic image of God. They restrict a woman's ability to use her own experience as a revelation of God's qualities and activities. They can even alienate a woman from her own experience when she presumes that "the holy" cannot be like her.

Research by Ana-Maria Rizzuto, professor of psychiatry at Tufts Medical School, suggests just how damaging this distortion of revelation is and how problematic are the consequences for women's spirituality. Rizzuto shows how a person's God-image is formed and developed, and she demonstrates the image's potential for generating belief or unbelief. Although the principal research was done with Dr. Rizzuto's patients, later research showed no significant difference between her medical staff and patients in their way of relating to God. Her conclusion draws a direct correlation between belief, personal experience, and the God representation at a given developmental moment. That is, belief in God, or its absence, depends upon whether or not a *conscious "identity of experience"* can be established between the God representation of a given developmental moment and self-representations needed to maintain relatedness and hope.[2]

Implications for women's spirituality are profound. On the

one hand, if women retain a God-image that implies a denial or denigration of women's worth and ability for full leadership and ministry, this probably indicates unresolved developmental issues. On the other hand, a woman experiencing a shift in self-understanding from dependence and conformity to self-direction and spiritual freedom can be expected to feel a strain in her relation to God if the image she has absorbed works to reinforce lack of self-esteem or restricts hope. Such a woman, in order to maintain her spiritual development, must drop that God-image; she must cease believing in that God.

HOW THESE ISSUES AFFECT WOMEN IN MINISTRY

All of these problematic issues are affecting the way women give and receive ministry. For ministry has become an integral dimension of women's experience of love, search for truth and goodness, discernment of God's presence and direction in their lives. In other words, ministry has become the most obvious manifestation of women's spirituality.

Although this was not always the case, it has become true for Catholic women in the past twenty-five years. Formerly, both public roles and professional ministry were exceptions rather than the rule for women. Most women were socialized to value primarily private work such as homemaking, teaching, or nursing, rather than leadership in these fields or public roles in law or medicine. Even more unusual was any mention of *ministry* for women, because the term ministry was considered Protestant, and ordained ministry meant priesthood which, of course, excluded women. Now, however, New Testament theology of baptism and mission has enabled Catholics to realize the universal call to ministry, and women's desire for full involvement has sent thousands into professional ministry.

What have been the effects of ministry on women's spirituality, that is, on their self-understanding as they reach out in love, service, prayer, leadership? Sandra M. Schneiders has noticed some negative and positive effects.[3] Exclusion from ordained ministry has affected women negatively in four ways. Some women conclude they are not called to ministry at all, because they interpret their service to their family, to the sick or to their students as simple "works of mercy" or assistance to the clergy. Second, women develop a sense of sacral unworthiness since they cannot be welcomed into the sanctuary to serve mass or to preach, even if their theological education surpasses the priest's. Third, an inferior sacramental position results in total sacramental dependence that is often very painful. Women speak of their suffering when, as chaplains, they cannot meet their patients' request for absolution from the first person who gave them a sense of God's mercy. Or other women weep at denial of sacraments because they found divorce and remarriage the only solution to desertion or domestic abuse. Finally, this exclusion reinforces their subordination in all spheres because it divinizes maleness and excludes femininity from the divine sphere. However, not all the effects are negative.

Feminist consciousness has raised awareness of values that can now be seen as positive and present for women in non-ordained ministry. This is *not* intended to legitimate women's exclusion from ordination, but simply to notice effects on spirituality that can honestly be appreciated. First, women's ministry has not been "ritualized," that is, that individuality of the minister has not been subsumed into an activity that is repeated. In other words, women's ministry has always been the personal service of one human to another for the love of Christ. This is so significant because women have effected experiences that are the substance of the sacraments—meals as experiences of Christian unity; reconciliation; initiating children into Christian community—but these have never lost their entirely personal and interpersonal experience. Second, women's ministries have seldom contributed to the pervasive sense of God as stern father-figure intent upon punishment. In fact, spiritual directors testify to the fact that healing of oppressive God-images is often manifest in experience of God as having qualities one recognizes from relationships with women: sisters, wives, mothers, lovers. Lastly, women ministers, generally, have less difficulty understanding and practicing their ministry as service rather than as power, as ministry *with* persons and in Christ, rather than power over the sacraments and over people. Women's experience of being excluded, undervalued, humiliated has given them, as Schneiders notes, a special capacity for identification with the great minister, Jesus, who was himself a simple layman persecuted and disowned by the religious authorities of his day, and who found in his solidarity with the poor and marginalized the basis for a nonritualized ministry of personal service characterized by gentleness and powerlessness that were singularly revelatory of the true God.

RESOURCES FOR WOMEN'S SPIRITUALITY
AND MINISTRY

Having summarized the problematic nature of women's spirituality and noted ways in which these issues influence women's ministry as well as ways ministry shapes spirituality, I wish to complete this chapter by suggesting resources which meet these needs in ministry. From my perspective as a spiritual director, teacher of women preparing for professional ministry, consultant to programs for ministry, and friend and colleague of women involved in diverse ministries, women need resources in order to *be* who they are: female Christians ministering in the contemporary church. This involves two struggles: (1) finding a Christian tradition that affirms women; (2) ministering in the style of church that is emerging. Given the discussion above, it is clear that the first struggle requires new resources from feminist theology.

What can support the second struggle? That is, what characterizes the emerging church and where are the resources needed to minister effectively? Catholicism today has fewer priests, religious sisters and brothers; Hispanics will be the majority at the turn of the century; there is a movement toward smaller church communities; ambiguity about possibilities for women's leadership in ministry is pervasive; there is dawning awareness of the interconnectedness between oppression of women and the domination of the poor and of the earth itself; a crisis of credibility regarding authority is evident. Attention to all these issues is beyond the scope of this chapter, but the movement toward smaller communities is so important I want to select it as the primary focus. Small church communities place greater emphasis on personal self-revelation, radical equality of members, shared ministry, compassion within the group and social outreach beyond it.[4] Resources for ministry in this setting include tools for self-knowledge and for the integration of psychological and spiritual development.

Christian Self-Knowledge for Ministry with Small Groups

All ministry needs self-knowledge, but work with smaller communities makes this requirement more evident. In order to pay attention to people's lives a minister must know herself, know how and why she feels and thinks the way she does so that her own concerns can be attended to in ways that do not block effective listening and collaboration. Small groups are even more demanding in this regard because ministers are with people for more hours, are drawn into greater self-revelation, have a more personal impact on others, and have more opportunities for informal counseling. In this context, Christian self-knowledge is a necessary resource for empathy, empowerment of others, and prayer.

What makes self-knowledge Christian, and how can it have these effects in ministry? On the one hand, self-knowledge is Christian when one consciously commits oneself to primary identity as a disciple of Jesus in the community of believers given over to the liberating, reconciling work of Christ. On the other hand, self-knowledge can be Christian if that knowledge is gained and sustained in a style characteristic of Christian tradition's admonitions regarding self-knowledge. My focus is this second sense of the phrase.

Great spiritual teachers, such as Catherine of Siena, Teresa of Avila, and Jane de Chantal, promote self-knowledge for several specific reasons and encourage a particular way of holding or having knowledge of oneself.[5] From their experience of mature spirituality these teachers learned that the best way to have self-knowledge is gently and loosely. Picture self-knowledge functioning like knowledge of riding a bicycle or a horse; it enables one to act without dominating one's consciousness. Guard against the kind of introspection that becomes self-preoccupation, or, what is worse for spirituality, an introspection that becomes a subtle kind of control that desires to force oneself toward a spiritual "progress" of one's own design. Put in positive terms, the only way to have self-knowledge is in a reciprocal way, in an interpersonal way—interpersonal with God and with others whom we choose as well as those we chance upon in ministry and life. We learn about ourselves, according to these great teachers, through reflection upon the ordinary experiences of work and prayer and especially in living closely with others. This learning *through* process is essential because our identity is the result of interrelationships. We do not have some kind of "true self" prior to reciprocity, but, rather, we become true by gradually facing our false operative notions that we are either autonomous or we are the roles and values others impugn to us. Appreciating this Christian tradition which honors the complexity, subtlety, and interpersonal process that goes into our identity makes me suspect that many books and workshops on the Meyers-Briggs and Enneagram personality-types are useless and counter-productive because they are taught and used without critical perspective and with exaggerated and unfounded claims for their accuracy, origins, or appropriate use.

If the way to have self-knowledge is gently, why have it? The most basic reason is for the sake of love, of prayer, which is the human experience of loving the Trinity and everyone from within that relationship. Self-knowledge frees us from projections that block availability to God and others, and it actually becomes a milieu for prayer because it opens us to the constant movement of God's presence and direction in our lives. It supports love because it enables us to value vulnerability as a human quality capable of generating empathy for others. That is, I learn to admit and cherish my mistakes as bonds with all who do the same foolish things and as insight into universal human experience. Self-knowledge teaches us, from experience, that life comes only through a kind of death: a death to the old way of understanding and feeling about ourselves and others, in order to move into a more inclusive and compassionate way of living, a way that we would not and could not create ourselves. We could not create it precisely because we did not yet have the self-knowledge to see that our present "self" was too narrow to hold the possibilities the Spirit was opening out for us through the ordinary situations and persons in our life. Self-knowledge also teaches us to examine critically how socialization affects our perception and feelings about self. This reason for self-knowledge brings me directly to specific resources for women.

Women's Self-Knowledge for Ministry

By now it is commonplace to notice the distinctive developmental patterns of women and men without rooting this distinction in separate natures. One human nature is shared by both females and males, but the meaning of this biological sex is created by social custom and traditional assumptions. Society's definition of female becomes the expectation of "the feminine." Socialization into these patterns of understanding, feeling, and action are the primary roots of the way women and men develop, according to the most verifiable research. Familiarity with different psychological approaches to these patterns can be very useful for ministry, so the following resources are suggested for that study which enables ministers to develop empathy and promote authentic maturity.

1. *Structural Developmental Approach.*[6] First, it is important to distinguish this approach to development from "life-span development" made famous by Erik Erikson. Erikson explains how each era of biological life brings a crisis, such as the adolescent crisis of identity, which each person meets with the uniqueness of her or his personality and the particular expectations of the culture. Whether or not one successfully resolves this crisis of identity, life continues to bring the subsequent developmental task, such as intimacy or generativity. Development, in this perspective, concentrates on how we resolve life's inevitable tasks; "ready or not," we meet the next phase of development which emerges because of our psychosocial situation. Women, in this perspective, have the same tasks as men. But the sequencing of tasks follows women's pattern of socialization. For example, men are taught to put identity before intimacy, whereas most women are taught to form intimacy *through* identity, especially with males.

In contrast, from a structural perspective, development does not happen necessarily or inevitably. A next stage of development may never happen because it results from the complex interaction of outer events and inner decisions to do the work that development requires. Each phase of development is a balancing of the two basic human longings: for independence and attachment. Like chicks we "hatch out" of shells of meaning (of ourselves and others) that have become too narrow to account for the way our world has become. For example, children can "hatch out" of the sphere of their family into a bigger world, or they can remain embedded in patterns of feeling and thinking that continue to conform to what "they say" it means to be a woman, mother, Christian, or good person. At each phase, the balancing movement tilts toward autonomy or relationship as one tries to have independence precisely for the sake of deeper and more inclusive relationships. Both autonomy and attachment are inseparable at every stage, from this perspective, but one quality can be stronger at a given stage. Women are socialized to remain at the stage that stresses attachment, but once they move beyond the fear of independence they tend to ease into a phase that integrates relationship with autonomy more quickly than men who are more universally socialized to view autonomy as "the end of the line" developmentally.

2. *Psychodynamic Approaches.* As the name implies, these approaches assume that humans live from dynamic energies rooted in biology and formed by the relationships of infancy and childhood. Whereas the earliest theories of this school of thought imagined these dynamics modeled on a rather fixed and mechanistic model, contemporary theory stresses the primacy of interpersonal relationships to shape the dynamic energy of personality. Another contrast distinguishes the earlier theory from later: Freud stressed male-centered issues of early childhood such as the oedipal complex and penis-envy, whereas contemporary re-examination of these issues now stresses the earlier period of infant/primary-parent bonding, and values female experience equally with male. Some practitioners notice the need to focus primarily on female experience, so they have developed a new psychology of women.

Jean Baker Miller,[7] for example, explains that autonomy as the goal of maturity is a carry-over from men's experience and implies that one should be able to give up affiliations in order to become separate and self-directed. Women actually seek more than autonomy as was defined for men because they seek to encompass relationships *simultaneously* with the fullest development of themselves. Too often women are misinterpreted or penalized for affirming to men a basic truth: *everyone's* individual development proceeds only through affiliation as well as differentiation. And this process involves conflict which is inevitable and not necessarily harmful. Regarding this last point, women need to learn to value the positive outcome possible when conflict is faced rather than avoided under the guise of "charity" of tolerance.

An example of the creative possibilities of facing conflict comes from mother-daughter issues. Feminist psychologists notice how "femininity" is constructed principally within mother-daughter relationships. Conflict arises when a mother's unconscious identification with her daughter can make a mother annoyed at seeing her daughter reveal her needs and insist on equal dignity rather than avoid conflict as she (i.e. mother) learned to do in order to be "feminine" in the only way that earned respect: being long-suffering and self-effacing. Women who interpret their roles as mothering (e.g. teachers, counselors, spiritual directors) may feel this same annoyance and be called to grow by struggling creatively with this conflict.

This is a new, uncomfortable position that women may interpret as regressive or aggressive unless they can find a community of correct interpretation and mutual support. Therefore, women in ministry need to understand these dynamics and create a community of candid discussion and evaluation of these issues.

3. *Jungian Psychology.* Because Jung's psychology values religion and seems so sympathetic toward "the feminine," religiously sensitive women often accept it without the necessary reservation or evaluation. Feminist scholarship provides a critique that notices Jung's male-centered view of women's development and provides a needed corrective for topics such as the "anima" and "animus." Jung's work is not totally rejected by most of this scholarship. Rather, these therapists and researchers enable one to appreciate some aspects of Jung's theory of archetypes while they also reveal and confront the sexist assumptions which influence his theory of "the feminine."[8]

When women and men understand these issues better and struggle with their consequences, women's spirituality in ministry can develop more easily and fruitfully. For they will be able to affirm the inseparable connection between spiritual and psychological development by realizing how self-transcendence is inherent in both. That is, spiritual tradition demonstrates that maturity is a matter of becoming one's true self by gradually facing the false operative notions that one is either autonomous or is the sum of roles that others impugn to us. Rather one's true self is a matter of reciprocity, of gradually *becoming* a self who is related most basically to the Trinity and to all persons and the cosmos by way of being "with and in" the holy mystery. Drawing closer to the holy mystery, paradoxically, enables one to become "one's own person," to have one's unique way of being Christian, not be merely absorbed into generic Christianity. In a similar way, developmental psychology presents maturity as a matter of becoming ever more differentiated (independent from fused relationships) precisely for the sake of deeper and more inclusive relationships. When examined together, from the perspective of Christian feminist spirituality, these two perspectives clearly reinforce the traditional maxim that "grace builds on nature."

I believe the task of finding and creating a theological tradition that includes and affirms women is even more urgent than the previous task of noting useful psychological resources. Most training programs for ministry are already convinced of the need for experiences such as clinical pastoral education which stress psychological awareness, and need only make the next expansive step to include equal time—at least—to psychology based on women's experience. Here research has produced many excellent resources available in ordinary bookstores. Unfortunately, this is not yet the case with feminist theology. Not only is the problem lack of mainstream resources, but also lack of experience of ways theology can function at least as therapeutically as popular psychology.

Finding and Creating a Theology That Functions Therapeutically for Women

What I mean here by "function therapeutically" is that appropriate theology can help women understand who they really are and promote action that expands their chances for deeper maturity, which is what most forms of psychology aim to do. In other words, a theology that enables women to flourish as much as men by giving women inclusive and affirming *meaning* and by legitimatizing women's *full ministry in the church* is a theology that functions therapeutically. Finding and creating this theology is the long-range and pioneering task of feminist theology. I wish to support women's spirituality in ministry precisely by describing this threefold task, which gives new meaning for women in Christian ministry, and by including examples of recent accomplishments in this field of life-giving theology.

Because the basic need for meaning and identity requires imagination, women in ministry need resources for picturing their own past and creating a vision for the future church that includes them in every way. This is the goal of feminist theology which is young, yet already developed into three phases. As in human growth, tasks of earlier stages remain significant even as later tasks emerge.

1. *Recover and Evaluate.* In the first phase of feminist theology the primary concern was recovery and evaluation. The picture of Christian tradition that women inherited was male-centered with a few women like Mary and Mary Magdalene imagined as receptive and obedient, or women like Clare and Jane de Chantal imagined as the subservient daughters of spiritual giants: Francis of Assisi and Francis de Sales. Therefore feminist scholars searched the landscape for lost women or took a second look at those they knew. Here the goal was at least to balance the picture of saints, leaders, and theologians held up as models and teachers.

Because Catholic Christianity sustains orthodoxy, which is continuity with the founding experience, through concrete historical persons in the communion of saints, it is important to have this communion accurately portray female embodiment of the body of Christ. So many notable women are missing from the tradition that new resources are needed to raise and expand consciousness. Two recent lectionaries present recovered women from the Bible and early Christianity in a format that encourages inclusion in daily public and private prayer. *WomanWord* is a feminist lectionary and psalter in two volumes (Hebrew Scripture and New Testament) that features all the biblical passages highlighting women.[9] It explains the context for each passage, gives points for reflection, offers a creative psalm based on a theme connected with each

woman, and concludes with a brief prayer. Another type of
lectionary is *Silent Voices, Sacred Lives: Women's Readings for the
Liturgical Year* compiled by four scholars, friends, religious of the
Sacred Heart.[10] Intended as supplemental reading for liturgy,
faith-sharing, or informal prayer, there is a selection from accounts
of "lost women in the tradition" appropriate for each day of the
liturgical year. The compilers hope this lectionary can contribute to
the therapeutic goal I mentioned above. In other words, these
readings can correct wounded memories, fill in gaps in one's identity, help us all identify vicariously with the human-religious experiences of the women whose lives mirror our own.

A second goal of this phase of feminist theology is evaluation.
Feminist theologians notice how the sources we do have usually
ignore, demean, or romanticize women. Because these texts have
been used to restrict or even oppress women, they require evaluation and sometimes repudiation. Saint Clare, for example, has
traditionally been regarded as Francis of Assisi's disciple, a holy
"nobody" in her own right. Recent scholarship shows that this is so
far from the truth that Clare can now be seen as co-founder of
Franciscan spirituality and preserver of authentic Franciscan values when friars were losing sight of Francis' charism.[11] Another
comparable example is Saint Jane de Chantal, who was assumed to
be Francis de Sales' "product," one who simply repeated the teaching of her spiritual friend and director. A careful examination of
the sources has revealed that Jane, who, like Clare, lived on long
after her friend and colleague died, was an accomplished spiritual
director in her own right, as well as an original interpreter of theological convictions she shared with Francis, her co-founder of the
Order of the Visitation.[12] Sources which demean women as "misbe-
gotten males" or the "gateway of the devil" have been carefully
repudiated as founded on pure bias or ignorance.[13] Recovery of
fascinating women's lives continues to offer new hope to women
seeking models and mentoring.

2. *Original, Creative Interpretations.* Phase two of the feminist theological, therapeutic task involves creative interpretation
and expansion of theology's very foundations. Here, a first desire
is to interpret sources so that they lose their power to intimidate
or restrict women; indeed, the goal is survival. Why frame the

situation in such dire terms? Because I agree with Mary Jo Weaver who describes the data this way: "As I have talked with Catholic women over the past ten years, I have heard stories of profound dislocation from women of all ages and in a variety of circumstances. Reduced to the simplest terms, many Catholic women find themselves in a double bind: living with misogyny and oppressive institutional structures is torture, but rejecting a church suffused with rich spiritual symbolism and a sacramental reality is starvation."[14]

What helps these women? My experience shows that help comes from returning to the rich wellspring of tradition with a faith-filled Christian feminist perspective, that is, with the energy of the "loyal opposition" within a patriarchal church. Such a return to "springs of water in a dry land" can yield the realization that saintly women like Teresa of Avila were true to their own religious insight in spite of male opposition and cleverly used the "rhetoric of femininity" to cover the spiritual teaching that actually violated Paul's injunction against women doing that very thing.[15] Or, for another example, such a return notices that a saint like Thérèse of Lisieux (the Little Flower), who was used to legitimatize an ideal sanctity as hidden obedience and absorption with trivial issues, actually was the author of her own original spirituality and was most comfortable with images of God that supported friendship and a kind of "equality with God."[16] What is more, such a return can inspire renewed appreciation of traditional themes of spiritual quest, priesthood, fasting, prayer, and almsgiving that "give no quarter" to patriarchy yet give no acquiescence to goddess worship either. Such a project is equipped to clarify how simplistic are the unfounded or exaggerated claims for the goddess, while still appreciating the disillusionment and desires that inspire the search for her.[17] This return has even yielded a thorough evaluation of the foundational texts regarding the Trinity and demonstrated how and why there is no need to interpret this doctrine in any way that legitimates church structures of domination. On the contrary, this scholarship makes very clear that a traditional patristic theology of the Trinity supports only interpersonal relationships that are mutual and collaborative, and only social structures that are collegial and interdependent.[18]

A particularly significant breakthrough in this phase is an

expansion of the very foundations and boundaries of theology in order to face and repudiate ecclesial sexism. Sandra M. Schneiders has explained with amazing clarity and precision how and why the Bible can be both divine revelation and an expression of sinful sexism.[19] Combining profound Christian faith and comprehensive biblical scholarship she lays out her position and demonstrates it through a case study interpreting the story of the Samaritan woman in John's gospel. Anyone using scripture in their ministry would be wise to study Schneiders' work with prayerful intensity.

In order to synthesize the accomplishments described above, a new book presents all the basic topics of theology from this renewed perspective. *Freeing Theology: The Essentials of Theology in Feminist Perspective* offers not a review of what is problematic in male-centered theology, but rather creative and original presentations of ten theological areas viewed positively in feminist perspective.[20] All the issues needed for contemporary ministry are included: theological method, biblical theology, revelation, the Trinity, Christology, anthropology, church, sacraments, moral theology, and spirituality. Chapters are written by today's most respected women theologians who provide a comprehensive introduction to the topics vital to spirituality and ministry today.

3. *Constructive Theology of the Divine Mystery.* A new third phase of this feminist theological task has begun. Here the movement is into uncharted waters: creative construction of theology of the holy mystery using women's experience as the primary and focal reference. Elizabeth Johnson, who received Vatican approbation of Catholic orthodoxy when she was promoted to professor at The Catholic University of America, has drawn on all her skill as a teacher and writer in presenting an inspiring and challenging presentation of the divine mystery of the Trinity and its implications (such as a response to the mystery of evil).[21] So many wounds of patriarchy could be healed by the meaning presented here and so many new challenges for contemplative love in ministry could be heard and answered by meditative study of this resource.

CONCLUSION

Mention of contemplative love brings me to the final resource for women's spirituality and ministry: experience of impasse and the "dark night."[22] Both the experience and its interpretation constitute the resource. For without the interpretation the experience may bear less fruit. When many women today describe their spirituality and ministry as "inability to communicate with God or with people in the ways that used to work," or as "constant effort to get priests to understand what I'm talking about," or as "longing to find satisfaction in the eucharistic liturgy but feeling lonely and left out because of the male-centered language and style," or as "seeing so many pastoral needs and feeling frustrated at my inability to effect a collaborative style of operation around here so these needs could be met," I recognize *some* signs of what the riches of tradition call "the dark night." If, and only if, this difficulty with communication and this fatigue in the struggles of ministry are accompanied by an experience of the gift of desire and energy enough to keep struggling, to keep trying to be Christ's reconciling love in the world, can one discern this as spiritual darkness. This darkness is not death in spirituality or ministry, though one may easily draw that conclusion without the wise advice of contemplative ministers such as John of the Cross. His contemplative experience in ministries of spiritual direction, parish administration, religious community administration, and contemplative presence to the needs of the world enabled him to interpret this darkness as the loving action of the Spirit drawing a person or community into a deeper and more inclusive love. It is a love that constitutes a new "taste" that one has not yet acquired but will later recognize as a deeper joy and life than one could previously appreciate. When many women who feel this dryness or profound uneasiness in ministry find this contemplative tradition, they shed tears of relief because they finally have found a satisfying interpretation of their experience. For this darkness is not divine abandonment or simply the effects of a dysfunctional church, but the Spirit's gradual transformation of our desires accomplished precisely through what means most to these women: their spirituality and ministry. Finally these women grasp the reason why they are able to keep dancing in the dark, to keep attending to their call to ministry. They can trust that they are in the midst of a dark transition into a more inclusive and mature church.

NOTES

1. Margaret O'Brien Steinfels, "The Church and Its Public Life," *America* (10 June 1989), pp. 550–58 as quoted in Rodger Van Allen, *Being Catholic: COMMONWEAL* (Chicago: Loyola University Press, 1993), pp. 131–32.

2. Ana-Maria Rizzuto, M.D., *The Birth of the Living God* (Chicago: University of Chicago Press, 1979), pp. 180–202.

3. Sandra M. Schneiders, "The Effects of Women's Experience on Their Spirituality," *Spirituality Today* (Summer 1983), pp. 100–116, as reprinted in Joann Wolski Conn, ed., *Women's Spirituality: Resources for Christian Development* (New York: Paulist Press, 1986), at 33–35.

4. I am grateful to Donald F. Brophy, of Paulist Press, for this characterization of small church community and the suggestion to correlate it with spirituality.

5. See, for example, Rowan Williams, *Teresa of Avila* (Ridgefield: Morehouse Publishers, 1991) and Wendy Wright, *The Bond of Perfection* (New York: Paulist Press, 1985).

6. For a more detailed explanation and application to pastoral counseling and to spiritual direction see Joann Wolski Conn, *Spirituality and Personal Maturity* (New York: Paulist Press, 1989; Lanham: University Press of America, 1994, reprint edition); for application to individual and community spiritual direction see Elizabeth Liebert, *Changing Life Patterns* (New York: Paulist Press, 1992).

7. Jean Baker Miller, *Toward a New Psychology of Women* (Boston: Beacon Press, 2nd ed. 1986). Dr. Miller, along with her associates at The Stone Center for the Study of Women (Wellesley, MA), have developed an entirely women-centered psychology which they present in terms of their therapeutic practice.

8. See, for example, Polly Young-Eisendrath and Florence Wiedemann, *Female Authority: Empowering Women Through Psychotherapy* (New York: The Guilford Press, 1987).

9. Miriam Therese Winter, *WomanWord: A Feminist Lectionary and Psalter* (New York: Crossroad, 1992).

10. Barbara Bowe, R.S.C.J., Kathleen Hughes, R.S.C.J., Sharon Karam, R.S.C.J., Carolyn Osiek, R.S.C.J., *Silent Voices, Sacred Lives:*

Women's Readings for the Liturgical Year (New York: Paulist Press, 1992).

11. Regis Armstrong ed. and trans., *Clare of Assisi: Early Documents* (New York: Paulist Press, 1988). Margaret Carney, "Francis and Clare: A Critical Examination of the Sources," *Laurentianum* 30 (1989), pp. 25–60.

12. See, for example, Joann Wolski Conn, "A Developmental View of Salesian Spirituality," *Review for Religious 52/1* (January-February 1993), pp. 56–68.

13. Anne Carr, *Transforming Grace* (San Francisco: Harper & Row, 1988).

14. Mary Jo Weaver, *Springs of Water in a Dry Land: Spiritual Survival for Catholic Women Today* (Boston: Beacon Press, 1993), p. xii.

15. Alison Weber, *Teresa of Avila and the Rhetoric of Femininity* (Princeton: Princeton University Press, 1990).

16. Joann Wolski Conn, "A Feminist View of Thérèse," *Experiencing Saint Thérèse Today*. Edited by John Sullivan, O.C.D. Carmelite Studies Vol. 5. (Washington, D.C.: Institute for Carmelite Studies, 1990), pp. 119–139.

17. Mary Jo Weaver, *Springs of Water,* pp. 78–95.

18. Catherine M. LaCugna, *God for Us: The Trinity and Christian Life* (San Francisco: Harper Collins, 1991).

19. Sandra M. Schneiders, *The Revelatory Text* (San Francisco: Harper Collins, 1991).

20. Catherine M. LaCugna, ed., *Freeing Theology: The Essentials of Theology in Feminist Perspective* (San Francisco: Harper Collins, 1993).

21. Elizabeth Johnson, *She Who Is: A Feminist Interpretation of the Holy Mystery* (New York: Crossroad, 1992).

22. The now classic article on this issue is Constance FitzGerald, O.C.D., "Impasse and Dark Night," reprinted in Joann Wolski Conn, ed., *Women's Spirituality* (New York: Paulist Press, 1986), pp. 287–311.

Feminist Spirituality: Christian Alternative or Alternative to Christianity?

Sandra M. Schneiders

Let us consider the issue of feminism in relation to Christian spirituality, i.e. to the area of lived experience of the faith. It must be noted, however, that the term "spirituality" is no longer an exclusively Christian, nor even an exclusively religious, term. Not surprisingly, therefore, feminist spirituality is not necessarily a Christian or even a religious phenomenon. In fact, however, as we shall see, feminist spirituality whether Christian or not tends to be deeply religious. Consequently, our first task is to define spirituality and specify the meaning of Christian spirituality so that we can then raise the question of how feminism is related to spirituality and finally how feminist spirituality is related to Christian spirituality.

Elsewhere I have traced the history of the term spirituality from its Christian biblical roots as a designation of that which is brought about by the influence of the Holy Spirit, through its development in Christian history to designate primarily the inner life of the Christian striving for more than ordinary holiness, to its contemporary usage not only for religious experience but also for non-religious and even anti-religious life-organizations such as secular feminism and atheistic Marxism.[1] I defined spirituality, as the term is being used today, as "the experience of consciously striving to integrate one's life in terms not of isolation and self-absorption but of self-transcendence toward the ultimate value one perceives."[2] This definition is open enough to include both religious and non-religious life projects but specific enough to exclude aimless spontaneity, partial projects, or religious dilettant-ism. Its essential elements are conscious effort, the goal of life integration through self-transcendence, and the finalization of the project by ultimate value. Its marked difference from the tradi-tional Christian definition lies in its openness concerning the na-ture of "ultimate value."

Christian spirituality involves a specification of this definition in terms of the participation of the person in the paschal mystery of Jesus the Christ. For the Christian the horizon of ultimate concern is the holy mystery of God revealed in Jesus Christ and experienced through the gift of the Holy Spirit within the life of the church.[3] Thus, Christian spirituality, as Christian, is essen-tially trinitarian, christocentric, and ecclesial. Given the way in which the tradition has presented the trinitarian God, viz. as three male "persons," the recent presentation of the theological signifi-cance of the maleness of Jesus by the Sacred Congregation for the Doctrine of the Faith,[4] and the church as a hierarchical (i.e. sacralized patriarchal) structure within which women, on the basis of their sex, are excluded from full participation, it is not surpris-ing that women, once their consciousness has been raised, have problems with the living of their faith in terms of the principal coordinates of traditional Christian spirituality. In other words, Christian spirituality will become problematic for any woman who becomes a feminist in the sense in which we have been using the term.

II. FEMINISM AND SPIRITUALITY

A. The Background and Development of Feminist Spirituality

The term "feminist spirituality" began to be used very early in the "second wave" of the modern feminist movement, arising in the United States in the 1970s and appearing in Europe in the 1980s.[5] It was mainstreamed in the feminist movement in this country with the publication in 1979 of the groundbreaking work *Womanspirit Rising: A Feminist Reader in Religion*,[6] which was followed ten years later by its sequel, *Weaving the Visions: New Patterns in Feminist Spirituality*.[7] While some of the feminists using the term spirituality were practicing members of one or another recognized religious tradition, and religion and/or theology was central to the academic feminist interests of most of them, feminist spirituality did not arise within or in terms of any particular institutional church or recognized religion.

Catherina Halkes is probably correct in locating the origin of feminist spirituality not in religion or even in the critique of religion but in the realization by feminists that women's estrangement and oppression are fueled not primarily by sex role polarization but by the dichotomy between spirit and body, with the former assigned to the male and the latter to the female, which is intrinsic to patriarchy.[8] In other words, male control of female sexuality, as it developed over the centuries, led eventually to the identification of women with their sexual/reproductive function and their consequent identification with the realm of the body which led to their gradual exclusion from the realm of the spirit. This spiritual realm, presided over by the male God who reigns in heaven, was opposed to the realm of nature which was relegated to the once universally powerful but now discredited Mother Goddess, the feminine divinity who was finally dethroned and definitively banished by the triumph of patriarchal monotheism.[9]

Feminist spirituality is the reclaiming by women of the reality and power designated by the term "spirit"[10] and the effort to reintegrate spirit and body, heaven and earth, culture and nature, eternity and time, public and private, political and personal, in short, all those hierarchized dichotomous dualisms whose root is the split between spirit and body and whose primary incarnation is the split between male and female.[11]

It is well beyond the scope of this work to enter into the complex and much disputed discussion of how a single, all-powerful male God came to take the place of the Great Goddess and the pantheon of lesser gods and goddesses who were worshiped everywhere in the ancient world before the relatively late advent of patriarchal monotheism in the west.[12] However, certain conclusions from the immense amount of research which has been done on this subject can be accepted as established.

As far back into antiquity as western religion can be traced the supreme deity was female. The Great Goddess was not merely an earth mother, a mate for a male god, or a fertility goddess whose cult justified sexual license. She was the all-powerful Creator, Source of life and of destruction, the Queen of Heaven, the Ruler of the universe. As a number of scholars have argued, this does not prove that there was ever a matriarchal society, a theory for which there is no hard evidence.[13] But even in patriarchal societies in which men controlled the myth and symbol systems, the supreme deity was female and the mediators between the Great Goddess and humans were usually female priests.

Patriarchy, however, was compatible with matrilocal and matrilineal kinship patterns, and strong patriarchal monarchies did not develop until the economic, social, and military conditions for this type of political organization arose. The Israelite monarchy, for example, did not emerge until centuries after the tribes arrived in Canaan, and a major political and military project of the first kings, Saul and David, was to centralize political power. An important aspect of this effort was the unification and centralization of the cult in Jerusalem. David's son Solomon was unable to maintain the fragile unity, and part of his failure to do so was his inability and/or unwillingness to stamp out the religion of the Great Goddess which, in many forms, was alive and well in his kingdom despite the official sanction of Yahwistic monotheism (cf. 1 Kgs 11:1–14).

Gerda Lerner in her very important study *The Creation of Patriarchy* describes the pattern observable in archaic societies which developed strong male monarchies.

> The observable pattern is: first, the demotion of the Mother-Goddess figure and the ascendance and later domination of her male consort/son; then his merging with a storm-god into a male Creator-God, who heads the pantheon of gods and goddesses. Wherever such changes occur, the power of creation and of fertility is transfered [sic] from the Goddess to the God.[14]

In other words, the source of the power of the Goddess, her originating relation to all life, must become the sole possession of the male God if he is to assume unique divinity.[15]

This is precisely the pattern which can be observed in the

development of Yahwism. The consolidation of the collection of Hebrew tribes into a single patriarchal monarchy required, as legitimation, patriarchal monotheism. As Elizabeth Dodson Gray says, with compelling clarity:

> When the holy space of a religion is sacred for male sexuality (as in the marking of the covenant upon the male phallus in circumcision), and sacred for blood-sacrifice presided over by males; and when that same holy space is contaminated by female blood and female fertility (as in menstruating and in giving birth), we are dealing with a male fertility cult, no matter what its other lofty spiritual insights may be.[16]

It is not surprising, furthermore, that the second version of the creation myth, the Jahwistic (the so-called J) account in Genesis 2:4b–25 which dates from the early days of the monarchy, presents the creator as a male deity, creating a male human being, from whose side a woman is "born" even though, as everyone knows, all men are actually born from a woman's womb. What is accomplished by the story is the mythical transference of the power of creation and of fertility from Goddess to God and from woman to man. And to put the final seal on the process the woman is then made responsible for the man's moral fall, thus legitimating his dominion over her even though, from creation, she is his equal, "bone of his bone and flesh of his flesh."

The Great Goddess, however, did not die easily in the Hebrew tradition. In fact, she never died completely. In the Old Testament we find not only continual prophetic denunciations of goddess worship (which would not have been necessary if such worship were not prevalent) but also, even in the canonical literature speaking of the one true God of Israel, occasional feminine images of God. In the figure of Holy Wisdom, we have a well-developed feminine personification of God (cf. Wis 8:1–9:6; Wis 6:12–11:1; Prov 8:1–9:12).[17] Nevertheless, there is no question that the Yahwistic commitment to monotheism involved, at least at the human level, a political commitment to patriarchal religion.

To expose the patriarchal political agenda involved in the development of the Jewish religion is not to deny the divinity of the Judaeo-Christian God, the theological truth and importance of monotheism, nor the revelatory character of the biblical text. As Matthew Lamb says in discussing the relation of hermeneutics to dialectics:

> To acknowledge ideological distortions does not imply a total rejection of either faith or science [in our case, feminist historical analysis] in order to find some other 'pure' realm of meaning, nor any lapse into anarchistic incoherence; instead it demands attention to an interpretative heuristics open to dialectical criticism.[18]

But it is to call for a demythologizing of the biblical account for the purpose of distinguishing its patriarchal overlay from its theology of God, its androcentrism from its theology of humanity, and its sexist ideology from its revelatory content just as we must distinguish its scientifically untenable three-tiered cosmology from its doctrine of creation. Monotheism is not necessarily patriarchal any more than Judaism or Christianity is necessarily monarchical. In fact, just as the God of mercy and justice is distorted by the vindictive warrior *persona* assigned to God in some parts of the Old Testament, so the Spirit God who is utterly beyond sex is often deformed by the patriarchal mythology in which the biblical God is usually presented.

The foregoing discussion provides the necessary background for understanding the emergence of contemporary feminist spirituality. Western religion and, in particular, the Judaeo-Christian tradition is deeply patriarchal, not only in its institutional organization but in its theology of God and of humanity. God is presented, not exclusively but overwhelmingly, as a male being. Males, who are perceived to be unequivocally in God's image, are God's representatives and ministers. Women, by virtue of their female sex which is unlike the sex attributed to God, are regarded as deficient images of the divine, unfit to represent God to the worshiping community or minister to him in official cult. Women are subordinate to men, helpers to men in the work of procreation, and thus defined primarily in terms of their sexuality, i.e. their relation to men as wives and mothers, and their participation in the natural processes by which human beings come into existence and thus become subjects of the spiritualization processes over which men preside.

The dichotomous dualism between male divine creator and female natural creation within which the male human is assimilated to the divine sphere and the female human to the natural sphere is the paradigm for the endless series of superior/inferior dichotomies that is characterized as masculine/feminine. Thus, at the male pole are divine creativity, power, intelligence, initiative, activity, goodness, independence, and at the female pole are natural passivity, weakness, instinct and emotionality, receptivity, evil, dependence. The short-hand cipher for this pervasive dualism is the spirit/body dichotomy, spirit representing everything divine and body representing everything natural. The spirit is male; the body is female. Culture is the triumph of male spirit over female nature.

Feminist spirituality, as we have already noted, began as women reclaiming spirit, refusing to be reduced to body. However, it virtually immediately expanded and deepened to include a reevaluation of body.[19] What feminists in the spirituality movement realized was that the root disorder was not women's confinement to the realm of body but the dichotomy itself which split reality along the spirit/body axis creating an unending and unwinnable war between a supposedly superior spiritual (i.e. male) half of reality and a supposedly inferior bodily (i.e. female) half of reality. They realized that this leads not only to male oppression of females, their exclusion from the realms of "spirit" such as religion, education, politics, and culture, but also to wars between nations struggling to prove their superiority to one another by reducing their enemies to subhuman status, to racial and colonial oppressions of people viewed as intrinsically inferior, and to the mindless rape of the natural environment by man who sees himself as having absolute dominion over nature.

The essence of feminist spirituality, then, is a reclaiming of female power beginning with the likeness of women to the divine, the rehabilitation of the bodily as the very locus of that divine likeness, and the right of women to participate in the shaping of religion and culture, i.e. of the realm of "spirit." This explains the generally religious character of feminist spirituality and, at the same time, its marginality to the mainstream religious traditions which are the principal sources of women's exclusion from the world of "spirit." Against this background we can examine some of the main features of feminist spirituality before looking at the specifically Christian form of the movement.

B. *Main Features of Feminist Spirituality*

1. Outside the Institutional Context

Feminist spirituality has tended to develop outside the institutional context of either church or academy. This is easily understandable since both these institutions were developed as cultural shrines of the life of the spirit, a life from which women have been excluded, in which they are supposed not to be interested, and for which they have been deemed unequipped. Thus the rituals and texts of religion as well as the research techniques, the canon of classical texts, and the teaching methods of the academy include very little of women's experience or history and even less that would be empowering of women. There is little place for women or for the experience or exercise of feminine power in either church or academy. In fact, a major function of both institutions has been to restrict women to the private sphere, the domestic environment, the ancillary roles, while power was possessed and exercised by men. The economic arrangements which support both church and academy are such that funding is usually not available for so-called "alternative" projects, i.e. for projects that fall outside the patriarchal interests already in place.[20]

Consequently, feminist spirituality both in theory and in practice has developed on the fringes of institutional culture. This allows feminists a certain freedom to tell their individual and corporate stories which are mutually empowering and to experiment with new theories that are *anathema* in the academy and new rituals which seem frivolous or shocking to mainstream religion. However, it has also kept scholars in feminist spirituality both from the variety and scope of critical exchange in the academy that would profit both women feminist scholars and their non-feminist dialogue partners and from full participation in their respective religious traditions which would be empowering for feminists and purifying and enriching for their churches.

2. The Discovery of Goddess[21]

An aspect of feminist spirituality which is most disturbing to mainline religion is discourse about Goddess. No doubt there is a deep, visceral awareness, especially among the guardians of patriarchal religion, that the reemergence of the goddess is potentially the greatest conceivable threat to the religious status quo. However, because of the importance of the Goddess theme, no discussion of feminist spirituality which avoids this issue can be even minimally adequate.

Basically, Goddess is the symbol of female divinity, i.e. of feminine sacred power, just as God is the symbol of male divinity or masculine sacred power. There are two main questions about the symbol for divinity: Is the divinity symbolized in masculine or feminine form actually male or female? How are real males and females related to the divinity? Various strands of feminist spirituality answer these questions differently. Three of these strands are of major significance for an understanding of feminist spirituality.

Thealogy: The most radical form of feminist spirituality involves the worship of the Great Mother Goddess who is conceived of as the one, true, ultimate divinity.[22] The study of her nature and her relations with creation and humanity is called thealogy, i.e. discourse about Goddess, rather than theology or discourse about God. However, a major difference between the understanding of Goddess is conceived as ultimately immanent rather than ultimately transcendent. More exactly, her transcendence is her all-embracing, all-empowering immanence. She is transcendently immanent. Thus, Goddess not only divinizes the feminine and its life-giving mysteries but also negates the ruinous split between transcendent and immanent, spirit and body, divinity and nature, heaven and earth with all their Manichean progeny in the realms of thought and action. A feminine deity allows women to experience themselves as truly "like Goddess," as imaging divinity in their very life-giving powers. Rather than being unclean because of their bodily capacity to give life, they are divine because of it. Women are rehabilitated in the rehabilitation of the body which is not the opposite of spirit but the enspirited vessel of divine creativity.

Closely related to Goddess religion and spirituality but not necessarily identical with it is the revitalization of Wicca, or pre-Christian, European traditions of pagan religion.[23] The deity of these nature religions is female and her devotees are predominantly although not exclusively women. They come together in "covens" and often call themselves "witches," a deliberately provocative practice which not only intends to unmask the irrational male fear of female religious power but also to expiate the murder of millions of women throughout Christian history who have been executed on the charge of witchcraft.[24]

Witchcraft is not the "black magic" or nocturnal sexual orgies feared by the religious establishment but a ritual participation in the life-giving and healing powers of nature which are seen as divine. For Wicca, which means "wisdom" or the "wise ones," the universe is not an inert thing but a living reality in which everything is intimately interconnected. Human beings are the priestesses of creation, not its lords. Spirituality includes sexuality without being either reduced to it or dominant over it. Life and love are supreme values which are not at odds with truth. Ritual plays a very important role in witchcraft because it is the place where spirit and nature meet and interact, sacralizing all of reality and uniting us to ourselves, to one another, and to the universe.[25]

God/dess: A less radical form of feminist spirituality, and one with whose approach to divinity many Christian feminists are much more comfortable, is well symbolized by respelling the verbal symbol of divinity as G-o-d / d-e-s-s. What such women are doing is appropriating for women all that is true in the theological and religious tradition about God. While repudiating the patriarchal and masculinizing deformation of the God-tradition, they continue to relate to the deity of Judaeo-Christian revelation. They emphasize the feminine aspects of the biblical deity, insist on a compensatory highlighting of feminine biblical metaphors for Yahweh, demand the use of gender inclusive language for both divine and human being in prayer and worship, and struggle toward a reimagining, for themselves and others, of the male God in female terms. In other words, they refuse to allow the biblical God to be appropriated by men and used against women. They see themselves as fully in the image and likeness of God/dess, not only because they possess intellect and will, i.e. spiritual faculties, but also because they participate bodily in the great divine work of giving and nurturing life. Thus they attempt to achieve much the same appropriation of spiritual power, rehabilitation of the body, and reintegration of the dichotomized spheres of reality that more radical Goddess worshippers do, but they seek to do this without separating themselves from the Judaeo-Christian biblical and sacramental tradition.[26]

Therapeutic or Psychological Approach to the Goddesses: A third way in which feminist spirituality has incorporated the goddess is basically psychological and therapeutic. Basing themselves on the archetypal theory of Carl Jung, but repudiating or modifying Jung's animus/anima dichotomy, some feminist psychotherapists have seen the potential of goddess archetypes for healing the profound self-hatred and self-rejection which patriarchal culture has inculcated in women by teaching them to identify with the inferior qualities regarded as "feminine" while assigning the superior human qualities to men.[27] Jung recognized the potentiality of transcultural intrapsychic patterns, which he called archetypes, to constellate the complexes of thought and feeling which are operative in our daily experience. A fundamental pair of archetypes, according to Jung, are the anima or the feminine principle in the male psyche, and the animus or the male principle in the female psyche.

The major problem with Jung's theory, from a feminist perspective, is that Jung assigned the culturally stereotypical masculine qualities, i.e. those associated with spirit such as logical reason, initiative, creativity, etc., to the masculine principle and the culturally stereotypical feminine qualities, i.e. those associated with body, such as emotion, instinct, receptivity, passivity, etc., to the feminine principle. The net result was that men were enabled to draw upon the resources of the dark, inferior, and less differentiated feminine qualities which, in small doses, make life richer, more exciting, and more beautiful without ever having to identify with them, whereas women could reach above themselves into the higher sphere of spirit, mind, and creativity but could never claim these qualities as their own. They would always experience these qualities as recessive in themselves, foreign to their true nature, borrowed for special occasions when they had to act in spheres not their own, e.g. in the academy, political life, or religious leadership. Despite Jung's effort to valorize both the feminine and the masculine, his dichotomous approach had the effect of canonizing the traditional sexual stereotypes and the cultural hierarchizing of masculine and feminine which alienates women from the realm of "spirit."

Feminist Jungian psychotherapists have revised the schema by agreeing that there are indeed archetypes of the masculine and the feminine in the psyche but that they are multiple.[28] Women have a plurality of archetypes of the feminine within themselves as men have a plurality of masculine archetypes. Using the ancient Greek goddesses to describe the archetypes of the feminine in women, these therapists have explained the ascendency in certain women, or in the same woman under different circumstances, of the inner paradigms not only of mother, child, and wife but also of solitary huntress, warrior and strategist, alchemical lover, contemplative virgin, goal-focused achiever, leader, thinker, intellectual mentor, artist, craftsperson, spiritual guide, and so on. Neither the bodily nor the spiritual is either more or less "natural" in women. The spiritual does indeed have a feminine persona in a woman, but it is not a recessive masculinity. It is her own feminine power active in a sphere from which real women have been traditionally excluded. The psychological task of women is to actualize all the inner goddesses, all the archetypes of female power.

3. Salient Characteristics of Feminist Spirituality

Against this background it is fairly easy to identify the salient characteristics of feminist spirituality and to see their interconnections. First, feminist spirituality is both rooted in and oriented toward *women's experience,* especially their experiences of disempowerment and of empowerment. For this reason storytelling, the narratizing and sharing of the experience of women which has been largely excluded from the history of mainline religion, is central.[29] Story-telling is both a technique for consciousness-raising and a source of mutual support. By telling their own stories women appropriate as significant their own experience which they have been taught to view as trivial. By listening to the stories of other women they come to see the commonalities and the political power in women's experience which they have been taught to believe is purely personal and private.

Second, as we have already seen, feminist spirituality is deeply concerned with the reintegration of all that has been dichotomized by patriarchal religion. This involves rehabilitating what has been regarded as inferior and reappropriating that which has been alienated. The fundamental reintegration is that of body with spirit. Thus, feminist spirituality is concerned with giving voice to and celebrating those aspects of *bodiliness* which religion has covered with shame and silence, particularly those feminine experiences associated with life-giving which have been reduced to sex and those aspects of sexuality which have been regarded as unclean.[30]

Very closely related to the emphasis on the goodness and holiness of the body is a third characteristic, a profound *concern with non-human nature*. Feminist theorists have explicated exhaustively the intimate connection between male possessiveness and exploitative violence toward women and that same possessiveness and exploitative violence toward nature. As men have raped women for their own pleasure and utility, so have they raped the environment for the same purposes. Feminists are convinced that only a spirituality which values both women and all those elements of the universe that have been "feminized," including nature, children, the poor, the disabled, the aged, and the infirm, can contribute to a renewed and livable world.[31]

A fourth characteristic of feminist spirituality is its rejection of cerebral, rationalistic, and abstract approaches to religious participation. The emphasis on *ritual* that is participative, circular, aesthetic, incarnate, communicative, life-enhancing, and joyful is a deliberate rejection of the rigidly unemotional, overly verbal, hierarchical, and dominative liturgical practice of the mainline churches. And feminists choose to organize themselves religiously not in the hierarchical institutional structures of patriarchal religion with its insistence on obedience and conformity but in communities that are inclusive and participative. Consequently, feminists involved in the spirituality movement are committed to a reenvisioning of ministry, liturgy, theology, teaching, community building, and ecclesiastical organization.

A final, but perhaps the most important, characteristic of

feminist spirituality is that from the very beginning it has involved commitment to the intimate and intrinsic *relationship between personal growth and transformation and a politics of social justice.*[32] The feminist rallying cry, "the personal is political," means not only that the problems women have experienced as their personal and private concerns are actually systemically caused and can only be rectified through structural reform, but also that societal transformation is only possible through and on the basis of personal transformation. Thus, unlike the traditional spiritualities of the churches which constantly (and often unsuccessfully) seek a point of intersection between a process of personal spiritual growth and a commitment to social justice, feminist spirituality starts with a commitment which faces simultaneously inward and outward. The changes and growth which must happen in women if they are to be and to experience themselves as fully human, daughters of divinity and its bearers in this world, are the same changes that must occur in society, namely, the reintegration of what has been dichotomized, the empowerment of that which has been marginalized and abused, the liberation of that which has been enslaved.

The word which has progressively come to serve as a cipher for feminist spirituality is "interconnectedness." In every area feminists involved in the spirituality movement are seeking ways to reunify everything that has been divided by the all-pervasive dichotomous dualism of the patriarchal system, to replace the win-lose, either-or, we-they, in-out, right-wrong bases of mutual destruction with a both-and-inclusiveness which will both achieve and be achieved by reconnecting that which has been separated. Feminist spirituality prefers networks to chains of command, webs to ladders, circles and mosaics to pyramids, and weaving to building.[33] It wants discourse to be both rational and affective, dialogue to replace coercion, cooperation rather than competition to be our usual mode of operation, power to be used for empowerment rather than mastery, persuasion to take the place of force, and all of this to be not merely the way individuals function but the way society functions. In short, feminist spirituality is a commitment to bringing about, in oneself and in the world, that alternative vision which is integral to feminism as a comprehensive ideology.

III. FEMINIST SPIRITUALITY AND
CHRISTIAN SPIRITUALITY

We come finally to the question of the relationship of Christian women and men who are feminists to feminist spirituality. Certain tensions, and also many points of convergence, should already have become obvious. However, just as there is considerable diversity among secular and post-Christian religious feminists involved in feminist spirituality, so Christians who are feminists occupy a variety of positions on a continuum running from very traditional Christian spirituality to very revisionist approaches. One way to distinguish among Christians who are feminists and who are involved in feminist spirituality is to examine the points of departure from which various feminists have come to identify themselves with the spirituality movement.

A. *Varieties of Christian Feminist Spirituality*

Not all women's spirituality is feminist just as not all women's movements are feminist. It is entirely possible for women to have a very patriarchal spirituality. In fact, it may well be the case that the spirituality of most women in the church is still at least unreflectively if not militantly patriarchal. However, there are women who claim the designation of feminist for spiritualities which most feminists would not recognize as such and might even consider anti-feminist.

Sometimes the designation feminist is simply an anachronism, a matter of assigning the term feminist to a woman who had a positive spiritual self-image and maintained her integrity in the face of patriarchal power.[34] Sometimes the term is appropriated by women who exalt the role in their religious experience of precisely those qualities, such as receptivity and passivity, which men have devalued and assigned to women. Sometimes people simply equate the spirituality of women, especially insofar as it seems to contrast with the spirituality of men, with feminist spirituality.

As has been said in relation to feminism itself, feminist spirituality is necessarily informed by a developed feminist consciousness which is quite different from a positive self-image as a woman or even a basic commitment to the well-being of women.

Feminist consciousness begins in an appropriated and criticized experience of sexual oppression and involves a critique of patriarchy as the cause of that oppression, an alternative vision of a non-patriarchal future, and a commitment to structural change to realize that vision.

A first group of Christians whose spirituality is genuinely feminist are people who have been deeply involved with personal and/or social spirituality within the Christian tradition and who came to feminist consciousness at some point and began to realize that it had serious implications for their spiritual life.[35] Many Catholic religious women and other ministers have had this experience. They have become sensitized to the oppressive masculinity of the language of prayer and celebration and the way that this linguistic hegemony functions to legitimate and reinforce ecclesiastical patriarchy. They are estranged from a male God in whose likeness they cannot imagine themselves and who is, for all practical purposes, men-writ-large. They have become progressively alienated from a sacramental system in which males exercise sacred power over women to grant or deny access to God and use sacramentally based office to exclude women from full participation in the church. They have come to recognize the ways in which male-controlled theology, moral formation, and spiritual guidance have functioned to infantilize and demonize women. In short, their consciousness-raising has extended to the sphere of spirituality and they have begun to judge traditional Christian spirituality as seriously flawed, even destructive of women.[36]

A second type of Christian feminist is the person whose coming to feminist spirituality began in her or his involvement in feminist liberationist praxis.[37] As this person has grown in awareness of the ways in which women are marginalized, excluded, victimized, degraded, and oppressed in family and society, he or she has begun to see that women undergo the same oppression in the church and that the church is a major legitimator of the oppression of women in family and society. The social analysis which enables such people to identify patriarchy as the root of women's social, economic, and political oppression is extended to the church where it is identified as the cause of women's religious oppression. However, such people recognize that the situation in the church is complicated by the spiritual element. It is not merely that the church as social institution is patriarchal but that patriarchy has infected the inner life of the church as a community. Sexual apartheid in the church, like racial apartheid in South Africa, is not just an evil social structure but a deadly cancer of the spirit which is destroying not only its intended victims, women, but all believers whose spiritual experience is patriarchally deformed.

A third type of Christian who becomes interested in feminist spirituality is the woman who has experienced personal oppression and violence in the church. She may be a religious whose congregation's constitutional revision process has been violated or who has been threatened with serious sanctions for exercising her basic human rights; a married woman enraged by church law on contraception, divorce, or abortion formulated by male celibates without any input from those who bear the brunt of those decisions; a woman in ministry who has been summarily fired without explanation from a post she has filled with distinction for many years because the new pastor is not comfortable with women; a woman seminary student who cannot accept that her vocation to priestly ministry is simply denied without testing on the basis of her sex; a wife who completes the diaconate formation program with her husband who is then ordained while she is quietly dropped from consideration; a woman who is raising the child she conceived with a priest who continues to function in good standing while she bears the onus of single parenting and the ecclesial opprobrium of adultery; a parent whose child has been sexually molested by a cleric who is protected by the system. This type of experience, because it is so personally painful and is inflicted by church officials who claim to be acting in the name of God, frequently creates a crisis in the spirituality of the victims. They can no longer relate to the God who is presented and represented in this way and they are forced, through a crisis of faith, to find a new approach to God or even a new God to approach.

A fourth type of Christian feminist is the person who has become involved in the secular or post-Christian feminist spirituality movement and gradually finds it more satisfying, more lifegiving, than participation in traditional patriarchal church life. She may continue to go to mass on Sunday and try to pray as before, but she finds herself overcome with anger at the sexist language of the liturgy and the unrelieved maleness of ministry; she can no longer read or listen to the paternalistic pronouncements of the hierarchy exhorting her to accept with humble joy her second class status in the church; she is unable to read or meditate on a biblical text that suppresses her history and violates her sense of self-worth; ministering under the domination of clerics is becoming intolerable. Little by little she finds herself identifying with the community of feminists with whom she celebrates inclusive and empowering rituals and disassociating herself from the oppressive experiences of mainline Christian spirituality.

In summary, women who are both Christian and feminist come to see the relevance of feminism to their Christian spirituality in a number of different ways. For some, feminist insight comes as an addition to and an enrichment of a basically traditional experience of growth in the Christian spiritual life. For others, their feminist consciousness, raised in other circumstances or in relation to other issues, begins to enlighten their Christian spirituality and to call into question the assumptions of that spirituality insofar as these are patriarchal and oppressive. Others come to feminist spirituality out of an experience of ecclesiastical oppression, and still others out of an alienation that is intensified by its contrast with liberating feminist experience. What all of these paths have in common is that they lead directly into the area of spirituality, i.e. they touch not just institutional participation but the lived experience of the faith, the intimate place where the human person encounters the Holy Mystery of being, life, and love. This is why the issue of feminist spirituality is for most Catholic women whose consciousness has been raised a much more serious issue than questions of institutional reform. It raises questions of whether the God of the Judaeo-Christian tradition can be God for a self-respecting woman; whether Jesus is a savior or an oppressor of women; whether sacraments can be experienced as symbolic encounters with God or only as the sacred ritualization of male domination; whether one can find oneself as a person and grow healthily in a community in which one's personhood and Christianity will never be fully recognized. The agony of the Catholic who is a feminist is experienced primarily in the area of spirituality.

B. Responses to the Effect of Feminism on the Spirituality of Catholics

No matter how the Catholic woman who is a feminist comes to see the connection between her feminism and her Catholic spirituality, seeing the connection will present at the very least a major challenge in the area of faith life and in all probability a major crisis.

One response to the crisis, and one which is becoming, unfortunately, ever more common, is abandonment of the Christian tradition. Raised feminist consciousness makes the person simply unable to absorb the incessant spiritual abuse of a resolutely patriarchal institution and she opts for her personhood, her self-respect, and her continuing spiritual growth which she realizes cannot be pursued in such an oppressive environment. Such feminists often refer to themselves as post-Christian, indicating that their roots are in the Christian tradition and that their feminist position is not neutral in relation to that tradition. But they no longer consider themselves Christians and no longer recognize the claim of the Christian community or institution upon them.

The responses with which I am most concerned in this chapter, however, are those of feminists who do not leave, or at least have not yet left the institution even though many of these admit that remaining is a daily painful choice. There seem to be at least two general groups of women who are both Christian and feminist: 1) those who are basically within the mainstream of the Christian tradition and whose spirituality remains recognizably Christian but who are involved in a continuous and radical criticism of the tradition; 2) those who are still formally within the institutional church but who have, to a large extent, relocated their spirituality into what has been named "womenchurch." These two groups are by no means totally distinct, and most Christian women who are feminists probably have some affiliation with both. I am distinguishing them for the sake of clearer description and analysis.

1. Mainstream: Feminist Catholics

For purposes of clarity I will call the first group "feminist Catholics," making Catholic the substantive and feminist a modifier. These feminists are usually women who have spent most of their lives developing a personal spirituality within the Catholic Christian tradition. Theirs is not a purely institutional spirituality, a matter of accepting church teaching, keeping church laws, and "practicing the faith" according to current church norms.

These women, many of whom are or were members of religious congregations, have developed a deep personal prayer life nourished by prolonged meditation on the scriptures that has formed in them a Christ-consciousness which is now integral to their personalities. Often this Christ-consciousness has been deeply marked by a personally appropriated study of one or another of the church's great spiritual traditions and/or personalities, such as Benedictine liturgical spirituality or Teresian contemplative spirituality. These women responded with spiritual joy and enthusiasm to the renewal of sacramental and liturgical life in the conciliar period and were delighted to replace the somewhat wooden and impersonal preached retreats of their youth with intense experiences of personal growth in solitary directed retreats. Spiritual vitality overflowed in their adult years in committed and energetic ministry which became more and more creative as the decline in numbers of clergy and a renewed ecclesiology conspired to open previously clerical ministries to the non-ordained.

In short, the feminists in this first group are people with mature, personally appropriated spiritualities. Their spirituality was born within and nourished by the Catholic tradition. Jesus is central to their faith life which is trinitarian and communal, and their ministry is an integral expression of their spiritual lives. Christianity, specifically in its Catholic incarnation, is not merely an institutional affiliation of which they can divest themselves like a person leaving her country club, or an ideological commitment which one might lay aside by conviction like a Marxist leaving the Communist Party, or even a cherished vocation which one might surrender for a greater good like a teacher retiring in order to raise a child. These people do not *belong* to the Catholic Church; they *are* Catholics. And their Catholic identity is constituted much more by their spirituality, their lived experience of the faith, than by institutional affiliation. Even if these feminists chose to sever their institutional connection they would find it virtually impossible to de-Catholicize their spirituality because Catholicity constitutes that spirituality in a fundamental way.

While it is certainly not possible to give a single description of the spiritual journey of such a large and diverse group of people, it might be possible to suggest, in a general way, the effect of heightened feminist consciousness on such women and the ways in which the encounter of their two commitments, viz. Catholicism and feminism, influences their spirituality. One way to organize this description is to talk of the inner and the outer faces of the experience.

Feminist consciousness, once raised, can only deepen. Consciousness-raising makes it impossible to ever "go home again." Once sensitized to the reality and the effects of patriarchy, one can only become ever more aware of its pervasiveness, more convinced of its destructiveness, more resistant to its influence on oneself and one's world. The feminist Catholic may begin with a mildly disturbing realization that the religious language of her tradition is heavily sexist, that she is being victimized in her ministry by the irrational fear and hatred of women that has been bred into an all-male, celibate clergy, that the God-imaging in the tradition is overwhelmingly masculine, that she is being restricted in totally unnecessary ways in the exercise of her sacramental life because of her sex. But once she has begun to see, begun the critical process of analysis, she will necessarily gradually be overwhelmed by the extent, the depth, and the violence of the institutional church's rejection and oppression of women. This precipitates the inward crisis which the feminist Catholic inevitably faces: a deep, abiding, emotionally draining anger that, depending on her personality, might run the gamut from towering rage to chronic depression.

This experience, which must be distinguished from the episodic anger we all experience in the face of frustrations or everyday mistreatment, should probably be called existential anger. It is not a temporary emotion but a state of being. Members of oppressed races and social classes know this experience well. Waking up in the morning angry and going to bed at night angry, especially for a person who has been socialized to women's responsibility for keeping peace in family and community and who has learned from childhood that a good Christian does not even feel, much less express anger, is a personally shattering experience. There are no categories or techniques in the repertoire of Christian spirituality for understanding or dealing with existential anger.[38]

The onslaught of existential anger faces the feminist Catholic with a new and all-embracing spiritual agenda for which the tradition offers little help. The data of the experience are conflicting. In her heart the feminist Catholic knows that her anger is not only justified but mandatory, just as was Jesus' anger at the oppressive hypocrisy of the clergy of his day, but this does not allay the guilt that arises from a lifetime of socialization and indoctrination about the unacceptability of this passion. At some deep level she believes in the Catholic faith tradition, but she sees more and more clearly that every aspect of it is not just tainted but perverted by the evil of patriarchy. It is not that the tradition has some problems; the tradition is the problem. She wants to hope that institutional purification and conversion are possible, but there is very little evidence that the male guardians of the patriarchal establishment have any intention of even addressing the problem. She wishes she could focus her anger on institutional arrangements and doctrinal positions, but the source of her suffering and the cause of her anger are most often real people, usually males in power positions who really cannot be honestly excused on the grounds of stupidity or ignorance because they *do* know what they are doing. These people are simultaneously her personal oppressors and those for whose salvation Jesus died.

Not only are the data of the situation conflicting but the behavioral alternatives, at times, are all simultaneously unacceptable or ineffective. Walking out of offensive liturgies not only deprives her of sacramental experience but usually has little effect on the offending presider; but remaining only enrages her and confirms the offender in his oppressive practice. Expressing her anger to males who are sufficiently sensitized to the issue to understand what she is saying risks alienating potential allies; but expressing it to those who most need to hear it is a waste of time; and not expressing it at all is psychologically dangerous. Furthermore, the institutional powers are in agreement that a woman accused of "being angry," like the woman once accused of "being a witch," can be disposed of with impunity. Thus, expressing her anger can cost her her job, her reputation, and any leverage she might have for bringing about change, while repressing her anger destroys her own integrity and psychological balance and makes her an accomplice in the oppression of her sisters.

While these descriptions are indicative rather than exhaustive, they should suffice to make the point. The feminist Catholic is in the sociological position in the church of the person of color in South African society. Sexual apartheid works exactly like racial apartheid. Oppression, frustration, discouragement, and hopelessness fuel an existential anger that is overwhelming, unquenchable, and utterly exhausting. The spiritual agenda of the feminist Catholic often consists primarily in searching for some constructive way to deal with existential anger, to become in her own way a spiritual Nelson Mandela or Rosa Parks or Joan of Arc.

A Carmelite, Constance FitzGerald, in a widely read article entitled "Impasse and the Dark Night,"[39] has suggested a way of conceptualizing, in the mystical categories of the Carmelite contemplative tradition, the experience of being totally blocked that is central to the existential anger of many feminist Catholics. Carolyn Osiek, in her book *Beyond Anger*,[40] has tried to suggest ways to both affirm the anger and to use it without becoming paralyzed by it. Elsewhere I have suggested that women's experience might be a resource for a renewed theology of the cross[41] as well as for an appropriation of ministerial gifts.[42]

These psychological and spiritual resources, some explicitly Christian and religious, some therapeutic, some sociological, are gradually emerging as feminist Catholics share their experiences of alienation and search for a way out. Two major fora for this sharing that have proved immensely strengthening for many feminist Catholics are spiritual direction, especially with a feminist woman director,[43] and support groups in which women come together to strengthen one another in suffering, to strategize for change, and to celebrate both traditional Catholic liturgies and alternative rituals. Their experience is not unlike that of the earliest Jewish Christians who, while continuing to participate in temple and synagogue, also met together in their homes to share and celebrate their Christian identity and faith which could not find expression in the Jewish assembly. Years of intense living of Christian spirituality has strengthened these women in their conviction that there are resources within them for living even the passion and crucifixion of ecclesial patriarchy and that resurrection is worth their hope.

The outward expression of feminist Catholic spirituality usually takes the form of active commitment to ecclesiastical reform. Many of these women are active in the Women's Ordination Conference, Catholics Speak Out, the Association for the Rights of Catholics in the Church, Mary's Pence, and other groups involved in ongoing challenge to the institution. Often they serve as well on diocesan pastoral councils, associations of religious and/or lay women, and advisory groups to church leaders.

Feminist Catholics in the academy are involved in a full-scale revisionist criticism of the Catholic tradition. Women scholars in church history, pastoral theology, biblical studies, systematic theology, sacramental theology, and moral theology are creating an alternative body of theological reflection which serious theologians can no longer ignore.[44] They are demonstrating that what has been blithely regarded as "the tradition" of the church is, at most, half the tradition. Church history is not the history of the church but of what men have preserved of male experience for male purposes. Much that the hierarchy would like to present as simply "theology" is the local theology of those in power often developed for ideological ends. Biblical interpretation has been done almost exclusively by exegetes wearing, unconsciously but really, sexual blinders. And while moral theology has been developed by male celibates unenlightened by the contribution of at least half of those who lived that morality, pastoral theology has been distorted by the exclusion of the ministerial experience of half the church.

Feminist Catholics, especially those directly involved in pastoral ministry, are pouring immense energy into the reform of life in the grassroots communities of the church. They are refusing to tolerate gender exclusive language in daily discourse or liturgical celebration; they are taking effective action, sometimes even legal action, to protect their rights against clerical privilege and the arbitrary use of hierarchical power; they are changing the dominative procedures of the ecclesiastical workplace in the direction of feminist models of cooperation and participation; they are building alternative models of religious community.

Feminist Catholic parents and teachers are committed to raising the next generation of Catholics as feminists. They want the
boys they deal with to eschew anything, including the ordained
ministry, from which their sisters are excluded. They want girls to
recognize their exclusion whenever and wherever it occurs and to
protest it loudly and effectively. Above all, they want the girls and
boys they are raising and educating to experience themselves as
equals and to treat each other that way so that there will not be
replacements for the generation of patriarchs that is dying.

What all of this activity has in common is that it is constructive expenditure of energy for the transformation of the church.
Not only does it channel the existential anger with which feminist
Catholics wrestle interiorly, but it is having an effect. The concerns of feminists can no longer be trivialized or ignored by
church officials.[45] Although it often seems that no progress has
been made and no change seems likely, the extent and depth of
change is actually astounding when one realizes that the Catholic
feminist movement is less than thirty years old. Institutional arrangements have not been modified in any significant way. But
the foundations on which those arrangements rest have been seriously undermined and the flow of personnel, money, and commitment necessary to sustain those arrangements is drying up. Like
the Berlin Wall and South African apartheid, the church's patriarchal sexism appears immovable, but it is built on the sand of
oppression, and history is on the side of liberation and justice.

2. Womenchurch

A second group of women who are both feminist and Catholic are those we might call Catholic feminists. Here the substantive is feminist and the adjective is Catholic. The primary social
location and focus of personal commitment of these women is to
feminism, and this is what characterizes and determines the extent and the quality of their participation in the Catholic tradition.
Most of these women find their spiritual home not in Catholic
parishes or alternative communities but in the movement called
"Womenchurch."[46]

Womenchurch defines itself as church, i.e. as a community
of religiously engaged and motivated people who are women-

identified. Their starting point is the experience of women, not any particular institutional religious tradition, although the movement originated among Catholic women moving beyond the goal of ordination into a self-understanding as an exodus community, a community not in exile from the church in sectarianism or schism but the community of church in exodus from patriarchy. Their goal is the full personhood of women, not the maintaining or improving of the religious institution or the saving of disincarnate souls, their own or anyone else's. The criterion by which they judge the genuinely religious quality of any experience, project, or process is whether it is life-giving for women.

Women in the Womenchurch movement now come from many different religious traditions, Christian and other, and from no tradition, although most of its members probably are or were originally Catholic and most Catholic women in the movement remain Catholics. Many Catholic women who experience themselves primarily as feminists but who have not abandoned institutional affiliation with Catholicism find themselves most at home in Womenchurch settings. And many feminist Catholics, such as those described in the previous section, participate in and are nourished by Womenchurch events even though their primary religious affiliation remains the institutional church.

The spirituality of Womenchurch is essentially feminist spirituality rather than the spirituality of mainline Christianity. Consequently, Womenchurch easily brings together for story-sharing, analysis, strategizing, political action, and ritual feminists who share a deep concern for religion but no common ecclesiastical or cultural history. Catholics, Protestants, Buddhists, native Americans, and devotees of pagan Wicca; whites and women of color; ordained women, lay women, and women religious all come together in Womenchurch on the basis of shared feminist theory and praxis which is the fundamental shaper of the reflection, action, and ritual of the community.

We might illustrate the difference between feminist Catholics and Catholics in Womenchurch as follows. A group of feminist Catholics might celebrate eucharist without an ordained presider but they would probably use the basic format of Catholic eucharist and they would be concerned about the question of how their celebration is related to the sacramental tradition of the church.

A group of Catholic feminists at a Womenchurch event, if they chose to celebrate eucharist (which is less likely because they would have trouble with its patriarchal presuppositions no matter who presided and because they would be unlikely to be in an all-Catholic group), would probably not be concerned with that question. They would be much more likely to develop a ritual, perhaps involving the sharing of a communal meal of bread and wine, which they would not see themselves as "borrowing" from a male church which owns the sacraments but would see as an organic expression of their own power to celebrate their spirituality.

Characteristic, then, of Catholic feminists is their primary self-location in the church of women, i.e. Womenchurch, whatever other institutional religious affiliations they might maintain. Second, their spirituality is essentially feminist rather than Christian or non-Christian, although it is usually enriched by those elements of the Catholic tradition which they still find meaningful. Its primary characteristics are those we discussed above under the heading of feminist spirituality, viz. non-institutional location, rootedness in women's experience rather than ecclesiastical tradition, a profound concern to rehabilitate the bodily while reclaiming the spirit for women and thus healing the dichotomous dualisms characteristic of patriarchy, ecological sensitivity, a deep commitment to social transformation as integral to personal transformation, and a concern that all of their interaction be characterized by interconnectedness expressed in full participation, circularity of organization and shared leadership, artistic beauty, inclusiveness, and joy.

Catholic feminists, along with religiously committed feminists from other traditions, are not content to await, actively or passively, the reform of the institutional church. They have undertaken to develop rituals which not only do not oppress them but will give them life and hope. They do not hesitate to rewrite the stories of the tradition from the standpoint of women's experience, to repudiate the stories from the tradition which marginalize, demonize, or degrade women, and to write new stories which carry the non-patriarchal content of the tradition in ways that are meaningful for women.[47] These feminists are also not waiting for the institutional church to ask for their opinion about or to reform the official positions on moral matters that affect women. They are not controlled by guilt in relation to the institution, and many have taken anti-establishment positions on such issues as contraception, divorce and remarriage, homosexuality, and abortion. In short, they are busy *being* church rather than trying to reform the male establishment which is usually regarded as church. However, they both hope for and expect that men of good will will eventually join them in the reshaping of a church for all believers. Thus their separatism is neither total nor ideological but practical and provisional, although no one in the movement thinks that the reintegration will happen anytime soon.

C. Catholic and Feminist: The Future of Women's Spirituality in the Catholic Church

While some women who are both Catholic and feminist could locate themselves clearly in one or the other of the two positions described above, many others would find it very difficult to do so. Depending on the situation, the issue, the occasion, or the participants, they would identify primarily with their Catholic tradition or primarily with their feminist affiliation. Against the background of the descriptions given above I would suggest two conclusions about the future of women's spirituality in the Catholic Church.

1. Complementarity of Feminist Catholicism and Catholic Feminism

First, feminist Catholics and Catholic feminists are making a complementary contribution to the transformation of both Catholic spirituality and the institutional church. In the area of spirituality it seems clear that the interior life of feminist Catholics is the "place" where the fierce inner battle over ecclesiastical apartheid is being lived in all its agonizing intensity. The church is certainly involved in an institutional power struggle that is theological and political. But, as with every authentic liberation struggle, at its heart lies a spiritual struggle. In every such struggle the victims must find a way between the Scylla of death-dealing oppression by the power structure they are fighting and the Charybdis of soul-destroying hatred that would make political victory meaningless. Community support is essential in this struggle, but ultimately individuals must face, live through, and emerge from the ultimate threat to their selfhood that the struggle constitutes. Engaging this inner struggle, finding within themselves the truth-power that will make genuine conversion possible, is a major contribution to feminist Catholics whose spirituality has been subsumed into this paschal experience of death in hope of new life.

However, in the passage through the dark night of external oppression and inner desolation it is crucial that the imagination be enlivened with new possibilities. The exiles must have hope, and they cannot sing the songs of Sion in the Babylon of ecclesiastical violence. What Catholic feminists, especially those who are active in Womenchurch, are contributing to the spirituality of women who are both Catholic and feminist is a whole new repertoire of songs, new liturgical forms for the imagination, a proleptic image of a new church. These women have bravely moved ahead and begun to live what they believe, not waiting for permission or until the rest of the church is ready to move. And their living is an assurance that there is reality in the hope of those who live the exile. If exile is the primary self-image for feminist Catholics, exodus is the primary self-image for Catholic feminists.

In fact, there is much mutually empowering interchange between the two groups. While feminist Catholics may sometimes fear that their Womenchurch sisters have "thrown out the baby with the bath" and set sail for a non-existent promised land and Catholic feminists may sometimes deplore what looks like fearful conservatism in their still "churched" sisters, the two groups are increasingly respectful of each other. Not only is internecine struggle among feminists damaging to the movement; it is contrary to the very inclusiveness and connectedness that feminists want to promote and it plays directly into the patriarchal agenda of separating women from women. There is more than one kind of suffering, more than one kind of fear, and more than one kind of courage. The gifts of all must meet the weaknesses of each as the struggle continues.

In regard to the institutional church all women who are both Catholic and feminist desire passionately the conversion of the institution from the sin of sexism and know that this requires a full and final repudiation of patriarchy. Feminist Catholics are struggling to find within the tradition the resources for bringing about this massive transformation. The work of feminist Catholic theologians, ministers, and parents toward this end is carried on in the firm hope that one can use the master's tools to dismantle the master's house and that from the debris of the house of ecclesiastical patriarchy we will be able to construct the home of equal discipleship within which the reign of God can be realized.

By contrast, Catholic feminists tend, if not to give up completely on the institution, to regard it as not worth their life's blood. For them the best way to bring about a new church is to start being that church now. If the real life energy of the church is diverted into the swelling torrent of feminist spirituality, the patriarchal institution will soon be a dried up river bed, an arid trace of a lifeform that refused to change and so remains as a more or less interesting crack in the surface of history. Like other lifeforms that could not change, the patriarchal church will become an interesting historical fossil while the real church moves into the future as a discipleship of equals.

Again, the two approaches are not so much contradictory as complementary. The common aim is a new religious dwelling for the disciples of Jesus. Whether one rebuilds on the ancestral site or buys new land in a distant location is a prudential decision. In either case, a pre-condition of the new construction is that the old hovel of patriarchy must come down because it is unfit for human habitation. What the two groups of feminists in the church have in common is their diagnosis of the problem and their commitment to solving it. While feminist Catholics bring pressure to bear for transformation from within, Catholic feminists are serving notice that if the transformation is not undertaken in earnest, and soon, increasing numbers of believers will look elsewhere for spiritual nourishment.

2. Spirituality as the Place of Crisis for Women Catholics Who Are Feminists

The second conclusion I would draw from the foregoing reflections on the spirituality of women Catholics who are feminists is that spirituality, the lived experience of the faith, is the place of crisis for women whose consciousness is raised as well as for the church as institution.

What began for most women as a problem with the institution has become in recent years a problem of faith. When the first Women's Ordination Conference met in Detroit in 1975 the women who attended were focused on the transformation of the power arrangements in the institutional church specifically through the admission of women to orders. By the time the second Women's Ordination Conference met in Baltimore three years later, the women who attended were already aware that the "add women and stir" recipe for church reform was totally inadequate. Since 1978 women have come to realize that, in reality, we are not talking about how to organize the institution. We are talking about whether the God of Judaeo-Christian revelation is the true God or just men-writ-large to legitimate their domination; whether Jesus, an historical male, is or can be messiah and savior for those who are not male; whether what the church has called sacraments are really encounters with Christ or tools of male ritual abuse of women; whether what we have called church is a community of salvation or simply a male power structure. In other words, because the issue has moved from the realm of politics to the realm of spirituality, the stakes are now very high.

IV. CONCLUSION

At no time in its history, except perhaps at the time of the Protestant reformation, has the church faced a crisis of such proportions. However, the Protestant reformation involved a relatively small segment of the church in the tiny theater of western Europe. Feminism involves over half the church in every location in the world. All of the mothers of future Catholics are women and, despite the exclusion of women from orders, by far the majority of the church's professional ministers are women. While not all Catholic women are feminists, time and historical process is on the side of rising liberationist consciousness, not on the side of oppressive ideology. The church as institution cannot survive the final disillusionment of women although women, as church, can probably survive the demise of the patriarchal institution. The conclusion is that because the issue is in the arena of spirituality it must be taken with utter seriousness. If anything is to be learned from the Protestant reformation it is that when reform is urgent it may be deferred but it cannot finally be avoided and the price of deferral can be disastrously high.

However, precisely because the feminist issue within the church has resituated itself in the realm of spirituality, there is some reason to hope that the institutional church may be able to meet this monumental challenge to grow from a male power structure imprisoning the word of God into a fitting locus for the epiphany of the reign of God in this world. Women who are feminists and Catholics bring to the church not only a powerful critique and the very real possibility of massive withdrawal but enormous resources for transformation. They bring an image of a renewed church that is derived from the gospels rather than from imperial Rome, the feudal middle ages, and the divine right monarchies of the sixteenth and seventeenth centuries. They also bring a spiritual strength tempered in intense suffering and a loyalty that has survived twenty centuries of exclusion and oppression. To this vision of faith and this strength of hope they add a love of Christ, of the church itself, and of the world that has fueled a burning commitment to ministry since the earliest days of the church's history and which is still unquenched despite what raised consciousness has enabled them to see.

The feminism of Catholic women is both the church's ultimate and most serious challenge and its best hope for a future worthy of its gospel roots. When the male disciples of Jesus returned from the town of Samaria where they had gone to buy lunch they found Jesus in deep theological conversation with a woman. We are told that they were shocked and could not imagine what Jesus wanted from a woman or why he would bother to talk to her. But they knew better than to challenge Jesus' designs whose horizons were obviously well beyond their culture-bound ken. So the woman, like other apostles who left boats and nets and father and tax stall to follow Jesus and announce the good news, left her water jar and went off to announce Jesus and to present her fellow townspeople with the only question that really matters: "Can this be the Christ?" Women today are asking this same question of the institutional church. Can you recognize in us, in our persons and in our experience, the image of Christ, and will you choose to act accordingly?

NOTES

1. See Sandra M. Schneiders, "Theology and Spirituality: Strangers, Rivals, or Partners?" *Horizons* 13 (Fall 1986) 257–260.

2. Schneiders, "Theology and Spirituality," 266.

3. Sandra M. Schneiders, "Spirituality in the Academy," *Theological Studies* 50 (December 1989) 684.

4. An English translation of *Inter Insignores* is available as *Declaration on the Admission of Women to the Ministerial Priesthood* (Washington, D.C.: United States Catholic Conference, 1976). See pp. 11–15. See also Sandra M. Schneiders, *Women and the Word* (New York: Paulist Press, 1986) 3–5, on the maleness of Jesus.

5. Catherina Halkes, "Feminism and Spirituality," tr. Joan van der Sman, *Spirituality Today* 40 (1988) 220.

6. Carol P. Christ and Judith Plaskow, eds., *Womanspirit Rising: A Feminist Reader in Religion* (San Francisco: Harper and Row, 1979).

7. Judith Plaskow and Carol P. Christ, eds., *Weaving the Visions: New Patterns in Feminist Spirituality* (San Francisco: Harper and Row, 1989).

8. Halkes, "Feminism and Spirituality," 220.

9. For a readable but very informative account of the origin of western religion as the religion of the Great Goddess and the gradual triumph of the male warrior God of the Indo-European and Hebrew peoples, see Joseph Campbell with Bill Moyers, *The Power of Myth*, ed. Betty Sue Flowers (New York: Doubleday, 1988) 164–183. For a scholarly discussion of the original supremacy of the Goddess, her eventual replacement by the male God, and the relationship of this transformation of mythology to the actual social condition of women, see Gerda Lerner, *The Creation of Patriarchy* (New York: Oxford University Press, 1988) 141–160.

10. Carol P. Christ has been a primary figure in the theoretical development of feminist spirituality both through her literary analyses of women's literature of transformation and through her work on the function of "the goddess" in women's psychological development through the appropriation and inner divine power and outward political power. For examples of her work in these areas, see her essays, "Margaret Atwood: The Surfacing of Women's Spiritual Quest and Vision," *Signs* 2 (Winter 1976) 316–330; "Why Women Need the Goddess: Phenomenological, Psychological, and Political Reflections," in *Womanspirit Rising: A Feminist Reader in Religion*, 273–287.

11. See, for example, the explanations of this fundamental character and agenda of feminist spirituality by Shelley Finson, "Feminist

Spirituality Within the Framework of Feminist Consciousness," *Studies in Religion* 16 (1987) 65–77; Patricia Schechter, "Feminist Spirituality and Radical Political Commitment," *Journal of Women and Religion* 4:1 (Spring 1981) 57; Sally B. Purvis, "Christian Feminist Spirituality," *Christian Spirituality: Post-Reformation and Modern,* Louis Dupré and Don E. Saliers, eds. [*World Spirituality: An Encyclopedic History of the Religious Quest*] vol. 18 (New York: Crossroad, 1989) 500–519.

12. See Lerner, *The Creation of Patriarchy,* for a comprehensive treatment.

13. Lerner, *The Creation of Patriarchy,* 36, refers to the hypothesis of an original matriarchy as the creation of a compensatory myth for which there is no compelling evidence. Other feminist scholars who reject the hypothesis of an original matriarchy are the following: Elizabeth Dodson Gray, *Patriarchy as a Conceptual Trap* (Wellesley, MA: Roundtable Press, 1982) 28–29; Halkes, "Feminism and Spirituality," 221; Rosemary R. Ruether, "Feminism and Religious Faith: Renewal or New Creation?" *Religion and Intellectual Life* 3 (Winter 1986) 8; Merlin Stone, "When God Was a Woman," in *Womanspirit Rising: A Feminist Reader in Religion,* 126–130; Deborah Streeter, "The Goddess: Power and Paradox," *Journal of Women and Religion* 1 (Fall, 1981) 13–14.

14. Lerner, *The Creation of Patriarchy,* 145.

15. Ruether, in "Feminism and Religious Faith: Renewal or New Creation?" 9, explains this process, and its continuation in Christianity, as follows: " . . . the more one studies different religious traditions and their early roots, the more one is tempted to suggest that religion itself is essentially a male creation. The male, marginalized from direct participation in the great mysteries of gestation and birth, asserted his superior physical strength to monopolize leisure and culture and did so by creating ritual expressions that duplicated female gestating and birthing roles, but in such a way as to transfer the power of these primary mysteries to himself. This would perhaps explain why mother-goddess figures predominate in early religion, but do not function to give women power. This ritual sublimation of female functions, as transfer of spiritual power over life to males, is continued in Christianity. The central mysteries of Baptism and the Eucharist duplicate female roles in gestation, birth and nourishment, but give the power over the spiritualized expression of these functions to males, and only males who eschew sex and reproduction."

16. Gray, *Patriarchy as a Conceptual Trap,* 26. (This citation is in italics in the original text.)

17. For an accessible but well-developed treatment of Wisdom as a feminine personification of God in the Judaeo-Christian tradition, see Susan Cady, Marian Ronan, and Hal Taussig, *Sophia: The Future of*

Feminist Spirituality (San Francisco: Harper and Row, 1986). Elizabeth Johnson, in "Jesus, Wisdom of God: A Biblical Basis for a Non-Androcentric Christology," *Ephemerides Theologicae Lovanienses,* LX 1:4 (December 1985) 261–294, suggests the theological potential of this biblical tradition for dealing with contemporary problems in christology.

18. Matthew L. Lamb, "The Dialectics of Theory and Praxis Within Paradigm Analysis," in *Paradigm Change in Theology: A Symposium for the Future,* Hans Küng and David Tracy, eds., Margaret Kohl, tr. (New York: Crossroad, 1989) 96.

19. Some feminist spirituality involves a lyrical celebration of the bodily as sacred. See, e.g., Starhawk (Miriam Simos), "Witchcraft and Women's Culture," Christ and Plaskow, eds., *Womanspirit Rising,* 263. See also Elisabeth Schüssler Fiorenza, "Feminist Spirituality, Christian Identity, and Catholic Vision," Christ and Plaskow, eds., *Womanspirit Rising,* 127–138, for the connection between goddess spirituality, which we will take up below, and the reclaiming of the bodily power to give life in the image of divinity.

20. Plaskow and Christ, eds., "Introduction," *Weaving the Visions,* 6–11.

21. I have attempted to distinguish between divinity presented in feminine form and particular feminine personifications of divinity by referring to the former as "Goddess" (without the article and capitalized, as we use the term God) and to the latter as "the goddess" or "a goddess" (with article and in lower case, as we would speak of the gods).

22. In answer to the question of whether Goddess is simply "female power writ large" or a real entity, Carol Christ, in "Why Women Need the Goddess," Christ and Plaskow, eds., *Womanspirit Rising,* 278–279, replies that different women answer that question differently. Some see Goddess as a real divine protectress to whom one can pray. Others see her primarily as symbol of either life-death-rebirth or of the beauty and legitimacy of female power.

23. Miriam Simos, who is a leading practitioner and theorist of witchcraft and who is known by her wicca name of Starhawk, provides an excellent explanation of this ancient religious tradition and its fate in Christian Europe in "Witchcraft and Women's Culture," in Christ and Plaskow, eds., *Womanspirit Rising,* 259–268.

24. Ibid. 261–262.

25. Ibid. 263.

26. Rosemary Radford Ruether, in "Feminist Theology and Spirituality," in *Christian Feminism: Visions of a New Humanity,* Judith L. Weidman, ed. (San Francisco: Harper and Row, 1984) 11, puts it well: "Feminist theology starts with the affirmation that God, the ground of

being and new being, underlies, includes, supports, and promotes female personhood as much as male personhood. Woman is not subordinate or 'included under,' but equivalent as imago dei."

27. An important contribution to this discussion is Christine Downing's *The Goddess: Mythological Images of the Feminine* (New York: Crossroad, 1981).

28. An excellent study on the goddesses as archetypes of the feminine is Jean Shinoda Bolen's *Goddesses in Every Woman: A New Psychology of Women* (San Francisco: Harper and Row, 1984).

29. Cf. Elizabeth Dreyer, "Recovery of the Feminine in Spirituality," *New Catholic World* 227 (1984) 71–72. Purvis, in "Christian Feminist Spirituality," 503–504, calls story-telling the creative moment in Christian feminist spirituality.

30. See, e.g., Christ, "Margaret Atwood," in Christ and Plaskow, eds., *Womanspirit Rising,* 329–330, who insists, in regard to menstruation, pregnancy, and childbirth, that "it seems to me far wiser for women as persons and as critics to name the power which resides in our bodies and our potential closeness to nature positively, and to use this new naming to transform the pervasive cultural and religious devaluation of nature and the body."

Purvis, in "Christian Feminist Spirituality," 504–514, names "embodiment" as one of the major characteristics of feminist spirituality. It involves a rejection of male fear of sexuality and an embracing of the erotic as a source of passion for union in love, for social justice, and for encountering God.

Schüssler Fiorenza, describing the effect of goddess consciousness, says in "Feminist Spirituality, Christian Identity, and Catholic Vision," in Christ and Plaskow, eds., *Womanspirit Rising,* 127–138: "The Goddess is the giver and nurturer of life, the dispenser of love and happiness. Woman as her image is therefore not 'the other' of the divine. She is not body and carnality in opposition to spirit and soul, not the perpetuator of evil and rebellion. Being a woman, living in sisterhood under the aegis of the Goddess, brings us in touch with the creative, healing, life-giving power at the heart of the world."

31. Cf. Streeter, "The Goddess: Power and Paradox," 9; Riley, *Transforming Feminism,* 97, says, "For radical feminism, the primary root [of war] is men's will to dominate women. From this root come all other forms of domination. The will to dominate appears subtly in the patriarchal social structures and the cultural ideology that supports those structures. It appears overtly in all acts of violence: rape, torture, sexual abuse, incest, pornography, domestic violence, the destruction of the earth. It finds its ultimate expression in war. . . . "

32. Some authors who explicate this connection are the following: Margaret Galiardi, "Bonding, The Critical Praxis of Feminism," *The Way* 26 (1986) 134–44; Patricia Schechter, "Feminist Spirituality and Radical Political Commitment," *Journal of Women and Religion* 4:1 (Spring 1981) 51–60; Rosemary R. Ruether, "Feminism and Religious Faith: Renewal or New Creation?" *Religion and Intellectual Life* 3 (Winter 1986) 7–20; Dermot A. Lane, "Christian Feminism," *Furrow* 36 (November 1985) 663–675; Plaskow and Christ, eds., "Introduction," *Weaving the Visions,* 1–11 and Maria Riley, *Transforming Feminism* (Kansas City: Sheed and Ward, 1989).

33. Purvis, "Christian Feminist Spirituality," 509.

34. I suspect most feminists would not recognize as feminist the approach taken by Mary E. Giles, in *The Feminist Mystic and Other Essays on Women and Spirituality* (New York: Crossroad, 1982) 5. Giles objects to much of contemporary feminism and reveals her own approach, which most feminists would label at least anachronistic, when she says, on p. 30, "Catherine and Teresa were free, joyous, loving and creative, alive in and through their being women. As such they were feminists."

35. One can see this kind of development, for example, in the work of Joann Wolski Conn who, in her first major work on spirituality, *Women's Spirituality: Resources for Christian Development* (New York: Paulist, 1986) 8–27, was hesitant to use the term "feminist" and preferred to speak of "women's spirituality." However, she has since become quite explicitly feminist in her treatment of spirituality. See e.g., "Discipleship of Equals: Past, Present and Future?" *Horizons* 14 (Fall 1987) 231–261.

36. Carol Christ, in the chapter "A Spirituality for Women," in *Laughter of Aphrodite: Reflections on a Journey to the Goddess* (San Francisco: Harper and Row, 1987) 56–72, describes this process as she experienced it. In her case it led to an abandonment of the Christian tradition in favor of Goddess spirituality.

37. A very good personal account of this type of journey is given by Riley in *Transforming Feminism,* 1–11.

38. See Fran Ferder, "Zeal for Your House Consumes Me: Dealing with Anger As a Woman in the Church," *Women in the Church I,* ed. Madonna Kolbenschlag (Washington, D.C.: Pastoral Press, 1987) 95–113 for a discussion of the psychological as well as spiritual dimensions of this experience.

39. In Joann Wolski Conn, ed., *Women's Spirituality: Resources for Christian Development* (New York: Paulist Press, 1986) 287–311.

40. Carolyn Osiek, *Beyond Anger: On Being a Feminist in the Church* (New York: Paulist, 1986).

41. Sandra M. Schneiders, "Women and Power in the Church: A New Testament Reflection," *Proceedings of the Catholic Theological Society of America* 37 (June 10–13, 1982) 123–128.

42. Sandra M. Schneiders, "The Effects of Women's Experience on Their Spirituality," *Spirituality Today* 35 (Summer 1983) 100–116.

43. See Kathleen Fischer, *Women at the Well: Feminist Perspectives on Spiritual Direction* (New York: Paulist, 1988) 175–194.

44. For a good treatment of the impact of feminist scholarship on the theological academy see Carr, *Transforming Grace*, 63–94.

45. This fact has been recognized by the undertaking by the U.S. bishops of the writing of a pastoral letter on women's concerns. See National Conference of Catholic Bishops, "Partners in the Mystery of Redemption: A Pastoral Response to Women's Concerns for Church and Society," *Origins* 17 (April 21, 1988) 758–788.

46. See "Women-Church: A Feminist Exodus Community," in Rosemary R. Ruether, *Women-Church: Theology and Practice of Feminist Liturgical Communities* (San Francisco: Harper and Row, 1986) 57–74, for a succinct summary description and analysis of the history and present shape of this movement.

47. Cf. Ruether, "Feminism and Religious Faith: Renewal or New Creation?" 17.

Cancer in the Body of Christ

Mary Jo Weaver

When I wrote *New Catholic Women* ten years ago, I focused on the women's movement within the Catholic Church with the institutional church as a primary reference point. Although the book sketched a vexed past and a troubled present, it was redolent with hope for a better future. Naively, as I now think, I believed in those years that the transformative power of feminism would join the vibrant confidence of Catholicism to create a more inclusive and therefore stronger community. Although I was aware that women's initiatives were being thwarted by ecclesiastical officials, I imagined that Catholic feminism, like justice or truth, would eventually triumph.

In the years between *New Catholic Women* and *Springs of Water in a Dry Land,* I learned from women that I needed to change my focus. As I addressed groups of Catholic women trying to cope with institutional anguish and personal despair, I had to admit more openly that the church was obviously failing many women. The institution that had welcomed the enormous ecclesiastical changes of the Second Vatican Council, that met the world with self-assurance in the 1960s, had, by the 1980s become polarized, fearful, and intransigent. Rather than opening expansive new possibilities, Catholic feminism had disclosed a morbid narrowness that cramped the future.

Springs of Water in a Dry Land, therefore, was an attempt to find strategies or to publicize efforts aimed to subvert or bypass the institution. It explored the metaphor of the desert where it seemed possible to sustain oneself prayerfully within, outside of, nearby, or quite apart from the tradition. What counted was a personal spiritual life that could be lived out even in the austerity of exile. I tried, in that book, to make some aspects of a feminist spirituality accessible to people who felt they were starving to death within the church.

If I did not exactly ignore the church, I treated it as if it were virtually irrelevant. The real question in my mind was not whether the church could welcome feminism, but whether Catholic feminists could nourish their religious lives in an institution hostile to any suggestion that the church might adapt itself more compellingly to feminism.

Since *Springs of Water in a Dry Land,* I have been increasingly troubled by an ecclesiastical conundrum: sacramentally and strategically, I do not see how we can ignore the church even though, in feminist terms, it seems impossible to engage it. The "people of God" are stuck. Or, to use an ancient metaphor, the "body of Christ" is ill. Because I have spent the past year or so dealing with cancer, focusing on the concrete pain and imaginative fears of the body, I wonder if some of what I have learned about my body, mind, and spirit might be usefully applied to the ecclesiastical body? Put bluntly: if the church is the "body of Christ," what would it mean to talk about that body as if it had cancer?

NO ESCAPE

First there's the inescapability of it. Whether it is my body or the body of Christ, I cannot leave it without committing suicide. I look in the mirror and see something that has delivered me into the hands of a chronic condition that I might learn to live with or might have to learn to die with. Many women in the church live in a body that has betrayed us and continues to do so. If, physically, we have managed to live in the illusion that we can control the body—dieting, medical makeover, hair coloring, endurance training—once marked with this disease, we are quickly and inexorably plunged into the cold waters of reality. Yeats says that in old age we realize that our hearts are "attached to a dying animal."[1] Cancer is a more dramatic route to that awareness in the body as perhaps recent papal statements are in the body of Christ.

FEAR AND ANGER

After the numbing physical shock, comes the emotional chaos of fear and anger. I feared mutilation, treatment, recurrence, and death and was angry at the environment, the medical establishment, and myself. In the ecclesiastical body, many women and men in the church live in a cascade of emotional pain every time they go to church. They may fear to say anything to their pastor or their partner, or they may be seethingly angry. Of these two emotions, fear is the most dangerous because it attaches so easily to surrender. Bernie Siegel, whose work I found helpful in the early days of my illness, says that sick people who are fearful give up too quickly: they feel helpless or hopeless and often have a powerless conception of themselves. In the body of Christ we might ask if a history of disparaging images of women in the church along with contemporary hostility to even minor ameliorations of sexism within the church produces a similar sense of despair so that some people give up (leave the church) rather than fight against those who have made their spiritual environment carcinogenic.

Unlike fear, anger can be a good friend when you are sick because it will not allow submissiveness. It tells you that being a "good patient" can be bad for you. Siegel claims that there is a 100% correlation between being a bad patient and having an active immune system. Anger helps us to ask questions, be pesky about our treatment, and refuse to be treated as a statistic.

Sexism in the body of Christ is insidious because it can jolt these same emotions of fear and anger to life in ways that threaten men and women of faith who have been trained for self-denial. Some of the profiles of cancer patients I have seen paint pictures of repressors with strong commitments to social norms who are expected to suffer loss and depression quietly (offering it up). They may have a hard time with boat-rocking individuality, because their religious training expects them to conform, to accept authority, and to respond with a cheery "I'm fine" even when their world is falling apart. Women and men who feel this way in the body of Christ might consider turning the gospel on its ear: in the case of injustice, it is not perfect love that "casteth out fear," but focused rage. We can put anger to good use in the church. When bishops and priests act like supercilious surgeons, telling us what is good for us without our consultation, we can badger them with questions, insist on clear and complete information, and reserve the right to make our own decisions, as if our lives depended on it.

TEARS AND GRIEF

Although anger is helpful in the early days of disease, it is usually overtaken pretty quickly by tears and grief. For me, for months after surgery, the tears simply would not stop: sometimes they came, like sneezes, uninvited and inescapable, other times they accompanied engulfing waves of sadness. The freedom to weep almost anywhere may be a cultural blessing of womanhood, but for me it was a hard practice to accept. I remember once thinking that the only springs of water I could find in my dry land were tears, and that reminded me that the "gift of tears" was part of the ancient understanding of spiritual growth.

Traditionally, within the body of Christ, the "gift of tears" was attached to self-condemnation and repentance. In the converted life of early monasticism, tears were thought to be an essential part of a process toward God that cleanses the soul and solidifies virtue. Men and women were supposed to weep endlessly for their sins. At the same time that ancient monks—and medieval saints like Catherine of Siena or Teresa of Avila—praise tears shed for sins, however, they condemn depression. Tears shed for one's own pain are not holy; tears shed in judgment of someone else's sins threaten salvation.

I think that view is short-sighted, like parents who look at a weeping child and say, "Quit crying, or I'll give you something to cry about." We *have* something to cry about: God may live in the church, but the church may be dying, and that is cause for keening grief in the body. A contemporary version of the "gift of tears" is the grief people feel *for* the church. The tears of the saints, shed for the body, ought to be heard in the church. Tears of bewildered pain turn into tears of rage when they are ignored. In the human body, as in the ecclesiastical body, pain, rage, and tears are visible signs of weakness that, like tears of repentance, clarify the need for help beyond our own resources.

In the body of Christ these days, quite apart from so-called "women's issues," there are many reasons to grieve: the scandalous disclosures of sexual abuse that have opened our eyes to intense pain in victims and perpetrators even while they have thoroughly damaged the popular perception of the priesthood; the mean-spirited perception of right-wing Catholics that all feminists are bitter, destructive, neo-pagan, abortion-mongers; the inner-city and rural parishes that have had to close leaving mostly elderly and poor people without pastoral care; the loss of a generation of young Catholics to ignorance about their own tradition; the grief of an older generation that has lost an entire culture and can see no way to retrieve it; and the rigid and merciless refusal of church leaders to discuss birth control, celibacy, homosexuality, and divorce.

All these reasons to grieve manifest the vulnerability of the body which, in turn, can open to healing. Grief draws us, seductively and darkly, into a deeper awareness of pain, despair, and depression. In the body of Christ, as in the physical body, the first reaction to illness is dread and confusion, normal but ineffective emotions. Grief is more helpful because it can teach us to embrace pain as the first step toward healing. Put another way, grief is part of a process of self-awareness that can lead toward a compassion rooted in self-acceptance. Without grief there can be no healing.

HEALING THE BODY

Unlike anger, fear, rage and pain that come along with illness uninvited, healing requires our cooperation. We lure it toward us by dropping bread crumbs of awareness for pain to feast on. In the physical body, healing demands a deep appreciation for one's own body and one's specific suffering even as it assures us that we do not suffer alone. Spiritual directors in all religious traditions have been saying similar things for years, but sometimes it takes the physical experience of the body to make the life of the spirit more vivid.

Healing is hard work because, in a culture dedicated to numbing all pain, it feels counter-intuitive. We are supposed to become more deeply aware of the body, to stay in a painful moment in order to soften around it. Like prayer, healing is partly a matter of focus and partly a matter of letting go. The task is to unfetter the body from the critical, worrying, racing-ahead, over-rationalizing, theorizing, and comically "in control" mind. The trick is learning to do this when you have been diagnosed with cancer.

We sometimes have to do some of the most important work of our lives in one of the worst conditions of our lives which is a difficult place to begin, and, as Carl Simonton says, "also a very powerful position because we now have a compelling reason to learn whatever we need to know to change the course of our lives."[2] The deep opening into one's own pain is necessary because we are—in our sick and hurting body—the only place where the work of healing can be done. In the physical body and in the body of Christ, a practice of awareness, the embrace of pain is the pathway into ourselves, toward healing and toward God which, in my mind, are the same realities.

Stephen Levine, whose work balances compassion with an unstinting look at the realities of cancer, has been my teacher in this process. If he were a monk, he would be a contemplative, someone who brings a habit of attention to the moment. In one of the most moving passages in *Healing into Life and Death* he says this about the relationship between healing and illness:

> Just as pain uncovers deep holdings within us—ancient fears, subliminal imprints, long unnoticed desires for control—so the investigation of illness begins to heal these underlying tendencies. Thus we have seen that for many working with illness in the body means working with the discomforts of the mind—a healing of one's deepest clingings and fears—which led them to the discovery of joys unimagined and a spaciousness never dreamed of. Illness causes us to confront our most assiduous doubts about the nature of the universe and the existence of God. It tears us open. It teaches us to keep our hearts open in Hell.[3]

In my own body, the most radical act of faith I can make for myself is to believe that whether I live or die, life will come out of my learning to keep my heart "open in Hell." Put less dramatically, I believe that meditations teach me about shared suffering and draw me into a more universal awareness of pain that will, eventually, heal me. When I work toward healing in myself, I use Levine's meditations to quiet the mind and draw awareness into the heart and toward the world. They make experiential sense to me on a personal level as I hope they might work for the ecclesiastical body.

THE BODY OF CHRIST

The church as the body of Christ is an ancient and complex metaphor used in the Pauline writings. It is a very rich concept in terms of the body in pain. Consider this passage from Colossians 1:24: "I rejoice in my sufferings for your sake, and in my flesh I complete what is lacking in Christ's afflictions for the sake of his body, that is, the church." What an astonishing sentence! The author rejoices in (or embraces) his suffering for the sake of others (the body) and, by so doing, somehow completes what is *lacking* in the sufferings of Christ.

Is it absurd, therefore, to believe that what we do in our physical bodies and what we suffer in the church also, somehow, completes or participates in the sufferings of Christ? If we accept Luke Johnson's reading of this passage—that suffering was the progressive opening of Jesus' humanity to the divine—I think we can say that the present suffering in the body of Christ, embraced for the sake of others, opens that body (the church) to the transforming power of God, what we used to call grace.

But how can we embrace suffering in the body of Christ? I suggest that we do something similar to what Levine suggests for healing in the physical body. The images he uses regularly are mind, heart, body, and breath, concepts that, for him, are clearly Buddhist but can also be profoundly Christian. Paul says in 1 Corinthians that we are the body of Christ, and that we are infused with the spirit or breath of God. He also says, in a rather startling passage (1 Cor 2:16), that we have the "mind of Christ." In Paul's understanding, as in the tradition of the church, our way to God is through Christ, and our way to Christ is to be baptized into his *body*. It is in this body, says Paul, that God "discloses the purposes of the heart" (1 Cor 4:5).

THE BODY OF CHRIST IN PAIN

Healing images are present, therefore, in Paul's writings: the body, mind, spirit, and heart of Christ are available to us even as, in some way, we constitute them or share in them. Spiritual growth, like healing, requires the body: it is only in the body that we meet the God who willingly participates in human suffering and can somehow lead us through it. In contrast with Buddhism which began with the teaching of the way to enlightenment, Christianity began in pain. From the earliest moments of the birth of Jesus in an animal shelter, to his public ministry, the life of Jesus is that of the lowly, homeless, self-forgetful man whose message of peace, love, and sympathy led in the end to suffering, agony, and final despair—and, in the faith of the Christian church, to salvation.

How does one find victory in that defeat? That is the genius of Paul: he blends his soul, rooted in ancient Judaism, with his startling *experience* of the risen Lord to find in the life and death of Jesus a God whose continuity is manifest in extraordinary reversals. In Christ, Paul says, God enters into a world of confusion and ambiguity where the divine purposes work in contradictions and turn human wisdom on its head. In Jesus, God works through events of conflict and rupture to open new possibilities made available only because Jesus embraced the pain that broke him open to his divinity. The image of God to which we are expected to conform has been made manifest in the image of the suffering Christ. The body of Christ is a body in pain.

For many of us in the church right now, that pain is all too real and seems only to get worse. For example, the publication of a universal catechism is a brilliant idea, but translating it deliberately and with "full consent of the will" into sexist language is painful to my generation and absurd to the next. In the dismay or anger stimulated by official decisions, the temptation to sever oneself from insensitive leaders in order to escape unnecessary suffering is overwhelming. When I am tempted to avoidance, I try to combine Paul's understanding of the ecclesiastical body with Levine's meditations for the physical body in order to sense the connections between healing and a deepening experience of hurt.

In religious terms, we cannot experience conversion and repentance without going down into the chaotic waters of Christ's death where the Spirit moves to make us into something new. Put another way, religion, like healing, is an experience of being unmade and remade, an experience where "the heart is broken so as to make space for others, for compassion. It is learning a new capacity for love."[4]

Learning to love through suffering is a fact of adult life for which, according to the New Testament, we have a model. The author of the epistle to the Hebrews says that Christ was made perfect through suffering, a phrase that has sometimes led to zealous masochism in search of spiritual perfection, but that is not what that epistle means at all. The author says that through sufferings Christ is allowed to experience human life and, at the same time, disclose a God identified with humanity in its suffering. Christ has gone before us into the dark places of doubt, fear, and weakness. If we follow, push through, those dismal places—not by creating suffering, but by embracing it for the sake of the body—we will come to the hidden God, what Levine calls "the great heart."

EMBRACING THE HUMAN

The identification of God with humanity was made perfect in the mind, heart, and body of Jesus whose spirituality was fully human. In the modern language of process thought, God began an adventure in Jesus that is necessarily connected with our lives. Because we are members of the body of Christ, God is passionately interested in our human lives. In the ancient language of the early church, "the glory of God is the human being fully alive."[5]

Jesus was more profoundly united to God than anyone else, and was more human, more free, more alive, more his own person because of it. The church as the body of Christ, therefore, achieves its perfection when it is most perfectly human, embracing the full range of its experience including sickness, suffering, and possible death. The body of Christ is the place where believers experience conversion as a thousand moments of change wrought by anguish, darkness, and the merciful embrace of the pain we all share. Speaking of conversion, Rowan Williams says that "loud cries and tears are what open the long-closed door between God and our hearts" and that going through that door is responding "to the trials encountered simply in living as a believer, living in the insecurities of faith."[6]

Unfortunately, many of the "insecurities of faith" these days come from those responsible for nurturing the body of Christ. Those ecclesiastical officials whose decisions cause pain to the body seem to have gotten confused about their purpose. By attempting to block out all discordant elements, church officials anesthetize the body and inhibit healing. We must remember that this body—the church—was formed by the life of Jesus, who entered a world of disharmony and discord, and was able to see a larger, more inclusive pattern within it. Jesus welcomed questions and new possibilities: his community was made up of the troubled and the troublemakers whose lives and ideas befuddled the religious authorities of the day.

His relationship to God was radically new and disconcerting. His God was not a control freak or a moral imperialist. On the contrary, as Jesus grew toward the God at the center of his heart, he found one willing to offer the divine heart as a means to transform cosmic suffering. And he entered into it, as we are called into it, into healing toward the great heart in the body of Christ. In religious terms, the great heart is the adventure of God's own life, the place where divine love takes risks.

EMBRACING THE PAIN

Life in the body of Christ is radical openness to startling disconnections. As Jesus opened himself to divine love through the shared pain of the world around him, the church should be dedicated to maintaining, extending, and strengthening the sphere of that influence. The body of Christ is open to God's love through the shared pain of its members and, finally, the shared pain of the universe. Healing in the body of Christ begins with merciful awareness of the pain caused by those who live in denial of the radical openness of Jesus, who use their power to squelch the new ideas that are the spirit and the mind of Christ.

This body which is not even permitted to *think about* women's ordination, for example, cannot breathe. This body, which stiffens and scowls at the notion that Christ would welcome homosexuals, divorced and remarried couples, and married people who have learned to celebrate their sexuality without always longing for off-spring, is gravely ill. This body which requires the anguished self-denial of sexual expression for its ministers radiates pain. This body that treats women from a vantage of hierarchy, privilege, emotional distance, and xenophobia has cancer.

The inescapability of this cancer is heightened by the realiza-tion that those who often cause the pain are members of the same body. In the ecclesiastical body as in the human body, everything is connected. There is a battle in progress between good cells and cancerous ones where it is possible that the body might not re-cover. When a human body has cancer, even extreme measures like radiation and chemotherapy do not destroy all the disease. Rather, they weaken it, send it into remission, and give the body a chance to handle the rest of it with our immune system. I am not sure I see how that works in the body of Christ except through determined participation in our own healing.

Learning to live with cancer—in my body, or in the body of Christ—might mean accepting that healing can lead to death as well as life and that death is not a failure, and healing is not fruit-less. Whether healing practices *change* the institutional church or not, they *touch* it: "Each person who works to open their [sic] hearts, touches the heart of us all," Levine says.[7] The inexorable connections within our own bodies and within the body of Christ mean that our efforts to participate in healing have a salubrious effect on others.

A HEALING MEDITATION

Meditations about healing usually ask us to imagine our-selves as part of a giant wave of human experience so that we can know, in our bodies, minds, and hearts, that there is no such thing as isolated suffering. In the body of Jesus, God emptied the divine self into time and history. In the body of Christ, we participate in healing by assuming the mind of Christ, i.e., by becoming an environment that opens new possibilities for those around us. I want to try one of Stephen Levine's healing meditations that I have adapted to the body of Christ in pain. The slippages between one's own body and the ecclesiastical body are intentional. This meditation should be read by you or to you slowly.

Make yourself comfortable and let attention settle into the body. Just feel what sits here and receive the body of sensation in a clear, gentle awareness.

Make an imaginative leap to the body of Christ of which you are an integral part and let the sensations of that body come into your awareness. You will feel them in your body, but try to sense the larger body as well.

Notice how sensations vary in type and intensity: some sensations are pleasant; some sensations are unpleasant. Stay with them.

Notice any sense of self, of "me" or "mine," imposed around areas of discomfort. Notice the tension where you hold on to "my suffering." There is nothing to judge here. Simply notice whatever tension or fear may hold discomfort in this body.

Notice and deepen awareness: Does the body attempt to shut off discomfort? Does the body close like a fist around pain? Does anything seem to "hold on" to the discomfort?

Notice any tendency to pull the pleasant forward or push the unpleasant away. Watch the natural aversion to the unpleasant. Focus on the resistance itself.

As awareness begins to meet discomfort, let the body soften, allow sensations to float. Allow the fist to open, to expose the tender sensations arising from moment to moment. Allow awareness to receive the moment-to-moment sensations arising in the body of discomfort.

You are the body of Christ, St. Paul says. Feel this body. Let awareness explore the varying sensations that compose this body.

Imagine other members of this body elsewhere in the world experiencing this same discomfort. Not taking on their pain, but healing it with your soft mercy.

Sense the body of discomfort shared by so many. Sense the thousands of members of the body of Christ experiencing this same sensation at this same moment.

And sense this discomfort not as "my pain" but as "the pain." Gently feel "the pain" in "the body."

Sense the thousands of children, and women, and men who, in this very moment, feel this same discomfort in this same body.

Softly allow the pain to float in the body we all share.

Letting go of the holding around pain, softening gently to allow sensation to float in the shared body, begin gradually to cradle the pain.

Take your time.

There is no rush now in meeting softly that which has so often been met with hardness.

Sense the moment of the woman, sick and lonely, in a small town with no priest, this same pain touching this same body.

Touch the discomfort of an alcoholic priest unable to rise from his sleepless bed, with a merciful awareness.

Picture a woman divorced and remarried afraid to go to church, longing for the sacraments.

Imagine a once-vibrant parish divided and acrimonious because of a sexist pastor who only likes docile women.

Touch the women with vocations to the priesthood driven from the body of Christ with no real alternative.

Let their pain be healed by your mercy and awareness as it touches these same sensations in this same body.

Receive their experience in sweet mercy. Feel the shared body softening and expanding into the spaciousness of the shared heart.

Feel the connectedness in the body of Christ. No one alone. The shared body with the mind of Christ met in the shared heart.

A vaster sense of being. Not alone in pain, but as one with all those in discomfort. Meeting the moment in mercy and kindness. A new tenderness arising relating to its own pain, relating to all pain.

Let the mind float.

Let the images come and go.

Feel all those others sharing this same moment, shared sensations floating in this shared body of Christ. Nothing to create, just receiving this moment shared.

Experiencing all these members of the body in the one heart, in our common mercy. Let the images come. Let them be gently experienced. Let them go. Constantly sharing the healing. Touching with mercy our pain so as to free the pain of the church.

Healing the body of Christ by touching this moment with mercy and awareness.

Feel the single experience of the shared heart.

Sensation floating free in the body of Christ.

Let awareness meet all the members of the body of Christ healing into the immensity of the Great Heart, the adventurous, loving God.

Let your heart merge with all that share the greater body.

Softening all about sensations to let them float in the shared body. To heal *this moment* with mercy and loving kindness.

Feel it. Let it be.

Feel it. Let it go.

Take each breath into the body that we all share.

Let the breath come.

Let the breath go.

In shared body.

In the vast heart that merges with all.

In this moment meeting our pain in our heart, the heart opens to universal healing.

Touching with mercy and loving kindness the pain we all share, we receive the healing we each took birth for.[8]

NOTES

1. "Sailing to Byzantium," in *The Collected Poems of W. B. Yeats.* New York: Macmillan, 1959, p. 191.

2. *The Healing Journey: Restoring Health and Harmony to Body, Mind, and Spirit.* New York: Bantam Books, 1992, p. x.

3. Stephen Levine, *Healing into Life and Death.* New York: Doubleday, 1982, p. 30.

4. Rowan Williams, *The Wound of Knowledge: Christian Spirituality from the New Testament to St. John of the Cross.* Boston: Crowley Publications, 1990, pp. 12f. Williams is a brilliant analyst of spiritual passion and pain, and much of my interpretation of the body of Christ in pain is indebted to his work.

5. Irenaeus of Lyons, *Adversus Haereses,* IV.34.

6. Williams, *The Wound of Knowledge,* p. 11.

7. Levine, *Healing into Life and Death,* p. 11.

8. Adapted from Stephen Levine's "Meditation on Great Heart," in *Healing into Life and Death,* pp. 73–76. Most of the language *not* specifically about the church as body of Christ is from Levine.

Woman-Body, Man-Body: Knowing God

Wendy M. Wright

It seemed like such a simple question. And the answer seemed almost as straightforward. "Do men and women know God differently because they are differently embodied?" "Yes, although one way of knowing should not be considered superior to the other." My own experience of being wife and mother had given me intimations of divine life that were distinct from my husband's. Furthermore, it was not simply my biological experience as woman that taught me about God. It was my gendered identity, my being a woman in this culture and time, and the subtle roles assigned to me here that shaped my ways of knowing God.

Once I had the question posed and my tentative answer, I began to be attentive to what others might say on the subject. I was not surprised at what I heard.

A middle-aged, married laywoman sat in my office reflecting pensively on her long faith journey. "I always felt sort of 'unspiritual.' God was always 'out there' somewhere, outside family, outside my most intimate womanly experiences. No one ever affirmed them for me as an experience of God's presence."

A forty-five-year-old Jesuit visual-artist sat on a park bench beneath the changing colors of autumn and spoke of his prayer: "I have always stood before God as a man. Somehow, my masculinity is part of my God-knowing."

Another Jesuit colleague in his mid-fifties, involved in formation work, commented on the difference he perceives between the men and women to whom he listens as spiritual director. "Women seem more likely to speak interpersonally, to dwell on relationships as the place where they find God. Men, on the other hand, seem to focus more on work, on the activities of discipleship."

Two single female friends attended a women's ritual group where they explored fresh and invigorating ways of worshiping God and shared the unique woman-stories of their lives.

I studied an article on the topic of spirituality written by a Jewish scholar, which included an emphatic, unfootnoted comment:

> We should recognize that men and women/boys and girls may experience this spirituality differently precisely because of their physical differences. Women's spirituality is a whole way of viewing the relationship of women to the Divine in a way which is different from men's spirituality.

As I listened to these and other voices, I felt confirmed in my answer. Yet I also felt strangely perplexed at the unanimity of the responses. Eventually I found myself raising question after question. This article is an attempt to follow the leads of those questions, not so much to arrive at a definitive answer as to explore the various dimensions of the questioning. My propensity for being attentive to others' responses to the query, "Do men and women know God differently because they are differently embodied?" took me first to the voices of contemporaries. Next, it alerted me to the Buddhist spiritual tradition. Then it led me to the Christian past and the startling variety of responses found there. It teased me back to the contemporary scene and the new scholarship on mysticism. Finally, I found myself once again in the Christian past, this time focusing not on the issue of men and women but on the modalities of knowing God.

THE PREVAILING CONTEMPORARY ANSWER

We in late-twentieth century America generally assume that the way a person knows God is shaped by sexual and gender identity. Our bookstore shelves are stocked with numerous titles treating men's and women's spirituality. We wonder whether spiritual traditions which reflect men's experience can adequately articulate women's spiritual lives. We pore over the literary artifacts of our religious foremothers to detect the themes that dominated their religious quests. We contrast these with the lives and writings of their male counterparts. Within Christian denominations, we trouble ourselves about the question of whether women can see themselves imaged in an exclusively male savior or identify with a deity whose only name is Father. We peruse the literature of the social sciences, which explores the distinctive quality of women's and men's conversations, social interaction, moral reasoning and learning styles, and use that literature to reflect upon religion. We look to contemporary literary analysis, which asserts that a new narrative shape and language is being forged from the particularity of women's experience. We draw upon the thinking of the modern women's and men's movements, which seek to disclose the group perceptions and symbolic milieus best suited to the two halves of the human whole.[1]

Yet the bulk of late twentieth century thinking about the topic, while it celebrates and affirms male and female ways of knowing God, shies away from the assertion that men can know God more adequately than women or vice versa. Both genders have equal access to divine intimacy. They are different but equal. We tend to say that men's spiritual narratives are shaped by the adventure of the hero, that autonomy and separation are the masculine ideals that shape the quest, that pride and self-assertion are men's sins, and abstract principles the key to male moral reasoning. We would at the same time claim that women's knowing is, on the whole, relational, acknowledges interdependence and seeks to make and maintain connections, that diffuseness and a lack of self-definition are female sins, and that women's moral reasoning is motivated by an ethics of care.

While thus affirming that our experience of God is rooted in our embodied human experience as male and female, we observe also that within their own groups, women and men have a diversity of life experiences which mediate their knowledge of God. Add to that race, ethnic and cultural identity, economic status and geographical region, and you have a complex of factors that, if God-knowing begins with unique experience, will influence a person as much as gender.

This is basically where we find ourselves today, especially in the American Christian community. God, for us, is not known primarily as uncreated, but is known through the medium of creation. And, fascinated by creation's variousness, we want to celebrate and give voice to all the various ways of being human. This includes the diverse and sexually differentiated ways of knowing God.

It should be noted that, in contemporary discussions that range over the above-cited territory, the assertion is often made that God, in God's essence, is not knowable. Language about God and the human perception of the ultimate (if one can separate the two) are always analogical, metaphorical and symbolic. All such knowledge is mediated. To the extent that we can "know" the sacred ground of being, we know according to the languages, geographies, cultures, ethnic and religious traditions, eras and genders in which we find ourselves embodied.

TRADITIONAL RESPONSES TO THE QUESTION

My questioning of the prevailing contemporary answer began when I considered a Buddhist story. I am aware that the metaphysical worlds of Buddhism and Christianity are in many ways far apart and that the question of "knowing God" is a thorny one to deal with cross-culturally. Yet the story heightened my interest. The raging question in Mahayana Buddhist circles in the early part of the common era was whether women could obtain buddhahood. Did their femaleness exclude them from the possibility? The conservative camp argued that women could not master the subtle arts of perception necessary for that attainment. The progressive camp argued otherwise in a series of tales that bear the title, "The Changing of the Female Body." In them, female adepts astound learned *arhats* with their grasp of Buddhist notions like emptiness. Yet their detractors scoff and refuse to validate their attainments, whereupon the women change from female to male before the astonished eyes of all. The texts underscore the Mahayana teaching that sex and gender are secondary characteristics, unimportant in the spiritual life. In Buddhism there is no permanent self. Femaleness or maleness is part of the ephemeral self that does not contribute to the attainment of *nirvana*.[2]

It occurred to me that the earliest Christian communities seem to convey an analogous message. Further hindsight reflection revealed that the cumulative Christian tradition presents one with multivocal and paradoxical answers to the question, and provides an understanding of why contemporary affirmations are what they are.

In the earliest Christian communities, neither maleness nor femaleness seemed to equip one for sacred intimacy. The baptismal formula of the ancient church—"There is neither Jew nor Greek, there is neither slave nor free, there is neither male nor female, for you are all one in Christ Jesus" (Gal 3:28)—made it clear that the distinctions which kept some people excluded from participation in the community were abolished with the coming of the promised one. In the nascent community the subordination of women to men was abolished, social roles that identified the genders shifted, and maleness and femaleness were neither necessary for nor barriers to intimacy with God.

The second century passion narrative of Sts. Perpetua and Felicitas pushed this point to its logical conclusion. Faced with being offered to the beasts should they accept baptism, a band of martyrs, led by two women, elect to go triumphantly to their deaths. The heroines of the narrative personified all that the prevailing culture saw as unfit to know God. They were female, one a young Roman matron with a baby at the breast, the other a pregnant slave. Linked to the body and to the transitory created world through childbearing, legally subordinate to the male heads of their households, considered less intrinsically spiritual, these women nonetheless had visions, dreamed dreams, prophesied, and proceeded with joy to the second bloody baptism which they believed to be the portal to resurrected life. The "leap-frogging of the grave" that the exultant martyrs practiced was also a "leap-frogging" of the gendered body, in the sense that neither women nor men were defined as such in their relationship with divinity.[3]

The radical egalitarian community of the early persecuted church did not continue as a social reality for long, but it persisted as a spiritual reality for many centuries. Martyrdom was replaced by the "white martyrdom" of the ascetic life. As with its bloody counterpart, the ascetic life was in some ways a very bodily experience, despite the fact that it attempted to overcome the natural demands of the body. But it was not a sexually differentiated life. Women and men alike became followers of Christ, consecrated themselves to virginity, practiced sexual continence and lived, as they said, like the angels.[4]

The institutionalized ascetic life of monasticism became the image of what human beings in the promised kingdom could hope for. Gone were the male and female distinctions, both the social inequities and the presumably differing capacities of man and woman; gone too were the pain and burdens of childbearing, and the supposed animality of sexual passion. Instead, the rational appetites ruled supreme and the intellect was freed to pursue its ascent to God. Being man or woman, at least in theory, was peripheral to the task of becoming more clearly the image and likeness of God in whom humanity was created.

Over the centuries, the ways Christians named God and described the experience of knowing God evolved. The language of human relationship and desire, as well as the language of human reproduction, became prominent in medieval Christianity. Expressions of the passionate love of bride and bridegroom, of gestation, birth and lactation—all these are derived from sexual, gendered embodiment. As a growing appreciation for the *humanity* as well as the divinity of Christ emerged from the eleventh century on, so too medieval Christians explored the God-experience with the language of the body. But theirs was primarily a metaphorical language. Bernard of Clairvaux rhapsodically related his sense of divine presence using the erotic texts of the Song of Songs. Guerric of Igny homilized on the gestation of Christ in the human soul, admonishing his listeners to be careful lest they harm the fetal Christ-life growing within. Catherine of Siena nursed at the wounds of the God-man from which the breast-blood flowed in life-sustaining abundance.

Language drawn from human sexual identity abounded. Yet it was articulated primarily within the context of that eschatological, asexual, ungendered life of the angels. Women mystics might know God through the language of birth, but this was not because they had actually given birth. Men used the same birthing language to describe their God-experiences. When medieval monastic males spoke of passionate union with God, they saw themselves not as exercising agency as partners in the relationship, but as the female of the pair. They were, as were women, the recipients of God's passionate embrace. Like the Virgin Mary, they were earthly vessels into which divine agency flowed. All creation was imaged as the receptive female in which God, as male potency, invested his spirit-seed in order to generate new, spiritual life. The use of language derived from male and female embodiment was rampant in the medieval church, yet it was primarily a metaphorical language.

As for the actual experience of being female or male and its relationship to knowing God, the story was quite different. Biological maleness, despite the radical disclaimers of the early Christian community, was often perceived as an advantage in knowing God. The virtue, intellectual superiority and strength of character men were presumed to possess were seen as enabling them to apprehend God. Women's potential for intimacy with the divine was viewed less positively. By nature weak, suggestible, not possessed of the strength of character necessary for spiritual realization, women were only great God-knowers when they emphatically overcame their biological destinies. The functions of the body, especially the female body, were deeply suspect, and certainly regarded as having nothing positive to do with the apprehension of God.

Gradually the church came to be more favorable toward the body in the sense that marriage and family life and the sexual processes associated with them were conditionally affirmed. Biological motherhood, for instance, moved gradually over the centuries from first being an obstacle to acknowledged holiness, to a surmountable barrier, and then finally became a possible arena in which one's sanctity might be realized. This gave rise to new answers to the question of male and female knowledge of God.[5]

Although the shift, albeit not spelt out, had begun much earlier, it was during the period of the Protestant and Catholic reforms that the Christian community came to articulate clearly a spirituality for women that was based on their biological capacity for childbearing. Particularly in Protestant circles, where any spiritual vocation other than the ordinary path of householder and citizen was suspect, the domestic sphere became the only one in which women could pursue Christian righteousness. In the eyes of most of the magisterial reformers, women were by nature (and thus by God's design) created primarily for childbearing. Their very embodiment as women, equipped with womb and breasts, signaled that their spiritual destinies could be realized only in the domestic sphere. Their presumed weakness of character, and the correspondingly presumed strength of male character, led naturally to the male headship of the family. Male and female were thus destined for specific social roles and could know God only by playing out those roles. One knew God in the ordinary and distinctively embodied roles in which one was engaged in society.

The Catholic reform world still held out the possibility of a superior way of knowing God that required one to "leap-frog" the body. This way was open to men and women as long as they transcended their natural sexual and socially gendered identities. However, a spiritual path of male and female embodiment began to develop for laypersons with families, living "in the world." Perhaps the most famous manual for such Christians was Francis de Sales' *Introduction to the Devout Life,* penned at the turn of the seventeenth century. Written primarily, but not exclusively, for non-cloistered women seeking to pursue a life of serious devotion in the midst of their familial duties, the *Introduction* assumed that knowing God is a matter of fidelity to one's "state in life," and that that state was determined in great part by one's male or female embodiment.[6]

Up to this point I had discovered that the tradition had answered the question "Do men and women know God differently because of their embodiment?" in two main ways. Either the gendered body was seen to be irrelevant to spiritual matters, or, if sexual difference did matter, one sex (generally the male) was intrinsically more suited to the spiritual quest. A third alternative began to emerge clearly in the wake of the reforms. The Quakers, or Society of Friends, posited that men and women were equal in their spiritual capacities. No leap-frogging of the body was necessary, in the sense that Friends embraced marriage and family as the normal way of Christian life. Yet the call of the Spirit was not different for men and women, and a sexually differentiated life was no hindrance to hearing that call.[7] If we turn our attention to American Christianity in the nineteenth and early twentieth centuries, we see all of the previous models existing side by side. Traditional Catholic religious life in both its apostolic and monastic modes expressed the "truth" that men and women do not know God differently when they transcend their biologically and socially differentiated identities. The magisterial Protestant model, which was adopted almost wholesale in the socially mobile immigrant Catholic layworld, championed differing spiritualities for women and men. In the emergent "cult of true womanhood" women emerged as the more intrinsically spiritual gender: the wife-mother in her domestic haven nurtured the souls and bodies of her offspring, practiced Christian virtue and provided a safe haven of spiritual calm for her husband. The alternative egalitarian approach articulated by the Quakers, supported by the thought world of the enlightenment which challenged the divine origin of social institutions, became more widespread. This perspective held that equality—of race, class and gender—not only should be realized in some eschatological future, but should also be incarnated in the community of believers and from there enter society. Thus Quakers, especially Quaker women, were at the forefront of all major American reform movements: the abolition of slavery, temperance and women's suffrage. In this way radical, egalitarian thinking entered the mainstream of American social life early. It has since become an almost normative perspective and shapes the way many of us think about men and women and God.

THE QUESTION OF KNOWING GOD

The issues that this survey of the Christian past raised for me were several. Is it simply the case that in the past we have given inadequate attention to differing ways of knowing God? Is the problem that literate, European, male experience has been deemed representatively human to the exclusion of experience that is female, non-European etc.? I want to say yes. But I want to qualify the yes. So I return to "The Changing of the Female Body" stories of Buddhism and to their parallels in early Christianity. Here we have counter-claims, not only that knowing God is a genderless undertaking, but that embodiment itself has little to do with knowing God. I call to mind as well the contemporary expression of our awareness that all knowledge of God is analogical and metaphorical.

This idea that human knowledge of God is limited is, of course, not new. At all stages in Christian development the spiritual tradition says as much, without the corresponding contemporary interest in the variety of equally valid ways of embodied knowing. Yet the tradition also posits that we can achieve intimacy with God as much by unknowing as by knowing, that there is a way of divine darkness, a *via negativa,* a path of loving, that provides us with an experiential, still incomplete, yet finally more "accurate" kind of knowledge than that which can be grasped either by the mind or through the avenue of sensory data.

While we are vehement today about exploring varied ways of knowing, we claim that God is only known in this fashion by analogy, and then we leave it at that. We echo the traditional caveat, yet do not posit that there is a mode of divine intimacy that pushes us beyond knowing into unknowing—the *"nada"* of John of the Cross, the "cloud" of the author of *The Cloud of Unknowing,* or the "Godhead beyond God" of Meister Eckhart. This unknowing is, in the literature of Christian mysticism, a profound sort of ecstatic love that takes one beyond all that is ordinarily apprehendable. This unknowing is more like the desiring, seeking and yearning of love than the clarity of rational knowledge or directness of sense experience. It strips one of all the particularity and diversity of the human condition.

Does this "apophatic" tradition have anything to contribute to our query about gendered and embodied knowledge of God? I think so. Yet I have two cautionary observations. First, the apophatic tradition has its roots in a neoplatonic thought world that conceptualizes divine reality as the one from which all created multiplicity comes. Knowledge derived from such created sources, while valuable, is insufficient when it comes to experiencing God. Does this ancient tradition simply lead us into an unacceptable philosophical impasse by assuming a dualism between body and spirit? Second, one current, compelling debate in the academic study of mysticism would question as epistemologically impossible any sort of direct, unmediated apprehension of the divine that is not shaped in some way by the confines of thought and language.[8] While both of these cautions condition my query, still the traditional claim, that the ecstatic unknowing, the abyss of divine darkness, is a part of our "knowing" of God, is compelling.

What the apophatic tradition does suggest, and this may be a significant way in which the past can illuminate the present, is that as human beings and God-seekers we are challenged both to know the vast diversity and multiplicity of what is, and to unlearn all that we know. We are drawn, by the sheer complexity of being, into mystery. We are drawn by our paradoxical capacity for imagining the unimaginable somehow to transcend what we as embodied persons can know. It is love, not only as physical pleasure, solicitous attachment, romantic ardor or wide-reaching responsibility for human welfare, that is operative here. The love suggested here is that wide, painful, joyous opening of the person to hold within himself or herself the paradoxes that cannot otherwise be borne. When categories and constructs are confounded, when multiple interpretations collide, when meaning fails and we can do no more than wait in silence, it is then that we are initiated into the love that begins the process of unknowing. This is emphatically part of knowing God.

Is this apophatic experience gendered? Is this loving unknowing the same for men and women? Is the embodied language of desire an apt language with which to attempt to speak of this distinctive type of knowledge? Has the Christian tradition framed this entry into the divine darkness in terms exclusively derived from either men's or women's embodiment? Does the Song of Songs, which provides scriptural metaphors for this kind of self-transcending excursion into divine desire, present a gender-biased portrait of human sexuality? I know of no studies which address these issues. They remain for me questions. What intrigues me is the idea that while particular embodied experience, including the experience of gender, does clearly shape our knowledge of God, it may be possible to speak of a kind of God-knowledge which begins to unravel all that we know, which can hear the silence beneath our varied voices, and through which, while respecting our differences, we can discover ourselves as one in our capacity for radical divine love.

NOTES

1. The literature on the topics mentioned is enormous, but it might be helpful to enumerate a few "modern classics" on male and female differences that have had an impact in the realm of spirituality. In moral development the names of Carol Gilligan and Nel Nodings loom large. Psychologist Gilligan's *In a Different Voice: Psychological Theory and Women's Development* (Cambridge: Harvard University Press, 1982) and philosopher Nodings' *Caring: A Feminine Approach to Ethics and Moral Education* (Berkeley: University of California Press, 1984) have set the agenda for the discussion. Also influential in the field of psychology has been Mary Belenky et al., *Women's Ways of Knowing: The Development of Self Voice and Mind* (New York: Basic Books, 1986). Christian theology has been profoundly affected. The names of Elisabeth Schüssler Fiorenza and Sandra Schneiders in scripture studies, and Rosemary Radford Ruether, Sallie McFague and Elizabeth Johnson in systematics, define the theological field. In the field of spiritual literature a variety of titles seem to have made the rounds. Included might be Patrick Arnold, *Wildmen, Warriors and Kings: Masculine Spirituality and the Bible* (New York: Crossroad, 1991); James Nelson, *The Intimate Connection: Male Sexuality, Male Spirituality* (Philadelphia: Westminster Press, 1988); Robert Johnson, *He* (New York: Harper and Row, 1989); Joann Wolski Conn, ed., *Women's Spirituality: Resources for Christian Development* (Mahwah: Paulist Press, 1986); Sherry Ruth Anderson and Patricia Hopkins, *The Feminine Face of God* (New York: Bantam, 1991); Maria Harris, *Dance of the Spirit: The Seven Steps of Women's Spirituality* (New York: Bantam, 1989).

2. This text can be found in translation in *An Anthology of Sacred Texts by and about Women,* edited by Serenity Young (New York: Crossroad, 1993), pp. 320–321. This theme is echoed in Gnostic Christian literature, especially the Gospel of Thomas, in which Jesus is reported as saying that Mary might be included in the inner circle if she becomes male. The scholarly debate about the actual meaning of the passage is heated.

3. The passion of Perpetua and Felicitas is translated in *Medieval Women's Visionary Literature,* edited by Elizabeth A. Petroff (Oxford: Oxford University Press, 1986), pp. 70–77. The phrase "leap-frogging the grave" comes from historian Peter Brown. It is certainly possible at this point to stop and insist that such "leap-frogging" is in fact gendered behavior, that the very renunciation of bodiliness was implicit in a spirituality shaped by male perspectives found in the Greco-Roman world. I would, however, like to hold that critique in abeyance.

4. For a survey of two theologies—of subordination and equivalence—that dominate the Christian past and shape the changing views of female embodiment, see Rosemary Radford Ruether's article in *Women in World Religions,* edited by Arvind Sharma (Albany: SUNY Press, 1987). See also Karen Jo Torjesen, *When Women Were Priests* (San Francisco: Harper San Francisco, 1993).

5. For a history of motherhood, see Clarissa W. Atkinson, *The Oldest Vocation: Christian Motherhood in the Middle Ages* (Ithaca: Cornell University Press, 1991).

6. Francis de Sales, *Introduction to the Devout Life,* translated by John K. Ryan (Garden City: Doubleday, 1982).

7. On Quaker women in America, see Margaret Hope Bacon, *Mothers of Feminism* (San Francisco: Harper and Row, 1986).

8. Cf. Steven T. Katz, ed., *Mysticism and Philosophical Analysis* (New York: Oxford University Press, 1978), and *Mysticism and Religious Traditions* (New York: Oxford University Press, 1983).

Jesuits and the Situation of Women in Church and Civil Society

Jesuit General Congregation, 1995

INTRODUCTION

1. General Congregation 33 made a brief mention of the "unjust treatment and exploitation of women."[1] It was part of a list of injustices in a context of new needs and situations which Jesuits were called to address in the implementation of our mission. We wish to consider this question more specifically and substantially on this occasion. This is principally because, assisted by the general rise in consciousness concerning this issue, we are more aware than previously that it is indeed a central concern of any contemporary mission which seeks to integrate faith and justice. It has a universal dimension in that it involves men and women everywhere. To an increasing extent it cuts across barriers of class and culture. It is of personal concern to those who work with us in our mission, especially lay and religious women.

THE SITUATION

2. The dominance of men in their relationship with women has found expression in many ways. It has included discrimination against women in educational opportunities, the disproportionate burden they are called upon to bear in family life, paying them a lesser wage for the same work, limiting their access to positions of influence when admitted to public life, and, sadly but only too

frequently, outright violence against women themselves. In some parts of the world, this violence still includes female circumcision, dowry deaths, and the murder of unwanted infant girls. Women are commonly treated as objects in advertising and in the media. In extreme cases, for example, in promoting international sex tourism, they are regarded as commodities to be trafficked in.

3.   This situation, however, has begun to change, chiefly because of the critical awakening and courageous protest of women themselves. But many men, too, have joined women in rejecting attitudes which offend against the dignity of men and women alike. Nonetheless, we still have with us the legacy of systematic discrimination against women. It is embedded within the economic, social, political, religious, and even linguistic structures of our societies. It is often part of an even deeper cultural prejudice and stereotype. Many women, indeed, feel that men have been slow to recognize the full humanity of women. They often experience a defensive reaction from men when they draw attention to this blindness.

4.   The prejudice against women, to be sure, assumes different forms in different cultures. Sensitivity is needed to avoid using any one simple measurement of what counts as discrimination. But it is nonetheless a universal reality. Further, in many parts of the world, women, already cruelly disadvantaged because of war, poverty, migration, or race, often suffer a double disadvantage precisely because they are women. There is a "feminization of poverty" and a distinctive "feminine face of oppression."

THE CHURCH ADDRESSES THE SITUATION

5.   Church social teaching, especially within the last ten years, has reacted strongly against this continuing discrimination and prejudice. Pope John Paul II in particular has called upon all men and women of good will, especially Catholics, to make the essential equality of women a lived reality. This is a genuine "sign of the times."[2] We need to join with interchurch and interreligious groups in order to advance this social transformation.

6.   Church teaching certainly promotes the role of women within the family, but it also stresses the need for their contribu-

tion in the church and in public life. It draws upon the text of Genesis which speaks of men and women created in the image of God (1:27) and the prophetic praxis of Jesus in his relationship with women. These sources call us to change our attitudes and work for a change of structures. The original plan of God was for a loving relationship of respect, mutuality, and equality between men and women, and we are called to fulfill this plan. The tone of this ecclesial reflection on scripture makes it clear that there is an urgency in the challenge to translate theory into practice not only outside but also within the church itself.

THE ROLE AND RESPONSIBILITY OF JESUITS

7. The Society of Jesus accepts this challenge and our responsibility for doing what we can as men and as a male religious order. We do not pretend or claim to speak for women. However, we do speak out of what we have learned from women about ourselves and our relationship with them.

8. In making this response we are being faithful, in the changed consciousness of our times, to our mission: the service of faith, of which the promotion of justice is an absolute requirement. We respond, too, out of the acknowledgement of our own limited but significant influence as Jesuits and as male religious within the church. We are conscious of the damage to the people of God brought about in some cultures by the alienation of women who no longer feel at home in the church and who are not able with integrity to transmit Catholic values to their families, friends, and colleagues.

CONVERSION

9. In response, we Jesuits first ask God for the grace of conversion. We have been part of a civil and ecclesial tradition that has offended against women. And, like many men, we have a tendency to convince ourselves that there is no problem. However unwittingly, we have often contributed to a form of clericalism which has reinforced male domination with an ostensibly divine sanction. By

making this declaration we wish to react personally and collectively, and do what we can to change this regrettable situation.

APPRECIATION

10. We know that the nurturing of our own faith and much of our own ministry would be greatly diminished without the dedication, generosity, and joy that women bring to the schools, parishes, and other fields in which we labor together. This is particularly true of the work of lay and religious women among the urban and rural poor, often in extremely difficult and challenging situations. In addition, many religious congregations of women have adopted the Spiritual Exercises and our Jesuit Constitutions as the basis for their own spirituality and governance, becoming an extended Ignatian family. Religious and lay women have in recent years become expert in giving the Spiritual Exercises. As retreat directors, especially of the Exercises in daily life, they have enriched the Ignatian tradition and our own understanding of ourselves and of our ministry. Many women have helped to reshape our theological tradition in a way that has liberated both men and women. We wish to express our appreciation for this generous contribution of women, and hope that this mutuality in ministry might continue and flourish.

WAYS FORWARD

11. We wish to specify more concretely at least some ways in which Jesuits may better respond to this challenge to our lives and mission. We do not presume that there is any one model of male-female relationship to be recommended, much less imposed, throughout the world or even within a given culture. Rather we note the need for a real delicacy in our response. We must be careful not to interfere in a way that alienates the culture; rather we must endeavor to facilitate a more organic process of change. We should be particularly sensitive to adopt a pedagogy that does not drive a further wedge between men and women who

in certain circumstances are already under great pressure from other divisive cultural or socio-economic forces.

12.   In the first place, we invite all Jesuits to listen carefully and courageously to the experience of women. Many women feel that men simply do not listen to them. There is no substitute for such listening. More than anything else it will bring about change. Unless we listen, any action we may take in this area, no matter how well intentioned, is likely to bypass the real concerns of women and to confirm male condescension and reinforce male dominance. Listening, in a spirit of partnership and equality, is the most practical response we can make and is the foundation for our mutual partnership to reform unjust structures.

13.   Second, we invite all Jesuits, as individuals and through their institutions, to align themselves in solidarity with women. The practical ways of doing this will vary from place to place and from culture to culture, but many examples come readily to mind:

13, 1.   explicit teaching of the essential equality of women and men in Jesuit ministries, especially in schools, colleges and universities;

13, 2.   support for liberation movements which oppose the exploitation of women and encourage their entry into political and social life;

13, 3.   specific attention to the phenomenon of violence against women;

13, 4.   appropriate presence of women in Jesuit ministries and institutions, not excluding the ministry of formation;

13, 5.   genuine involvement of women in consultation and decision making in our Jesuit ministries;

13, 6.   respectful cooperation with our female colleagues in shared projects;

13, 7.   use of appropriately inclusive language in speech and official documents;

13, 8.   promotion of the education of women and, in particular, the elimination of all forms of illegitimate discrimination between boys and girls in the educational process.

Many of these, we are happy to say, are already being practiced in different parts of the world. We confirm their value, and recommend a more universal implementation as appropriate.

14.   It would be idle to pretend that all the answers to the issues surrounding a new, more just relationship between women and men have been found or are satisfactory to all. In particular, it may be anticipated that some other questions about the role of women in civil and ecclesial society will undoubtedly mature over time. Through committed and persevering research, through exposure to different cultures, and through reflection on experience, Jesuits hope to participate in clarifying these questions and in advancing the underlying issues of justice. The change of sensibilities which this involves will inevitably have implications for church teaching and practice. In this context we ask Jesuits to live, as always, with the tension involved in being faithful to the teachings of the church while at the same time trying to read accurately the signs of the times.

CONCLUSION

15.   The Society gives thanks for all that has already been achieved through the often costly struggle for a more just relationship between women and men. We thank women for the lead they have given and continue to give. In particular, we thank women religious, with whom we feel a special bond, and who have been pioneers in so many ways in their unique contribution to the mission of faith and justice. We are grateful, too, for what the Society and individual Jesuits have contributed to this new relationship, which is a source of great enrichment for both men and women.

16.   Above all we want to commit the Society in a more formal and explicit way to regard this solidarity with women as integral to our mission. In this way we hope that the whole Society will regard this work for reconciliation between women and men in all its forms as integral to its interpretation of Decree 4 of GC 32 for our times. We know that a reflective and sustained commitment to bring about this respectful reconciliation can flow only from our God of love and justice, who reconciles all and promises a world in which "there is neither Jew nor Greek, there is neither slave nor free, there is neither male nor female, for you are all one in Christ Jesus" (Gal 3:28).

NOTES

1. GC 33, D 1, n. 48.

2. John Paul II, apostolic letter *Mulieris Dignitatem* and apostolic exhortation *Christifideles Laici:* Message for the World Day of Peace, 1 January 1995.

Section II

Women's Psychological Development

In a Different Voice: Visions of Maturity

Carol Gilligan

Attachment and separation anchor the cycle of human life, describing the biology of human reproduction and the psychology of human development. The concepts of attachment and separation that depict the nature and sequence of infant development appear in adolescence as identity and intimacy and then in adulthood as love and work. This reiterative counterpoint in human experience, however, when molded into a developmental ordering, tends to disappear in the course of its linear reduction into the equation of development with separation. This disappearance can be traced in part to the focus on child and adolescent development, where progress can readily be charted by measuring the distance between mother and child. The limitation of this rendition is most apparent in the absence of women from accounts of adult development.

Choosing like Virgil to "sing of arms and the man," psychologists describing adulthood have focused on the development of self and work. While the apogee of separation in adolescence is presumed to be followed in adulthood by the return of attachment and care, recent depictions of adult development, in their seamless emergence from studies of men, provide scanty illumination of a life spent in intimate and generative relationships. Daniel Levinson (1978), despite his evident distress about the exclusion of women from his necessarily small sample, sets out on the basis of an all-male study "to create an overarching conception of development that could encompass the diverse biological, psychological and social changes occurring in adult life" (p. 8).

Levinson's conception is informed by the idea of "the Dream," which orders the seasons of a man's life in the same way that Jupiter's prophecy of a glorious destiny steers the course of Aeneas' journey. The Dream about which Levinson writes is also a vision of glorious achievement whose realization or modification will shape the character and life of the man. In the salient relationships in Levinson's analysis, the "mentor" facilitates the realization of the Dream, while the "special woman" is the helpmate who encourages the hero to shape and live out his vision: "As the novice adult tries to separate from his family and pre-adult world, and to enter an adult world, he must form significant relationships with other adults who will facilitate his work on the Dream. Two of the most important figures in this drama are the 'mentor' and the 'special woman' " (p. 93).

The significant relationships of early adulthood are thus construed as the means to an end of individual achievement, and these "transitional figures" must be cast off or reconstructed following the realization of success. If in the process, however, they become, like Dido, an impediment to the fulfillment of the Dream, then the relationship must be renounced, "to allow the developmental process" to continue. This process is defined by Levinson explicitly as one of individuation: "throughout the life cycle, but especially in the key transition periods . . . the developmental process of *individuation* is going on." The process refers "to the changes in a person's relationships to himself and to the external world," the relationships that constitute his "Life Structure" (p. 195).

If in the course of "Becoming One's Own Man, this structure is discovered to be flawed and threatens the great expectations of the Dream, then in order to avert "serious Failure or Decline," the man must "break out" to salvage his Dream. This act of breaking out is consummated by a "marker event" of separation, such as "leaving his wife, quitting his job, or moving to another region" (p. 206). Thus the road to mid-life salvation runs through either achievement or separation.

From the array of human experience, Levinson's choice is the same as Virgil's, charting the progress of adult development as an arduous struggle toward a glorious destiny. Like pious Aeneas on his way to found Rome, the men in Levinson's study steady their lives by their devotion to realizing their dream, measuring their progress in terms of their distance from the shores of its promised success. Thus in the stories that Levinson recounts, relationships, whatever their particular intensity, play a relatively subordinate role in the individual drama of adult development.

The focus on work is also apparent in George Vaillant's (1977) account of adaptation to life. The variables that correlate with adult adjustment, like the interview that generates the data, bear predominantly on occupation and call for an expansion of Erikson's stages. Filling in what he sees as "an uncharted period of development" which Erikson left "between the decades of the twenties and forties," Vaillant describes the years of the thirties as the era of "Career Consolidation," the time when the men in his sample sought, "like Shakespeare's soldier, 'the bauble Reputation' " (p. 202). With this analogy to Shakespeare's Rome, the continuity of intimacy and generativity is interrupted to make room for a stage of further individuation and achievement, realized by work and consummated by a success that brings societal recognition.

Erikson's (1950) notion of generativity, however, is changed in the process of this recasting. Conceiving generativity as "the concern in establishing and guiding the next generation," Erikson takes the "*productivity* and *creativity*" of parenthood in its literal or symbolic realization to be a metaphor for an adulthood centered on relationships and devoted to the activity of taking care (p. 267). In Erikson's account, generativity is the central stage of adult development, encompassing "man's relationship to his production as well as to his progeny" (p. 268). In Vaillant's data, this relationship is relegated instead to mid-life.

Asserting that generativity is "not just a stage for making little things grow," Vaillant argues against Erikson's metaphor of parenthood by cautioning that "the world is filled with irresponsible mothers who are marvellous at bearing and loving children up to the age of two and then despair of taking the process further." Generativity, in order to exclude such women, is uprooted from its earthy redolence and redefined as "responsibility for the growth, leadership, and well-being of one's fellow creatures, not

just raising crops or children" (p. 202). Thus, the expanse of
Erikson's conception is narrowed to development in mid-
adulthood and in the process is made more restrictive in its definition of care.

As a result, Vaillant emphasizes the relation of self to society
and minimizes attachment to others. In an interview about work,
health, stress, death, and a variety of family relationships, Vaillant says to the men in his study that "the hardest question" he
will ask is, "Can you describe your wife?" This prefatory caution
presumably arose from his experience with this particular sample
of men but points to the limits of their adaptation, or perhaps to
its psychological expense.

Thus the "models for a healthy life cycle" are men who seem
distant in their relationships, finding it difficult to describe their
wives, whose importance in their lives they nevertheless acknowledge. The same sense of distance between self and others is evident
in Levinson's conclusion that, "In our interviews, friendship was
largely noticeable by its absence. As a tentative generalization we
would say that close friendship with a man or a woman is rarely
experienced by American men." Caught by this impression, Levinson pauses in his discussion of the three "tasks" of adulthood
(Building and Modifying the Life Structure, Working on Single
Components of the Life Structure, and Becoming More Individu-
ated), to offer an elaboration: "A man may have a wide social
network in which he has amicable, 'friendly' relationships with
many men and perhaps a few women. In general, however, most
men do not have an intimate male friend of the kind that they recall
fondly from boyhood or youth. Many men have had casual dating
relationships with women, and perhaps a few complex love-sex
relationships, but most men have not had an intimate non-sexual
friendship with a woman. We need to understand why friendship is
so rare, and what consequences this deprivation has for adult life"
(p. 335).

Thus, there are studies, on the one hand, that convey a view
of adulthood where relationships are subordinated to the ongoing
process of individuation and achievement, whose progress, however, is predicated on prior attachments and thought to enhance
the capacity for intimacy. On the other hand, there is the observation that among those men whose lives have served as the model

for adult development, the capacity for relationships is in some sense diminished and the men are constricted in their emotional expression. Relationships often are cast in the language of achievement, characterized by their success or failure, and impoverished in their affective range:

> At forty-five, Lucky, enjoyed one of the best marriages in the Study, but probably not as perfect as he implied when he wrote, "You may not believe me when I say we've never had a disagreement, large or small."

> The biography of Dr. Carson illustrates his halting passage from identity to intimacy, through career consolidation, and, finally, into the capacity to *care* in its fullest sense . . . he had gone through divorce, remarriage, and a shift from research to private practice. His personal metamorphosis had continued. The mousy researcher had become a charming clinician . . . suave, untroubled, kindly and in control . . . The vibrant energy that had characterized his adolescence had returned . . . now his depression was clearly an *affect;* and he was anything but fatigued. In the next breath he confessed, "I'm very highly sexed and that's a problem, too." He then provided me with an exciting narrative as he told me not only of recent romantic entanglements but also of his warm fatherly concern for patients (Vaillant, 1977, pp. 129, 203–206).

The notion that separation leads to attachment and that individuation eventuates in mutuality, while reiterated by both Vaillant and Levinson, is belied by the lives they put forth as support. Similarly, in Erikson's studies of Luther and Gandhi, while the relationship between self and society is achieved in magnificent articulation, both men are compromised in their capacity for intimacy and live at great personal distance from others. Thus Luther in his devotion to Faith, like Gandhi in his devotion to Truth, ignore the people most closely around them while working instead toward the glory of God. These men resemble in remarkable detail pious Aeneas in Virgil's epic, who also overcame the bonds of attachment that impeded the progress of his journey to Rome.

In all these accounts the women are silent, except for the

sorrowful voice of Dido who, imploring and threatening Aeneas in vain, in the end silences herself upon his sword. Thus there seems to be a line of development missing from current depictions of adult development, a failure to describe the progression of relationships toward a maturity of interdependence. Though the truth of separation is recognized in most developmental texts, the reality of continuing connection is lost or relegated to the background where the figures of women appear. In this way, the emerging conception of adult development casts a familiar shadow on women's lives, pointing again toward the incompleteness of their separation, depicting them as mired in relationships. For women, the developmental markers of separation and attachment, allocated sequentially to adolescence and adulthood, seem in some sense to be fused. However, while this fusion leaves women at risk in a society that rewards separation, it also points to a more general truth currently obscured in psychological texts.

In young adulthood, when identity and intimacy converge in dilemmas of conflicting commitment, the relationship between self and other is exposed. That this relationship differs in the experience of men and women is a steady theme in the literature on human development and a finding of my research. From the different dynamics of separation and attachment in their gender identity formation through the divergence of identity and intimacy that marks their experience in the adolescent years, male and female voices typically speak of the importance of different truths, the former of the role of separation as it defines and empowers the self, the latter of the ongoing process of attachment that creates and sustains the human community.

Since this dialogue contains the dialectic that creates the tension of human development, the silence of women in the narrative of adult development distorts the conception of its stages and sequence. Thus, I want to restore in part the missing text of women's development, as they describe their conceptions of self and morality in the early adult years. In focusing primarily on the differences between the accounts of women and men, my aim is to enlarge developmental understanding by including the perspectives of both of the sexes. While the judgments considered come from a small and highly educated sample, they elucidate a contrast and make it possible to recognize not only what is missing in women's development but also what is there.

This problem of recognition was illustrated in a literature class at a women's college where the students were discussing the moral dilemma described in the novels of Mary McCarthy and James Joyce:

> I felt caught in a dilemma that was new to me then but which since has become horribly familiar: the trap of adult life, in which you are held, wriggling, powerless to act because you can see both sides. On that occasion, as generally in the future, I compromised. (*Memories of a Catholic Girlhood*)

> I will not serve that in which I no longer believe, whether it calls itself my home, my fatherland or my church: and I will try to express myself in some mode of life or art as freely as I can and as wholly as I can, using for my defense the only arms I allow myself to use—silence, exile and cunning. (*A Portrait of the Artist as a Young Man*)

Comparing the clarity of Stephen's *non serviam* with Mary McCarthy's "zigzag course," the women were unanimous in their decision that Stephen's was the better choice. Stephen was powerful in his certainty of belief and armed with strategies to avoid confrontation; the shape of his identity was clear and tied to a compelling justification. He had, in any case, taken a stand.

Wishing that they could be more like Stephen, in his clarity of decision and certainty of desire, the women saw themselves instead like Mary McCarthy, helpless, powerless, and constantly compromised. The contrasting images of helplessness and power in their explicit tie to attachment and separation caught the dilemma of the women's development, the conflict between integrity and care. In Stephen's simpler construction, separation seemed the empowering condition of free and full self-expression, while attachment appeared a paralyzing entrapment and caring an inevitable prelude to compromise. To the students, Mary McCarthy's portrayal confirmed their own endorsement of this account.

In the novels, however, contrasting descriptions of the road to adult life appear. For Stephen, leaving childhood means renouncing relationships in order to protect his freedom of self-expression.

For Mary, "farewell to childhood" means relinquishing the freedom of self-expression in order to protect others and preserve relationships: "A sense of power and Caesarlike magnanimity filled me. I was going to equivocate, not for selfish reasons but in the interests of the community, like a grown-up responsible person" (p. 162). These divergent constructions of identity, in self-expression or in self-sacrifice, create different problems for further development—the former a problem of human connection, and the latter a problem of truth. These seemingly disparate problems, however, are intimately related, since the shrinking from truth creates distance in relationship, and separation removes part of the truth. In the college student study which spanned the years of early adulthood, the men's return from exile and silence parallels the women's return from equivocation, until intimacy and truth converge in the discovery of the connection between integrity and care. Then only a difference in tone reveals what men and women know from the beginning and what they only later discover through experience.

The instant choice of self-deprecation in the preference for Stephen by the women in the English class is matched by a child-like readiness for apology in the women in the college student study. The participants in this study were an unequal number of men and women, representing the distribution of males and females in the class on moral and political choice. At age twenty-seven, the five women in the study all were actively pursuing careers—two in medicine, one in law, one in graduate study, and one as an organizer of labor unions. In the five years following their graduation from college, three had married and one had a child.

When they were asked at age twenty-seven, "How would you describe yourself to yourself?" one of the women refused to reply, but the other four gave as their responses to the interviewer's question:

> This sounds sort of strange, but I think maternal, with all its connotations. I see myself in a nurturing role, maybe not right now, but whenever that might be, as a physician, as a mother . . . It's hard for me to think of myself without thinking about other people around me that I'm giving to.
>
> (Claire)

I am fairly hard-working and fairly thorough and fairly responsible, and in terms of weaknesses, I am sometimes hesitant
about making decisions and unsure of myself and afraid of
doing things and taking responsibility, and I think maybe that
is one of the biggest conflicts I have had . . . The other very
important aspect of my life is my husband and trying to make
his life easier and trying to help him out.

(Leslie)

I am a hysteric. I am intense. I am warm. I am very smart
about people . . . I have a lot more soft feelings than hard
feelings. I am a lot easier to get to be kind than to get mad. If I
had to say one word, and to me it incorporates a lot, *adopted*.

(Erica)

I have sort of changed a lot. At the point of the last interview
[age twenty-two] I felt like I was the kind of person who was
interested in growth and trying hard, and it seems to me that
the last couple of years, the not trying is someone who is not
growing, and I think that is the one thing that bothers me the
most, the thing that I keep thinking about, that I am not
growing. It's not true, I am, but what seems to be a failure
partially is the way that Tom and I broke up. The thing with
Tom feels to me like I am not growing . . . The thing I am
running into lately is that the way I describe myself, my behavior doesn't sometimes come out that way. Like I hurt Tom a
lot, and that bothers me. So I am thinking of myself as somebody who tried not to hurt people, but I ended up hurting him
a lot, and so that is something that weighs on me, that I am
somebody who unintentionally hurts people. Or a feeling,
lately, that it is simple to sit down and say what your principles
are, what your values are, and what I think about myself, but
the way it sort of works out in actuality is sometimes very
different. You can say you try not to hurt people, but you
might because of things about yourself, or you can say this is
my principle, but when the situation comes up, you don't
really behave the way you would like . . . So I consider myself
contradictory and confused.

(Nan)

The fusion of identity and intimacy, noted repeatedly in
women's development, is perhaps nowhere more clearly articulated

than in these self-descriptions. In response to the request to describe themselves, all of the women describe a relationship, depicting their identity *in* the connection of future mother, present wife, adopted child, or past lover. Similarly, the standard of moral judgment that informs their assessment of self is a standard of relationship, an ethic of nurturance, responsibility, and care. Measuring their strength in the activity of attachment ("giving to," "helping out," "being kind," "not hurting"), these highly successful and achieving women do not mention their academic and professional distinction in the context of describing themselves. If anything, they regard their professional activities as jeopardizing their own sense of themselves, and the conflict they encounter between achievement and care leaves them either divided in judgment or feeling betrayed. Nan explains:

> When I first applied to medical school, my feeling was that I was a person who was concerned with other people and being able to care for them in some way or another, and I was running into problems the last few years as far as my being able to give of myself, my time, and what I am doing to other people. And medicine, even though it seems that profession is set up to do exactly that, seems to more or less interfere with your doing it. To me it felt like I wasn't really growing, that I was just treading water, trying to cope with what I was doing that made me very angry in some ways because it wasn't the way that I wanted things to go.

Thus in all of the women's descriptions, identity is defined in a context of relationship and judged by a standard of responsibility and care. Similarly, morality is seen by these women as arising from the experience of connection and conceived as a problem of inclusion rather than one of balancing claims. The underlying assumption that morality stems from attachment is explicitly stated by Claire in her response to Heinz's dilemma of whether or not to steal an overpriced drug in order to save his wife. Explaining why Heinz should steal, she elaborates the view of social reality on which her judgment is based:

> By yourself, there is little sense to things. It is like the sound of one hand clapping, the sound of one man or one woman,

there is something lacking. It is the collective that is important to me, and that collective is based on certain guiding principles, one of which is that everybody belongs to it and that you all come from it. You have to love someone else, because while you may not like them, you are inseparable from them. In a way, it is like loving your right hand. *They are part of you;* that other person is part of that giant collection of people that you are connected to.

To this aspiring maternal physician, the sound of one hand clapping does not seem a miraculous transcendence but rather a human absurdity, the illusion of a person standing alone in a reality of interconnection.

For the men, the tone of identity is different, clearer, more direct, more distinct and sharp-edged. Even when disparaging the concept itself, they radiate the confidence of certain truth. Although the world of the self that men describe at times includes "people" and "deep attachments," no particular person or relationship is mentioned, nor is the activity of relationship portrayed in the context of self-description. Replacing the women's verbs of attachment are adjectives of separation—"intelligent," "logical," "imaginative," "honest," sometimes even "arrogant" and "cocky." Thus the male "I" is defined in separation, although the men speak of having "real contacts" and "deep emotions" or otherwise wishing for them.

In a randomly selected half of the sample, men who were situated similarly to the women in occupational and marital position give as their initial responses to the request for self-description:

Logical, compromising, outwardly calm. If it seems like my statements are short and abrupt, it is because of my background and training. Architectural statements have to be very concise and short. Accepting. Those are all on an emotional level. I consider myself educated, reasonably intelligent.

I would describe myself as an enthusiastic, passionate person who is slightly arrogant. Concerned, committed, very tired right now because I didn't get much sleep last night.

I would describe myself as a person who is well developed intellectually and emotionally. Relatively narrow circle of friends, acquaintances, persons with whom I have real contacts as opposed to professional contacts or community contacts. And relatively proud of the intellectual skills and development, content with the emotional development as such, as a not very actively pursued goal. Desiring to broaden that one, the emotional aspect.

Intelligent, perceptive—I am being brutally honest now—still somewhat reserved, unrealistic about a number of social situations which involve other people, particularly authorities. Improving, looser, less tense and hung up than I used to be. Somewhat lazy, although it is hard to say how much of that is tied up with other conflicts. Imaginative, sometimes too much so. A little dilletantish, interested in a lot of things without necessarily going into them in depth, although I am moving toward correcting that.

I would tend to describe myself first by recounting a personal history, where I was born, grew up, and that kind of thing, but I am dissatisfied with that, having done it thousands of times. It doesn't seem to capture the essence of what I am, I would probably decide after another futile attempt, because there is no such thing as the essence of what I am, and be very bored by the whole thing . . . I don't think that there is any such thing as myself. There is myself sitting here, there is myself tomorrow, and so on.

Evolving and honest.

I guess on the surface I seem a little easy-going and laid back, but I think I am probably a bit more wound up than that. I tend to get wound up very easily. Kind of smart aleck, a little bit, or cocky maybe. Not as thorough as I should be. A little bit hardass, I guess, and a guy that is not swayed by emotions and feelings. I have deep emotions, but I am not a person who has a lot of different people. I have attachments to a few people, very deep attachments. Or attachments to a lot of things, at least in the demonstrable sense.

I guess I think I am kind of creative and also a little bit schizo-phrenic . . . A lot of it is a result of how I grew up. There is a kind of longing for the pastoral life and, at the same time, a desire for the flash, prestige, and recognition that you get by going out and hustling.

Two of the men begin more tentatively by talking about people in general, but they return in the end to great ideas or a need for distinctive achievement:

I think I am basically a decent person. I think I like people a lot and I like liking people. I like doing things with pleasure from just people, from their existence, almost. Even people I don't know well. When I said I was a decent person, I think that is almost the thing that makes me a decent person, that is a decent quality, a good quality. I think I am very bright. I think I am a little lost, not acting quite like I am inspired—whether it is just a question of lack of inspiration, I don't know—but not accom-plishing things, not achieving things, and not knowing where I want to go or what I'm doing. I think most people especially doctors, have some idea of what they are going to be doing in four years. I [an intern] really have a blank . . . I have great ideas . . . but I can't imagine me in them.

I guess the things that I like to think are important to me are I am aware of what is going on around me, other people's needs around me, and the fact that I enjoy doing things for other people and I feel good about it. I suppose it's nice in my situation, but I am not sure that is true for everybody. I think some people do things for other people and it doesn't make them feel good. Once in awhile that is true of me too, for instance working around the house, and I am always doing the same old things that everyone else is doing and eventually I build up some resentment toward that.

In these men's descriptions of self, involvement with others is tied to a qualification of identity rather than to its realization. Instead of attachment, individual achievement rivets the male imagina-tion, and great ideas or distinctive activity defines the standard of self-assessment and success.

Thus the sequential ordering of identity and intimacy in the transition from adolescence to adulthood better fits the development of men than it does the development of women. Power and separation secure the man in an identity achieved through work, but they leave him at a distance from others, who seem in some sense out of his sight. Cranly, urging Stephen Daedalus to perform his Easter duty for his mother's sake, reminds him:

> Your mother must have gone through a good deal of suffering . . . Would you not try to save her from suffering more even if—or would you?
> If I could, Stephen said, that would cost me very little.

Given this distance, intimacy becomes the critical experience that brings the self back into connection with others, making it possible to see both sides—to discover the effects of actions on others as well as their cost to the self. The experience of relationship brings an end to isolation, which otherwise hardens into indifference, an absence of active concern for others, though perhaps a willingness to respect their rights. For this reason, intimacy is the transformative experience for men through which adolescent identity turns into the generativity of adult love and work. In the process, as Erikson (1964) observes, the knowledge gained through intimacy changes the ideological morality of adolescence into the adult ethic of taking care.

Since women, however, define their identity through relationships of intimacy and care, the moral problems that they encounter pertain to issues of a different sort. When relationships are secured by masking desire and conflict is avoided by equivocation, then confusion arises about the locus of responsibility and truth. McCarthy, describing her "representations" to her grandparents, explains:

> Whatever I told them was usually so blurred and glossed, in the effort to meet their approval (for, aside from anything else, I was fond of them and tried to accommodate myself to their perspective), that except when answering a direct question, I hardly knew whether what I was saying was true or false. I really tried, or so I thought, to avoid lying, but it

seemed to me that they forced it on me by the difference in
their vision of things, so that I was always transposing reality
for them into terms they could understand. To keep matters
straight with my conscience, I shrank, whenever possible,
from the lie absolute, just as, from a sense of precaution, I
shrank from the plain truth.

The critical experience then becomes not intimacy but choice,
creating an encounter with self that clarifies the understanding of
responsibility and truth.

Thus in the transition from adolescence to adulthood, the
dilemma itself is the same for both sexes, a conflict between integrity and care. But approached from different perspectives, this
dilemma generates the recognition of opposite truths. These different perspectives are reflected in two different moral ideologies,
since separation is justified by an ethic of rights while attachment
is supported by an ethic of care.

The morality of rights is predicated on equality and centered
on the understanding of fairness, while the ethic of responsibility
relies on the concept of equity, the recognition of differences in
need. While the ethic of rights is a manifestation of equal respect,
balancing the claims of other and self, the ethic of responsibility
rests on an understanding that gives rise to compassion and care.
Thus the counterpoint of identity and intimacy that marks the
time between childhood and adulthood is articulated through two
different moralities whose complementarity is the discovery of
maturity.

The discovery of this complementarity is traced in the study
by questions about personal experiences of moral conflict and
choice. Two lawyers chosen from the sample illustrate how the
divergence in judgment between the sexes is resolved through the
discovery by each of the other's perspective and of the relationship between integrity and care.

The dilemma of responsibility and truth that McCarthy describes is reiterated by Hilary, a lawyer and the woman who said
she found it too hard to describe herself at the end of what "really
has been a rough week." She too, like McCarthy, considers self-
sacrificing acts "courageous" and "praiseworthy," explaining that
"if everyone on earth behaved in a way that showed care for

others and courage, the world would be a much better place, you wouldn't have crime and you might not have poverty." However, this moral ideal of self-sacrifice and care ran into trouble not only in a relationship where the conflicting truths of each person's feelings made it impossible to avoid hurt, but also in court where, despite her concern for the client on the other side, she decided not to help her opponent win his case.

In both instances, she found the absolute injunction against hurting others to be an inadequate guide to resolving the actual dilemmas she faced. Her discovery of the disparity between intention and consequence and of the actual constraints of choice led her to realize that there is, in some situations, no way not to hurt. In confronting such dilemmas in both her personal and professional life, she does not abdicate responsibility for choice but rather claims the right to include herself among the people for whom she considers it moral not to hurt. Her more inclusive morality now contains the injunction to be true to herself, leaving her with two principles of judgment whose integration she cannot yet clearly envision. What she does recognize is that both integrity and care must be included in a morality that can encompass the dilemmas of love and work that arise in adult life.

The move toward tolerance that accompanies the abandonment of absolutes is considered by William Perry (1968) to chart the course of intellectual and ethical development during the early adult years. Perry describes the changes in thinking that mark the transition from a belief that knowledge is absolute and answers clearly right or wrong to an understanding of the contextual relativity of both truth and choice. This transition and its impact on moral judgment can be discerned in the changes in moral understanding that occur in both men and women during the five years following college (Gilligan and Murphy, 1979; Murphy and Gilligan, 1980). Though both sexes move away from absolutes in this time, the absolutes themselves differ for each. In women's development, the absolute of care, defined initially as not hurting others, becomes complicated through a recognition of the need for personal integrity. This recognition gives rise to the claim for equality embodied in the concept of rights, which changes the understanding of relationships and transforms the definition of care. For men, the absolutes of truth and fairness, defined by the concepts of equality and reciprocity, are called into question by experiences that demonstrate the existence of differences between other and self. Then the awareness of multiple truths leads to a relativizing of equality in the direction of equality and gives rise to an ethic of generosity and care. For both sexes the existence of two contexts for moral decision makes judgment by definition contextually relative and leads to a new understanding of responsibility and choice.

The discovery of the reality of differences and thus of the contextual nature of morality and truth is described by Alex, a lawyer in the college student study, who began in law school "to realize that you really don't know everything" and "you don't ever know that there is any absolute. I don't think that you ever know that there is an absolute right. What you do know is you have to come down one way or the other. You have got to make a decision."

The awareness that he did not know everything arose more painfully in a relationship whose ending took him completely by surprise. In his belated discovery that the woman's experience had differed from his own, he realized how distant he had been in a relationship he considered close. Then the logical hierarchy of moral values, whose absolute truth he formerly proclaimed, came to seem a barrier to intimacy rather than a fortress of personal integrity. As his conception of morality began to change, his thinking focused on issues of relationship, and his concern with injustice was complicated by a new understanding of human attachment. Describing "the principle of attachment" that began to inform his way of looking at moral problems, Alex sees the need for morality to extend beyond considerations of fairness to concern with relationships:

> People have real emotional needs to be attached to something, and equality doesn't give you attachment. Equality fractures society and places on every person the burden of standing on his own two feet.

Although "equality is a crisp thing that you could hang onto," it alone cannot adequately resolve the dilemmas of choice that arise in life. Given his new awareness of responsibility and of the actual consequences of choice, Alex says: "You don't want to look at just equality. You want to look at how people are going to be able to handle their lives." Recognizing the need for two contexts for judgment, he nevertheless finds that their integration "is hard to work through," since sometimes "no matter which way you go, somebody is going to be hurt and somebody is going to be hurt forever." Then he says, "you have reached the point where there is an irresolvable conflict," and choice becomes a matter of "choosing the victim" rather than enacting the good. With the recognition of the responsibility that such choices entail, his judgment becomes more attuned to the psychological and social consequences of action, to the reality of people's lives in an historical world.

Thus, starting from very different points, from the different ideologies of justice and care, the men and women in the study come, in the course of becoming adult, to a greater understanding of both points of view and thus to a greater convergence in judgment. Recognizing the dual contexts of justice and care, they realize that judgment depends on the way in which the problem is framed.

But in this light, the conception of development itself also depends on the context in which it is framed, and the vision of maturity can by seen to shift when adulthood is portrayed by women rather than men. When women construct the adult domain, the world of relationships emerges and becomes the focus of attention and concern. McClelland (1975), noting this shift in women's fantasies of power, observes that "women are more concerned than men with both sides of an interdependent relationship" and are "quicker to recognize their own interdependence" (pp. 85–86). This focus on interdependence is manifest in fantasies that equate power with giving and care. McClelland reports that while men represent powerful activity as assertion and aggression, women in contrast portray acts of nurturance as acts of strength. Considering his research on power to deal "in particular with the characteristics of maturity," he suggests that mature women and men may relate to the world in a different style.

That women differ in their orientation to power is also the theme of Jean Baker Miller's analysis. Focusing on relationships of dominance and subordination, she finds women's situation in these relationships to provide "a crucial key to understanding the psychological order." This order arises from the relationships of difference, between man and woman and parent and child, that create "the milieu—the family—in which the human mind as we know it has been formed" (1976, p. 1). Because these relationships of difference contain, in most instances, a factor of inequality, they assume a moral dimension pertaining to the way in which power is used. On this basis, Miller distinguishes between relationships of temporary and permanent inequality, the former representing the context of human development, the latter, the condition of oppression. In relationships of temporary inequality, such as parent and child or teacher and student, power ideally is used to foster the development that removes the initial disparity. In relationships of permanent inequality, power cements dominance and subordination, and oppression is rationalized by theories that "explain" the need for its continuation.

Miller, focusing in this way on the dimension of inequality in human life, identifies the distinctive psychology of women as arising from the combination of their positions in relationships of temporary and permanent inequality. Dominant in temporary relationships of nurturance that dissolve with the dissolution of inequality, women are subservient in relationships of permanently unequal social status and power. In addition, though subordinate in social position to men, women are at the same time centrally entwined with them in the intimate and intense relationships of adult sexuality and family life. Thus women's psychology reflects both sides of relationships of interdependence and the range of moral possibilities to which such relationships give rise. Women, therefore, are ideally situated to observe the potential in human connection both for care and for oppression.

This distinct observational perspective informs the work of Carol Stack (1975) and Lillian Rubin (1976) who, entering worlds previously known through men's eyes, return to give a different report. In the urban black ghetto, where others have seen social disorder and family disarray, Stack finds networks of domestic exchange that describe the organization of the black family in poverty. Rubin, observing the families of the white working class, dispels the myth of "the affluent and happy worker" by charting the "worlds of pain" that it costs to raise a family in conditions of social and economic disadvantage. Both women describe an adult-hood of relationships that sustain the family functions of protec-tion and care, but also a social system of relationships that sustain economic dependence and social subordination. Thus they indi-cate how class, race, and ethnicity are used to justify and rational-ize the continuing inequality of an economic system that benefits some at others' expense.

In their separate spheres of analysis, these women find order where others saw chaos—in the psychology of women, the urban black family, and the reproduction of social class. These discover-ies required new modes of analysis and a more ethnographic ap-proach in order to derive constructs that could give order and meaning to the adult life they saw. Until Stack redefined "family" as "the smallest organized, durable network of kin and non-kin who interact daily, providing the domestic needs of children and assuring their survival," she could not find "families" in the world of "The Flats." Only the "culturally specific definitions of certain concepts such as family, kin, parent, and friend that emerged during this study made much of the subsequent analysis pos-sible . . . An arbitrary imposition of widely accepted definitions of the family . . . blocks the way to understanding how people in The Flats describe and order the world in which they live" (p. 31).

Similarly, Miller calls for "a new psychology of women" that recognizes the different starting point for women's development, the fact that "women stay with, build on, and develop in a context of attachment and affiliation with others," that "women's sense of self becomes very much organized around being able to make, and then to maintain, affiliations and relationships," and that "eventu-ally, for many women, the threat of disruption of an affiliation is perceived not just as a loss of a relationship but as something closer to a total loss of self." Although this psychic structuring is by now familiar from descriptions of women's psychopathology, it has not been recognized that "this psychic starting point contains the possi-bilities for an entirely different (and more advanced) approach to living and functioning . . . [in which] affiliation is valued as highly as, or more highly than, self-enhancement" (p. 83). Thus, Miller points to a psychology of adulthood which recognizes that develop-ment does not displace the value of ongoing attachment and the continuing importance of care in relationships.

The limitations of previous standards of measurement and the need for a more contextual mode of interpretation are evident as well in Rubin's approach. Rubin dispels the illusion that family life is everywhere the same or that subcultural differences can be assessed independently of the socioeconomic realities of class. Thus, working-class families "reproduce themselves not because they are somehow deficient or their culture aberrant, but because there are no alternatives for most of their children," despite "the mobility myth we cherish so dearly" (pp. 210–211). The temporary inequality of the working-class child thus turns into the permanent inequality of the working-class adult, caught in an ebb-tide of social mobility that erodes the quality of family life.

Like the stories that delineate women's fantasies of power, women's descriptions of adulthood convey a different sense of its social reality. In their portrayal of relationships, women replace the bias of men toward separation with a representation of the interdependence of self and other, both in love and in work. By changing the lens of developmental observation from individual achievement to relationships of care, women depict ongoing attachment as the path that leads to maturity. Thus the parameters of development shift toward marking the progress of affiliative relationship.

The implications of this shift are evident in considering the situation of women at mid-life. Given the tendency to chart the unfamiliar waters of adult development with the familiar markers of adolescent separation and growth, the middle years of women's lives readily appear as a time of return to the unfinished business of adolescence. This interpretation has been particularly compelling since life-cycle descriptions, derived primarily from studies of men, have generated a perspective from which women, insofar as they differ, appear deficient in their development. The deviance of female development has been especially marked in the adolescent years when girls appear to confuse identity with intimacy by defining themselves through relationships with others. The legacy left from this mode of identity definition is considered to be a self that is vulnerable to the issues of separation that arise at mid-life.

But this construction reveals the limitation in an account which measures women's development against a male standard and ignores the possibility of a different truth. In this light, the observation that women's embeddedness in lives of relationship, their orientation to interdependence, their subordination of achievement to care, and their conflicts over competitive success leave them personally at risk in mid-life seems more a commentary on the society than a problem in women's development.

The construction of mid-life in adolescent terms, as a similar crisis of identity and separation, ignores the reality of what has happened in the years between and tears up the history of love and of work. For generativity to begin at mid-life, as Vaillant's data on men suggest, seems from a woman's perspective too late for both sexes, given that the bearing and raising of children take place primarily in the preceding years. Similarly, the image of women arriving at mid-life childlike and dependent on others is belied by the activity of their care in nurturing and sustaining family relationships. Thus the problem appears to be one of construction, an issue of judgment rather than truth.

In view of the evidence that women perceive and construe social reality differently from men and that these differences center around experiences of attachment and separation, life transitions that invariably engage these experiences can be expected to involve women in a distinctive way. And because women's sense of integrity appears to be entwined with an ethic of care, so that to see themselves as women is to see themselves in a relationship of connection, the major transitions in women's lives would seem to involve changes in the understanding and activities of care. Certainly the shift from childhood to adulthood witnesses a major redefinition of care. When the distinction between helping and pleasing frees the activity of taking care from the wish for approval by others, the ethic of responsibility can become a self-chosen anchor of personal integrity and strength.

In the same vein, however, the events of mid-life—the menopause and changes in family and work—can alter a woman's activities of care in ways that affect her sense of herself. If mid-life brings an end to relationships, to the sense of connection on which she relies, as well as to the activities of care through which she judges her worth, then the mourning that accompanies all life transitions can give way to the melancholia of self-deprecation and despair. The meaning of mid-life events for a woman thus reflects the interaction between the structures of her thought and the realities of her life.

When a distinction between neurotic and real conflict is made and the reluctance to choose is differentiated from the reality of having no choice, then it becomes possible to see more clearly how women's experience provides a key to understanding central truths of adult life. Rather than viewing her anatomy as destined to leave her with a scar of inferiority (Freud, 1931), one can see instead how it gives rise to experiences which illuminate a reality common to both of the sexes: the fact that in life you never see it all, that things unseen undergo change through time, that there is more than one path to gratification, and that the boundaries between self and other are less clear than they sometimes seem.

Thus women not only reach mid-life with a psychological history different from men's and face at that time a different social reality having different possibilities for love and for work, but they also make a different sense of experience, based on their knowledge of human relationships. Since the reality of connection is experienced by women as given rather than as freely contracted, they arrive at an understanding of life that reflects the limits of autonomy and control. As a result, women's development delineates the path not only to a less violent life but also to a maturity realized through interdependence and taking care.

In his studies of children's moral judgment, Piaget (1932/ 1965) describes a three-stage progression through which constraint turns into cooperation and cooperation into generosity. In doing so, he points out how long it takes before children in the same class at school, playing with each other every day, come to agree in their understanding of the rules of their games. This agreement, however, signals the completion of a major reorientation of action and thought through which the morality of constraint turns into the morality of cooperation. But he also notes how children's recognition of differences between others and themselves leads to a relativizing of equality in the direction of equity, signifying a fusion of justice and love.

There seems at present to be only partial agreement between men and women about the adulthood they commonly share. In the absence of mutual understanding, relationships between the sexes continue in varying degrees of constraint, manifesting the "paradox of egocentrism" which Piaget describes, a mystical respect for rules combined with everyone playing more or less as he pleases and paying no attention to his neighbor (p. 61). For a life-cycle understanding to address the development in adulthood of relationships characterized by cooperation, generosity, and care, that understanding must include the lives of women as well as of men.

Among the most pressing items on the agenda for research on adult development is the need to delineate *in women's own terms* the experience of their adult life. My own work in that direction indicates that the inclusion of women's experience brings to developmental understanding a new perspective on relationships that changes the basic constructs of interpretation. The concept of identity expands to include the experience of interconnection. The moral domain is similarly enlarged by the inclusion of responsibility and care in relationships. And the underlying epistemology correspondingly shifts from the Greek ideal of knowledge as a correspondence between mind and form to the Biblical conception of knowing as a process of human relationship.

Given the evidence of different perspectives in the representation of adulthood by women and men, there is a need for research that elucidates the effects of these differences in marriage, family, and work relationships. My research suggests that men and women may speak different languages that they assume are the same, using similar words to encode disparate experiences of self and social relationships. Because these languages share an overlapping moral vocabulary, they contain a propensity for systematic mistranslation, creating misunderstandings which impede communication and limit the potential for cooperation and care in relationships. At the same time, however, these languages articulate with one another in critical ways. Just as the language of responsibilities provides a weblike imagery of relationships to replace a hierarchical ordering that dissolves with the coming of equality, so the language of rights underlines the importance of including in the network of care not only the other but also the self.

As we have listened for centuries to the voices of men and the theories of development that their experience informs, so we have come more recently to notice not only the silence of women but the difficulty in hearing what they say when they speak. Yet in the different voice of women lies the truth of an ethic of care, the tie between relationship and responsibility, and the origins of aggression in the failure of connection. The failure to see the different reality of women's lives and to hear the differences in their voices stems in part from the assumption that there is a single mode of social experience and interpretation. By positing instead two different modes, we arrive at a more complex rendition of human experience which sees the truth of separation and attachment in the lives of women and men and recognizes how these truths are carried by different modes of language and thought.

To understand how the tension between responsibilities and rights sustains the dialectic of human development is to see the integrity of two disparate modes of experience that are in the end connected. While an ethic of justice proceeds from the premise of equality—that everyone should be treated the same—an ethic of care rests on the premise of nonviolence—that no one should be hurt. In the representation of maturity, both perspectives converge in the realization that just as inequality adversely affects both parties in an unequal relationship, so too violence is destructive for everyone involved. This dialogue between fairness and care not only provides a better understanding of relations between the sexes but also gives rise to a more comprehensive portrayal of adult work and family relationships.

As Freud and Piaget call our attention to the differences in children's feelings and thought, enabling us to respond to children with greater care and respect, so a recognition of the differences in women's experience and understanding expands our vision of maturity and points to the contextual nature of developmental truths. Through this expansion in perspective, we can begin to envision how a marriage between adult development as it is currently portrayed and women's development as it begins to be seen could lead to a changed understanding of human development and a more generative view of human life.

REFERENCES

Erikson, Erik H. *Childhood and Society.* New York: W. W. Norton, 1950.

Gilligan, Carol, and Murphy, John Michael. "Development from Adolescence to Adulthood: The Philosopher and the 'Dilemma of the Fact.' " In D. Kuhn, ed. *Intellectual Development Beyond Childhood.* New Directions for Child Development, no. 5. San Francisco: Jossey-Bass, 1979.

Joyce, James. *A Portrait of the Artist as a Young Man* (1916). New York: The Viking Press, 1956.

Levinson, Daniel J. *The Seasons of a Man's Life.* New York: Alfred A. Knopf, 1978.

McCarthy, Mary. *Memories of a Catholic Girlhood.* New York: Harcourt Brace Jovanovich, 1946.

McClelland, David C. *Power: The Inner Experience.* New York: Irvington, 1975.

Miller, Jean Baker. *Toward a New Psychology of Women.* Boston: Beacon Press, 1976.

Murphy, J. M., and Gilligan, C. "Moral Development in Late Adolescence and Adulthood: A Critique and Reconstruction of Kohlberg's Theory." *Human Development* 23 (1980): 77–104.

Perry, William. *Forms of Intellectual and Ethical Development in the College Years.* New York: Holt, Rinehart and Winston, 1968.

Piaget, Jean. *The Moral Judgment of the Child* (1932). New York: The Free Press, 1965.

Rubin, Lillian. *Worlds of Pain.* New York: Basic Books, 1976.

Stack, Carol B. *All Our Kin.* New York: Harper and Row, 1974.

Vaillant, George E. *Adaptation to Life.* Boston: Little, Brown, 1977.

Conflict, Leadership, and Knowledge Creation

Robert Kegan

"Happy families," Tolstoy said, "are all alike." But I'm not so sure. Consider two happy marriages, that of the Ables and that of the Bakers. Both couples have been married twenty-five years. All four spouses are about fifty. Let us look at the way these two couples experience and construct difference and conflict.

If the Ables spoke in a single voice, here is what they might say:

> Twenty-five years? Sometimes we can hardly believe it ourselves. Where did all those years go? We wouldn't kid you and say it's been nonstop wine and roses, but the truth is we both feel enormously grateful for our relationship and for each other. If you asked us, we'd say we have a very good marriage. Of course, it hasn't always been the *same* marriage. But at this point we'd give it very high marks, and we'd say we deserve them, because we've worked hard at it.
>
> So you wanted to know about conflict and differences, and on that subject we could tell you a lot. That certainly has been a part of our hard work. It took us years even to learn how to fight. It's a funny thing. You marry someone because you feel you've found a soul mate, someone whose way of thinking and feeling about things is so much like your own. So you get married, and what do you start to notice? All the *differences!* Where you want to live, how to raise the children, what's a fun vacation, how much mayonnaise to mix into the tuna fish. The truth is we really are very different people.

131

When we are tired at the end of the day and need a recharge, one of us wants to exercise and the other one wants a nap. One of us takes a much more political view of how the world is organized and how we'd like it to change, the other looks at things more aesthetically. One of us is contemplative, the other more active. One is stricter with the kids but looser with the money, and the other is more laissez-faire with the kids but is always saying we need to make a budget. What a riot! In many respects we are like night and day.

This is something we can talk about, even laugh about, *now*. Earlier in our marriage our differences were less discussable, more threatening, more disguised. We were both probably acutely aware of the situations or topics likely to highlight important differences too starkly. We mostly avoided those situations and topics, usually without even being aware we were doing so. Today we would say that our differences are one of the great strengths of our marriage. We won't deny we still get on each other's nerves occasionally, but for the most part we have developed a lot of respect for each other's way of looking at and relating to the world. And, to tell the truth, we've probably each developed a lot of respect for our *own* way of looking at and relating to the world as well. We are both a lot clearer that we each have a way it took us fifty years of living to create, that it's who we are and we're comfortable with it. We're probably more comfortable with each other because we're a lot more comfortable with ourselves.

Anyway, we've become a good team. We find that our differences are often complementary. One picks up what the other one misses. Yes, we still fight sometimes. We don't always listen or consider that there might actually be a whole different take on a matter besides our own that also makes sense. Or we don't always, in truth, have an easy time finding the sense in the other's view. We can get stubborn and dig in behind our own positions. But more often the fights lead to a better result. They make one or both of us come over and take a look from the other one's point of view, and we see that there's a good reason why it looks different to the other one. We are a good problem-solving team. Neither of us feels we have to do it our way all the time. We compromise. We take turns. And sometimes we even find a way to create a solution that includes a lot of both of our views. We stopped trying to get the other person to change a long time ago. We are who we are. At this point, we're not so sure we'd even *want* the other one to change. Our differences are an asset for the most part.

Not every problem has a solution, either, and sometimes you just have to live with that. That goes with the territory of two strong people with minds of their own. And once in a while we've noticed an odd thing. All the strife and struggle can go out of an issue we've been fighting about without our ever having solved it at all. We feel back together, feel like everything's fine again, and actually nothing's been decided or changed regarding the problem but somehow it doesn't seem like much of a problem anymore. We both find that odd. It's a little irrational, but it does happen once in a while.

Now let's hear from the Bakers:

Twenty-five years? Sometimes we can hardly believe it ourselves. Where did all those years go? We wouldn't kid you and say it's been nonstop wine and roses, but the truth is we both feel enormously grateful for our relationship and for each other. If you asked us, we'd say we have a very good marriage. Of course, it hasn't always been the *same* marriage. But at this point we'd give it very high marks, and we'd say we deserve them, because we've worked hard at it.

Now you wanted to know about conflict and difference, and on that subject we could tell you a lot. Certainly that's been a part of our hard work. First we had to learn how to fight, to figure out what we really thought, apart from what the other one thought, and trust we would not scare ourselves or the other one too much in the process. But that was early on. For better or worse, neither of us has much problem telling you where we stand on anything now. In fact, these days, it is the way we've been able to let up a little on how proud we are of our stands that has been the most difficult and the most rewarding thing about how we currently handle conflict.

If you asked our children or our friends or, to be honest, if you asked us, you'd hear this very clear description and distinction between the two of us. One of us would be described as athletic, the exerciser, the other as sedentary. One looks at the world like a politician, tends to see things in terms of power, the other looks at the world like a visual artist, tends to see things in terms of balance and form. The one who is tough on the kids is carefree about the money, and vice versa. These are the ways we're known and have known ourselves for years. When we're at our very best, though—and this is definitely only in the last few years of our relationship—we are able to stop pretending that these differences and opposites can only be found in the *other* person, or that the battles we get into are only with the other person. We realize that this polarizing or dichotomizing serves a purpose for each of us, and we are less enamored with that purpose. We see it's not the whole truth.

When we are at our best, we get a good glimpse at the fact that the activist, for example, also has a contemplative living inside him. The one who is strict with the kids has a part of herself that has a whole other, looser way of feeling about them. And on and on. It isn't easy, and it doesn't happen all the time, but our favorite fights are the ones in which we don't try to solve the conflicts but let the conflicts "solve us," you could say. We mean by that that if a conflict doesn't go away after a while we've found it's a good bet that one of us, or both of us, has gotten drawn back into being too identified with our more comfortable position. Like the end we're holding onto so passionately is our whole story, our whole truth in the matter. When we can get out of the grip of our more familiar side then the fight doesn't feel as if the other one is trying to make us give up anything. The fight becomes a way for us to recover our own complexity, so to speak, to leave off making the other into our opposite and face up to our own oppositeness.

Working out our conflicts this way generates a different kind of intimacy than we've ever known. We've laughed and said there's still a lot of kicking and screaming in our fighting, but it's more a matter of the way our relationship is now dragging us out of the fiction that we're so "day and night," that one of us is all "this way" and the other all "that way." More and more we're refusing to act out the other's opposite, to be the "stand-in" for the other's own oppositeness. This makes each of us get connected to the quieter, less comfortable side of ourselves. And as we do that, we are connected to each other in a different way too. We would say that we have always felt a lot of intimacy in our relationship, but this is definitely a different kind of intimacy than we've experienced in the past.

If the epistemological underpinning of modernism is actually the fourth order of consciousness,* then it is clearly a modern marriage that the Ables depict in their account of how they experience conflict and difference. Theirs is a story of surviving the disillusionment of an earlier romantic truth, in which their bond was based on their sharing a common identity. But the loss of this truth does not leave them like lonely statues, standing near but coldly, with no interest in or possibility of connecting, like some caricature of postromantic "modernism." Giving up the romantic truth does not mean giving up their hopes for closeness. It means discovering a new form of closeness. The Ables have created a different but deep connection. It seems to be rooted in a mutual appreciation of the other's capacity to enter relation as a distinct and whole human being. They each seem to recognize and respect both the other and themselves as complicated persons who bring something important and different, but often complementary, to the relationship.

As self-possessed persons who share a commitment to sustaining a relationship they treasure, they do not seem surprised by the appearance of differences, nor do they take them as a suspension of their connection, nor expect that the differences will be resolved if one of them simply molds herself or himself to the preferences of the other. Not only does the relationship continue in the face of the difference, but they seem to find their successful, collaborative handling of the differences to be an especially satisfying aspect of the relationship. Both their closeness as a couple and their evaluation of the quality of their decisions are enhanced, rather than troubled, by their difference. Difficult though it may be, they ultimately value the experience of being forced by the other, or by their commitment to the relationship, to take seriously the integrity of the different world view from which the differing preference, opinion, or plan of action arises. Like respectful and enlightened anthropologists, they regularly visit, and deeply appreciate, the other's "culture of mind." At their best,

---

*The fourth order of consciousness is the ability to construct a sense of self-in-relationship so that one takes responsibility for one's true feelings/thoughts and does not take responsibility for what are truly those of others.

they suspend the tendency to evaluate the other's "culture" through the lens of their own, and seek rather to discover the terms by which the other is shaping meaning or creating value. Not only does each seem to benefit from frequent "travel" to the other's "culture," but the one who is "being visited" also seems to appreciate the experience of having the other come in with a nonimperial stance to see how reality is being constructed.

Of course we could imagine many couples with these same fourth order capacities for self-authorship and personal authority who would not have the generosity, personal comfort, freedom from self-absorption, or interest in intimacy to fashion such a rich connection. The point is not that everyone who constructs the world at the fourth order would necessarily sustain such bonds, but that there is nothing about the fourth order or about modernism that necessarily prevents a highly satisfying, mutually nourishing, deep form of intimacy.

However intimate the fourth order might be, it is clear that the Bakers' account reflects a qualitatively different way of constructing conflict and difference. Theirs is *also* a story of surviving disillusionment, but the truth they have been seeing as an illusion is not the truth of romance, it is the truth of modernism. Long ago, they say, they set aside the truth that the source of their closeness lay in their sharing the same identity. The truth they are now in the process of setting aside is that the source of their closeness lies in the respectful cooperation of psychologically whole and distinct selves.

Unlike the Ables, the Bakers are prouder of the way they suspect rather than honor their sense of their own and each other's wholeness and distinctness. At least they are suspicious of any sense of wholeness or distinction that is limited to an identification of the self with its favorite way of constructing itself. They are suspicious of their own tendency to feel wholly identified with one side of any opposite and to identify the other with the other side of that opposite.

When they take this suspicion to their experience of conflict or difference in their relationship, a quite different picture emerges from that sketched by the Ables. The Ables consider themselves at their best when, in the face of difference, they do not disdain the other but seek to discover how the other's point of view arises out of a "culture of mind" with its own coherence and integrity. But what is never open to question is that the respectful anthropologist is visiting a foreign culture. In contrast, the Bakers consider themselves at their best when, in the fact of difference, they stop to see if they haven't, in fact, made the error of identifying themselves wholly with the culture of mind that gives rise to their position (which now shows up as a kind of ideology or orthodoxy) and identifying their partner wholly with a foreign culture of mind that gives rise to their partner's position (which now shows up as an opposing ideology or heterodoxy). Mr. Able comes over to discover the world of Mrs. Able, but in all his respectful discovering he never questions his premise that this is not his world. When Mr. Baker comes over to try on the perspective he has identified with Mrs. Baker, however, he is vulnerable to discovering another world within himself.

The Ables value conflict as a confirmation of the good working of the self and a satisfying recognition on the part of the other of how that self works. So do the Bakers. The difference is that the Ables are constructing *fourth* order selves, so for them the good working of the self and its recognition by the other begin with the shared premise that each brings a distinct and whole self *to* the relationship. The relationship is a context for the sharing and interacting of two whole, distinct, self-possessed, self-authoring selves. Two distinct selves will inevitably have conflicts. This is a part of their interacting, and it has its origins in their very wholeness and distinctness. If they were not whole and distinct, but romantically shared a common identity, as they might have done when they were constructing third order selves, they would be less likely to have conflict.

The Bakers, in contrast, are constructing fifth order selves (or, more precisely, are somewhere in the transformation from the fourth to the fifth order). As depicted in Figure 9.1, the fifth order moves form or system from subject to object, and brings into being a new "trans-system" or "cross-form" way of organizing reality. For the Bakers, the good working of the self and its recognition by the other begins with a refusal to see oneself or the other as a single system or form. The relationship is a context for a sharing and an interacting in which both are helped to experience their "multipleness," in which the *many* forms or systems that *each self is* are helped to emerge. While the Ables begin with the premise of their own completeness and see conflict as an inevitable by-product of the interaction of two psychologically whole selves, the Bakers begin with the premise of their own tendency to *pretend to* completeness (while actually being incomplete) and see conflict as the inevitable, but controvertible, by-product of the pretension to completeness.

Both the Ables and the Bakers satisfy the demands of the modernist curriculum to construct the self as a system or form. At the heart of the difference between their constructions of conflict are these two related questions about that self: (1) Do we see the self-as-system as complete and whole or do we regard the self-as-system as incomplete, only a partial construction of all that the self is? (2) Do we identify with the self-as-form (which self then *interacts with* other selves-as-forms) or do we identify with the process of form creation (which brings forms into being and subtends their relationship)? Another way of putting this second question is: Do we take as prior the *elements of* a relationship (which then enter into relationship) or *the relationship itself* (which creates its elements)?

The idea that a relationship can be prior to its parts may sound strange, but when we start to think about it, the idea that things exist first and then enter into relationship can come to sound just as strange.[1] An example I have often used is this: Imagine a glass cylinder or tube that is open at each end lying on its side. Inside the cylinder is a marble. We are going to push the cylinder so that it is rolling, and we wonder out of which of the cylinder's two ends the marble will escape. As we discuss this, it is perfectly natural for us to distinguish between the two ends or openings of the cylinder (if we are standing on the same side of the cylinder, we might refer to them as the "right opening" and the "left opening"). If we began to pay a lot of attention to these two openings (perhaps they are not identically shaped and we think one end is a more likely exit for the marble) we could conclude that what the cylinder really is, is two openings connected by a glass tube. We could see the glass tube as the connector or relater of the two ends. Although this is an unfortunately static, reified image of a relationship, the tube is, in a sense, the bond or link between the parts, the two ends. The parts "have a relationship" to each other and the tube defines it. But it would make just as much sense to say, "Wait a minute! The cylinder does not *connect* the two openings. There wouldn't be any openings without the cylinder. It *creates* the openings. All there really is, is one thing, a cylinder. The cylinder has the openings, not the other way around. The relationship has the parts. The parts do not have a relationship."

These kinds of questions—about the completeness or priority of the self-as-a-form—are actually hiding behind all manner of contemporary analyses of adult experience. Whether it is marriage psychologists or labor mediators thinking about conflict, educational theorists or family therapy theorists thinking about the very usefulness of a concept like the self, critical theorists thinking about the ideological nature of our intellectual disciplines, political scientists thinking about leadership and followership, or a host of others, questions like these underlie the distinctions these theorists are making between two different ways of understanding. These kinds of questions—about the completeness or priority of the self-as-form—are in fact epistemological questions about the difference between the fourth and fifth orders of consciousness. The question "Do we take as prior the self-as-form or the process of form creation?" could as easily read "Do we take *as subject* the self-as-form (the fourth order) or do we take the self-as-form *as object* (the fifth order)?" And these same kinds of questions, it is also true, go directly to the distinction between modernism and postmodernism. What "postmodernism" even is, is still up for grabs and will continue to be so until we stop calling it "postmodernism" and are able to name what it is rather than only what it is not.

In this chapter I am going to state what I think postmodernism is. I am going to suggest that at the frontiers of our various noncommunicating disciplines, which implicitly or explicitly say what we must do to be successful in our private and public lives, there is, in fact, a collection of mental demands that are different from those calling for personal authority. Like the demands of modernism, these can also be analyzed in terms of their epistemological complexity. By considering the postmodern curriculum in three exemplary areas—the meaning of conflict or difference, good leadership, and knowledge creation—I hope to demonstrate

	SUBJECT	OBJECT	UNDERLYING STRUCTURE
			LINES OF DEVELOPMENT
			K COGNITIVE **E** **INTERPERSONAL** **Y** INTRAPERSONAL
1	PERCEPTIONS *Fantasy* **SOCIAL PERCEPTIONS** IMPULSES	Movement Sensation	Single Point/ Immediate/ Atomistic Durable Category
2	CONCRETE *Actuality* Data, Cause-and-Effect **POINT OF VIEW** **Role-Concept** **Simple Reciprocity (tit-for-tat)** ENDURING DISPOSITIONS Needs, Preferences Self Concept	Perceptions Social Perceptions Impulses	
3	ABSTRACTIONS *Ideality* Inference, Generalization Hypothesis, Proposition Ideals, Values **MUTUALITY/INTERPERSONALISM** **Role Consciousness** **Mutual Reciprocity** INNER STATES Subjectivity, Self-Consciousness	Concrete Point of View Enduring Dispositions Needs, Preferences	Cross-Categorical Trans-Categorical

	SUBJECT	OBJECT	UNDERLYING STRUCTURE
4 M O D E R N I S M	ABSTRACT SYSTEMS *Ideology* Formulation, Authorization Relations between Abstractions INSTITUTION **Relationship-Regulating Forms** **Multiple-Role Consciousness** Self-Authorship Self-Regulation, Self-Formation Identity, Autonomy, Individuation	Abstractions Mutuality Interpersonalism Inner States Subjectivity Self-Consciousness	System/Complex
5 P O S T - M O D E R N I S M	DIALECTICAL *Trans-Ideological/Post-Ideological* Testing Formulation, Paradox Contradiction, Oppositeness INTER-INSTITUTIONAL **Relationship between Forms** **Interpenetration of Self and Other** SELF-TRANSFORMATION Interpenetration of Selves Inter-Individuation	Abstract System Ideology Institution Relationship-Regulating Forms Self-Authorship Self-Regulation Self-Formation	Trans-System Trans-Complex

Figure 9.1   The Five Orders of Consciousness

what these curricular demands all have in common: they all require an order of consciousness that is able to subordinate or
relativize *systemic knowing* (the fourth order); they all require
that we move systemic knowing from *subject* to *object*. In other
words, they are all "beyond" the fourth order.

How the curricular demands differ is that some represent an
earlier, and some a later, moment in the transformation from the
fourth to the fifth order of consciousness. In other words, I am
going to suggest that what we call "postmodernism" is not just a
different way of thinking, it is identifiable on the continuum of the
evolution of consciousness; that the different "strands" or "faces"
of postmodernism others have identified correspond to slightly
different places on this continuum; that what postmodernism is
"post" to is the fourth order of consciousness. Such an analysis
will lead us naturally to a set of perplexing implications and questions: If a given threshold of consciousness must be reached in
order to comprehend the implicit demands of postmodernism,
what does it mean that, although we are told we are living in "a
postmodern age," the best empirical evidence shows that very few
of us have actually reached this threshold and even then never
before mid-life? Thinking of the "students" of this curriculum,
how will postmodern demands be experienced when understood
according to a traditional or modernist consciousness? Thinking
of the "teachers" of this curriculum, if the growing edge for most
adults is not the move to postmodernism but to modernism, then
even if their long-range goal is that more people master the *post*-
modern curriculum, won't they need to have far greater sympathy
and respect for the process of mastering modernism?

What are the unrecognized demands of this newer curriculum? We might return for a bit to the subject of conflict not as it
applies to the private realm of intimate relations but as it applies
to the public realm of social controversy and protracted dispute.
Developments in the field of conflict resolution among representatives of antagonistic positions, groups, or states mirror the distinction between the marriages of the Ables and the Bakers.

Since the 1960s, a group of social scientists has endeavored
to develop a theory and practice for creating productive contexts in which disputing parties can break the patterns of stale-

mate or escalation of their conflict.[2] Though the various action-research projects differ somewhat among themselves, they all share features of the Ables' mutually respectful, enlightened, and modernist approach to conflict. Coming largely from the field of social psychology rather than international diplomacy or labor negotiation, these ground-breaking pioneers suggest that when conflicting parties can recognize each other's needs, views, and fears, and consider solutions which reassure the other that their most precious interests will be respected, a new dynamic for unsticking their conflictual relationship can replace the traditional dynamics of threat, deterrence, and force. These traditional dynamics arise from unilateral strategic analyses of advantage and vulnerability and essentially assume that the only changes that will occur in protracted conflicts are changes in behavior, not changes in attitude.

In contrast, the social psychologists, like the Ables, who try to avoid simply finding ways to get the other to mold to their preference, seek ways to change the actual thinking and feeling of each party. It should also be noted that, like the Ables, the social psychologists assume the wholeness and distinctness of the conflicting parties. That is, the kind of learning they promote is about the willingness and ability of each party to understand and respect the position of the other. Although in their writings they often refer to their goal of "transforming" the relationship, what they are actually transforming are the attitudes each party has about the other's capacity to respect their position, not the positions themselves. The changes in thinking and feeling they effect involve improved understanding of the other's and one's own position, altered attitudes about the other's capacity and willingness to understand one's own position, and new thinking about the possibility of developing solutions that preserve the most precious features of each other's positions. In situations of protracted conflict, especially in the international arena, such changes could be of historic and life-saving proportion.

But these changes also differ from those the Bakers attempt in their disputes and those that are implicitly sought by newer contributors to the field of public dispute. It is one thing to seek a process for resolution in which each side respectfully visits the preconstructed constraints and genius of the other's way of seeing the world, and each transforms its attitude about the possibility of solutions that preserve the integrity of both (the so-called "win-win" solution). It is quite another to seek a process that uses the conflict to transform one's identification with one's own "side," one's sense of its inevitability or intractable integrity, one's need to have that side "win" even if the other side also wins. It is one thing to provide mutual assurance of respect for the *integrity* of the other's position. It is another thing to mutually suspect that what passes for integrity (one's own and the other's) is also *ideology*, necessarily partial, and an unworthy prize, finally, over which to risk one's entire treasure.

This second, postmodern approach to conflict and its resolution does not assume the wholeness, distinctness, or priority of the competing parties. It does not begin the story with, "Once upon a time there was Position X, and it lived and existed happily enough until one day it ran into Position Not-X, and then there was conflict." Even the most enlightened, nonstrategic, non-power-based approaches to conflict implicitly start the story this way and confirm, in their practice designs, the disputants' perceptions of the logical priority of their distinct existences. Though much is made of the distinction between the win-lose and win-win processes of conflict resolution—and the distinction *is* and important one—a postmodern conception suggests that both positions (win-win and win-lose) share an axiomatic faith in the prior distinctness of the disputing parties.

Thus, whether the conflictual process is marked by domination, a willingness to meet in the middle, or even a commitment to mutually preserving win-win results, any of the outcomes of these processes is guaranteed to keep hidden from view, and thus untransformed, the assumption-taken-as-truth: that each side has no need of the other for its existence and that their relationship is an after-the-fact inconvenience with which they must contend. Even from the most enlightened of these perspectives, the designs for dispute resolution will confirm each party's quite natural feeling that "my life, or my people's life, would be so much better if the other side would just disappear, but since the protracted nature of our conflict suggests they will not, we have to find the best resolution possible."

The postmodern view suggests a quite different conception, something more like this: "The protracted nature of our conflict suggests not just that the other side will not go away, but that it probably *should* not. The conflict is a likely consequence of one or both of us making prior, true, distinct, and whole our partial position. The conflict is potentially a reminder of our tendency to pretend to completeness when we are in fact incomplete. We may have this conflict because we need it to recover our truer complexity."

From the postmodern view, the relationship Palestinians and Israelis, pro-choice and pro-life proponents, environmentalists and land developers, rich and poor, black and white, men and women all find themselves in is emphatically *not* an after-the-fact matter in which each side just happens to be in a conflict because, in addition to the existence of its own take on the world, there just happens, inconveniently enough, to be a contrary take that it runs into. The "left opening" of the hollow cylinder does not just "happen to" have a relationship with the right opening; the "left opening" has its very existence *because of* the "relationship," because of the cylinder. From the postmodern view, the conflictual relationship creates the parties; the parties do not create the relationship.

To this the modernist replies, "Wait a minute. If the conflictual relationship exists prior to the parts, how come many disputants not only experience their independence and self-sufficiency from their opponent once the conflict is joined, but also experience a long history of happily existing before they ever knew of or ever experienced themselves as in a conflictual relationship with their opponent? How can my conflictual relationship with a poor person, a black person, or a woman, be prior to my existence as rich or white or male, when I've been rich or white or male for a long time without any experience of being in a conflictual relationship with these others?"

To this the postmodernist replies, "The fact that you haven't experienced a conflictual relationship before now certainly doesn't mean it hasn't existed before now. If you are in the more powerful position in this relationship, you might not have experienced any pain that would cause you to even be aware of the existence of the relationship, and if you are in the less powerful position, you may

have had a need *not* to experience your pain in terms of a relationship to someone or something to whom you would then have to see
yourself as opposed."

In essence, the postmodern view bids disputants to do several
things: (1) consider that your protracted conflict is a signal that
you and your opponent have probably become identified with the
poles of the conflict; (2) consider that the relationship in which
you find yourself is not the inconvenient result of the existence of
an opposing view but the expression of your own incompleteness
taken as completeness; (3) value the relationship, miserable
though it might feel, as an opportunity to live out your own multiplicity; and thus, (4) focus on ways to let the conflictual relationship transform the parties rather than on the parties resolving the
conflict. Postmodernism suggests a kind of "conflict resolution" in
which the Palestinian discovers her own Israeli-ness, the rich man
discovers his poverty, the woman discovers the man inside her.[3]

Though they don't spell it out quite this overtly, this approach
to conflict resolution is implicit in the work of those who come to
the field from family therapy theory[4] and the Chris Argyris wing of
organizational theory.[5] Except for William Torbert, who explicitly
incorporates a constructive-developmental perspective, none of
the psychological approaches to conflict resolution—not the efforts of pioneering social psychologists, nor the more recent work
of the family therapists or the organization developmentalists—
attend to the individual's development of consciousness. As a result, none of these theorist-practitioners is in a position to consider
the demands their respective curricula make on mental capacity or
to assess a person's readiness to engage their designs.

Argyris, however, has been candid in reporting that even
highly advantaged, graduate-educated, organizationally high-
ranking adults have a great deal of difficulty mastering—or simply
cannot master—what it is he is teaching.[6] But this should be no
surprise, because what he and the other postmodern conflict resolu-
tionists are asking people to do is to organize experience at a level
of complexity beyond the fourth order of consciousness, something
few people are yet able to do.[7] Refusing to see oneself or the other
as a single system or form, regarding the premise of completeness
as a tempting pretense, constructing the process of interacting as
prior to the existence of the form or system, facing protracted

conflict as a likely sign of one's own identification with false assumptions of wholeness, distinctness, completeness, or priority—all of these ways of constructing reality require that the epistemological organization of system, form, or theory be relativized, moved from subject in one's knowing to object in one's knowing.[8] They all require a "trans-systemic," "multiform," or "cross-theoretical" epistemological organization. In other words, they all require the fifth order of consciousness.

In an illuminating essay, Ronald Heifetz and Riley Sinder review the various conceptions of leadership and criteria for leadership success that exist in their field.[9] They note a remarkable convergence of expectations among contributors to the topic irrespective of their political, ideological, or scholarly differences. The successful leader, these thinkers agree, must combine two talents: an ability to craft and communicate a coherent vision, mission, or purpose; and an ability to recruit people to take out membership in, ownership of, or identification with that vision, mission, or purpose. The first requires powers of conception and communication; the second tests interpersonal skills and capacities. We can imagine people who might be especially talented in one of these abilities, but who would still fail as leaders because they lacked the other.

Although these expectations might be directed to different aspects of personal competence, together they form a single demand on consciousness. In somewhat different terms they are an echo of the fourth order expectation upon parents as leaders of the family to shape a value-generating vision or theory by which the family will be led, and to induct their followers, the younger generation, into this vision. Heifetz and Sinder's review amounts to yet another identification of the pervasive modernist demand for fourth order consciousness in yet another domain, this time that of public leadership.

But Heifetz and Sinder's purpose in their essay is to propose an alternative to the highly agreed-upon vision. Here, in what amounts to quite a different but equally unacknowledged mental claim, they begin to lay out the postmodern "honors curriculum" for reconceiving the successful leader. However benign, admirable, or "inclusive" the leader's vision happens to be, it is still a unilaterally constructed one that comes into existence prior to its contact with prospective followers. From the view of established wisdom—the modernist view—this preconstructed vision is the leader's "gift," it is the "goods" she has to deliver, the way she shows she's got the right stuff to be taken seriously as a leader.

In contrast, Heifetz and Sinder call for an exercise of leadership on behalf of *providing a context* in which all interested parties, the leader included, can *together* create a vision, mission, or purpose they can collectively uphold. Heifetz and Sinder are aware, as Lahey and I have discussed,[10] that this kind of leadership practice will have to contend with the dismay of those followers who have a different construction of what a leader should be and do. "What kind of a leader are you?!" some people will certainly think. "You say you want to lead us to a better place, but when we say, 'We're ready to follow you, show us the way, show us your plan,' you say, 'We need to figure that out together.' So what you're saying is you haven't *got* a plan! If you've got nothing to stand up for, how can you lead us? And if you can't lead us, don't stand up and say you can!"

In reply, whether she says it only to herself or to those who are challenging her, the kind of leader Heifetz and Sinder are proposing might think something like this: "I agree with you that I don't have a whole cut-and-dried plan for how we can get to where we want to go. I have my ideas to add, of course, but so do you. And I even agree that a person has no business posing as a leader if he doesn't have something to stand up for. But that's exactly why I think I *am* a leader, why I think I'm actually *being* a leader right now in refusing to treat my ideas and plans as whole and complete, however internally consistent and comprehensive they may be in their own terms. I *am* standing up for something right now, for the importance of our suffering through this inevitably frustrating and awkward process of cobbling together a collectively created plan for getting where we want to go. And once we have the plan, you know what? I'll want to lead by continuing to stand up for the likelihood of *its* incompleteness, and for our need to keep seeking the contradictions by which it will be nourished and grow."

The leader Heifetz and Sinder describe in their essay not only transcends an identification with the internally consistent system, form, or theory. She goes beyond the discovery we identified in our consideration of conflict that the form is neither prior to its relationship nor complete. Having created a disjunction between herself and fourth order structures (form, system), having dislodged it from the place of "subject" in her epistemology, she has come to a place beyond merely disdaining or deconstructing the claim of any internally consistent theory or form to objective truth. She is doing something more than determining that any self-consistent theory is inevitably "ideological" either in the Mannheimian sense of being a system of explanation or in the Foucaultian sense of being necessarily partial and power-delineating, covertly privileging some interests and disadvantaging others.[11]

In other words, it would be possible to recognize the fact that the established view of the good leader falsely presumes the completeness and priority of the leader's vision and nonetheless have quite a different kind of reply to the claim of the dismayed follower. This reply could be something more like this: "You're right that I have no plan, at least none I would think to offer you as being right for more than me. And maybe you're right that I'm not much of a leader either. Maybe I'm the leader who has come to put an end to leaders. Any plan I would give you, any plan anyone else you'd like to lead you will give you, any plan any of you might come up with, and, for that matter, *any plan we might collaboratively come up with,* is still going to be a plan. It is going to make decisions. It is going to say yes to something and no to something else. It is going to establish what is 'in' and what is 'out.' It is going to create difference, normativeness, hierarchy. It is going to say what is true, what is important, what counts now, and what is not and does not. Thus, any plan is going to be inevitably saturated with ideology and unworthy of your identification with it. Identifying yourself with any plan essentially brings you back to a position of reification and reunion with the assumptions of distinctness, priority, and completeness you have already rejected."

Both of these leaders are "postmodern." Both challenge the unacknowledged epistemological assumptions behind modernist conceptions of the unilateral leader. But while the first finally does have a place to stand and lead from, it is more questionable whether the second one does. Even if it were to be suggested that the second leader *is* leading on behalf of the position that it is important to remain skeptically disengaged from any plan or system for arriving at plans, it can be asked, "But is this not also a position? And if so, by the speaker's own logic, why should it be credited with any authority or granted any legitimacy?" But the second leader has a question, in turn, for the first leader: "Since you *do* have a place to stand and you *do* hold out the hope of a plan, or a system for arriving at plans, with which you would advocate our identification, how is this not a backsliding reification—a reauthorizing or relegitimizing of that which we both know to be false?"

The distinction between these two kinds of postmodern leaders illustrates a lively division of thinking that runs throughout postmodern writing in general, especially recent considerations of knowledge creation. I refer to this division as the distinction between *deconstructive* postmodernism and *reconstructive* postmodernism, but I am certainly not the first to have noticed it. In a wonderfully clarifying essay on the implications of postmodernism for the goals and practice of education, Nicholas Burbules and Suzanne Rice make essentially the same distinction between what they call an "anti-modern" brand of postmodernism (what I call "deconstructive") and a brand of postmodernism that seeks to reelaborate and reappropriate modernist categories (such as reason, freedom, equity, rights, self-determination) on less absolutistic grounds (what I call "reconstructive" postmodernism).[12]

Burbules and Rice begin by identifying three features they say are common to *all* postmodern writing (and in the process they give us a sense of how certain postmodern theorists talk):

> First is the rejection of absolutes. Postmodernists usually insist that there can be no single rationality, no single morality, and no ruling theoretical framework for the analysis of social and political events. The conventional language here, deriving from Jean-François Lyotard, is that there are no "meta-narratives" that are not themselves the partial expressions of a particular point of view. As Zygmunt Bauman[13] puts it: "The philosophers' search for the ultimate system, for the complete order, for the extirpation of everything unknown and unruly, stems from the dream of having a firm soil and a secure home,

and leads to closing down the obstinately infinite human potential. Such search for the universal cannot but degenerate into a ruthless clamp-down on human possibilities."

Second is the perceived saturation of all social and political discourses with power or dominance. Any metanarrative is taken to be synonymous with the hegemony of a social and political order. [As Lather puts it:] "To learn to see not only what we do but also what structures what we do, to deconstruct how ideological and institutional power play in our own practices, to recognize the partiality and open-endedness of our own efforts, all of this is to examine the discourses within which we are caught up. Imploding canons and foregrounding the power/knowledge nexus by deconstructing "natural" hierarchies demonstrate that what had seemed transparent and unquestionable is neither. All of this is to participate in the radical unsettling that is postmodernism in ways that have profound implications for pedagogy and curriculum . . . In this context of ferment, educational inquiry is increasingly viewed as no more outside the power/knowledge nexus than any other human enterprise."[14]

A third idea that recurs in the Postmodern literature is the celebration of "difference." Rather than attempting to judge or prioritize the explanatory or political significance of given elements in a social situation, the Postmodern trend is to argue that, because all signifiers are mere constructions, there is no clear reason to grant any one special significance of value over others. [Bauman again:] "What the inherently polysemous and controversial idea of *postmodernity* most often refers to . . . is first and foremost an acceptance of the ineradicable plurality of the world—not a temporary state on the road to the not-yet-attained perfection, sooner or later to be left behind, but the constitutive quality of existence. By the same token, postmodernity means a resolute emancipation from the characteristically modern urge to overcome difference and promote sameness . . . In the plural and pluralistic world of postmodernity, every form of life is *permitted on principle;* or, rather, no agreed principles are evident which may render any form of life impermissible."[15]

All three of these ways of thinking reflect the disjoining of fourth order "system" from its ultimacy as epistemological *subject.* Each way of thinking relativizes the attributions of wholeness, distinctness, and priority. But, having thus relativized the truth of the form or system—that is, having discovered its subjectivity—what now becomes the nature of one's knowing?

One pattern is forever repeated in the evolution of our structures of knowing, whether we are looking at mental development in infancy or the highly elaborated order of consciousness that underlies postmodernism. That pattern can be described like this: *differentiation always precedes integration.* How could it be otherwise? Before we can reconnect to, internalize, or integrate something with which we were originally fused, we must first distinguish ourselves from it. The two-year-old's "No" is literally its first *objection,* a declaration that it is *making into object* the people and things with which it had formerly identified itself. What can feel to the parents like a contrariness directed at *them* is as much directed at the child's old organization of self, the expression of a need to maintain a hard-won and still tenuous differentiation. When the disjunction comes to feel secure, and closeness to the parents no longer threatens reabsorption into the old organization, the negativism subsides and the child can reconnect with the parents on new terms. Differentiation precedes integration, that is, it simply precedes it in time; I do not intend to imply any *philosophical* priority.

This same pattern is observable in all the qualitative evolutions of mind subject-object psychology studies. In our longitudinal study of adult development, in which a majority of the subjects are gradually navigating the evolution from the third to the fourth order, one continually sees that a critique of one's identification with the values and loyalties of one's cultural or psychosocial surround precedes the construction of a fourth order system that can act upon those values, set them aside, or modify and reappropriate them to a new place within a more encompassing organization. Differentiation precedes integration. Conflict precedes *resolution.* This does not mean that actual social or personal distance must precede relational reconnection, as in Shakespeare's *Macbeth:* "In order to make Society the sweeter welcome / we will keep ourselves till suppertime alone." The differentiation that must precede integration is epistemological. Whether or not it is also accompanied by separation from real persons and social arrangements depends on the support those persons and social arrangements are able to extend to the processes of evolution.

Likewise, the three "common" features of postmodernist thinking that Burbules and Rice identify all reflect the fact that no matter what else has happened to one's way of knowing, one has differentiated from the fourth order system. But what about the next question: Is postmodern thinking also about a new kind of integration? For the kind of postmodern thinking Burbules and Rice call "antimodernism" it is not:

> The antimodernist position is characterized by a strong antipathy to the language, issues, and values of modernism . . . it defines itself in opposition to modernism, not as a position growing out of and moving beyond modernist concerns. Hence it is not concerned with recapturing and reformulating modern values, such as reason or equality, but with deconstructing them. Not surprisingly, this tradition in particular has been more convincing in pointing out the limitations and contradictions of modernism than in reformulating positive alternatives.[16]

Antimodernism is clearly the position of differentiation before integration, a position whose energy is necessarily devoted to maintaining a valuable disjunction and whose gift it is to make clear the good reasons for doing so. The prospect of reconnection with what one is working hard to differentiate from can only be known at this position in the unacceptable terms of reabsorption into a former discredited organization. The problem with this position is that, although it makes very clear where one should not stand, it has no place where it can stand, indeed, no place where it can stand in order to promote the values implied in its differentiation. Although Burbules and Rice tell us that postmodern thinking does "not attempt to judge or prioritize the explanatory significance" of various differences, the most valuable part of their essay, to my mind, finds them judging and prioritizing the difference between this antimodern brand of postmodernism and another, more integrating brand of postmodernism:

> We do not question for a moment the relations of dominance, or histories of conflict and hostility, or gulfs of non-understanding or misunderstanding across differences, that undercut conventional educational aims and practices. In-

deed, identifying and criticizing these is the necessary starting point for any new thinking on the problems of education. But unless one conceives freedom only negatively (as the mere avoidance or removal of such impediments), it is not clear what follows from this critique for educational or political practice. Antimodernism lacks a clear conception of a "positive freedom" that identifies social conditions in which freer thought and action are possible; lacking this, antimodernism has not been able to articulate a clear and defensible educational theory . . . The view we have termed antimodernism has been largely content with emphasizing points of critique. The educational practices that are generated from the antimodern perspective seem largely dependent upon the preferences of those who advance them. This is not necessarily to denigrate such practices, but merely to stress, again, that antimodernism cannot justify them by reference to generalizable values. As a result, value assumptions that actually do underlie these practices are frequently left implicit and unexamined . . . On the one hand, post-modernism provides strong reasons for valuing diversity, for not assuming homogeneity when it does not exist, and for avoiding modes of discursive and non-discursive practice that implicitly or explicitly exclude subjects who do not participate in dominant modes of thought, speech, and action. This position might even be pushed a step further, to insist that, given occasions of conflict and misunderstanding, we ought to err on the side of respecting the self-identification and worldview of others, especially for members of groups who have been traditionally *told* who they are, what is true, and what is good for them.

However, at some points in the literature, this position lapses over into claims that are much more problematic. Specifically, the celebration of difference becomes a presumption of incommensurability, a denial of the possibility of intersubjective understanding, and an exaggerated critique that *any* attempt to establish reasonable and consensual discourse across difference inevitably involves the imposition of dominant groups' values, beliefs, and modes of discourse upon others. These views are antimodern in their rejection of such goals as dialogue, reasonableness, and fair treatment of alternative points of view; such legacies of the modernist tradition are not only regarded as difficult and sometimes impossible to attain—which they are—but as actually undesirable ends.

In our view, this antimodernist position is unsustainable either intellectually or practically. It derives from a deep misunderstanding of the nature of difference and has counter-educational implications for pedagogy. The literature that espouses this view is often internally contradictory, suggesting that such a severe critique is difficult to sustain consistently; many authors who advocate strong antimodern critiques later find themselves reversing direction when the time comes to offer positive recommendations.[17]

In contrast to "antimodernism," and without acknowledging that they are violating a supposed postmodern proscription against judging and prioritizing among differences, Burbules and Rice clearly prefer what I call a "reconstructive postmodernism," one that seeks not only a differentiation from the forms of modernism but their reintegration into a new way of knowing that abjures the absolutism of the forms, that does not take the forms as complete, distinct, or prior.

There is no reason to assume that dialogue across differences [necessarily] involves either eliminating those differences or imposing one group's views on others; dialogue that leads to understanding, cooperation, and accommodation can sustain differences within a broader compact of toleration and respect. Thus what we need is not an antimodern denial of community, but a postmodern grounding of community on more flexible and less homogeneous assumptions . . .

As Nancy Harstock has pointed out, it is exceedingly ironic that at the very time that traditionally disadvantaged groups are beginning to find their voice, an epistemological view has gained currency that legitimated relativizing their claims to credibility and respect.[18]

The distinction between deconstructive and reconstructive postmodernism introduces the possibility that not every "theory," "stand," or "way" is necessarily absolutistic or ideological. Not every "differencing," normatizing, or hierarchizing is necessarily a hidden and arbitrary privileging of a special interest. Not every kind of judging or prioritizing is impermissible modernist domination. To return to the imagined dialogue between the two postmodern leaders, the possibility of a reconstructive postmodernism suggests that one could in fact advocate identification with a theory, a stand, or a way, and that such advocacy need not necessarily be a backsliding reification of one kind of modernist authority or another. An example would be a theory that was really a theory about theory-making, a theory that was mindful of the tendency of any intellectual system to reify itself, to identify internal consistency with validity, to call its fourth order brand of subjectivity "objectivity." The expression of such a theory's "maturity" would not be the modernist capacity to defend itself against all challenges, to demonstrate how all data gathered to it can find a place within it, but to assume its incompleteness and seek out contradiction by which to nourish the ongoing process of its reconstruction.[19]

This distinction between a deconstructive and a reconstructive relation to theory suggests two dramatically different postmodern relationships to the intellectual disciplines. Like the two postmodern leaders I have described, one uses the limits of a given discipline, theory, or scholarly approach to demonstrate its unacknowledged ideological partiality and therefore its unacceptability. This is the stance of the deconstructive university professor, who has essentially come to teach that any of our disciplines, theories, or scholarly approaches is ultimately unworthy of our commitment to it, and, by implication, that ultimately the only intellectual activity that is worthy is deconstruction. By this definition, the well-educated person would be the one who has discovered the separate bases for deconstructing the widest range of intellectual disciplines.

In contrast, the reconstructive approach would have an equal interest in bringing the limits of the disciplines and its theories to center stage in our learning, but for the purpose of nourishing the very process of reconstructing the disciplines and their theories. We could argue that the purpose of this reconstructing—this creating of better and better theory—is to arrive eventually at the Complete Theory, but a truly reconstructive view would actually be more likely to associate such a "victory" with death. As long as life goes on, the process will need to go on. We nourish reconstruction not as a means to the end of the Complete Theory but as an end in itself. When we teach the disciplines or their theories in this fashion, they become more than procedures for authorizing and validating knowledge. They become procedures about the reconstruction of their procedures. The disciplines become generative. They become truer to life.[20]

A theory that is also a theory about theory-making and a stand-taking that is also about the *way* we take a stand will by necessity make judgments about and deprioritize those procedures, theories, and stands that are not self-conscious about their own tendency toward absolutism. Although they are judgmental and hierarchizing in this fashion, they themselves are not necessarily being absolutistic. Thus, the fact that a theory or system does indeed "privilege" or "valorize" something (two favorite postmodern words) is *not* sufficient evidence that it is modern, absolutistic, partial, or ideological.

In the same way we need to reconsider equating generalization and universality with impermissible modernist absolutism. Not every generalization or proposed group universal is necessarily a forcing of the excluded or marginalized into terms or categories that fit only the dominant group. Universals or generalizations—about the processes of meaning-making, for example (that differentiation precedes integration or that negentropic processes of greater complexity, increased organization, and more highly concentrated energy characterize all living systems) or about the forms of meaning-making (that they can be analyzed with respect to the question of what they can look at, or take as object, and what they are embedded in, or take as subject)—are not necessarily, ipso facto, absolutistic (whereas the assumption that they are or must be *is* absolutistic!).

Reconstructive postmodernism thus reopens the possibility that some kinds of normativeness, hierarchizing, privileging, generalizing, and universalizing are not only compatible with a postideological view of the world, they are necessary for sustaining it. Once these possibilities have been reopened, it is only a quantitative, not a qualitative leap for postmodernists to consider the outlandish and heretical idea that a theory such as the one I have outlined in this book—in spite of the judgments, generalizations, and claims to universality it makes and in spite of its unabashed privileging of "complexity"—is at least potentially an ally, not an enemy of postmodernism.

Indeed, subject-object theory might be much more than that. It may actually be a sympathetic guide to the long and arduous labor of gradually creating a postmodern view of the world. For the self may indeed by multiple, not unitary, as postmodernists are fond of arguing, but *not* right away. Multiselved postmodern parents do not mate and give birth to multiselved postmodern babies. Half a lifetime, if not more, precedes these discoveries. And good company is required every step of the way.

And good company—sympathetic support—is required even after one has left the modern world behind. Burbules and Rice at times sound downright put out with the antimodernists. They call the antimodernist position "unsustainable," "deriving from a deep misunderstanding," "countereducational," "exaggerating," "unnecessarily prejudicial," "counterproductive," and "oversimplifying." How would they help these wrong-headed folk to give up the error of their ways? Are they hoping to argue the antimodernists out of their view by the sheer force of their presentation of the alternative? Do they expect a deconstructive modernist to read their essay and slap himself of the forehead exclaiming, "But of course! Why didn't I see this all along? My deconstructionist thinking is flawed. I'm switching to reconstructivism!"? I doubt it. But what happens if they take seriously the possibility that the antimodernist position actually "derives" less from any "deep misunderstanding" than from the fact that it represents an earlier stage of complexity in the gradual evolution from the fourth to the fifth order of consciousness?

The first thing Burbules and Rice might reconsider is their claim that the position is "unsustainable." Anyone making this claim should read through our years of subject-object interview transcripts. ("Do you think Senator Humphrey's position on the war is untenable?" Eugene McCarthy was asked by an interviewer during a presidential primary season. "Well, I don't think we can say it's *untenable*," the former Jesuit and Latin-literate McCarthy responded, "because he's been *holding* to it for quite a while now.") The antimodern position may be unsustainable from the standard of fifth order logic, but from its own position (just enough beyond the fourth order to critique its limits but not yet able to create a new order) it is completely sustainable—and the self is sustained in creating the world in this way. The antimodernist cannot move from a deconstructive to a reconstructive position without disturbing the self.

The next thing Burbules and Rice might do is to stop characterizing the antimodern position as "oversimplifying." This term suggests that the antimodernist not only expresses a simpler order of mental complexity but could alter it as if it were an "error" he could "correct" without cost. If Burbules and Rice tried on a developmental formulation of the distinction between the two positions, they would see that characterizations like "overly simple" and "counterproductive" are egocentric on their part; that is, they view the situation only from their own vantage point, not from that of the antimodernists, whose position is anything but simple to them and is at the same time completely "productive" of the mind's integrity as the mind is currently constituted.

Finally, if they were to conduct their own "dialogue across differences" (the title of their essay) in this constructive-developmental way, it would promote the possibility of dwelling for a time in the home of the other and developing an empathy for the coherence of the other's position and the costs that leaving it might entail. This kind of dialogue across difference might help in fashioning a bridge that is more respectfully anchored on both sides of the chasm, instead of assuming that such a bridge already exists and wondering why the other has not long ago walked over it.

I do not say all this to chastise Burbules and Rice, whose essay I obviously admire. Their annoyance with antimodernism I can readily identify in myself, since I have spent twenty years developing a theory that turns to dust in antimodernist hands; yet I notice that my own sense of annoyance is transformed to one of connection when I take seriously the developmental possibility. Their preference for reconstructive postmodernism is one I share. My intention is to resolve the unrecognized contradictions of their essay by showing how it is possible for us to enter a judging, prioritizing, generalizing, and universalizing theory like subject-object psychology *on behalf of* the postmodern project.

Let me conclude this chapter by summing up some of the specific ways subject-object theory might in fact be helpful. First, it demonstrates that privileging consciousness complexity (which subject-object psychology certainly does) need not necessarily entail absolutism. On the contrary, it can be a saving tool for avoiding absolutism. And it can help us preserve the distinction between the rejection of absolutes on the one hand, and the rejection of the possibility of any nonabsolutist ground on the other.

Second, subject-object theory makes explicit the conditions under which a judging and status-conferring relationship to difference (such as Burbules and Rice construct) is in fact consistent with postmodernism. For example, antimodernist positions are prized ahead of modernist positions and reconstructive postmodern positions are prized ahead of antimodernist positions, but not because the advantaged position is closer to some dominating, ideological absolute. Rather, each is preferred because it is closer to a position that in fact protects us from dominating, ideological absolutes. Constructions beyond the complexity of the fourth order of consciousness are prized above those embedded in the fourth order, and fifth order constructions are prized above those that are just a little beyond the fourth order, but not because complexity itself is a virtue. They assume an advantaged position because with each, the next way of constructing reality provides even more protection from the captivation and dominance of other reality constructions.

Finally, subject-object theory makes operational the criteria for determining whether one position is actually more complex than the other or merely fancies itself so. A status-conferring or judging relationship to difference is still a relationship: it does not have to create a discounting of what is less advantaged; it creates instead a connection to it. If one position is actually more complex than the other, it should be able to understand the other's position *on the other's own terms,* to extend empathy for the costs involved in altering that position, and to provide support for, rather than dismissal of, the prior position. If the positions are of equal complexity, each may be able to understand the other, but neither can build the bridge between orders of consciousness its false claim to superiority would imply. If one position is actually less complex than the other, it should not even be able to understand the other on terms that allow the other to feel that its being is adequately understood.

NOTES

1. For further consideration of this essentially "dialectical" point, see the discussion of the transformation from the fourth to the fifth order in L. Lahey, E. Souvaine, R. Kegan, R. Goodman, and S. Felix, *A Guide to the Subject-Object Interview: Its Administration and Interpretation* (Cambridge: The Subject-Object Workshop, 1988); E. Souvaine, L. Lahey, and R. Kegan, "Life after Formal Operations: Implications for a Psychology of the Self," in C. N. Alexander and E. J. Langer, eds., *Higher Stages of Human Development: Perspectives on Adult Growth* (New York: Oxford University Press, 1990); and M. Basseches, *Dialectical Thinking and Adult Development* (Norwood, N.J.: Ablex, 1984).

2. My thanks to Ariela Bairey, who gave me a background in this field. See J. W. Burton, *Conflict and Communication: The Use of Controlled Communication in International Relations* (London: MacMillan, 1969); Burton, *Resolving Deep-Rooted Conflict: A Handbook* (Lanham, Md.: University Press of America, 1987); J. W. Burton and F. Dukes, *Conflict: Practices in Management, Settlement and Resolution* (New York: St. Martin's Press, 1990); L. W. Doob, ed., *Resolving Conflict in Africa: The Fermeda Workshop* (New Haven: Yale University Press, 1970); Doob, "Adieu to Private Intervention in Political Conflicts?" *International Journal of Group Tensions,* 17 (1987): 15–27; L. W. Doob and W. J. Foltz, "The Belfast Workshop: An Application of Group Techniques to a Destructive Conflict," *Journal of Conflict Resolution,* 18 (1973): 237–256; R. J. Fisher, "A Third-Party Consultation Workshop on the India-Pakistan Conflict," *Journal of Social Psychology,* 112 (1980): 191–206; Fisher, "Third Party Consultation as a Method of Conflict Resolution: A Review of Studies," *Journal of Conflict Resolution,* 27 (1983): 301–334; Fisher, *The Social Psychology of Intergroup and International Conflict Resolution* (New York: Springer-Verlag, 1990); Fisher, *Conflict Analysis Workshop on Cyprus: Final Workshop Report* (Ottawa: Canadian Institute for International Peace and Security, 1991); H. C. Kelman, "The Problem-Solving Workshop in Conflict Resolution," in R. L. Merritt, ed., *Communication in International Politics* (Urbana: University of Illinois Press, 1972), pp. 168–204; Kelman, "An Interactional Approach to Conflict Resolution and Its Application to Israeli-Palestinian Relations," *International Interactions,* 6, no. 2 (1979): 99–122; Kelman, "Interactive Problem Solving: A Social-Psychological Approach to Conflict Resolution," in W. Klassen, ed., *Dialogue toward Inter-Faith Understanding* (Jerusalem: Ecumenical Institute for Theological Research, 1986), pp. 293–314; H. C. Kelman and S. P. Cohen, "The Problem-Solving Workshop: A Social-Psychological Contribution to the

Resolution of International Conflict," *Journal of Peace Research,* 13 (1976): 79–90; Kelman and Cohen, "Resolution of International Conflict: An Interactional Approach," in S. Worchel and W. G. Austin, eds., *Psychology of Intergroup Relations,* 2nd ed. (Chicago: Nelson-Hall, 1986), pp. 323–342.

3. This "union of opposites" Jung called "enantiodromia," depicted by the snake who eats its tail, the joining of the poles making a single whole. Interestingly, Jung associated the union of opposites with midlife.

4. L. Chasin, R. Chasin, M. Herzig, S. Roth, and C. Becker, "The Citizen Clinician: The Family Therapist in the Public Forum," *American Family Therapy Association Newsletter* (Winter 1991): 36–42; R. Chasin and M. Herzig, "Creating Systemic Interventions for the Sociopolitical Arena," in B. Berger-Gould and D. H. DeMuth, eds., *The Global Family Therapist: Integrating the Personal, Professional and Political* (Needham, Mass.: Allyn and Bacon, 1993); S. Roth, L. Chasin, R. Chasin, C. Becker, and M. Herzig, "From Debate to Dialogue: A Facilitating Role for Family Therapists in the Public Forum," *Dulwich Centre Newsletter,* no. 2 (1993): 41–48; C. Becker, L. Chasin, R. Chasin, M. Herzig, and S. Roth, "From Stuck Debate to New Conversation on Controversial Issues: A Report from the Public Conversations Project," *Journal of Feminist Family Therapy,* in press.

5. C. Argyris, *On Organizational Learning* (Cambridge: Blackwell Business, 1993); C. Argyris, *Overcoming Organizational Defenses: Facilitating Organizational Learning* (Boston: Allyn and Bacon, 1990); C. Argyris, R. Putnam, and D. M. Smith, *Action Science* (San Francisco: Jossey-Bass, 1985); C. Argyris, *The Applicability of Organizational Sociology* (Cambridge, England: Cambridge University Press, 1972); S. Srivastva and Associates, *The Executive Mind* (San Francisco: Jossey-Bass, 1983); C. Argyris, *Increasing Leadership Effectiveness* (New York: Wiley, 1976); Argyris, *Inner Contradictions of Rigorous Research* (New York: Academic Press, 1980); D. A. Schon, *The Reflective Practitioner* (London: Temple Smith, 1983); D. A. Schon, ed., *The Reflective Turn: Case Studies in and on Educational Practice* (New York: Teachers College Press, 1991); C. Argyris and D. A. Schon, *Theory in Practice: Increasing Professional Effectiveness* (San Francisco: Jossey-Bass, 1974); Argyris and Schon, *Organizational Learning: A Theory of Action Perspective* (Reading, Mass.: Addison-Wesley, 1978); D. A. Schon, *Intuitive Thinking?: A Metaphor Underlying Some Ideas of Educational Reform* (Cambridge: Division for Study and Research in Education, Massachusetts Institute of Technology, 1981); Schon, *Educating the Reflective Practitioner: Toward a New Design for Teaching and Learning*

in the Professions (San Francisco: Jossey-Bass, 1987); W. R. Torbert, *The Power of Balance: Transforming Self, Society and Scientific Inquiry* (Newbury, Calif.: Sage Publications, 1991); Torbert, *Managing the Corporate Dream: Restructuring for Long-Term Success* (Homewood, Ill.: Dow-Jones Irwin, 1987); Torbert, *Learning from Experience: Toward Consciousness* (New York: Columbia University Press, 1972); Torbert, *Creating a Community of Inquiry: Conflict, Collaboration, Transformation* (New York: Wiley, 1976).

6. Personal communication.

7. For an illuminating discussion and exploration of the mental demands implicit in Argyris's "action science," see E. Souvaine, "Creating Contexts for Effective Action and the Development of Meaning-Making" (unpublished qualifying paper, Harvard Graduate School of Education, 1985).

8. See Lahey et al., *A Guide to the Subject-Object Interview;* Souvaine et al., "Life after Formal Operations"; and Basseches, *Dialectical Thinking and Adult Development.*

9. R. A. Heifetz and R. M. Sinder, "Political Leadership: Managing the Public's Problem Solving," in R. Reich, ed., *The Power of Public Ideas* (Cambridge: Balinger, 1988).

10. R. Kegan and L. Lahey, "Adult Leadership and Adult Development," in B. Kellerman, ed., *Leadership: Multidisciplinary Perspectives* (New York: Prentice-Hall, 1983).

11. K. Mannheim, *Essays on the Sociology of Culture* (London: Routledge and Paul, 1956); M. Foucault, *Power/Knowledge* (New York: Pantheon Books, 1980).

12. N. C. Burbules and S. Rice, "Dialogue across Differences: Continuing the Conversation," *Harvard Educational Review,* 61 (1991): 393–416.

13. Z. Bauman, "Strangers: The Social Construction of Universality and Particularity," *Telos,* 28, no. 23 (1988–1989) (quoted in Burbules and Rice, "Dialogue across Differences").

14. P. Lather, "Post-Modernism and the Politics of Enlightenment," *Educational Foundations,* 3, no. 3 (1989) (quoted in Burbules and Rice, "Dialogue across Differences").

15. Z. Bauman, "Strangers"; Burbules and Rice, "Dialogue across Differences."

16. Ibid., p. 398.

17. Ibid., pp. 398–401.

18. Ibid., pp. 402–407.

19. Arlin identifies a stage of cognitive development beyond the fully formal operational "problem solving," which she calls "problem

finding," in which thinkers seek out and are nourished by contradiction. Are Arlin's "problem solving" and "problem finding" stages cognitive reflections of the fourth and fifth orders, respectively? See P. K. Arlin, "Cognitive Development in Adulthood: A Fifth Stage?" *Developmental Psychology,* 11 (1975): 602–606; Arlin, "Piagetian Operations in Problem Finding," *Developmental Psychology,* 13 (1977): 247–298; Arlin, "Adolescent and Adult Thought: A Structural Interpretation," in M. L. Commons, F. A. Richards, and C. Armon, eds., *Beyond Formal Operations: Late Adolescent and Adult Cognitive Development* (New York: Praeger, 1984); Arlin, "Wisdom: The Art of Problem Finding," in R. J. Sternberg, ed., *Wisdom: Its Nature, Origins and Development* (New York: Cambridge University Press, 1990).

20. Belenky et al. identify a "way of knowing" beyond "procedural knowing" which they call "constructed knowing," in which we become more aware of and responsible for the constructed nature of our procedures. Are "procedural knowing" and "constructed knowing" expressions of the fourth and fifth orders, respectively? See M. F. Belenky, B. M. Clinchy, N. R. Goldberger, and J. M. Tarule, *Women's Ways of Knowing* (New York: Basic Books, 1986).

The Development of Women's Sense of Self

Jean Baker Miller

The concept of the self has been prominent in psychological theory, but perhaps this is so because it has been one of the central ideas in western thought. While various writers use different definitions, the essential idea of "a self" seems to underlie the historical development of many western notions about such vast issues as the "good life," justice and freedom. Indeed, it seems entwined in the roots of several delineations of the fundamental human motive or the highest form of existence, as in Maslow's self-actualizing character.

As we have inherited it, the notion of "a self" does not appear to fit women's experience. Several recent writers have spoken to this point, for example, literary critic Carolyn Heilbrun (1979), and psychologist Carol Gilligan (1982). A question then arises, "Do only men have a self, and not women?" In working with women, the question is quite puzzling, but an examination of the very puzzle itself may cast new light on certain long-standing assumptions.

Modern American workers who write on early psychological development and, indeed, on the entire life span, from Erikson (1950) to Daniel Levinson (1978), tend to see all of development as a process of separating oneself out from the matrix of others, "becoming one's own man," in Levinson's term. Development of the self presumably is attained via a series of painful crises by which the individual accomplishes a sequence of allegedly essential separations from others, and thereby achieves an inner sense of separated individuation. Few men ever attain such self-sufficiency, as every woman knows. They are usually supported by numbers of wives, mistresses, mothers, daughters, secretaries, nurses and others (and groups of other men who are lower than they are in the social-economic hierarchy, if they are higher). Thus, there is reason to question whether this model accurately reflects men's lives. Its goals, however, are held out for all, and are seen as the pre-conditions for mental health.

Almost every modern psychiatrist who has tried to fit women into the prevalent models has had much more obvious difficulty, beginning with Freud, going through Erikson and others. Some haven't tried. In Erikson's scheme, for example, after the first stage, in which the aim is the development of basic trust, the aim of every other stage, until young adulthood, is some form of increased separation of self-development. I'm not referring at this point to the process by which each aim is attained (although that is an intimately related point—see below), but the aim itself, the goal. It is important to note that the aim is not something like development of greater capacity for emotional connection to others, or for con-tributing to an interchange between people, or for playing a part in the growth of others as well as one's self. When the individual arrives at the stage called "intimacy," he is supposed to be able to be intimate with another person(s), having spent all of his prior development geared to something very different.

Recently, a large amount of writing, which deplores men's incapacity to engage in intimacy, has come from the women's movement. But men have been making the same testimony. Al-most all of modern literature, philosophy and commentary in other forms portrays men's lack of a sense of community—indeed, even of the possibility of communicating with others.

Thus, the prevailing models may not describe well what oc-curs in men; in addition, there is a question about the value of these models even if it were possible to fulfill their requirements. These two questions are related, as I'll try to suggest. It is very important to note, however, that the prevalent models are power-ful because they have become prescriptions about what *should* happen. They affect men; they determine the actions of mental health professionals. They have affected women adversely in one way in the past. They are affecting women in another way now, if women seek "equal access" to them. Therefore, it behooves us to examine them carefully. It's important not to leap to the only models available.

THE BEGINNINGS

What the some of the questions which arise when we try to bring women's experience into the picture? We can take Erikson's theories as a starting point, not in order to attempt a thorough examination of them, but to use his formulations as a framework for consideration of a few of the many features in women's development.

In the first stage of life, Erikson says that the central goal is the infant's development of a sense of basic trust. There is another important dimension. Even at that early stage in all infants, but encouraged much more so in girls, the young child begins to be like and act like the main caretaker who, up until now, has usually been a woman—not to "identify" with that person as some static figure described only by gender, but with what that person *actually* is doing. I think that the infant begins to develop an internal representation of herself/himself as a kind of being that, for the moment I'll call by a hyphenated term—a "being-in-relationship." This is the beginning of a sense of "self" which reflects what is happening *between* people, as known by the relation between people. The infant picks up the feelings of the other person, that is, it has an early sense that "I feel what's going on in the other as well as what's going on in myself." Really, it's more complex because it's "knowing"—feeling—what's going on in that emotional field between us. The child experiences a sense of comfort only as the other is also comfortable, or, a little more accurately, only as they are both engaged in an emotional relationship that is moving toward greater well-being, rather than toward the opposite, i.e. only as the interactions in the emotional field between the infant and the adult are moving toward a "better" progression of events. In this sense, the infant, actively exerting an effect on the relationship, begins to develop an internal sense of herself/himself as one who changes the emotional interplay for both participants—for good or ill.

The beginnings of a mental construction of self are much

more complicated than those suggested by such commonly used terms as fusion, merger and the like for the mental constructions of the first stages of infancy, as drawn from Mahler (1975), object relations theorists and others. New research on infant-caretaker interactions also indicates the inappropriateness of those terms. (See, for example, Stern, 1980; Stechler and Kaplan, 1980; Klein, 1976. These points have been made in various ways by many theorists, such as M. Klein, H. S. Sullivan and several others. The features which they emphasize, however, are different.) This research suggests that these constructs are not likely to describe adequately the complex internal representations of the self and "the other," or rather the internal self-other relational patterns that the infant is likely to create even from the earliest age.

When we talk about a sense of self in this field, we have been referring to a "man-made" construct meant to describe an internal mental representation. The suggestion here is that from the moment of birth this internal representation is of a self which is in active interchange with other selves. Moreover, the kind of interaction has one central characteristic, and that is that people are attending to the infant—most importantly attending to the infant's core of being, which means the infant's emotions—and the infant is responding in the same way, i.e. to the other person's emotions. The beginning of mental representations of the self, then, is of a self whose core—which is emotional—is attended to by the other(s); and who begins to attend to the emotions of the other(s). Part of this internal image of oneself includes feeling the other's emotions and *acting on* the emotions coming from the other as they are in interplay with one's own emotions. This means that the beginnings of the concept of self are not those of a static and lone self being ministered to by another (incidentally, this construct has a strongly suggestive male flavor), but much more of a self inseparable from a dynamic interaction. And the central character of that interaction is one of attending to each other's mental states and emotions.

This early "interacting sense of self" is present for infants of both sexes, but the culturally induced beliefs of the caretakers about girls and boys enter the scene from the moment of birth. These beliefs are, of course, internalized even in the woman caretaker, although more so in fathers, according to suggestions from some studies (e.g. Rubin, et al., 1974, Block, 1978 and others). Girls are encouraged to augment their abilities to "feel as the other feels," and to practice "learning about" the other(s). Boy infants are systematically diverted from it, to their deprivation and detriment in my opinion. (In my opinion, this redounds, too, to the detriment of the whole construction of societal structure and of our models of thinking.)

Out of this interplay of experience one certainly develops a sense of one's self, that is, an internal or mental representation of one's self. Moreover, one develops a sense of one's self as a person who attends to and responds to what is going on in the relationships between two or more people.

Much of the prevalent literature tends to suggest that because she is the same sex as the caretaker, the girl cannot develop an internal sense of self; that is, that boys develop a sense of self because they separate themselves from the female caretaker. This is truly an incredible notion. First, it ignores all of the complexity of the interaction between caretaker and infant. It is as if there were no interaction because they are both of the same sex, i.e. female, an amazing negation of the very idea of girls and women.

Second, the prevalent literature has ignored the extraordinarily important character of the interaction—that of attending to and responding to the other. This is the essential feature of what comes to be called "caretaking." It is also the basis of all continuing psychological growth, i.e. all growth occurs within emotional connections, not separate from them. Current theories ignore, too, the likelihood that the early self is built on the model of this very process—as opposed to the very different kinds of interaction which exist in the current world. The very notion of true caretaking precludes anything that would lead the infant to feel submerged, fused or merged with the other. These are words which may describe some of the phenomena observed after *distortions* in caretaking have occurred, but they are unlikely to characterize the infant's prototypic sense of self.

Third, the current notions tend to ignore the very likelihood that the only possibility of having any sense of self at all is built on this core process. As suggested above, I believe that this is true for both sexes, but it is not allowed to flourish in boys. Instead, it begins to be discouraged early. For girls, it is encouraged, but complications are added at this and at each succeeding phase of development.

Surrey has suggested that this early mental representation of the self can be described as a more *encompassing* sense of self by contrast with the more boundaried, or limited, self that is encouraged in the boy from a very young age. She suggests, too, the term "oscillating" sense of self as compared to the more linear current model, and that the "oscillation" would follow from the ongoing growth of empathy in the child as well as in the mother (Surrey, 1984; Jordan, Surrey, Kaplan, 1982). Many implications follow. To mention just a few: Certain events in later life which are seen as detracting from the self, according to other models, are seen as satisfying, motivating and empowering. For example, to feel "more related to another person(s)" does not mean to feel one's self threatened, but enhanced. It doesn't feel like a loss of part of one's self, but the prospect of a step toward more pleasure and effectiveness—because it is the way the girl and woman feel "things should be," the way she wants them to be. Being in relationship, picking up the feelings of the other and attending to the "interaction between," becomes an accepted, "natural-seeming" way of being and acting. It is learned and assumed. It is not alien or threatening. Most important, it is desired; it is a *goal*—by contrast to a detraction or a means to some other end, such as one's own self-development. Thus, it forms a *motivation.*

We have come to think of this whole experience as so "foreign," I believe, because our cultural tradition has emphasized such a different direction. In the dominant and official culture, attending to the experience of others and of the relationships between people has been so lacking as a usual basis and *requirement* of all of life. It has been relegated to the alien and mysterious world of mothers and infancy—and misunderstood. Sometimes, when I've tried to talk about this, some psychiatrists have said, "Oh, I see what you mean. All right, I agree that women are more altruistic." That isn't what I mean. That's attempting to slot this description into the old categories. It suggests a "sacrifice" of parts of a kind of self which has developed in a different fashion. To engage in the kind of interaction I'm discussing is not a sacrifice; it is, in fact, a source of feeling better and more gratified, as well as more knowledgeable—about what's really happening. I believe it is closer to elementary human necessities from which our dominant culture has become unnecessarily removed.

Another implication relates to the topic of self-esteem or the sense of self-worth. The girl's sense of self-esteem is based in feeling that she is a part of relationships and is taking care of the relationships. This is very different from the components of self-esteem as usually described and, incidentally, as measured by most available scales. Another ramification involves the issue of competence or effectiveness. The girl and woman often feel a sense of effectiveness as arising out of emotional connections and as bound up with and feeding back into them. This is very different from a sense of effectiveness (or power) based on the sense of lone action and especially from acting against others or over others. This sense of effectiveness can develop further in the next and all subsequent ages, but it grows upon this base.

AGENCY WITHIN COMMUNITY

To move quickly through the next ages of life, I'll sketch a few suggestions about each of them, leading here only as far as adolescence. Erikson speaks about the second stage of childhood as one in which the goal is autonomy; others have spoken about separation and individuation. I would suggest, instead, that we could think of this as a period when the child has more abilities, more possibilities "to do" and more physical and mental resources to use. She or he also has an enlarged "point of view" on all events, as it were, i.e. a more developed sense of how she or he sees things. There is not, however, nor need there be, any increased separation. Instead, there are new configurations and new "understandings" *in the relationship*. Maintaining the relationship(s) with the main people in her or his life is still *the* most important thing.

We might think of this as something like a phase called "agency-in-community." These words are borrowed from Bakan (1966), but not used with his definitions. Instead, by "agency," I am searching for a word again, a word that means being active, using all of one's resources, but without the connotations of aggression, another large topic, but one that cannot be developed here (Miller, 1983). Here, again, what the "doing" is clearly is different from what has been described. Often for little girls, it's doing *for*—again, for the mother (and others)—following the model of what the mother is doing (Jordan, Surrey, Kaplan, 1982; Surrey, 1984). What the mother is still doing with little children is attending to their feelings and "*doing for*" them, although not totally. So the action, again, has a different character—it's doing for other(s) within a relationship, with the little girl using very increased powers and increased "opinions" about how and what she wants "to do," and an increased assertion of what she can do.

In her internal representation of herself, I would suggest that the girl is developing not a sense of separation, but a more developed sense of her own capacities and a sense of her greater capability to put her "views" into effect. That is, she has a sense of a larger scope of action—but still with an inner representation of a self that is doing this in relation to other selves. A larger scope of action is not equivalent to separation; it requires a *change* in her internal configuration of her sense of self and other, but not a separation.

The child can move on not only to a larger, but a more articulated sense of herself *only because* of her actions and feelings *in* the relationship. These may—inevitably are—actions and feelings different from the other person's. They are obviously not identical. The point is that she is attuned to the feelings of the other person and that her feelings are also in response to the other's feelings and, in turn, influence them as the others' influence hers. She has a wide range of feelings and actions, and they vary at different times with one or another in ascendancy, but they occur within the relational context.

Of course, the character of the relationship differs from that of infancy; new qualities come in. But this does not lead to a "separate" sense of self. It leads to a more complex sense of self in more complex relationships to other selves.

The whole notion of describing human interaction in geographic or spatial terms, along a scale of close or distant (i.e. separated), seems questionable. Surely it is the *quality* of the interaction that is the question—the interplay of "conceptualized feelings" (i.e. feelings *cum* concepts), the doing of good or bad to the other—in relation to the nature of the needs of each. A growing child has the possibility to do more than she or he could do before. The caretaker who recognizes and supports this enlarged ability does not become more distant. She or he becomes one step *more caring* in one more way—i.e. *more related*—and the child does, too.

CHILDHOOD

When we move to the next stage, which is based on the Oedipal stage, we may ask whether one reason that people, beginning with Freud, have had such trouble delineating this stage in girls is that it may not exist. There is no big crisis of "cutting off" of anything, and especially relationships. And there is no need to fulfill the goal of "identifying with an aggressor," i.e. the threatening and dominant male figure. (Several theorists believe that all of society, culture and thought is built on this Oedipal moment of identification with the aggressive father. It is interesting to think about the possibility that society need not be built on this base.) However, there is a message which may come in more forcefully at this time (though it begins earlier and it continues later, too), that the girl should now focus all of her attunement to the other person on the well-being and the growth and development of men. But the relationship to the mother and to other women continues. A pronounced turning away from the mother and toward the father may occur because of particular conditions in particular families, especially when the mother herself encourages and models this way of being. Western culture has dictated that mothers should uphold the superior importance and the power of the man. These forces begin to affect deeply the girl's sense of herself and her relationship to her mother, and to complicate the relationship in many ways. However, the relationship to the mother and to other women continues, although it may be less obvious and it may be made to seem less important. There are ethnic, class and historical variations in the degree of influence of the mother or father within the family, but the greater importance, value and power of the father—and the devaluation of the mother—seem to come through psychologically, in general.

In latency, or the period which, according to Erikson, has "industry" as its goal, there is increasing evidence that girls are not very latent. What girls may do is learn to hide more, if we're talking about sexuality, as Freud was when he initiated the use of the term. But certainly if we're talking about relationships, this is the time when the girls are very intensely involved in all of their relationships, especially with other girls. Many girls are very interested in men and boys, too, but the boys are often either not interested or actively deprecating and destructive to girls. The boys are out learning "industry," which others have talked about as "learning the rules of the game and how to play them" (Gilligan, 1982). Most of these, incidentally, seem directly traceable to war games. In a study on this period, Luria (1981) describes the events in a grade school playground. She talks about the boys learning not only how to be "warlike" and to win out over others, but how to cheat and get away with it. If she asks the girls what they are doing, they often say, "Nothing." The girls are hanging around the edges of the playground "just talking." What are they talking about? They are talking about the issues in their families and how to solve them. In discussing their families, the girls are, of course, very involved in an emotional interaction with each other. Surrey (1984) has pointed out that the vast amount of psychological development which occurs within the relationships between girls at this time has been one of the major neglected areas in psychological study.

ADOLESCENCE

Now, adolescence. Adolescence has been seen as a time when the individual has greatly increased capacities. Traditionally, psychologists have *divided* them in several ways: for example, sexual capacities, aggressive capacities—which I will call for the moment, agentic (the ability to act)—cognitive capacities, with the development of formal thought which does greatly expand the universe. However, many studies still indicate that this is a time when girls begin to "contract" rather than expand. Clara Thompson (1942) noted this long ago. She said that for boys, adolescence was seen as a period of opening up, but for girls it's a time for shutting down. In his terms, Freud said this too. Freud believed that girls now had to learn for good that they were not to use actively all of themselves and all of their life forces from a base centered in their own bodies and in their own psychological constructions. For Freud, this meant, of course, the derivatives of their sexual drive. Instead, these forces are to be turned, now, to the use of others—men, in the first instance, and to the service of the next generation, childbearing. That is, girls had to resolve their psychological issues by becoming passive and masochistic— i.e. to accomplish the necessary submission to the man and to "sacrifice" themselves for children.

Freud's observations may have reflected much of what happened—and still happens. That is, in regard to sexuality, most girls still learn that their own sexual perceptions, sensations, impulses are not supposed to arise from themselves, but are to be brought forth by and for men. Thus, girls still tend to experience their physical and sexual stirrings as wrong, bad, evil, dirty and the like. This is to say that part of what has been going on in the girl's earlier internal representations of herself has included several problematic parts. One of these involves bodily and sexual experience. This situation can lead to an attempt to deal with this experience by turning to passivity and submission. The girl picks up the strong message that her own perceptions about her bodily and sexual feelings are not acceptable. They acquire connotations of badness and evil. They become parts of her self which are shameful and wrong. She has sought to bring these parts of herself into relationships with others all along, but has had difficulty in doing so. She still seeks to act on these desires within relationships with others. But she meets opposition. In the face of this, the solution of "doing it for others" can seem to offer a ready answer. The problem is that this solution is one which attempts to leave her, and her sense of herself with all of her own psychological constructions, out of the relationship.

In heterosexual relationships, if the girl or young woman tries to have her own perceptions, to follow her own desires, and to bring them into sexual experience with boys, she still is destined for conflict. Despite all of the recent talk, the girl's attempt to act on the basis of her own sexuality still leads to conflict with her potential male partners. It will lead also to internal conflict with certain components of her sense of self. One is the part that says she should—and that she wants to—be attuned to others, which leads to a conflict if the other is behaving in ways which are excluding her perceptions and desires from the relationship. Another is the part that has made sexuality an unacceptable aspect of her internal sense of self and therefore prevents her from bringing a large part of herself into the relationship.

It is similar in regard to "agency," that is, the girl's whole capacity to perceive and to use her powers in all ways. Women were not supposed to do this, and have incorporated the idea that to do so is wrong and shameful. The girl has learned and done many things, until now, within a relationship. However, because of societal influences, she has also incorporated a sense—again to varying degrees—that she is not fully and freely to use all of her powers. At adolescence, however, she receives this as a much stronger message.

Thus, her sense of self as an active agent—in the context of acting within a relationship and for the relationship—has been altered to some degree all along by a sense of a self who must defer to others' needs or desires. However, at adolescence she experiences a much more intense pressure to do so. Her sense of self as developed so far now faces a more serious conflict with the external forces she confronts.

The question is how she will deal with this conflict. As with sexuality, I believe that the major tendency is for the girl to opt for the relationship both in her overt actions and also in an alteration of her internal sense of self. She will tend to want most to retain the self that wants to be a "being-in-relationship," but she will begin to lose touch with the definition of herself as a more active "being-within-relationships." If one part has to go, and until now it did, most girls lose more of the sense that they can bring their agency and sexuality, as they experience it, into the relationship.

To restate some of these points, at adolescence the girl is seeking fulfillment of two very important needs: to use herself, including her sexual and all of her capacities, but seeking to do so within a context that will fulfill her great desire to be a "being-in-relationship." This wish to do so has developed all through earlier ages. She wishes that the other person(s) will be able to enter into a relationship in this fashion. I believe that the boy really has the same needs, at bottom. However, he has been much more preoccupied with trying to develop "himself" and a sense of his independent identity. The culture has made the very heavy demand that he be so preoccupied. It has been doing so all along, but it does so at adolescence in an even more forceful way. He has also picked up the idea that the girl should adapt to him, and he has not been encouraged to continue the development of the sense that he is mainly a boy-in-relationship with a primary responsibility for others and a desire to concentrate on the relationship between him and others.

Thus, girls are not seeking the *kind* of identity that has been prescribed for boys, but a different kind, one in which one is a "being-in-relation," which means developing all of one's self in increasingly complex ways, in increasingly complex relationships.

The model of a "being-in-relationship" which women are seeking is not easy to attain in present conditions. As I've tried to suggest, it is a very valuable model and, I believe, a model more related to reality, the reality of the human condition. In the current situation, however, it still tends to mean for women the old kind of relationship with the suppression of the full participation of the woman's way of seeing and acting. This has been the historical pattern, certainly. For most women it is still the case. Even so, the woman's struggle continues into later life, but many more factors now complicate it.

PRACTICAL IMPLICATIONS

The practical implications are many. To suggest just a few, women probably do talk about relationships more often, and this is often misinterpreted as dependency. It's very important to listen carefully to what women are saying. Often it is not about wanting or needing to be dependent *or* independent, but about wanting to be in relationship with others, and, again, to really comprehend the other; to understand the other's feelings; to contribute to the other; wanting the *nature* of the relationship to be one in which the other person(s) is engaged in this way (see Stiver, 1984; Surrey, 1984; Jordan, Surrey, Kaplan, 1982). Thus, very often I've heard women described as dependent who are taking care of (and still developing psychologically from taking care of) about six other people. Sometimes they were doing so within a framework which contained many factors of realistic dependency, i.e. economic dependency or social dependency. Sometimes they had to adopt the psychological framework of the other because that is what their partners expected or demanded. But that is better described as the condition of a subordinate (Miller, 1976), which is still the social condition. This distinction is important.

It's not because of relationships per se that women are suppressed or oppressed. The issue is the *nature* of the relationships. In fact, without the recognition of the importance of relationships to women, we do not help women to find a path that leads them to growth and development. Some psychologists fall into a tendency to encourage "independence" or "separation," which is not what many women want. In the past, mental health professionals encouraged dependency with submission. The point is that the construction of concepts on that axis is inappropriate and misleading.

Perhaps I can illustrate these points by referring briefly to parts of the therapeutic work with one young woman, Ms. D. Ms. D., a twenty-three year old woman, had been depressed and had felt worthless in an extreme way since about the age of thirteen. She was clearly very intelligent and also had a profound quality of thought. She was exceptionally physically attractive.

She did not know where all of the troubles were coming from, and couldn't connect their onset with any specific events. She saw her father as a sort of nice guy; he was light, humorous and the parent she liked. By contrast, she perceived her mother as a difficult, agitated, "screaming" person—someone no one would want to be like or even to be around. This is one description of parents that therapists hear frequently.

There was one thing that seemed related to the trouble beginning at age thirteen, although Ms. D. didn't make this connection initially. The main part of her relationship with her father appeared to center around her tagging along with him in what seemed his major interest, football. From about age twelve or thirteen, he didn't let her tag along anymore, and didn't let her play with him and her brothers and the other boys around. This also is one fairly common occurrence.

She had two brothers, two and four years younger, to whom she felt very devoted. She had always been very sympathetic to them, felt she understood them, did a great many things for them, and always had, from young childhood.

Something else began around age thirteen: many boys began to pursue her, some clearly making a straightforward dash for sex; others seeming to seek her ability to hear their needs, to understand them, to be responsive, sympathetic, to help them, all of which she did. In neither case, however, were the boys interested in her feelings and concerns if she tried to bring these into the relationship. By the time of therapy, she had lost much of her ability to do so.

I will highlight in abbreviated fashion some of the features which emerged in therapy. Ms. D. came to see that she had developed in many ways, even with all that was bad and lacking in her life. She had related to others in a way that fostered their development. She did this and did it with pleasure and willingness, but she herself was not given much sense of self-worth and self-validation for the doing of it. No one recognized it fully, or gave her much affirmation for it. Thus, for one thing, she missed a huge portion of a basis for self-esteem which she could and should have had. Second, almost no one did this for her, that is, wanted to know and to respond to her needs and desires as she perceived and felt them.

Only after a while in therapy did she see that she indeed had worked at bolstering her father (which she felt was her task) and her brothers; most important, she connected some of this to the "life's work" that had pre-occupied her mother all along. She could see, for instance, that a great part of her mother's "ranting and raving," as she called it, resulted from the attempt to "shore up" her father and help her more valued brothers. Her father always had been shaky in his work, and there was a lot to do in the effort to help him "succeed." Her mother had been trying to do that. A large part of her mother's behavior was, however, both a cry for help at her felt obligation to accomplish an impossibility, and a "protest" against having to accomplish that impossibility. Late in therapy, Ms. D. could begin to feel a sense of connection to her mother in the recognition that they both had been engaged in that task. Both had gained little sense of value from it. Simultaneously, her mother had not been able to value her daughter as she had not been able to value herself.

After this recognition, Ms. D. was able to alter some of her resentment toward her mother, although acknowledging the ways that her mother failed her. Later, too, she came to see her father as someone who had never been prepared or able to hear her concerns, or to be responsive to her. She was able to perceive this only after she had first become able even to *think* of seeking this kind of interaction with him. When she tried to bring her own needs into discussions with him, she perceived his inability to relate to her in this way. It was not like football.

Ms. D. had to confront her anger. She had a large amount of anger at both her father and her mother, for different reasons. It took a long time, but she became more able to allow herself her anger, as she also became able to see how much she had really contributed to others' development. That is, she had first to feel some sense of value before she could tolerate a view of herself as a person with anger (see Miller, 1983). Then, the understanding and redirection of her anger further relieved her sense of worthlessness. Very importantly, she came to see that she would not have had a large amount of anger if she indeed had not had her own set of perceptions, expectations, wishes, desires and judgments, that is, the sense of self that she had thought she never had. She was angry because of the violation of the self she really had. She, like many people, particularly women, had said originally that she had no sense of self at all; she was able to discover one and then to go on to build on it.

Her biggest problem in a way remains: how to be the kind of self she wants to be, a being-in-relationship, now able to value the very valuable parts of herself, along with her own perceptions and desires—and to find others who will be with her in that way. She still encounters situations, particularly, but not only, with men, in which she feels annihilated as a person. I think she is experiencing situations which are common to all of us.

RICHER MODELS

To generalize from this example, then, the model of self-development as it has been defined so far does not help us to understand or to help women well. Many women perceive the prospects held out by this model as threatening, for good reason. I think their perception reflects at bottom a fear of forfeiting relationships. By contrast, men's fears occur in different forms. Indeed, most men see the prospect of self-development as not only desirable, but a basic definition of what they must do in life. Moreover, seeking to understand women opens paths to enlargement of a model of "a self" to one which encompasses more truthfully the range of human necessities and possibilities.

For Ms. D. there had been problems in relationships, especially in having directed a large portion of her life to relationships which benefited others, primarily. However, to have overlooked their value, and her value in them, would have robbed Ms. D. of the major source of her strength and her potential for greater strengths.

The features I've suggested are present even in many highly accomplished women, and women who, like Ms. D., don't care for families in the concrete sense. There is a small group of women today who seek a sense of self similar to that which has been advocated for men. But even many of these women express many of the same themes. They are often the relatively advantaged women who feel very pressured to advance in careers. They often find that their desires to live and work in a context of mutually enhancing relationships conflict with male norms. There is pressure to believe that the latter are better and to devalue the relational desires in themselves.

Important evidence is emerging from other parts of the psychological field. Notably, Gilligan's (1982) work in developmental psychology suggests that women's sense of self and of morality revolves around issues of responsibility for, care of and inclusion of other people. It is embedded in a compelling appreciation of context and an insistent unwillingness to make abstractions which violate their grasp of the complexities of the connections between people. Women were previously seen as deficient or at a low level of development as a consequence of their encompassing these realms of context and of psychological connection. These features are found even in as accomplished a group as current women Harvard students. In other studies, McClelland finds that women tend to define power as having the strength to care for and give to others, which is very different from the way men have defined power.

As always, the artists have said it long ago. It's interesting to note that in much of literature the man has been in search of his self, as in many examples: *David Copperfield, Portrait of an Artist* and many others. Women express desires, but they have tended to cast them in the overarching terms of wanting to make deep connection with another (others) and usually to enhance another, as in G. Eliot's *Middlemarch* or C. Bronte's *Villette.*

In the overall picture, then, the concept of a "self" as it has come down to us has encouraged a complex series of processes leading to a sense of psychological separation from others. From this there would follow a quest for power over others and power over natural forces, including one's own body. This would seem to be inevitable if one cannot be grounded in *faith* in the kind of interconnections I've tried to suggest. Have such definitions of a separated self become conceivable *only* because half of the species has been assigned to the realms of life which involve such necessities as attending to the complex particularities of building the day-to-day emotional connections with others? This means, in effect, primary attention to participating in and fostering the development of other people—and even direct concentration on the sustenance of the sheer physical life of others. Simultaneously, these realms delegated to women have been granted less value. They have not been incorporated into our perceptions as sources of growth, satisfaction and empowerment. It then becomes difficult to conceive of them as the wellsprings of true inner motivation and development. But they are.

Another way to put this, perhaps, is to say that women's actual practice in the real world and the complex processes which those practices entail have not been drawn upon, nor elaborated on, as a basis of culture, knowledge, theory or public policy. They then come to sound almost unreal or idealistic, but they are real; they are going on every day. If they were not, none of us would have lived and developed at all. But they've been split off from official definitions of reality.

An underlying question may be, "Has our tradition made it difficult to conceive of the possibility that freedom and maximum use of our resources—our initiative, our intellect, our powers— can occur within a context that requires simultaneous responsibility for the care and growth of others and of the natural world that we cannot hope that this will develop *after* the person develops first as a separated "self," as currently defined? Thus, I believe that the search for the more appropriate study of women in women's own terms can lead us all not only to understanding women, certainly valid in itself, but to clues to a deeper grasp of the *necessities* for all human development, and simultaneously to a greater realization of the realities of the vast untapped human capacities. This is not an easy thing to do because our whole system of thought, our categories, the eyes by which we see and the ears by which we hear have been trained in a system removed from this activity.

We've all been laboring under only one implicit model of the nature of human nature and of human development. Much richer models are possible. Glimpses of them have always been struggling to emerge, through the artists and the poets, and in some of the hopes and dreams of all of us. Now, perhaps, we can work at learning about them in this field.

REFERENCES

Bakan, D. *The Duality of Human Existence: An Essay on Psychology and Religion.* New York: Rand McNally, 1966.

Block, J. "Another Look at Sex Differentiation in the Socialization Behaviors of Mothers and Fathers." *Psychology of Women: Future Directions of Research.* New York: Psychology Dimensions, 1978.

Erikson, E. *Childhood and Society.* New York: W. W. Norton, 1950.

Gilligan, C. *In a Different Voice.* Cambridge: Harvard University Press, 1982.

Heilbrun, C. *Reinventing Womanhood.* New York: W. W. Norton, 1979.

Jordan, J., Surrey, J. and Kaplan, A. "Women and Empathy." *Work in Progress* 82–02. Wellesley: Stone Center Working Papers Series, 1982.

Klein, G. *Psychoanalytic Theory.* New York: International Universities Press, 1976.

Levinson, D. *The Seasons of a Man's Life.* New York: Alfred A. Knopf, 1978.

Luria, Z. Presentation, Stone Center Dedication Conference, Wellesley, Massachusetts, October 1981.

McClelland, D. *Power: The Inner Experience.* New York: Irvington, 1979.

Miller, J. B. *Toward a New Psychology of Women.* Boston: Beacon Press, 1976.

Rubin, J., Provenzano, F., Luria, Z. "The Eye of the Beholder: Views on Sex of Newborns." *American Journal of Orthopsychiatry* 44:512–519, 1974.

Stechler, G. and Kaplan, S. "The Development of the Self." *Psychoanalytic Study of the Child* 35:85–105, 1980.

Stern, D. "The Early Differentiation of Self and Other." Presentation at the Symposium, Reflections of Self Psychology, Boston Psychoanalytic Society, Boston, Massachusetts, October 1980.

Stiver, I. "The Meanings of 'Dependency' in Female-Male Relationships." *Work in Progress* 83–08. Wellesley: Stone Center Working Papers Series, 1983.

Surrey, J. "The Self-in-Relation: A Theory of Women's Development." *Work in Progress* 84–02. Wellesley; Stone Center Working Papers Series, 1984.

Thompson, C. "Cultural Pressures in the Psychology of Women." *Psychiatry,* 5:331–339. Reprinted in J. B. Miller, ed., *Psychoanalysis and Women.* New York: Brunner/Maxel and Penguin Books, 1973.

The Construction of Femininity

Luise Eichenbaum and Susie Orbach

Psychological development starts at birth and occurs within the context of the relationship the infant has with the caregiver. Women's psychological development is thus shaped in the mother-daughter relationship, the critical relationship in the formation of women's psychology.

Mothers and daughters share a gender identity, a social role, and social expectations. They are both second-class citizens within a patriarchal culture and the family. In mothering a baby girl a woman is bringing her daughter up to be like her, to be a girl and then a woman. In mothering her son she is bringing him up to be other, to be a boy and then a man. Because of the social consequences of gender, mothers inevitably relate differently to their daughters and their sons. Much of the difference is intentional and prescribed by the requirements of sex-role stereotyping—for example, encouraging an adolescent son's sexual adventures and restricting an adolescent daughter's. Some of the difference is subtle and mothers may not be aware of it—girls are encouraged to be neat, messiness is tolerated in boys; or girls are encouraged to be "pretty" and boys to be "bright." And some of the difference comes from a mother's unconscious feelings about being a woman and raising a daughter or raising a son.

In looking at the significance of the shared gender of mothers and daughters, the most obvious and most important point is that all mothers were and are daughters themselves. A second obvious and important point is that all daughters are brought up

185

by their mothers to become mothers. The third point is that all mothers learned from their mothers about their place in the world. In each woman's experience is the memory, buried or active, of the struggles she had with her mother in the process of becoming a woman, of learning to curb her activities and to direct her interests in particular ways. Mothers and daughters thus have a tremendous amount of common experience, although this is often obscured by the fact that they are always in different phases of their social role vis-à-vis each other. A fifty-year-old mother and a twenty-five-year-old mother each experiences similar emotional pushes and pulls in relation to their children. Yet the mothering requirements for each of them are very different. Adult women with girl children play two roles simultaneously in the mother-daughter relationship: they are their mother's daughters and their daughter's mothers.

The interplay between a woman's conscious and unconscious feelings about being both a daughter and a mother are an essential part of what she brings to the maternal nurturance. The psychology that the infant girl will embody in the process of becoming a person will be imbued with the mother's sense of self. Growing up female and being a woman means that one's sense of self reflects what each woman has had to learn in her development. Aspects of the mother's psychology that are inextricably bound up with being socialized to the feminine role are absorbed and then shared by the daughter in her own psychology.

In our practice we often hear women describe how startling it is to hear themselves speaking to their daughters just as their mothers spoke to them. As one woman put it, "I couldn't believe it came out of my mouth. The same tone of voice, practically the very same words. It was as if my mother's voice came from my lips." It is often after a woman has a child that she becomes more aware of the ways in which she is like her mother. The mother's influence becomes apparent as aspects of her personality resonate for the daughter in herself as mother. Traversing the generations from grandmother to mother to daughter is a particular psychology which has its roots and its flesh in the experience of being female in a patriarchal culture. The social requirements of deference, submission, and passivity generate many complicated feelings. Often women do not feel complete, substantial, or good within themselves. They feel afraid of their emotional needs, their insecurities and dependencies; they are fearful and guilty about their sexuality and their strivings for independence, nurturance, and power. The social requirements of patriarchy surround a girl from the moment of her birth. This means that she has a particular psychology which she transmits to her daughter.

Men's and women's psychologies reflect patriarchal attitudes in different ways. A boy will be raised to expect to be looked after and attended to, a girl to provide the looking after and attending.

For a woman, the process of pregnancy, giving birth, and becoming a mother can be a very satisfying experience. Having a baby may fulfill an important personal desire and enrich a woman's sense of self. Since motherhood is traditionally the apex of woman's social role, approved by family and society, giving birth enables a woman to feel a certain contentment. In turn she is able to transmit these positive feelings to her daughter. Mother reads the communications of her daughter and is responsive. The infant in turn expresses her pleasure, and this communication adds to mother's feelings of self-worth and potency. Positive interactions between mother and daughter establish a pattern of relating and a feeling of closeness between them. As a relationship forms, the mother experiences great pleasure in seeing her daughter's daily developments. Mother's time and care and tiring long hours of work through the day and night have moments of overpowering reward as she sees her daughter grow, and she continues to express her feelings of competence, strength, and ability to care and protect within the relationship. In this nurturing relationship the mother gives her daughter the essential emotional food that helps the infant establish her very sense of existence as well as her security and well-being. The daughter's psychological development is built on the feelings of acceptance and love in this first and most important relationship.

Beyond these positive feelings that mother has toward herself, however, lie mother's other experiences of self. The effect of having to curtail one's wants and desires over many years is that many women are not aware of the fact that they feel needy, and they have complicated feelings about their repressed needs. Over the years in our practice we have seen many women reveal the part of them that is needy and uncared for, undeserving, inadequate, and inarticulate. A woman often feels that nobody sees this part of her or gives her what she needs, and that even she herself cannot locate what she wants—"everybody sees me as so strong, they don't know that I have my moments, too, when I want to give up and weep and feel unsure and anxious." These negative and complicated feelings, conscious or unconscious, also have a profound effect on the daughter's psychology. The mother's negative self-image is as important a factor in the mother-daughter interaction, and hence in the daughter's psychology, as her positive experiences of self through motherhood and in other areas.

We can identify the following major aspects of the mother-daughter interaction which make for a particular shaping of a daughter's psychology. The first of these is that the mother will *identify* with her daughter because of their shared gender, for when a woman gives birth to a daughter she is in a sense reproducing herself. When she looks at her daughter she sees herself. Laura, a thirty-three-year-old mother of a daughter aged three and (an infant) son, talked about this point in her therapy. "When Ruth was an infant I can remember looking down at my body as I lay in a certain position in my bed and thinking it was Ruth's body. The shape of my knee or my arm looked to me like Ruth's body. And when she had her first cold I felt ill. It was very strange. These things have not happened with Barry. Somehow it just isn't the same. I've never had the feeling I *was* him or he *was* me."

Vivian, a forty-year-old woman, expressed it this way: "When my daughter was born, each time I looked at her I thought she *was* me; I couldn't tell at all that she was different from me. You know that feeling when you look at yourself in a mirror? Well, it felt something like that. When my son was born that never even crossed my mind. He was different, he was something else [motioning "out there" and "away" with her hand]. It was completely clear that he was a different person."

When a mother looks at an infant son she sees someone who is quite other, who is going to have a very different life, and for whom she can imagine a whole world of differing possibilities. But she knows that her daughter will follow her own footsteps. Mother must introduce her daughter to the ways of behaving and feeling that go along with being a girl. Mother must prepare her for a life spent, like hers, in taking care of others. Mother, whether she is consciously aware of it or not, must also prepare her daughter to take her place in society as a second-class citizen.

When a woman bears a son, the difference in sex and gender helps her to be more aware of her own boundaries. A woman does not have this aid with a daughter. The boundaries are blurred. When she looks at her daughter she sees mirror images of her own experience of being mothered, her own childhood and growing up; her whole life as a woman.

The second major aspect of the mother-daughter relationship is that a mother not only identifies with her daughter but also *projects* onto her some of the feelings she has about herself. Having superimposed these deeply buried feelings which are inaccessible and unconscious she experiences them as if expressed in her daughter. In this projection she is seeing her daughter not as another person but as an extension of herself. Thus when she holds her infant daughter in her arms she reads the child's communications in a particular way. She sees a vulnerable, undefended, expressive, eager little girl. This in turn reawakens—still at an unconscious level—the part of her that feels needy and wants to be nurtured, responded to, encouraged.

Such feelings are almost inevitable because of the importance in women's social role, and thus in their psychology, of deferring to and caring for others. Women today pay a high psychological price for the ability to nurture. In developing emotional antennae for the desires of others, women place their own needs second. The experience of receiving nurturance is not symmetrical for women and men. There is an unequal emotional exchange between men and women, and the emotional caretaking is not reciprocal. Because of this social-psychological construct a woman hides and represses many of her own emotional needs as she develops an adult stance in the world. She appears to be a person with little need. These needs do not disappear, however, and in experiencing and responding to the needs of her infant daughter the mother unconsciously first identifies and then projects her *own* needy parts, what we call her little-girl onto her daughter.

In responding to her daughter the mother is full of contradictory feelings, some conscious and some not. She wants to meet her daughter's needs: sometimes she is able to and at other times she is not. The reasons are complex. On the one hand she hopes for a fuller and less restricted life for her daughter, while on the other she is fearful for a daughter who does not learn the essential feminine characteristics of restraining her own needs and desires and curbing her moves toward independence. This conflict is often unconscious. Mothers generally raise and relate to their daughters much as they themselves were raised. Unbeknownst to them they are caught in a paradox. Mother has the difficult task of showing her daughter how to limit her strivings toward independence. At the same time she must wean her very early from relying, at an emotional level, upon having her dependency desires met. For mother to continue to meet them would go deeply against the grain of socialization to the feminine role. Mother knows that she has had to manage and contain her own desires for emotional nurturance; that she has had to swallow her disappointment and anger many times and that she has had to learn how to adjust her expectations for emotional care and relating.

Their own social experience prevents mothers from setting up false expectations about what awaits a daughter in womanhood. Unconsciously mother gives the message to the daughter. "Don't be emotionally dependent; don't expect the emotional care and attention you want; learn to stand on your own two feet emotionally. Don't expect too much independence; don't expect too much from a man; don't be too wild; don't expect a life much different from mine; learn to accommodate." Mother demonstrates these unconscious injunctions by relating to her daughter in this way herself. Consciously and unconsciously mother acts toward her daughter in the ways she experiences others relating to herself. Unable to respond continually and directly to her daughter's needs because her own needs have not been met in this way, she relates to the child inconsistently.

At times the mother is able to see her daughter as a separate little person and to respond to her freely. At other times, however, the mother's unconscious identification makes her annoyed with the child for displaying her needs and for not controlling them as she herself does. At these times mother is unconsciously driven to respond to her daughter with resentment and disapproval, thus transmitting the message that there is something wrong with her daughter, something wrong with her desires, something that needs to be kept at bay. Unwittingly, mother provides her daughter with her first lesson in emotional deprivation.

At the same time that mother pushes her daughter's neediness away she pulls her daughter to stay within the boundaries that she herself inhabits. There is a push-pull dynamic in the mother-daughter relationship. Mother wishes to see her daughter contented, but she is again caught in a paradox, for she herself does not have the experience of contentment. Mother has learned throughout her childhood to curb her desires and wants, to split her needs off, to hide that part of herself from others and not to expect to be responded to. Mother herself has a little-girl hidden inside herself.

This repressed little-girl inside mother is a third important shaper of the mother-daughter relationship. Mother comes to be frightened by her daughter's free expression of her needs, and unconsciously acts toward her infant daughter in the same way she acts internally toward the little-girl part of herself. In some ways the little daughter becomes an external representation of that part of herself which she has come to dislike and deny. The complex of emotions that results from her own deprivation through childhood and adult life is both directed inward in the struggle to negate the little-girl part of herself and projected outward onto her daughter.

A vivid example of this dynamic is the relationship between Beth and her daughter Alice. . . .

In Beth's therapy we were able to see the ways in which her daughter expressed many of Beth's own feelings and desires. Gradually Beth was able to see her identification with Alice and to see the ways she had rejected the child just as she rejected the little-girl part of herself.

This mother-daughter relationship illustrates the sensitivity that a mother can develop toward the needs and desires of a daughter, needs and desires that imitate her own. These features of mother-daughter interaction make for extreme intensity in the relationship. This intensity is often marked by a staccato quality, an inconsistency in the relating. The inconsistency stems from the way a mother copes with her feeling of identification with her daughter and her own deep feelings about herself as a woman. At those times when mother relates to daughter as a separate person she can be responsive and unambiguously caring. She can give her daughter what she needs and convey a sense of security and well-being. At other times, however, mother's sense of herself as a separate person dissolves and she experiences her daughter and herself as having the same feelings, thoughts, and desires.[1] When this occurs it is hard for a mother to be appropriately responsive; she may be withdrawn at one moment and overinvolved the next. She is acting on her unconscious feelings of identification and relating to her daughter in the same inconsistent way that she relates to the little-girl part of herself. Such toing and froing between a mother's sense of herself as separate and her merger with her daughter creates the staccato quality in the relationship.

The shape of this relationship, first established in infancy, is maintained throughout the daughter's life. As she slowly becomes her own person and needs her mother in different ways, the intense push-pull nature of the relationship persists. The daughter is absorbing essential lessons about what it means to be female, with her mother as both model and guide, and beyond that their relationship is absorbed by the daughter as a blueprint for other love relationships. The picture of mother that the daughter takes into herself is complex. Mother is the person who gives her what she needs—feeds her, bathes her, cuddles her, plays with her, talks to her, responds to her. She open up wider and wider horizons. At the same time mother is the person who can say no, who can disappoint or withhold, who can be short-tempered and can misunderstand. Mother holds tremendous power to please and to hurt.

Many of mother's actions are thus incomprehensible, because the daughter receives contradictory messages in the push-pull dynamic. She experiences her mother giving the unconscious injunctions of staying close by but not expecting too much for doing so. The little girl cannot fathom why mother is so approving and loving at times and so disappointed and disappointing at others. The little girl tries to make sense of mother's actions. The part of her that has felt nurtured and understood by mother has contributed to a psychological experience of solidity and goodness, but she has also experienced that some parts of herself are not acceptable. The little girl absorbs the idea that to get love and approval she must show a particular side of herself. She must hide her emotional cravings, her disappointments and her angers, her fighting spirit. She must hide *her self*. She comes to feel that there must be something wrong with who she really is, which in turn must mean there is something wrong with what she needs and what she wants. A feeling that she is inauthentic develops, and she is unsure in her reactions and distanced from her wants. This soon translates into feeling unworthy and hesitant about pursuing her impulses. Slowly she develops an acceptable self, one that appears self-sufficient and capable and will receive more consistent acceptance. Here in this first relationship with mother the little girl learns to fear and hide away the little-girl part of herself. And she comes to feel like a fraud, for an external part of her is developing that is different from who she feels she is inside.

Here we can begin to see the way in which a feminine psychology is reproduced from generation to generation. Girls' psychologies develop within the context of their social world and social role. In our practice we hear women talk about their needs with contempt, humiliation, and shame. They feel exposed and childish, greedy and insatiable. Mothers and daughters both attempt to curb their little-girl inside while showing only one part of themselves to others, a part they feel others will find acceptable because it is not needy.

This psychological split, which occurs in the first years of life, is not a conscious act but a protective feature of psychic structural development. The hidden part (the little-girl) does not disappear; it has to go underground and seek nurturance within the girl's inner world. And since this little-girl part of the developing psyche still yearns for nurturance, there is confusion about its rejection in the first place. This part of the psyche tends to carry feelings of isolation and depression, even despair. When contact with it is evoked she may be flooded with feelings of anger, disappointment, or rejection. Hurt by the mother's rejections, the daughter may not be able to show this needy part to anyone again, and so lives primarily in her inner world of relationships (internal object relations). These both excite and disappoint her little-girl inside. The girl constructs seemingly more satisfactory relationships in her inner world. Mother continues to live on inside, alternately presenting herself as giver and withholder. She is still very powerful and still much needed. Inside too, the little-girl is trying to challenge the deep conviction that if she shows herself she will continue to be rejected and disliked. In her private world the child tries to rewrite history, but time and again her previous painful experiences are reinforced. So the little-girl part builds boundaries; it is as though the needy, frightened part is surrounded by a fortress. She cannot send messages out and others cannot penetrate her defenses. Nobody can come in and hurt her and she cannot get out and hurt others or humiliate herself by exposing her needs. . . .

A daughter hides the little-girl part of herself because she has picked up a painful and powerful message from mother that tells her she should not have expectations of being looked after emotionally or of having her desires met, either by mother or by anyone else. Mother encourages her daughter to look to a man to be emotionally involved with; she teaches her daughter to direct her energies toward men and to someday depend on a man. But at the same time there is another message. As she lets her daughter know she must look to men, mother simultaneously transmits a message of disappointment and frustration. She conveys that her daughter must not expect a man to really help or understand her. Mothers often let their daughters know both overtly and covertly that men are disappointments. They may convey disdain and contempt for them. Mother's messages about men are thus more than a little ambivalent. She conveys both the necessity and the limitations of a daughter's emotional ties to a man.

Lorraine was perplexed by her mother's interest in the job status of the men she went out with. Her mother seemed terribly interested in these relationships, yet Lorraine always felt uncomfortable about discussing them with her mother because she realized that her mother had very little interest in what Lorraine felt about the personalities of her men friends. Indeed, her mother never discussed men in terms of emotional exchange or feelings. On a conscious level Lorraine felt pressure from her mother to find the right man and settle down, but on another level she felt that her mother dismissed men completely, that she didn't think of them as people capable of relationships or feelings. Consciously the mother was pushing her daughter to be with a man, but unconsciously, she was transmitting a message not to expect anything from a man except a house and children. Lorraine began to understand that essentially her mother thought of men as economic providers and that was all.

Even though a daughter comes to look toward men, she still yearns for mother's support and care. From girlhood to womanhood women live with the experience of having lost those aspects of maternal nurturance. This nurturance is never replaced. Women look to men to mother them but remain bereft. These needs for nurturance do not decrease any the less for loss. This loss, which causes tremendous pain, confusion, disappointment, rage, and guilt for the daughter, is buried and denied in the culture at large as well as in the unconscious of the little girl.

We have mentioned that infants who have had sufficient good contact to embody the caregiver's positive feelings within themselves come to feel secure. They are confident that their needs will be met and that the large world they can now see outside themselves and mother is full of exciting possibilities and new relationships. As the baby begins to separate from mother she or he acquires a sense of individuality. For the developing girl, still yearning for mother's reassurance, psychological separation and individuation can only be partial. The experience of the initial relating with mother means that the girl is left with feelings of deprivation, unworthiness, and rejection. As she still needs mother very badly it is hard for her to feel unambiguously receptive to new experiences or to have confidence that others will be receptive to her needs and desires. She tries to move toward others to express herself but she feels nervous, at once disloyal and abandoned. Enjoying being with an aunt may be complicated; she may seek contact with her and yet feel guilty for leaving mother and for getting nurturance from elsewhere. This is an example of the way in which the social requirement for women to be connected to others rather than full, autonomous people is reflected in the development of a feminine psychology.

Too often a little girl's attempts at separation take place under conditions of opposition from mother and consequent fear. There is no feeling of strength and wholeness to make the world outside seem exciting; instead it is tantalizing and frightening. In some ways it echoes aspects of the painful inner world of the child's reality. Mother is still a focal point; she encourages some attempts at separation—even forces them—and thwarts others. Because the little-girl part of the girl's psyche has been split off, it continues to be deprived of the nourishment and contact it needs for maturation. The girl both fears and longs to remerge with mother and to be held and cared for, but the inconsistencies in the relationship push her toward separation, with the construction of boundaries between self and the little-girl inside. These are in some sense false boundaries; they do not come from an integrated ego structure which can clearly distinguish between self and the outside world, but are internal boundaries, separating one part of herself from another part and keeping the little-girl inside shut away from the outside world.

At the same time, the daughter's sense of self is fused with her sense of mother, so that in her attempts to separate from mother she may not know who she herself is. Trying to be her own person, she is nevertheless confused about where she begins and mother ends. In her early development she has taken her mother into her, and now, because she does not have a strong sense of her own separate self, the sense of mother inside her may outweigh her own independent identity. Unlike her brother, she cannot use gender difference to differentiate herself. Psychologically and socially she is a miniversion of mother, someone who will have a life like mother's.

And so her sense of self as unique, separate, and other is entwined with a sense of mother. There is a shared social role, a shared prescription for life, and a shared psychology.

Inevitably, then, the daughter's attempts at separation are somewhat ambiguous and dovetail with mother's ambivalence. The message from mother during the period of infantile dependency has been, "Take care of yourself, don't depend on others, don't want too much," but these injunctions, which in effect seem to push the daughter away, have been combined with the unstated, unconscious message: "Stay close, don't stray, don't go too far, it's dangerous." As a result, the process toward separation has to contend with a tug to stay close to mother and share the boundaries she inhabits.

Ideally, as daughter tries to separate from mother, mother in turn must let go just enough. She must allow her daughter to explore the limits of her developing identity from a secure base. The broadening of boundaries and setting of new ones that daughter and mother negotiate require enormous emotional and psychological shifting for the mother. In the daughter's infancy the mother may experience a tension between her sense of the baby's utter dependency and helplessness, which confirms her essentiality, and her desires for the child's separateness. The mother may be reassured by being needed and simultaneously resent and begrudge her own loss of independence. If she worked outside the home before the birth and intends to do so again, she must shift her focus from her former job to that of child rearing and then remove herself psychologically and emotionally from her absorption in her infant's world back toward the outside world and her other work.[2]

There is a delicate pushing away and pulling together between mother and baby as each attempts to separate from the other. Mother's wish to keep her daughter close reflects her own psychology and social experience. Having a child has filled up her life, and if she has been living through her child, accruing an identity through mothering, she may have great difficulty letting her daughter separate. She may need to keep her daughter close to her to maintain this sense of herself, and this psychological need may exist whether or not she has worked outside the home. A daughter's moves toward independence are bound to diminish a mother's sense of being needed. Brought up to see her central role as that of mother, she may feel empty, depressed, confused about who she is; she may lose her sense of purpose. If she has not been able to separate psychologically from her mother, she may in turn cling to her daughter. The period of her child's separation-individuation can make the mother feel that she is already "losing" her child, in a foretaste of future separations (nursery school, adolescence) that jolts and hurts. She clings in the hope that her daughter will not abandon her.

If the mother's psychological development has been similar to her daughter's, and she herself has not had a solid experience of separation and selfhood, she too has false boundaries. Her daughter's moving away involves a loss at the psychic structural level because she has attempted to complete herself in her attachment to and merger with her daughter. The distinction between the two of them is blurred, so that the daughter's development toward independence brings feelings of loss as well as pride.

As a baby daughter reaches this stage, a woman often finds herself wanting another baby. "I thought I wanted only one child," said one of our clients. "I never intended to have more. But when Jennie was two I started having dreams about another baby and thinking about it every single day. I sort of forgot about my previous thoughts on the subject of how many children I wanted. It wasn't on a rational thinking level. I just *felt* intensely that I wanted another baby." Mother's unconscious feelings of loss as her daughter attempts separation constantly reinforce the jagged attachment between the two of them. As mother now pulls her daughter to stay close, as she indicates to her the shape of a girl's life, she instructs her in an essential feminine skill. She teaches her to look after others. The daughter, as she learns to hide her needy little-girl part, becomes extremely sensitive to neediness in others. She develops the radar to pick up the needs of others; *she learns to give what others need; and she gives to others out of the well of her own unmet needs.*

Once again we see the reproduction of a feminine psychology. Just as mother responds to and anticipates the needs of others, so the daughter comes to embody this same capacity for giving. And like mother, she too wishes for someone to respond to her needs. So the giving capacity starts very early on in her life and becomes an important part of her identity and self-image.

As the mother transmits to her daughter the importance of caring for others, she brings to the relationship her *own* unmet emotional needs. Inside each mother lives a hungry, needy, deprived, and angry little-girl. She turns to her daughter for nurturance, looking to the child to make up the loss of her own maternal nurturance and satisfy her continued yearnings.

The psychological attachment and lack of separation between mothers and daughters and daughters and mothers continues through generations of women. The daughter becomes involved in a cycle that is part of each woman's experience: attempting to care for mother. As the daughter learns her role as nurturer, *her first child is her mother.*

Women do not usually bring these same needs to their sons.

Built into a mother's experience with a son from the beginning of his life is the knowledge that he will become his own person in the world. She accepts the fact that he will become a man and move out into the world to create and commit himself to a family of his own. But although she expects her daughter to have a family too, she expects this to be an extension of her own family rather than a separate entity. Whether or not a woman still lives with her husband after her children are grown, her daughter tends to remain available and responsible for her care and companionship. In fact, we often see daughters-in-law taking on this responsibility as well. Although an adult daughter may resent this responsibility, at the same time she is consciously and unconsciously aware of her mother's needs. The social position of women, which often forces them to hide their loneliness or pain even from themselves, is a strong adhesive in the mother-daughter relationship.

Just as she transmits messages to her daughter about her role as a woman, a mother also transmits what her sexuality may be. The mother's feelings about her own body and her sexuality are a critical influence on the way a daughter will come to feel about herself. Nancy Friday writes: "When we were learning to walk, mother helped us to practice and her confidence in our success encouraged us to keep trying. When it came to sex her emotions became communicated to us too, this time what we learned from her was anxiety and failure."[3]

Our complex cultural attitudes toward women's bodies—that they are sexual, ugly, mysterious, extraordinary, dark, bloody, and bad smelling—find a place in each woman's sense of self. The female body is both degraded and deified; it is felt to be so powerful that men will destroy themselves or die for it. Female sexuality is held responsible for male sexuality and male aggression (an extreme example is the myth that it is a woman's fault if a man rapes her). Women, then, often come to their relationship with their daughters with, at the very least, apprehension about the female body and the power of female sexuality.

In the generational transmission of feminine sexuality it is mothers who begin the process of shaping a daughter's sexuality. But mother's sexuality has developed within particular constraints, so that many mothers feel uncomfortable within their own bodies and hide their sexual desires and needs. In our therapeutic work we rarely hear a woman say that sexuality was openly accepted, that the parents' sexuality was visible, that mother or father informed the girl of the changes her body would go through in a positive and exciting way, telling her that when her body became a woman's body it would be a proud, joyful transition. We hear instead remembrances of shame, embarrassment, fear; of women not liking their breasts because they are too big or too small, not liking their pubic hair, big hips or rounded bottoms. Women also recall adolescent warnings and restrictions (boys are encouraged to be experienced). Female sexuality seems to be dangerous; it is unknown, unspoken. You must have it to become a grown-up woman and yet you must hide it. Thus many adolescent girls and young women learn to be frightened of their own sexuality and to dislike their own bodies.

At the same time many daughters perceive their mothers as nonsexual and know that they do not want to be like mother in that respect. From quite an early age they may be aware of wanting to be quite a different sort of woman. A girl may want to be "sexy," like a movie star or the woman at the beauty shop. She may feel ashamed of the way her mother dresses or embarrassed by her behavior. Whether mother conveys her sexuality through dress or physicality or hides it, it will make an impression on her daughter. The daughter compares herself to her mother as she tries to find her own independent sexuality.

As the girl's sexuality explodes during adolescence, it drives her to seek freedom and independence from her family. Her new sexual body means that she comes face to face with both her reproductive and her erotic capacities. This is a painful time for many young women, because they are already uncomfortable with their sexuality and know that women's social heritage does not allow them to act on these new desires for freedom.

The thread of sexuality is entwined in the issues of separation and merger, although its meaning is not always confluent. Sexual connection with another is in part a demonstration of a woman's attempt to separate from mother. Her physical attachment to another symbolizes her relatedness outside the family, but this new relatedness highlights the complexities of separation and attachment. In many parts of society cultural law still dictates that the only way a woman can leave her family is by starting another family. Even if she lives apart from her parents, she leaves their home only to go into her husband's. In patriarchy the daughter is passed from father to husband, as ritualized in the wedding ceremony, when the bride is "given away" by the father. But often mother is crying nearby, filled with a sense of loss due to her daughter's new attachment. The paradox lies in the fruition of mother's ambiguous message. On the one hand, mother has instructed her daughter to go toward a man; on the other, when the daughter does so it brings mother tremendous pain, for she experiences the loss of her daughter. (Mother's own memory of leaving her mother may also be unconsciously re-evoked.) The marriage highlights the cultural prohibition against separation—psychological or social—for a woman. She must leave home and yet she cannot. Women are at psychic crossroads.

A daughter's personality takes shape in her relationship with her mother, a relationship weighted heavy with longing, identification, disappointment, betrayal, anger, and guilt. As mothers transmit the knowledge of how to survive within the structure that they and all women inhabit, they bind their daughters with the chains of femininity. Thus mothers and daughters share complex and powerful emotions of love, neediness, insecurity, low self-esteem, and identification. Many women never feel free of their mothers. They are not separate people, but experience mother as living inside, judging, binding, tempting, and disappointing. At the same time mothers and daughters often feel the pain of not being able to share honesty, to show themselves to each other in direct ways.

As Adrienne Rich writes, "Mother stands for the victim in ourselves, the unfree woman, the martyr. Our personalities seem dangerously to blur and overlap with our mothers." The consequence of this painful identification is that we deny that our mother has anything to do with us: "We develop matraphobia and try to split ourselves off from her, to purge ourselves of her bondage, in a desperate attempt to know where mother ends and daughter begins, we perform radical surgery."[4]

Although the nuances and particulars of each woman's experience vary, although what each woman brings to mothering is different, and although the specifics of each mother-daughter relationship are unique, these two crucial determinants—a mother's

feelings about herself and her identification with her daughter—
are reproduced in all mother-daughter relationships. They are the
key features in the development of a woman's psychology.

As a girl develops, her father's presence in her life continues
to be very different from her mother's. In a traditional family the
little girl learns that her father is very important to family survival, and that his daily abandonment is for the purpose of providing security, especially economic security, for the family. She
learns that she must rely on him in particular ways. She also sees
the complexity of mother's relationship with father. She sees how
mother defers to and depends on father and she also sees that
father depends on mother for many things. His daily life is an
expression of his need for a woman in order to survive. His dependency needs are met in an unstated way at home, emotionally and
physically.

The girl may feel excluded and pushed away from mother
when father is around. She senses that she does not have the
power to hold mother in the same way he does. She may feel
jealous of mother's availability to another, and she may feel excluded from her parents' relationship. In her infancy she and her
mother were a couple; as she develops, her awareness of the
world shifts and she is confronted by mother and father as a
couple. She takes in how important a man, a partner, is in a
woman's life. Whether the marriage is satisfactory and coopera-
tive or not, the little girl sees the intensity of her parents' relationship, and the seeds for her own future relating to a man are
fertilized. As she watches mother she learns to relate to father in
specific ways. For example, most little girls learn that an important part of the relationship with father is pleasing him. They are
encouraged to transfer their primary dependency from mother to
father, the embodiment of all future males. This is part of learning
to become a woman in a heterosexual society, and, because
mother is aware of this, and how she must help her daughter to
make this transfer of love and dependency needs from her to
father, there is a tension expressed in the mother-daughter relationship. It shows up in the push-pull dynamic.

Both parents encourage their daughter to look to father in
several ways. He is the link to the world outside the family and

the daughter must use him as access to that world. Because he is more secure and sure of himself in the world, she can imagine that he will protect her. However, she cannot fully identify with father because of his sexual identity. Father encourages his daughter to charm him and a male audience, to attract and hold his attention in specifically defined feminine ways, as she will later need to do. She learns that she must not attempt to make decisions which challenge his authority; she must not show too much independence and power.

Very few little girls have much contact with their fathers in the very early period of psychological development. Father plays a tremendously important role very soon, but he builds on the ego development that has occurred between mother and daughter. Father is a person with whom the daughter can identify when she is in the process of separation-individuation, and as she tries to differentiate herself from her mother, she may try to emulate him, incorporating characteristics she admires.[5] If he is outgoing, humorous, or a good storyteller, for example, the daughter may develop these aspects in her own personality.

The father's relationship with his daughter is complex. He stands outside the physical experiences of pregnancy, birth, and lactation. He may feel excluded from the mother-child relationship or inadequate to participate in it. He may appreciate the sensuality and tenderness it brings into his life, and he may very much want to participate fully, but he may be consciously or unconsciously unsure about his place. Because of his lack of preparedness he may feel inadequate in relating to the baby, and his own insecurities may be reinforced by the mother's anxiety about his capabilities at mothering. In her worry about his inexperience mother may unintentionally undercut his confidence. His feelings about having a daughter or having a son will inevitably influence his relationship to a new baby. And with a daughter, especially, he may feel in the dark about who she is, what to do with her, how to relate. With a boy child he can rely on his own experience of boyhood and maleness to aid him in building a relationship.

Father may feel excluded from the early mother-infant couple and become jealous. His relationship with his partner has changed with the entry of the third person, and his partner is no longer available to him in the same way. If the child is a girl, his feeling of being the "outsider" in the triangle may be increased. The closeness between mother and infant may also evoke happy or unsatisfactory experiences from his own infancy, when he was very close to a woman.

In our practice many women report having no real contact with their fathers. As adults they still wonder where father fits in their lives.[6] We often find that a daughter's relationship with father was not straightforward, that she experienced barriers and interceptions. The mother strongly affects the father-daughter relationship. A father's loving relationship with his daughter may cause friction, because mother may experience jealousy at his attention to daughter as well as anger because of what she feels is lacking in her life. Mother may feel that father shows gentle, caring affection to a daughter in ways he does not with her, and since her needy little-girl inside yearns for just this kind of attention, seeing it between her partner and their daughter can be painful. Mothers may unwittingly intercept this loving contact between a father and a daughter.

In addition, because father often spends very little time each day with a daughter, his availability to his daughter in those moments may stir up mother's resentment. She sees the child thrilled at father's attention and feels that all she gives is taken for granted or even negated. (She may also have a burden of unconscious jealousy: father's time at home used to be hers alone.)

These dynamics in the mother-father-daughter triangle are likely to be part of the girl's psychological development and they help explain why a daughter's relationship to her father is often undeveloped. Because she is so attuned to her mother, the daughter picks up mother's feelings, including any ambivalent feelings about daughter's relationship to her father. The daughter may have to hide the contact she does have with him. As one woman put it, "Each time I phoned my parents I essentially talked to my mother. If my mother answered, then I never even had a word with my father. I would just tell my mother to send him my love. When my father answered the phone we talked for ten seconds, very superficially, and then my mother would come on the phone. When I became aware of this I tried to talk longer to my father and then my mother actually started picking up the extension."

Another dynamic we have consistently seen in our practice is that of a daughter's alliance with mother about father's inadequacies. Women often express contempt and disdain for their fathers because they are involved in mother's anger. Indeed, the daughter often carries her mother's rage. Women report feeling their fathers to be weak because they did not "stand up" to mother, especially in relation to them. "He wasn't strong enough to stop my mother's interceptions." "He didn't fight for a relationship with me." Once again daughter and mother share an experience. Both feel disappointed with father, both feel disdain, and thus they tighten their unspoken bond.

Father's position in the emotional triangle of the family is a critical piece in the puzzle of why it is so difficult for women to separate psychologically. The father-daughter relationship no more provides for unambiguous relating than the mother-daughter one does. Father is outside daughter's primary ambivalent relationship with mother but cannot offer an unambivalent one himself. Adolescence, then, the time of struggle toward independence, creates a psychic hiatus. Mother continues to relate in the push-pull while father is confronted with a daughter who is now a sexual being. This may well make him uncomfortable and as a result distant and inconsistent with his relating. Women who had good contact with their fathers and felt it changed dramatically during adolescence are likely to feel that there is something dangerous and wrong with their sexuality and that they are being punished because of it. The adolescent girl living in an emotional storm has no constant buoy.

The father-daughter relationship illustrates one of the tragedies of patriarchy. A man's position in the family and the significance of gender in his early psychological development means that he is often both ill prepared to give nurturance and afraid of women.[7] Men do not provide the emotional stability girls and women need either in their early struggles for psychological separation or in adult heterosexual relationships.

Father, then, stands at once outside the mother-daughter relationship and as the representative of the patriarchal order. Symbolically he represents for his daughter many things that are outside the world of women, the world of her mother, the world she is supposed to enter.

A daughter's psychology, then, is created in this nexus of

family relations in a particular way. Like her mother before her, the woman's internal sense of self will be somewhat shaky and her psychological boundaries malleable.[8] She will have learned to hide her needy and would-be independent and initiating parts and will find herself searching in various ways for the missing connection in her life that will allow her the unambiguous nurturance she needs to continue her developmental task of separation. She will look to her husband and children to fill in the missing pieces, because the psychological merger with her mother thwarts her from achieving a solid sense of self and separateness. As a result she is well suited for her social role of handmaiden to others' activities. Her inner sense of unworthiness and unentitledness have been reinforced over and over again in the social constraints of her childhood and in the learning of her adult role. She has buried part of her self.

NOTES

1. Psychologists have observed this as part of "normal" development without considering the conditions that make this possible and the impact of mother-and-daughter psychology. For example, Winnicott, describing the mother's ability to respond to her infant's needs in the first year of life, writes: "Towards the end of the pregnancy and for a few weeks after the birth of a child the mother is preoccupied with (or better 'given over to') the care of her baby, which at first seems like a part of herself; moreover she is very much identified with the baby and knows quite well what the baby is feeling like. For this she uses her own experiences as a baby" (*Dependence Towards Independence: The Maturational Processes and the Facilitating Environment,* London, 1963). He writes of the mother's primary maternal preoccupation as an "extraordinary condition which is almost like an illness. . . . " (*The Family and Individual Development,* London, 1965, pp. 15–16.) In the period when the mother is providing for the needs of the infant, and "finding the part of her that identifies with the infant, the mother is herself in a dependent state and vulnerable" (*The Maturational Processes and the Facilitating Environment,* London, 1963).

2. Andrea Egan, who is doing a study on the experience of mothering, has informed us that many of the women she interviewed found that after the initial period of merger in infancy, as the baby turned more

toward the world at six months of age, so mother had to readjust and redirect some of her interests outside her baby.

3. Nancy Friday, *My Mother, My Self,* New York, 1977.

4. Adrienne Rich, *Of Woman Born,* New York, 1976, p. 236.

5. From Freud's development of the concept of the Oedipus complex onward throughout psychoanalytic theory we see the analyst's attempt to incorporate the father as the central figure in psychological development. Freud himself recognized the critical nature of the early years of life for the girl's psychology and called this preoedipal—that is, he had to keep father in the picture and name everything else in relation to the father's entry into the world of the child. Even Melanie Klein could not abandon the father and so saw the oedipal conflict as happening in the first year of life.

6. Signe Hammer, *Passionate Attachments: Fathers and Daughters in America Today,* New York, 1982.

7. Men's psychology is obviously not the subject of this book, but for an explication of men's fear of women see Robert J. Stoller, *Sex and Gender,* New York, 1968, London, 1969; Dorothy Dinnerstein, *The Mermaid and the Minotaur: Sexual Arrangements and Human Malaise,* New York, 1976; and Luise Eichenbaum and Susie Orbach, *What Do Women Want? Exploding the Myth of Dependency,* New York, 1983.

8. Nancy Chodorow, *The Reproduction of Mothering: Psychoanalysis and the Sociology of Gender,* Berkeley, Calif., 1978; Jean Baker Miller, *Toward a New Psychology of Women,* Boston, Mass., 1976; and Carol Gilligan, *A Different Voice,* Cambridge, Mass., 1982. All have a more positive view of the developmental repercussions of women's malleable boundaries. They point to the certainty of affiliation in relating and the ways in which a feminine view of the world provides for safety and containment.

The Problem of Anger

Kathleen Fischer

Anger is a difficult and troublesome emotion for most people, men as well as women. "Anger is a flood," the book of Proverbs tells us (27:4), and the church lists it as one of the seven deadly sins. The bible warns us not to be angry, and, if we are, not to let the sun go down on our anger. Yet in spite of admonitions, we continue to experience anger, and sunset frequently arrives before we have found a way to put it to rest.

While anger is a challenge for all Christians, it is especially problematic for women.[1] We have been discouraged from awareness of our anger and the direct expression of it. This suppression of anger results, in part, from the high value women place on caring and relationships. Anger is seen as endangering and perhaps destroying those relationships. What if we tell a spouse, a friend, a pastor, or a supervisor that we are angry? Will they be able to handle it, or will we lose their friendship and approval? We sense that anger will lead to conflict, and as women we have been taught that conflict is something frightening and evil. This reluctance to face conflict may prevent us from acknowledging and working through our anger.

Not only does anger threaten our relationships, it clashes with our ideas of goodness and holiness. The image of the ideal or good woman extols patience, kindness, and caring; anger is out of place in such an image. People speak disparagingly of "angry women." Anger in women threatens others, and so is labeled unfeminine, immature, even hysterical. These taboos against women's direct expression of anger make it easier to turn the anger inward rather than risk disapproval and the loss of important relationships.

The inhibition of women's anger would not be so problematic if we grew up in a church and culture with few or isolated instances giving rise to anger. However, this is not the case. In addition to the situations that lead to anger in every person's life—frustrations at work, difficulties in relationships, obstacles that block our goals—women must deal with the reality of sexism. Each specific aspect of oppression—the slighting of our gifts for ministry because we are women, the official statements that reiterate women's secondary place in the church, the fear of physical abuse, the lack of opportunity for job advancement—can fuel the fires of anger. In *Anger: The Misunderstood Emotion,* Carol Tavris quotes one woman as saying:

> Everything, from verbal assault on the street, to a 'well-meant' sexist joke your husband tells, to the lower pay you get at work (for doing the same job a man would be paid more for), to television commercials, to rock-song lyrics . . . everything seems to barrage your aching brain, which has fewer and fewer protective defenses to screen such things out.[2]

Since this increased awareness of situations generating anger is accompanied by prohibitions against expressing that anger directly, women fear anger. Sometimes we are not even aware that we are angry.

All these factors make anger a central concern in the spirituality of women. The issue of anger is tied to a woman's struggle to love others well without losing her own integrity, to her view of herself as a good or evil person, to her efforts to achieve personal peace and honesty in prayer, and to her struggle for justice and the coming of the reign of God. The way anger is dealt with in the spiritual direction context is also a touchstone for how well spiritual guides understand women's situation today. If a woman's anger is pacified, explained away, or seen simply as her personal problem in isolation from its cultural causes, the old destructive patterns of dealing with anger will continue.

Depending on a woman's personal experience with anger, the following can be helpful dimensions of spiritual guidance:

(1) recognizing and validating anger, (2) exploring the personal and social origins of anger, (3) finding ways to use anger for spiritual growth, and (4) clarifying the relationship between anger and forgiveness. The goal of spiritual friendship is to help women accept the experience of anger and direct its energy toward healthy growth, good relationships, and creativity. As Tavris says, we want to learn how to use the anger of hope to avoid falling into the anger of despair.

RECOGNIZING AND VALIDATING ANGER

As we have seen, a primary factor accounting for our difficulty in acknowledging and accepting anger is the fact that it seems incompatible with holiness. During a spiritual direction session a sister in her early fifties was describing problems she was experiencing in her prayer. She usually prayed early in the morning, from the scripture texts of the day. During the preceding few weeks, however, she had frequently become restless and unable to concentrate during prayer. Silence was uncomfortable, and she found herself stopping to get a cup of coffee, or terminating the attempt to pray altogether. This was uncharacteristic behavior for her, and she wondered if she was losing her ability to pray. When I asked her what else had been going on in her life during these weeks, it became apparent that she was angry, but not fully aware of this anger. Her administrator had changed her responsibilities without consulting her, moving her from the wing of the hospital where she was working effectively to another unit. She resented this action, but had said nothing about it. She felt she could not risk the possible consequences of dealing directly with the situation, yet the injustice of it continued to bother her. Anger did not fit her ideal of a good religious. She felt guilty even acknowledging its existence.

This sister is not alone in the difficulty she experiences with reconciling anger and holiness. As one woman expressed it,

When I was growing up I learned that if you loved someone you didn't get angry with them; and if you got angry, that meant you didn't love them.

Another woman found her inner peace disrupted by a relationship with a man who called her only when it was convenient for him and who made promises he never kept. At one point in recounting the way she accommodated him, she cried out, "Why am I so nice!" In exploring this issue she became aware of her spiritual ideal, "the good-girl self," as she called it. This ideal was reinforced in her early education and related to an image she had of Mary of Nazareth. However, another self was emerging, one that was willing to acknowledge the anger she felt when she was treated unfairly.

The psychological theories of Karen Horney help to illumine this ideal self as it functions in many women's spiritual lives. Horney believes that the desire to avoid conflict and disapproval causes certain emotions to be blocked, labeled wrong, and eventually repressed. This results in the creation of rigid self-ideals; the repressed need or emotion is expressed in characteristics that are the direct opposite of the hidden feeling. For example, repressed hostility is transformed into the self-ideal of being and acting totally loving and dutiful toward others. The most difficult aspect of change may be giving up exaggerated and unrealistic self-ideals. We may be busy trying to be perfect and blaming ourselves for not achieving that goal.[3]

This mixture of emotions helps explain why some women find it physically exhausting to be angry, and why it interferes with their ability to sleep, concentrate, or function well. We may fear that if we recognize our anger, after not acknowledging it for a long time, there will be an explosion. We also recognize on some level that anger signals the need for change in our actions and relationships, and such change may feel threatening. These conflicting feelings make anger an unpleasant experience; we would avoid it if we could. But when we do not acknowledge and express anger directly, it can take indirect forms and appear as depression, fatigue, or apathy.

An important function of spiritual direction is providing a safe place for a woman to explore and affirm her anger while she learns to use its energy in creative ways. This is especially important for those women who fear their anger will overwhelm them and others, or emerge in inappropriate and destructive ways. In the past, it was thought that venting anger was a helpful way to get rid of it. This theory is currently being challenged; venting may simply increase the anger, since it tells our body to keep it coming. Dealing with anger is not a matter of getting it out so that we can get rid of it; it is a matter of turning it from indirect and destructive forms of expression to those that are direct and constructive. While it is helpful to release the adrenalin created by the anger, this can be done in any number of physical activities— swimming, dancing, jogging, doing relaxation exercises, breathing deeply, cleaning the house, chopping wood. Since anger is a matter of both mind and body, we can continue to fuel the anger by mentally rehearsing the situation in which it occurred. This can often be exhausting and nonproductive. Instead of moving us forward, it keeps us stuck in a recycling of the pain.

What is a healthy Christian approach to anger? Anger is a message, a revelation. Looking at and understanding the conflict we experience is a key step in illuminating the situation we find ourselves in. What might God be revealing to me in this situation? How is my personhood being violated here? Or what valid needs of mine are not being met? If we are attempting to hear God's word, we must listen to anger as carefully as we listen to joy, peace, fear, and fatigue. This approach to anger has been articulated well by Fran Ferder. She speaks of anger as a gift.

> As such it was purposefully and lovingly created and shaped by God as a source of energy, as a source of fire. The only aspect of anger about which we have choices is how we let it move us. We do not have choices about whether or not we will experience it, unless we choose to cut off a very significant dimension of God's life in us.[4]

For many women, viewing anger as a gift of God rather than as an abnormal and sinful emotion requires a dramatic shift. We need new models to support such a change in perception. Ferder refers us to a central story from Jesus' life: Jesus' cleansing of the temple in John's gospel. In this story Jesus is clearly angry and does not hesitate to make the strength of his emotion known. It is an expression of his zeal for the reign of God. Our anger can contribute to the same purpose. First, however, we must acknowledge that we are angry. It is also helpful to know why.

EXPLORING THE ORIGINS OF OUR ANGER

Although we may initially experience anger as interfering with clear thinking, understanding the reasons for our anger can in fact lead to greater clarity about ourselves and our relationships. Spiritual direction can help women appreciate the personal and political origins of anger. Two key questions which help unlock these insights are: What am I really feeling? and Why am I feeling this way?

Recent research on anger illumines the first question, What am I really feeling? It indicates that anger is not a simple emotion. Many different feelings lie beneath the secondary response we name when we say, "I am angry." These emotions are fear, hurt, frustration, outrage, powerlessness. We may be feeling ignored, discounted, or treated unfairly. It is more helpful to identify these primary emotions and express anger in terms of them. Anger is the instinct of self-preservation. It signals us that we are in danger, that our needs are not being met, that our rights are being violated, that we are allowing others to define us, or that unfair demands are being made upon us.

An example may help. Sue was a young woman who had belonged for several years to a fundamentalist Christian group, and was trying to live out the biblical ideal of love. During spiritual direction she described how she was feeling increasingly guilty about the way she related to a woman who rented a room in her house. For several weeks they had grown more and more silent with one another, and Sue found that she avoided her housemate and barely greeted her when she came home. It took some time for Sue to realize that she was angry but afraid to admit it since she saw it as a sign that she was failing in love. When she was able to recognize and accept her anger, it helped her to look more closely at the underlying feelings. Beneath her anger Sue found that she felt hurt by the fact that her housemate ignored her and never shared anything that was happening in her life. Sue also felt that she was being treated unfairly because her housemate was not abiding by the rental agreement, which she acknowledged had not been very clear in the first place. Sorting out her underlying emotions helped Sue clarify the sources of her anger and pointed to some actions she might take in expressing it positively.

These insights can help us clarify the personal roots of our anger. But anger is not simply a personal problem. As with other issues in our lives, women need to recognize the political origins of much anger. A woman was once referred to me by a professor in a program in which she was enrolled. She told me that he wanted me to do some healing work with her around her anger against the church, which came out frequently in her class comments. He had suggested to the woman that she must have had some negative childhood experiences that were in need of healing. His approach implied that the anger was the woman's personal problem and that the solution lay in uncovering the psychic causes.

While many of us do indeed carry with us baggage from the past, we cannot understand our anger if we look only within ourselves for its origins. Such an approach runs the risk of muting the moral power of anger as a force against injustice. While it might have intersected with earlier hurts and rejections in her life, this woman's anger had a sufficient cause in the insults and barriers she was indeed experiencing in the institutional church. It needed to be affirmed as legitimate and as founded on the reality of injustice. For many women such acknowledgement is an important part of eliminating the guilt they feel about being angry. Once this point is established, it is possible to evaluate the effectiveness of various ways of expressing anger.

Recent reflection on assertiveness programs for women illumines this question of the personal and political roots of anger.[5] The direct expression of anger is a particular instance of the more general area of assertive behavior. Such direct expression of emotions is a choice in favor of clear communication. It is a goal of assertiveness training for women since that training is aimed at helping them express their feelings honestly and comfortably. During the past two decades, assertiveness training has been one of the most popular feminist therapy programs and the subject of numerous self-help books. Countless women have participated in assertiveness training workshops in the United States and Europe. Most of these programs are based on the assumption that women lack assertiveness and do not know how to stand up for their own rights. However, recent research challenges the view that males are assertive and females are nonassertive. Rather, the research shows that women have certain assets when it comes to assertion, and that they are nonassertive only under certain conditions: Women have greater difficulty than men in refusing requests, expressing negative feelings, and setting limits. On the other hand, women assert themselves more easily than men in giving expressions of love, affection, and approval to others.

More directly related to our point about the relationship between the personal and the political is the growing realization that focusing on areas of nonassertive behavior in women is not enough. Such an approach is based on the assumption that if individual women change, society's attitudes toward them will change. In fact, there is now a growing body of research that suggests a strong bias against assertive women. The results of their assertive behavior may therefore not be positive, not because of a woman's deficits, but because of society's deficits. This reinforces the conviction that we have to go beyond the personal and work for societal change.

> When half the population is targeted as needing to change their behavior in order to gain fair treatment by the system, we have to ask what system are those individuals trying to fit.[6]

Critics of assertiveness training suggest that individual work is not enough because it focuses on symptoms and blames the victim rather than addressing the larger issues and treating the system. This must be kept in mind as we look at ways in which women can direct the energy of their anger in positive ways.

USING ANGER FOR SPIRITUAL GROWTH

Like other aspects of reality, the experience and expression of anger has been distorted by the dichotomies imposed on human existence. Adrienne Rich, in her poem "Integrity," describes the hope of breaking through such dichotomies:

> Anger and tenderness: my selves.
> And now I can believe they breathe in me
> as angels, not polarities.

Anger and tenderness: the spider's genius
to spin and weave in the same action
from her own body, anywhere—
even from a broken web.[7]

Stereotypes about female and male behavior have restricted this aspect of human life along with others. When we search for creative ways to deal with anger, we find few models.

As women acquire the freedom to look at anger in fresh ways, they are developing new approaches to it. One woman describes her imaginative method.

The male hierarchy just angers me. My feminine spirit is stifled and cries constantly. I have gotten to the point of naming the different people inside of me—priestess, prophet, feminist, mother. Then I speak to them and say, 'Seth, it is not your season yet; I am going to let Elizabeth speak to these men right now.' It works for me and I am very creative with my energies. Each staff I have worked with finds that I do express what I feel, but I also am speaking the truth. I time things well.

What this woman's comments convey is the creative effort to preserve both the legitimacy of anger and the importance of relationships.

Through the spiritual direction process we can learn not only to look at our anger and accept it without guilt or self-recrimination, but to use it creatively for our own spiritual growth and our work for the reign of God. Miriam Greenspan describes this use of anger. Like love, anger takes many shapes, she says. There are hidden and self-destructive forms such as depression.

But there is another form of anger, the other side of which is love. Not only a growing love for ourselves and each other as women, but also a growing realization that we are all of us—men and women alike—mutually interdependent. This is not a rigid closing off of our energies but an opening up to a respectful compassion for ourselves as women, and a loving struggle with the men in our lives. Anger is the fuel we need to burn in the struggle to create a society without victims.[8]

We may have little choice about whether we will feel angry or not, since anger arises spontaneously and physically. However, once we are aware of this emotion, we have a choice about what we will do.

Anger is a state of being highly energized, and we can act in a number of ways when we are in that state. As Tavris summarizes it:

> The moral use of anger, I believe, requires an awareness of choice and an embrace of reason. It is knowing when to become angry—'this is wrong, this I will protest'—and when to make peace; when to take action, and when to keep silent; knowing the likely cause of one's anger and not berating the blameless.[9]

This choice also involves discriminating between the sources of anger we can do something about, and those we cannot. Aware of the limits of our energy, we learn to recognize when an expression of anger can be effective and when it is a waste of time.

The creative use of anger also includes the sense that we are addressing the source of the grievance. No matter what we do with our anger in the short run, it will not have served its purpose unless we address the situations and relationships which gave rise to the anger in the first place. The native American poet, Joy Harjo, writes of the sufferings of poor families where women face not only the struggle to provide bread and a roof, but where violence and alcohol make domestic life hell.

> angry women are building
> houses of stones
> they are grinding the mortar
> between straw-thin teeth
> and broken families[10]

Out of their anger women are strengthening their determination to change destructive patterns.

Anger that comes from a clear sense of injustice requires the channeling of its energy into alleviating that injustice. However, we may feel powerless to do anything about the situations that anger us. In her helpful book, *The Dance of Anger,* Harriet Lerner provides some approaches to assist women in dealing creatively with their anger.[11] Lerner emphasizes that anger operates within a system of relationships. Our behavior helps to support the behavior of others. This is what she calls the dance of anger. While we usually cannot change the behavior of others, Lerner says, we can change our own behavior and thus make it impossible for the dance to continue as before.

> We cannot make another person change his or her steps to an old dance, but if we change our steps, the dance no longer can continue in the same predictable pattern.[12]

This approach focuses on changing patterns of relationship rather than on blaming ourselves or the other persons involved. For example, a friend of mine who is the mother of three young children was exhausted and resentful because of their constant demands. As a way of dealing with her resentment and anger, she decided to change the way she related to them. She began to set limits and then she stuck with them. A woman who constantly picked up the pieces so that her male supervisor looked good, meanwhile resenting the fact that it was her talent and ingenuity he received credit for, simply stopped rescuing him.

Women have begun to change their behavior in relation to the church as well—making their discontent with sexism public, refusing to allow their experiences to be trivialized, contributing to biblical research and theology which illumine women's role in the church, targeting their donations to women's projects. As women change their steps in the old dance, it becomes more difficult for the patterns to continue.

But as Lerner points out, systems usually have an investment in our staying exactly the same. We can expect therefore that they will intensify their resistance as we change our behavior. Since they want the dance to go on as before, they will dance the same steps more insistently as we change our own part in it. This is a way of saying: "You're wrong; change back or else . . . " Lerner describes this powerful emotional counterforce as predictable and universal. If women are not prepared for it, however, such resistance can surprise and defeat them.

Women need to recognize that expressing anger frequently carries a practical price. We receive rewards for what is considered appropriate behavior; if we show anger we risk losing real rewards. Women who are already in poverty or situations of physical abuse are being realistic when they recognize the dangers involved in expressing their anger directly. As Jean Baker Miller insists, it is not useful to urge people who are in subordinate positions to conduct conflict as if they were not powerless and dependent. It is very difficult to initiate conflict when you are totally dependent on an individual or group for your elemental material and psychological means of existence.[13]

Viewing anger within patterns of relationship helps us understand another aspect of it. How we feel after expressing our anger depends a great deal on how it is received. Many people are as uncomfortable with another person's anger as they are with their own. They do not know how to respond. We may work with a woman in spiritual direction around her own expressions of anger and she may learn to handle them very well. Yet her interactions with a colleague, a husband, a friend, or a parent may leave her feeling inadequate and depressed because of the way her anger is received by them. Sometimes direct expressions merely worsen both the situation and our own feelings; another approach is then necessary. Lerner lists some questions that are helpful in sorting out approaches to anger:

What am I really angry about?
What is the problem and whose problem is it?
How can I express my anger in a way that will not leave me feeling helpless and powerless?
When I'm angry, how can I clearly communicate my position without becoming defensive or attacking?
What risks and losses might I face if I become clearer and more assertive?
If getting angry is not working for me, what can I do differently?[14]

These questions are useful as well for discernment in spiritual direction. They spell out the Christian ideal of telling the truth with love (Eph 4:15–16).

One aspect of discernment in relation to anger is how closely a woman will be associated with the institutional church. The continuum of involvement with the church runs all the way from simply belonging to working in a ministry that takes a woman close to the center of church structures.[15] For example, a woman who had worked in a diocesan chancery office for several years found that because of her anger with the church she needed to leave that job, but that she could still manage to be active in her parish as a volunteer. Other women can only attend liturgies on an intermittent basis or must stay away from such celebrations completely for a time. Still other women choose to change denominations or to leave the church completely. We often turn to spiritual friends for help in making these choices.

Women sometimes feel anger toward a person, perhaps a parent, who is no longer living. They cannot express their anger directly, yet they feel that something in the relationship is unfinished. In these cases, writing a letter that is later destroyed, speaking to the person in an empty chair, or developing some other ritual is a move toward closure.

All of these approaches can help us channel the energy of anger into spiritual growth and creative action.

ANGER AND FORGIVENESS

Like self-sacrifice, forgiveness is a Christian ideal that has been defined in ways restrictive for women; in the process the meaning of forgiveness has been distorted and, in fact, trivialized. Women have at times been led to believe that forgiveness is a one-time action that can follow quickly on the heels of being wronged. In spiritual direction, they frequently struggle with this, saying: "I know I should forgive this person, but I can't," or "I've tried to forgive, but the pain won't go away, and the anger keeps coming back when I think about it."

Forgiveness can in fact be a lengthy process with a number of stages.[16] One woman describes the shape this process takes for her.

> I take time for journaling, healing and prayer. I state my needs while working toward mutual reconciliation and joy. I don't accept what is destructive and devaluing of my person.

Forgiveness rests on awareness of the hurt or pain we have experienced and any anger that accompanies it. It moves to a recognition of how this has affected the relationship and what actions we must take. Finally, a time of healing may be necessary.

The act of forgiving is a way of saying that we will no longer dwell on the pain inflicted on us, or use the experience of being wronged as a weapon in the relationship. In other words, we will not harm another in return for being harmed. Forgiveness does not require that we excuse or minimize the wrong done to us, or take more than our share of responsibility for what happens in relationships. Nor does it imply that we will necessarily continue to relate to a person or stay in a harmful relationship. Because of the importance we give to affiliation, women experience the loss of a relationship as the loss of a dimension of the self. Some relationships must end, however, for the good of all involved, and recognition of this fact is a dimension of forgiveness.

Forgiveness usually requires a healing process, though it may vary in length. Ritual has been an important part of that healing for many women with whom I have worked in spiritual direction. One woman wanted to be free of some bitterness that she had experienced for years in a relationship. As she thought about this process of letting go, she recalled how as a child she used to take her hurts and pains and attach them to small wooden boats that she set out to sea. It helped her to revive this childhood ritual, this time attaching statements about her more recent feelings of resentment to the boats she made.

Once when I was working with a group of women on the use of ritual, one woman told us that she had developed a healing ritual around the pain of her divorce. On her wedding anniversary she went to the church where she had been married, and walked through the ceremony again alone. This time she expressed her pain, let go of some of her idealistic notions regarding her marriage, and asked for forgiveness where she was responsible for the difficulties that led to the divorce. Several women in the group were surprised that she had the courage to do this. Another woman was trying to move toward forgiveness in a relationship that had ended with no opportunity for her to express her emotions directly. As part of the healing process, she wrote out her feelings, burned the letter, and in the ashes planted flower seeds. It was a death/resurrection ritual that helped her deal with some of her feelings.

In commenting on the problems we all experience in dealing with anger, Jean Baker Miller offers an interesting challenge.[17] Neither women nor men, she says, have been able to experience or express the sort of anger that may be possible but which we are not yet able to conceptualize. The constraints for women are different and more restrictive than those for men, but men also learn to suppress and deflect anger. Our culture will not be able to solve its problems with anger, Miller believes, until we encourage each sex to examine and understand its own experience of anger more fully and truthfully. Meeting this challenge in new ways is a central part of working for the reign of God in our midst.

FOR PRAYER AND REFLECTION

1. Praying About Our Anger

Choose for the subject of your prayer a recent experience of anger. In the presence of God, reflect on this experience: What were you angry about? What feelings lay beneath the anger? What is God revealing to you in this anger? Acknowledge the feelings before God and let them be your own, a part of who you are.

Then decide on one thing you can change about your actions or responses in the situation that gave rise to the anger. In other words, how can you alter your steps in this dance of anger so that the dance cannot go on as before? As you weigh your choices, be aware of any areas of yourself that fear and resist change. Consider your choice before God, and then ask for strength to carry it out.

2. Journaling About Anger

Sometimes it is easier to write about our anger, since writing is a more controlled medium than speech. Journal about your anger. You may want to write your history of anger, including messages you heard about its religious meaning, ways you saw anger expressed or not expressed in your family, responses you have received from others when you have expressed anger, and your fears and hopes about the anger you experience in your life.

It may be helpful to draw a picture of your anger, and share this picture and your responses to it in a spiritual direction session.

3. Expressing Anger in Movement

Anger is a physical experience, a rush of energy and adrenaline meant to motivate, protect and empower for action. We have all learned how to clamp down physically and withhold our anger so as not to harm others. Eventually, we end up harming ourselves by bottling up this powerful force and not accessing it for choiceful living. This exercise suggests one way to express your anger in movement and, in doing so to restore the flow of energy throughout your body. You then have a choice for how to direct this flow into creative action in your life.

For this exercise, choose a safe environment where noise will not disturb others. Begin by grounding, feeling your legs connected to the earth. Notice where in your body you feel tight, held, restricted. These are the places from which you will focus on bringing out expression.

Now take a pillow. Hold the pillow over your head and arch back slightly, knees bent to maintain grounding. As if shooting an arrow, propel your top half forward with force, striking the floor (or bed) with the pillow. Let out a growl or aggressive sound. Repeat this as many times as you have energy for. Each time focus on bringing out expression from a different body part—jaw, shoulders and arms, belly, pelvis, legs. The more comfortable you become, experiment with other ways to move and express anger, e.g., stomping or kicking, biting, etc. When you are complete, practice grounding and softening again. Notice how your body feels now, and write results in your journal.

When working in a group, stand in a fairly large circle and use the energy of the group to support you. You can even take turns leading different aggressive movements that you discover. Share verbally with others as you complete.

4. Jesus' Anger: A Gospel Meditation

Meditate on the story of Jesus cleansing the temple in John 2:13–16. The following questions may help you enter into the story: What does the temple symbolize to you? In what areas of your life can you identify with Jesus' anger? How do you feel zeal for God's house? How are you called to express this zeal? What are your convictions about violence and nonviolence in relation to the expression of this zeal?

NOTES

1. See Alexandra G. Kaplan, et al., "Women and Anger in Psychotherapy," in *Women Changing Therapy,* pp. 29–40.

2. (New York: Simon & Schuster, 1982), p. 246.

3. See *Our Inner Conflicts* (New York: W.W. Norton, 1945); *Neurosis and Human Growth* (New York: W.W. Norton, 1950).

4. "Zeal for Your House Consumes Me: Dealing with Anger as a Woman in the Church," in *Women in the Church I,* ed. Madonna Kolbenschlag (Washington, DC: The Pastoral Press, 1987), p. 97.

5. Iris Goldstein Fodor, "Assertiveness Training for the Eighties: Moving Beyond the Personal," in *Handbook of Feminist Therapy. Women's Issues in Psychotherapy,* ed. Lynne Bravo Rosewater and Lenore E. A. Walker (New York: Springer Publishing Co., 1985), pp. 257–265.

6. "Assertiveness Training," p. 261.

7. Adrienne Rich, *The Fact of a Doorframe. Poems Selected and New. 1950–1984* (New York: W.W. Norton & Company, 1984), p. 274.

8. *A New Approach to Women and Therapy,* p. 315.

9. *Anger: The Misunderstood Emotion,* p. 253.

10. "Conversations Between Here and Home," in *Voices of Women. Poetry By and About Third World Women,* p. 25.

11. (New York: Harper & Row, 1985).

12. *The Dance of Anger,* p. 13.

13. *Toward a New Psychology of Women,* p. 122.

14. *The Dance of Anger,* p. 4.

15. A description of different levels of engagement can be found in Carolyn Osiek, R.S.C.J., *Beyond Anger. On Being a Feminist in the Church* (New York: Paulist Press, 1986), pp. 25–43.

16. Helpful insights on anger and forgiveness are presented in Evelyn Eaton Whitehead and James D. Whitehead, *Seasons of Strength. New Visions of Adult Christian Maturing* (New York: Doubleday, 1984), pp. 115–128.

17. "The Construction of Anger in Women and Men," *Work in Progress* (Wellesley, MA: Stone Center for Developmental Services and Studies, 1983), p. 8.

Group Psychotherapy as Spiritual Discipline: From Oz to the Kingdom of God

John McDargh

> ". . . and they sent me home. Home. And this is my room.
> And you're all here. Oh, Auntie Em, there's no place like
> home."
>
> Dorothy Gale, *The Wizard of Oz*

*It is 7:00 on a sultry summer evening in Boston's Back Bay.
Seven men and myself are reconfiguring the space in a small consulting room three stories above the street. We arrange wicker
chairs and carry in wooden chairs from the waiting room to allow
us to gather in some form of close circle for the next two hours.
Windows are thrown open to catch what little breeze rises up with
the street sounds from the boulevard below. Outside the tall windows, rays of the setting sun sluicing down the alley golden the grey
stone walls of an old Congregational church that is practically flush
against the building that houses this counseling practice, a clothing
designer's studio, and an antique bookstore. I have met with these
men in similar fashion once a week for nearly five years as their
therapist/group leader. We know one another well, and yet each
time we gather there is about these early moments that unique
mixture of uncertainty, expectation, wariness, and anticipation that
for each of us characterizes our every new human encounter and all
beginnings. Here in this room we re-enact the patterns of our lives
in slow motion—and equally slowly begin to change those patterns.*

The majority of the men in the room have been here from the
very beginning of the group, two years prior to my assuming its

leadership when the original therapist, a former student of mine, moved to the west coast. I had accepted his invitation to take over the group just as I was completing a one year sabbatical during which time I did a post-doctoral internship in community mental health. I had worked that year at a day treatment program for chronically mentally ill persons where I helped run several different kinds of groups. Taking over this established long-term therapy group, specifically designated for gay men who had grown up in alcoholic families, seemed at the time a good way to keep some connection to the sort of hands-on clinical practice which I found so challenging and meaningful, and such a shift of psychic gears from the more experience-distant work of teaching and research that is my full time professional occupation. The appeal of such an invitation was decidedly over-determined. Though conducted in a thoroughly secular context, group psychotherapy also offered some foothold in pastoral work which twenty years ago was the "road not taken" when I left military service to enter Harvard Graduate School rather than seminary or religious life. For the first few years of running the group, when asked about it, I would say something like, "it isn't the thing I do best, but it may be the best thing that I do." That is perhaps still true, but there is much more to say now. Over time, I increasingly have come to recognize the ways in which what I receive from the group is perhaps much greater than whatever I may offer as a servant of its process. This single weekly experience focuses in a highly condensed fashion all of what I am about in staking an intellectual position on the boundary of psychology and theology. The group is where I come up against the limits of my own personal, theoretical and practical integration of what I know and believe about the life of the Spirit and what I am coming to understand of the operation of the psyche. The "upper room" where the group meets has been alternately (and sometime simultaneously) a place of judgment, repentance, compunction, and grace. Finally, it is in the group that I understand what D. W. Winnicott (1971) meant when he dedicated *Playing and Reality*, "to my patients who paid to teach me."

On this particular evening as we settle into our familiar places with the same unquestioned territoriality that I regularly observe in classrooms my thoughts are far from these kinds of meta-critical reflections. Certainly I do not imagine that tonight's group might potentially provide that narrative through which I shall take up the questions of the Uppsala seminar. The session begins with what has become over the years one of the rituals that help define the "holding environment" which the group at its best attempts to create. I lead the group in a five minute breath mindfulness exercise, prefacing it unusually with a short teaching reminding the group members of the aim of this practice. The invitation to center one's attention on the sensations of the breath as it enters and leaves the body, and then anchored in that attention to simply notice without judgment or pursuit whatever other body sensations, thoughts or feelings one is carrying into the room this evening. This activity of contemplatively taking note of "how it is" with one at any given moment is a deployment of attention, I remind the group, that can and should be used through the session. I finally know enough about my own process to recognize that the impulse momentarily to fall back on a teaching mode in the group, even when the intervention may prove to be strategic and helpful, is a signal of my own anxiety. I am also preaching to myself in this moment. I am one who needs to be reminded to breathe and pay attention because this evening is already different and already difficult at more levels than I can keep track of.

The introduction of an opening centering meditation to begin the therapy group was made about four years ago. It coincided with my own deepening interest in the role of the body and of pre-thematic or pre-linguistic knowing in the processes of religious experiencing. Here the sources of this concern were multiple. Closest to heart was work I did with an earlier Jesuit spiritual director who introduced me to the "focusing" techniques of existential psychologist Eugene Gendlin (1981).[1] Wisely, this director figured out well before I did that like a great many persons who self-select for academic life, I was very good at knowing what I *thought* about a given subject but frightfully unaware of what I *felt*. If, as Gendlin argued, we most often "know more than we can say," then the capacity to identify our "felt sense" about our condition at any given time is perhaps the truest and most reliable guide to the kind of self-knowledge that is ultimately transformative. Indeed, Gendlin (1967) and his colleagues at the University of Chicago determined that the ability, innate or learned, to monitor one's "felt sense" and to bring that sense into speech by way of metaphor or imagery was perhaps the most significant predictor of constructive change in psychotherapy.

My own initial interest in these ideas, apart from their value for my own prayer and therapy, was the corrective that I felt they offered to the excessively conceptualist approach which I felt I had taken to the subject of my own original doctoral research at Harvard between 1974 and 1979 (McDargh, 1984b, 1986).[2] My interest then had been in the resources of contemporary psychoanalytic theory and especially British object relations theory as a way of investigating the formation, development and transformation of our very idiosyncratic, conscious and unconscious, images of "God." Certainly in that personal preoccupation with individual images or "object representations" of "God," in contrast to formal doctrines of concepts of the divine, there is to be seen a concern shared with H. Richard Niebuhr (1943) to find my way down to the roots of both faith and idolatry in the "imaginings of the human heart." But what is below (beneath?) our images of God? Is there a knowing of the Holy that is deeper than saying, and is it somehow writ into our bodily experiencing? It is a question I was taking up in several articles, though earlier still it was forced for me in my appreciative encounters with Buddhism where I found a psychology that was far more subtle and sophisticated in its understanding of the psychic sources of imagery than anything I had found in the traditions of Christian spirituality (McDargh, 1984a, 1992a, 1992b).[3]

It is perhaps characteristic of my own slowness to translate thinking into action that though I was experimenting personally with the practice of mindfulness (*vipassana*) meditation and attempting to integrate such practices into my own prayer, for a long time I kept the parameters of my work in the group defined rather strictly by a more traditional psychoanalytic notion of what constitutes a "talking cure." The purpose of the group was to talk about one's feelings and attend to the interactions within the group as clues to one's unconscious relational conflicts. Yet before one could talk about such feelings it was necessary to know that one *had* feelings, and this is no small step. Indeed, as I have begun to understand more about the condition of growing up in a

"dysfunctional" or abusive family I could see more clearly that for
all of the men in the group to some degree, and for some men to a
very great degree, there was a profound impairment in the ability
to be aware of their own flow of affect. The necessary adaptations
they made to childhood patterns of physical or emotional abuse,
unpredictable parenting, and violent or emotionally chaotic households involved learning to pay attention to the moods of others
but to be oblivious to their own. Like the "gifted children" in the
writings of Swiss psychoanalyst Alice Miller (1981), the persons in
the group were frequently precociously responsible for their sib-
lings and parents and such habits of generous, selfless caretaking
extended down to the present. What also was true is that to a man
they frequently found it difficult, if not impossible, to identify
with any conviction what *they* desired, what *they* felt, what *they*
wanted for themselves. Hence attention to "felt sense," what is
happening in the present moment, has become no small part of
the work of the group.

*So what is it that I am feeling as I allow my breath to steady my
attention? I become aware that my mind wants to wander to two
preoccupying thoughts. The first is, where is George?⁴ George is a
group member who for some time now has been exploring the
question of whether he is at a place in his own personal and professional life and psychological work that would make it timely to
terminate. George has been a faithful and hard working member of
the group for over four years and his weighing of a decision to
bring this work to a conclusion is completely appropriate. Still, for
these men who are dealing with how to trust a world that has been
marked by early abandonments and untimely departures, any consideration of a member moving on is freighted with immense conscious and unconscious significance. Usually on time, George's
absence at the hour we are scheduled to begin provokes a sensation
of dis-ease I notice between breaths. I wonder how his absence is
being experienced by the other members. The second more anxious
thought does not relate to an absence, but to a presence after long
absence. Jack has returned tonight to the group after being unable
to attend for nearly two months. The only member to be HIV
positive, Jack has suffered a debilitating series of opportunistic
infections that marked his assumption of a full AIDS diagnosis*

over two years ago. Since April he has been undergoing a number of hospitalizations for ailments that have left him seriously weakened and unable to work. Jack now occupies the empty chair which was kept for him during the time he was away. Like Elijah at the Passover table, his return has been as anticipated and in some measure as disbelieved. With one swollen foot from which a gangrenous toe was recently amputated propped up on the wicker coffee table, he hugs under one arm a canvas gym bag full of medications and towels ready should he need to make a hurried dash (on crutches) for the bathroom down the hall. Though still handsome, Jack is a good twenty pounds thinner than when last he sat here. His posture in the chair suggests that the effort to make it here tonight has already taken a toll on his limited reserves of energy. As gay men living in the midst of the epidemic, like men in wartime, several of us in the group have already borne more losses of friends and colleagues than my grandfather knew before he was ninety and outlived his generation. Remarkably, however, for a few of the men in the group Jack is the closest they have come to witnessing the long, relentless and unpredictable struggle that the disease exacts. For all of us, no matter where we have found ourselves on the front lines, Jack's own process claims our attention inescapably and the covenant to be truthful, at least in this room, about our feelings for and about him cuts off the evasions and compromises that are possible in other contexts. The thought arises, "Will we make room for Jack tonight?" If at first I imagine that I am worrying about the already cramped consulting room, at second I know I am thinking about the space in the heart needed to carry the almost unbearable sadness and hopefulness evoked by Jack's return, and the resurgent feelings of anger and helplessness which the course of his illness and his managing of it have pulled up.

In the middle of the meditation I hear the door open behind me and without opening my eyes follow George's steps as he carefully enters and takes his place on one end of the sofa. I silently make the decision to extend our centering meditation for a while longer to give him a chance to catch his own breath and find his way into the room in spirit as well as body.

Paul Tillich (1966) entitled his autobiography *On the Boundary,* and it has often struck me that this is also perhaps an apt emblem for the professional lives of most persons who have chosen academic careers that span disparate intellectual disciplines as well as the gulf between theory and praxis. I have often found myself "on the boundary" in pursuing the psychology of religious development in a Roman Catholic department of theology. There is about this work something that feels naggingly illegitimate and vaguely subversive. Perhaps that is why I sometimes describe myself with reference to one of Woody Allen's old jokes. "I once almost got kicked out of college," Allen quips. "It seems I was taking a theology examination and the professor caught me looking into my neighbor's soul." Maybe that is who I am, a theologian who cheats. Psychoanalysis, the practice of psychotherapy, the discipline of spiritual direction have all been for me a way of looking into my neighbor's soul as well as my own, and hence has been for me a place of theologizing—of seeking some understanding of the faith I find there.

Yet as I muse further on the matter of boundaries, of living on the margins, I recognize that an assignment to, if not a preference for, boundary living was forming well before I entered Harvard's Committee for the Study of Religion (itself a program that had no secure departmental home within the university). I was raised in the American South, but without the deep historical roots or family in the region which would have conferred status and identity. A Roman Catholic by baptism and thirteen years of parochial education, even that identity was a tangled one—being Jewish back a generation on my mother's side and on my father's side Presbyterian and Baptist. Moreover, to be Roman Catholic in the South in the fifties was always to feel like an odd minority and an outsider. (My earliest memories of the Sunday liturgy are of a circuit riding priest celebrating at a card table altar in a public school cafeteria.) When I finally encountered the ethnic Roman Catholicism of Boston I remember being appalled at my students' (and colleagues') unquestioned presumption of Roman superiority and their innocent ignorance of other ways of being Christian. Perhaps this is why in recent years I have felt most spiritually at home in a marvelously eccentric liturgically-serious, socially-radical Anglo-Catholic parish—a marginal tradition in a denomination which itself is sometimes uneasily camped on the boundary between Catholicism and Protestantism.

Finally, I am recognizing that this very old sense of being on the outside looking in also surely has something to do with the experience of growing up gay in a straight world. As I have prayed over this identification, it has increasingly come to me as the condition of possibility for a sensed solidarity with the suffering and the oppressed which as a white, higher educated, North American male, I might not otherwise be graced with. Insofar as this is also a touchstone for the revelation of God to me in the Christ crucified outside the city walls, my experience of being a gay man at this particular time in history is integral to my spiritual life.[5] This came to me most powerfully on a retreat my partner and I made a number of years ago with a group of Mexican nuns in Cuernavaca. Every evening when we would return to their convent to reflect on our day's experiences in the *colonias* or shanty towns in the ravines of that town, they would say, "Do not feel guilt or dismay over what you have seen today; you have some place in your lives where you can know for yourselves what it means to live as these. Tell us about it." I am not certain that the good sisters even quite grasped what I was trying to explain, though they made an honest effort. What is more important, I understood something on that retreat which is reaffirmed every week that I look around this group. These happen to be a cross section of middle class, and (mostly) middle-aged white men with the education and talent to hold positions as university and church administrators, business executives, city planners, government bureaucrats. The coincidence of sexual orientation, familial history, and now the historical circumstance of the AIDS epidemic in this country, combine in a different way for each man to draw forth a degree of care, courage, and wider identification than might ever have been expected or predicted. Many an evening I have left the group recalling Yeats' image for the astonishing depth of character he saw unexpectedly emerge in those who stepped forward to take a role in the Irish uprising—"A terrible beauty is born" (Finneram, 1989).

"Take three more mindful breaths and when you are ready, slowly open your eyes." The meditation over, we are in "check in," a process of going around the circle to describe whatever of the week past as it bears on the issues, concerns or feelings one is

bringing into the group this evening. Pedro, a writer and publicist, shares something of the trauma of unexpectedly finding out that a trusted supervisor had been maligning him behind his back—a betrayal that set off feelings of falling apart from which he has been a week recovering. He also picks up again the thread of an interaction he had last week with Michael the week before who had kindly but directly questioned the wisdom of a plan Pedro had announced to take a five-week break from the group in order to take a business course demanded for his professional development. Alerting us that he might have more to say on the matter, Pedro wants to thank Michael for his concern and let us all know that with some effort he had found an alternative course that would not conflict with the group meeting. Arnold announces plans to return for a vacation to his mother's home in Vermont where there may be some confrontation he will need to prepare for. Patrick and Michael check in with brief descriptions of their mood as they have become aware of it—depressed and grumpy respectively. George seem to want to short circuit any criticism of his late arrival by saying, "I'll take the blame for coming in late," and then goes on to discuss what he is truly apprehensive about, the decision he has come upon to set a date for termination at the end of the summer and then "see how that feels." Sean, following George, frankly admits the anxiety he has felt about this impending decision and his relative relief that it is now out on the table.

Finally, Jack takes a labored breath and begins his check-in. At first it is a straightforward and almost business-like synopsis of his medical condition and the economic consequences of his needing to apply for Social Security disability—the most serious of which is that he may soon have to move into subsidized housing and leave the apartment which it has taken him nine years to fully renovate. This will be a big loss. Jack further mentions that finally after many years he has told all members of his family about his diagnosis and has been surprised by their unpredicted compassion and support. The management of his medical care and monitoring of his complex treatment protocols, he explains, has absorbed most of his time and attention and given him a focus for his anger. As he talks the steely control he has had to exercise over his feelings begins to soften: "In dealing with the struggle to maintain myself there has been no time for me . . . my mind has been so jumpy."

There is a space of silence, like the stillness before a rain storm. A huge sob wells up and shudders Jack's chest. "I never knew there were so many ways my body could feel pain . . . Nothing can be taken for granted now . . . I feel that I have been in free fall ever since I got sick." The full silence that holds his check-in has about it a sense of both reverence and relief—there will be room for Jack again.

Into that silence I offer a brief comment that provides a segue to the rest of the evening. I remind the group that Jack's frustrating effort to "find a time for me" and his sense that he is living his life in "free fall" echoes a theme that with variations has been developing in the group for some time now as various members cope with heightened demands and pressures from work, family and significant others. The issue comes into clearer focus: how in the midst of constant reactivity does one make decisions for life from some center of genuine desire and personal truth. Later in the evening each group member will return to talk about some of his feelings towards Jack and what it is like to have him here again in the body, but at this juncture something unexpected happens. George claims the floor to talk further about how he wants to figure out if it is time for him to leave the group. The point of contact he makes with Jack to enter into that reflection is Jack's image of being in "free fall" and George's association is to the scene from The Wizard of Oz *in which Dorothy's house is tumultuously swept up on the cyclone finally to land with a great jolt in Oz. As George spins out his association and talks about the clues he is reading towards this decision there are actually two paradoxical metaphors that emerge. On the one hand he feels that the events of the last several months, including a solitary trip he took to Asia, have given him a certain sense of having "landed" in his own life. He has identified some "still point in the turning world" [T.S. Eliot's words, my unvoiced association] from which he now feels freer to decide for a life that is more satisfying and more agential. On the other hand, the felt-sense he has of his life now is that it is in fact moving, not in a chaotic spin, but with the promise of a direction and flow that means he is finally getting "unstuck" from the familial and professional roles that hitherto he has simply and successfully acquiesced to without noticing the high cost. George works to put into words this sense he has that he is now on some kind of "spring board" of his life, and that there is a ripeness or readiness he feels to leave this company of men who have helped him arrive at this place. As he speaks he looks at Jack. Their eyes lock for a long time and the unspoken questions hang in the between. Can it be alright to feel this excitement about moving on when it means leaving you behind? Can I ever have anything like this sense of promise in my life which now seems so unfairly foreshortened? Will I be able to both celebrate your movement and feel my own grief and loss? Can we both eventually say how much we have meant to each other?*

However problematic I sometimes may find the ordinary operations of the institutional Roman church, the group reminds me again and again that in some profound and undeniable way my spiritual sensibilities are deeply "Catholic." By that I mean in part that I operate from a belief that the Holy Mystery has so sown Its presence into the stuff of humanity that we cannot escape the activity of God's love and mercy if we live attentively and receptively to the world as it comes to us. Like the central character in Bernanos' *Diary of a Country Priest* who declines the last rites because "grace is everywhere," I realize that I live on my better days with some expectancy that I will be surprised by how homely and hospitable God turns out to be.[6] Such a conviction that grace builds upon nature (*gratia perficit naturam*) inclines me to look for continuities rather than discontinuities between psychological and spiritual accounts of human development (McDargh, 1985, 1990b, 1991b) allows me to find wisdom for religious living in unlikely places, like the journals of Etty Hillesum (1981), a twenty-seven year-old Dutch Jewish woman who died in Auschwitz, and whose writings I would hold to be a modern spiritual classic (McDargh, 1991a). In the context of the group, a sacramental imagination tutors me to notice how stories and images from popular culture can come to function as secular scriptures, conveying with power and appeal a saving revelation about God.

In the life of this psychotherapy group the narrative of *The Wizard of Oz* has spontaneously emerged from time to time as a communal myth illuminating both individual and shared group process. Not coincidentally, the movie classic starring Judy Garland has long been a favorite film in American gay male culture. (In the 1940s gay men would signal their identity to one another by asking, "Are you a friend of Dorothy?") Within this group, however, the imagery of the film has disclosed deeper levels of signification. Two weeks earlier Pedro, in describing the deeply destructive psychic assault he felt in his work place, referred to himself as feeling like the Scarecrow attacked in the haunted woods who has had the straw stuffing beaten out of him. It was a poignant and evocative image for the feeling of narcissistic depletion and emotional emptiness which Pedro experienced as a result of having his competence attacked and his credibility questioned by persons he had confided in and relied upon. The image at the time also provoked the question, "How shall I get re-stuffed and filled up again?" In the movie the Scarecrow is at once helpless and dependent on his two companions, the Cowardly Lion and the Tin Man, for their assistance, and at the same time he must exercise agency and initiative in directing them in the process. Pedro can be helped, but the straw is all his.

When George evokes the image of "landing" in his life there is an uncommented-upon irony. Escaping the tornado is not an ending, but only a beginning. It is what launches Dorothy on her journey to find a way home. "Finding one's way home" has often seemed to me an appropriate metaphor for group psychotherapy as spiritual process. Each of these men in his own way has been exiled from himself by the vicissitudes of his own history, in particular by the ways in which "home" as family of origin failed to be an environment welcoming and responsive to his own unfolding. I am drawn to using D. W. Winnicott's (1965) concepts of the "true" and "false" self to describe the organization of self-experience that disposes these individuals to feeling easily empty and impaired in the capacity to feel authentic, real, and capable of spontaneous gesture. Having "landed" in strange company they are on a quest alone but together to find that which each feels will make his life complete and worthwhile.

Who am I on this journey? In the transference I am frequently the Wizard who is believed to have the magic power to restore heart, head, and will to proper function by the assignment and enforcement of impossible tasks (show up, pay attention, bring me the broomstick of the Wicked Witch of the West). Accepting the role of group leader is to invite and to bear such expectations and idealizations, and also to allow the curtain to be pulled so that there is the disillusioning realization that though I may be a good man, as a wizard I am a humbug. Wherein then lies the power for healing? The myth would have it that it lies within, where courage, and compassion and luminous intelligence have always resided, albeit unrecognized and unrealized. The path "home" is also as close as one's own heart and the realization of its deepest desiring. This however the wizard cannot awaken, it is a gift from the ever elusive Other (in the movie, the slightly silly and unpredictably appearing Glinda, Good Witch of the North). That is the part that challenges my own faith and trust most radically. How many times I have sat in the group and succumbed to the fear that if I did not find the right lever to push (right words to say, correct interpretation to offer) that all would be lost. The circus would never find the park. In these moments, when I could surrender something of my own desire for perfection or control, and trust in the power that is there in truth-telling and in waiting, something would happen. Someone would be directed humbly to their own place on the earth, look to their feet if you will, and be inspired to offer a gift of self that truly is a foretaste of "home."

We are nearing the end of the session. Darkness has fallen outside and the sounds of the city on a summer night, including the jarring wail of car alarms and sirens, compete with our voices in speech. Pedro has returned to the topic of the distress he has been wrestling with during this most difficult of weeks. He rehearses for us the way the blows of these small but significant betrayals by coworkers and employers have fallen on his soul, shaking his sense of reality testing about himself and his abilities, resurrecting the horrid ghosts of his chaotic childhood in which his life was frequently threatened by his stepfather who was given to destructive rages. The small child he was then had no place to run and, worse, no one to whom he could tell his story. In consequence there was no one to assure that child that though his parental world was bad he was not, and that he could be safe. Then Pedro addresses Michael who the week before had directly voiced his concern for Pedro amidst the many difficult professional changes he was trying to navigate. "There is a big part of me," he says with a tremor in his voice, "that doesn't want to go on living." "But I see now," he continues, "that I have to stop throwing myself and my relationships away . . . I get it that I am a part of you, and you are a part of me. I have to believe that, and believe that it is worth living despite *the fact that I am not perfect,* despite *everything . . . my limitations . . . "* With these words Pedro seems to name not only his own *condition, but to speak to the longing of every person in the group. In the quiet pause after he finishes I ask simply, "What do you want from the group tonight?" Pedro replies softly, "Just to be told that there is hope, that I will get through." In the few minutes left before I must signal "check out" and we bring the group to an end by once more going around for concluding reflections, several men in the group give Pedro what he asks for, but again in an unexpected and deeply wise fashion. No one offers any glib words of encouragement or affirmation. No one even says the word "hope." What they do quite simply is share with Pedro what they have seen over five years of how he has endured and prevailed. Against his memories of failure and abandonment they counterpose their own memories of his survival and the faithfulness of Whoever or Whatever has seen him through. It is healing by* anamnesis.

"What do you hope for your clients?" "What enables you to bear with your own sense of helplessness in the face of your patients' pain?" These are all questions which, in the four summers that I have co-taught a seminar for Einstein Medical School on "Spirituality and Psychotherapy" for mental health workers, have driven us to locate where our convictions about the origins and trajectory of human suffering intersect with our most foundational beliefs about ultimate reality.[7] Do I believe that in the end we are alone, or do I believe that in the end, as in the beginning, God? Do I see the *telos* of human development, even psychologically described, as the achievement of sufficient autonomy and self-sufficiency to maintain one's independent existence in a world where finally and inevitably one must learn to do it alone? For me, part of the drama of the emergence of a relational perspective in psychoanalysis (Mitchell, 1988) and a feminist account of normative human development (Miller, 1984) is its convergence with a vision of human existence as profoundly and irreducibly corporate, a Trinitarian vision, if you will, in which created in the *imago dei* "I am a part of you and you are a part of me" because we belong to Christ and Christ belongs to God (McDargh, 1990a). For Pedro to be able to say, indeed to be able to *experience,* this fact of mutual inter-dependence, is to my mind both a psychological achievement and a gift of grace. It has required the consolidation of boundaries against the incursions of persons for whom mutuality really meant submission and was a prelude to violation. Only from a place of some trust and inner integrity could Pedro risk knowing how he and Michael have come to belong to one another's lives. The paradox is that this achievement of self-definition and differentiation was itself relationally mediated, the fruit of a long and patient process of committing to being together week after week, year after year.

What do I hope for? The conclusion of the group on this particular evening brought me back to think of the work of Jesuit philosopher and literary critic William Lynch. Based in part on his own experiences at St. Elizabeth's Mental Hospital, Father Lynch (1974) observed that one of the most destructive human modes of thought was what he termed the "absolutizing imagination." It is the tendency, very often aided and abetted by religious language and belief, to think in totalities and absolutes. Rather than hoping to human scale we tyrannize ourselves into thinking that the good person "hopes all things, believes all things, endures all things." Failing—inevitably—to meet this standard of perfection we are vulnerable to despair. Winnicott (1971) wrote of the "good enough" parent (and I think of the "good enough" therapist) with a genial wisdom about the way in which life uses our limited resources and makes them sufficient. Pedro is coming to embrace a life that is "just this much," as Stephen Levine (1987) so beautifully put it. For many years I thought that this approach was a kind of failure of spiritual nerve, a collapse of transcendence into a mode of stoic resignation. Now, slowly, I am being brought to see how it requires and rides a more profound if often less articulate sense of trust and surrender. Its cultivation requires a disciplined practice, as sure and committed as showing up weekly for group, but its fruition cannot be willed or asserted, compelled or coerced. Like the Spirit it is sheer gift. Like what transpired this night, it is beyond calculation.

The group breaks up, as it always does, with the shifting and reordering of chairs, the exchanging of hugs and handshakes, the writing of checks. The servant is worthy of his hire, or so the Book says. I make a mental note that Jack and I will soon need to discuss a sliding scale to accommodate his changed financial circumstances, and he anticipates me by mentioning as he leaves that he will be calling me at my office to discuss the matter of fee. The men in the group disperse, some to assist Jack home, others to go out for coffee. Below on the street I hear laughter and snatches of conversation. They are talking about book reviews in the local gay newspaper, plans for the weekend, the new Tina Turner flick. Group business is what stays in the room. Crossing Copley Square to go home I notice there is an open folk dance going on. A fiddler, a piper and a caller are playing on the square beneath the protective Romanesque bulk of Trinity Church. Several dozen adults and children of all ages and races spontaneously gathered are merrily weaving in and out and colliding with one another in their best approximation of an Irish reel. In the back of my mind I am still thinking of the dance we have just completed in the lee of another stone church, our missteps and collisions, intricate patterns and surprising symmetry. "Blessed be God forever" I murmur to myself for want of anything wiser and notice, somewhat to my surprise, that I am very near to tears.

NOTES

1. For a philosophical defense of the epistemological privilege of this order of experiencing see Gendlin (1987). A book that was influential in making these connections for me is *Religious Experiencing: William James and Eugene Gendlin* by John Shea (1987).

2. Both works are deeply indebted to the pioneering research of Ana Maria Rizzuto (1979) who has been both mentor and friend.

3. When I cite my encounter with Buddhism I have in mind both the person and the writing of Dr. Jack Engler who I was fortunate to have as my clinical supervisor while on sabbatical (see Engler, 1986).

4. Names and identifying information of group members have been changed to protect their confidentiality.

5. A growing edge in my own work as a writer and researcher has been to recognize that my observations and experience as a gay man are also potentially a relevant and fruitful resource for critical reflection on a range of religious and psychological issues. Two recent pieces of writing are efforts to explore this in a more public and self-conscious way: a

paper delivered at the Society for Values in Higher Education meeting in Colorado Springs the summer of 1992, "F.O. Mattheisen, Martin Duberman and Me: Reflections of a Gay Male Academic on the Problem of Masculinity"; and an essay offered to Donald Capps' and Richard Fenn's seminar on "Soul Death" at Princeton Seminary in September 1992, "Desire, Domination and the Life and Death of the Soul."

6. The "homeliness" of God, that is, God's condescension and unlimited welcome to God's creatures is a favorite theme of the fourteenth-century English anchorite, Blessed Julian of Norwich, for an introduction to whom I am indebted to Bishop Tom Shaw, S.S.J.E.

7. "Spirituality and Psychotherapy" has been a seminar presented by the Agosin Group yearly since 1990 (Mark Finn, Peter Cohen, Fredrica Halligan, Nancy Kehoe, R.S.C.J., and John McDargh) at the Cape Cod Institute of the Department of Psychiatry, Albert Einstein College of Medicine.

REFERENCES

Bernanos, G. (1937). *Diary of a country priest* (P. Morris, Trans.). New York: Macmillan.
Engler, J. (1986). Therapeutic aims in psychotherapy and meditation. In K. Wilber, J. Engler, & D. Brown (Eds.), *Transformations of consciousness: Conventional and contemplative perspectives on development*. Boston: Shambhala Press.
Finneran, R. (Ed.). (1989). *The poems of William Butler Yeats*. New York: MacMillan.
Gendlin, E. (1967). Focusing ability in psychotherapy, personality, and creativity. In J. Shlein (Ed.), *Research in psychotherapy* (Vol. 3). Washington, DC: American Psychological Association.
Gendlin, E. (1981). *Focusing*. New York: Bantam Books.
Gendlin, E. (1987). A philosophical critique of the concept of narcissism: The significance of the awareness movement. In D. Levin (Ed.), *Psychopathologies of the modern self: Post modern studies on narcissism, schizophrenia, and depression*. New York: University Press.
Hillesum, E. (1981). *An interrupted life: The journals of Etty Hillesum 1941–1943*. New York: Pantheon Books.
Levine, S. (1987). *Healing into life and death*. New York: Anchor Books.
Lynch, W. (1974). *Images of hope: Imagination as healer of the hopeless*. Notre Dame, IN: University of Notre Dame.

McDargh, J. (1984a). The life of the self in Christian spirituality and contemporary psychoanalysis. *Horizons, 11*(2), 344–360.

McDargh, J. (1984b). *Psychoanalytic object relations theory and the study of religion: On faith and the imaging of God.* Lanham, MD: University Press of America.

McDargh, J. (1985). Theological uses of psychology: A retrospective and prospective. *Horizons, 12*(2), 247–264.

McDargh, J. (1986). God, mother, and me: An object relational perspective on religious material in psychotherapy. *Pastoral Psychology, 34*(4), 251–263.

McDargh, J. (1990a, May). *Clues to transcendence: Contemporary psychoanalysis on the trail of mystery.* Opening plenary address to the American Association of Pastoral Care and Counseling, Annual meeting, Williamsburg, VA.

McDargh, J. (1990b). Theology and psychoanalysis. In R. Hunter et al. (Eds.), *Dictionary of pastoral care and counseling.* Nashville, TN: Abingdon Press.

McDargh, J. (1991a). A psychoanalytic appreciation of prayer. In W. Barry (Ed.), *A hunger for God.* New York: Sheed and Ward.

McDargh, J. (1991b). Spirituality and psychology. In M. Downey (Ed.), *New dictionary of Catholic spirituality.* Collegeville, MN: Liturgical Press.

McDargh, J. (1992a). The deep structure of religious representations: A case study. In M. Finn & J. Gartner (Eds.), *Object relations theory and religion: Clinical applications* (pp. 1–20). New York: Praeger Press.

McDargh, J. (1992b). Ralph Waldo Emerson and the life of the self: A psychoanalytic conversation. In R. Fenn & D. Capps (Eds.), *The Endangered Self* (Monograph Series No. 2, pp. 7–20). Princeton, NJ: Princeton Theological Seminary, Center for Religion, Self, and Society.

Miller, A. (1981). *The drama of the gifted child: The search for the true self.* New York: Basic Books.

Miller, J. B. (1984). *The development of women's sense of self* (Monograph Series). Wellesley, MA: Stone Center for Women's Studies.

Mitchell, S. (1988). *Relational concepts in psychoanalysis: An introduction.* Cambridge, MA: Harvard University Press.

Niebuhr, H. R. (1943). *Radical monotheism and western culture.* New York: Harper.

Rizzuto, A. M. (1979). *The birth of the living God.* Chicago: The University of Chicago Press.

Shea, J. (1987). *Religious experiencing: William James and Eugene Gendlin.* Lanham, MD: University Press of America.

Tillich, P. (1966). *On the boundary: An autobiographical sketch.* New York: Scribner.

Winnicott, D. W. (1965). Ego distortion in terms of true and false self. In *Maturational processes and the facilitating environment.* London: Hogarth.

Winnicott, D. W. (1971). *Playing and reality.* New York: Basic Books.

Response: An Invitation to Grace and Truth from the Margins

John Carter

There are many things to which I could respond in John McDargh's (1994) "Group Psychotherapy as Spiritual Discipline: From Oz to the Kingdom of God." First, McDargh identifies with a relational model of psychology (Mitchell, 1988) and a relational model of the *imago Dei.* Second, McDargh reports a commitment to a "grace builds on nature" (*gratia perficit naturam*) understanding of nature and grace. Third, McDargh apparently identifies with pilgrims in the land of Oz. All these issues are interesting in themselves and delicately woven into the fabric of his very sensitive piece on therapy, life, and healing. However, to address any of these in a cognitive, combative or even dialogic way is to miss the point of his effort.

Instead the implicit invitation of his article has been accepted: to engage in examination of my own psychodynamics and the path I have taken in becoming a therapist and writer on psychology and theology. I have lived on the edges of many groups, approaching all, but at home in none. I was raised the only male in a multigenerational female household. I had the only college educated parent in an extensive blue-collar neighborhood. I attended the Methodist Church on Sunday morning and was restricted to my house and yard the rest of the day while my Roman Catholic or non-religious friends took Sunday as a time for play and socializing. I commuted to a downtown high school instead of a local one like my friends. I read the Bible as a grade school child for myself. I was often frightened as well as fascinated when dragged to radical Pentecostal churches by my mother. At a local university in the 1950s evangelicals clustered in an InterVarsity Club defending themselves in what was a very hostile anti-religious environment. While attending a Baptist Seminary oriented to pastoral and mission work, I hung out with the intellectual clique and went to Presbyterian churches. Completing my doctorate on a part-time basis at a progressive European oriented graduate school, I found myself at odds with the mentality of the rather fundamentalist college where I was teaching. Perhaps it is this living in the border lands that has impelled me to wrestle with boundaries between the secular and sacred.

Growing up, God was always very real to me. The realness of God was my ground and organized an otherwise fragmented existence (Hedges, 1983). That is not to say that I have not had doubts or intellectual or personal crises of faith. My writings on the sacred and secular (Carter, 1977; Carter & Narramore, 1979), maturity (Carter, 1974) and the nature and scope of integration (Carter & Mohline, 1976; Fleck & Carter, 1981) all reflect my efforts to remove the artificially conceived boundary between nature and grace. With the Psalmist (24:1) and Kuyper (1909/1963), I believe there is no conflict between the sacred and the secular because all is sacred. The conflict arises because the human race in introducing corruption into nature now stands with it in need of redemption. This seems to be at odds with McDargh's "grace builds on nature" and his stress on the immanence of God (his homelessness) in the therapy process as a spiritual discipline. Without losing God's immanence (which McDargh seems to identify with catholicity) I would support a more redemptive "grace rebuilds nature."

McDargh, by grounding healing in a relational image of God, has invited us to examine the therapy process. I, too, feel the mystery of God's restoration of wounded persons, including myself in the therapy groups I lead and have attended. Sometimes I ponder the relationship of psychological healing and sanctification. I know all the theories (theologies) but I am less dogmatic in choosing one than I used to be. Like the spirit blowing where He wills, I see the effects but do not know how He moves (John 3:8). Healing is always by degrees in a context of mercy with integrity. Without understanding the healing process fully, some of the ingredients are grace, truth, and time in the "I and Thou" relationship illuminated by Buber (1923/1958).

This commentary has been an effort to accept John McDargh's invitation to explore the mystery of God's healing work in the kingdom of therapy. I do not feel I have done it justice, but I do feel I have come to know him better. I hope he has come to know me. However, I am struggling still with a puzzle in his article left unsolved: the relationship between the Land of Oz and the Kingdom of God which seems synonymous, yet his subtitle suggests there is movement from Oz to God's Kingdom. I hope he will clarify this at a later time. This is my invitation to continue the conversation.

REFERENCES

Buber, M. (1958). *I and Thou* (R. G. Smith Trans.). New York: Scribner's. (Original work published 1923)

Carter, J. D. (1974). Personality and Christian maturity: A process congruity model. *Journal of Psychology and Theology, 2,* 190–201.

Carter, J. D. (1977). Secular and sacred models of psychology and religion. *Journal of Psychology and Theology, 5,* 197–208.

Carter, J. D., & Mohline, R. (1976). The nature and scope of integration. *Journal of Psychology and Theology, 4,* 3–14.

Carter, J. D., & Narramore, S. B. (1979). *The integration of psychology and theology.* Grand Rapids: Eerdmans.

Fleck, J. R., & Carter, J. D. (Eds.). (1981). *Psychology and Christianity: Integrated readings.* Nashville: Abingdon.

Hedges, L. (1983). *Listening perspectives in psychotherapy.* New York: Aronson.

Kuyper, A. (1963). *Principles of sacred theology.* Grand Rapids: Eerdmans. (Original work published 1909)

McDargh, J. (1994) Group psychotherapy as a spiritual discipline: From Oz to the Kingdom of God. *Journal of Psychology and Theology, 22,* 290–299.

Mitchell, S. A. (1988). *Relational concepts in psychoanalysis: An introduction.* Cambridge, MA: Harvard University Press.

Reply to Carter

John McDargh

I am particularly grateful for John Carter's (1994) generous personal response to the tacit invitation of my article (McDargh, 1994) to share how his own psycho-theological perspective proceeds from the story of his own spiritual journey. There is much in his distinctive, yet oddly parallel, life process that stimulated my own serious reflection. However, in the spirit of this on-going dialogue it seems most appropriate to respond to his last question to me. Like the canny clinician I take him to be, Carter poses what is actually an analytic question: "What all might you have intended by linking 'Oz' and the 'Kingdom of God' in the sub-title of your article?" For the fact of the matter is that the title itself was written as a spontaneous response to the request of the Guest Editor of this Special Issue of *JPT* to supply a title to a piece that I had originally called simply "Tuesday Night Meditation." Thus Carter's query is rather like the invitation to explore the possible meanings of an association in therapy. Was there an intuitive wisdom operative here, or is the connection overstated and not to be taken too seriously?

As it happens, subsequent to the writing of this piece two events occurred that have confirmed for me that I was on target in connecting the myth of the 1939 American film classic *The Wizard of Oz* to the psychological challenges faced by gay men in general and this group of individuals in particular. The first event was that in the final termination meeting of the person called "George" in this narrative, he expectedly brought into the group a gift for each man and formally presented these with an explanation why he had chosen each one. Each group member, including myself, received a representation of a different character from *The Wizard of Oz*. No great surprise; I was indeed the man behind the green curtain. What was striking however is that I had never suggested this myself or shared with the group my own still unformed intuitions about the salience and centrality of this story for its life.

The second event was my discovery of a remarkable chapter

in a book by Jungian analyst Robert Hopcke, *Jung, Jungians and Homosexuality*, which argues that the narrative of this movie has captured the imagination of gay men precisely because it presents in imaginative, archetypal fashion the core psychological and spiritual issues of gay male development (Hopcke, 1989). Hopcke is himself deeply indebted in his analysis to the work of Union Theological Seminary professor Ann Bedford Ulanov who in her book *The Feminine in Jungian Psychology and Christian Theology* first proposed that this movie mirrors the coming to awareness and individuation of contemporary women in a culture still deeply patriarchal (Ulanov, 1971). Hopcke (1989) writes:

> Obviously the popularity of Dorothy's story among gay men is evidence that this myth of persona strikes a deep chord in the souls of gay men. The persona task for Dorothy in the movie is to see beneath "what seems" in Kansas in order to know more fully "what is" in Oz. The movie, that is the tale of her stripping off her persona to find her soul, is a story of transformation. Kansas, once stifling, now has new depth and richness. Moreover, her sojourn in Oz requires that she accomplish the same persona removal task there. She must see beneath the ineffectuality of her male companions to aid them in developing true intelligence, heart and fearlessness. She must unmask the Wizard, find the witch's vulnerability, and go beneath Glinda's bright surface to uncover the wisdom that will bring her home. All these tasks have deep symbolic resonance for gay men who must, in Malcolm Boyd's words, "Take off the masks" and make a journey behind the inhospitable outer face of convention to find the color, life and power of their sexuality within. (p. 151)

Granting the psychological salience of this analysis, the question would still remain, what is the relationship of this process of recovery of a "true self" as effected in the practice of group psychotherapy to the eschatalogical labor of bringing about in time and eternity the reign of justice, holiness and peace and the fulfillment of God's creative purposes for human kind which the Gospel names "The Kingdom of God." In the more personalist idiom that both John Carter and I have employed in our discussion here, this may devolve to the question, "How do we see our work as group psychotherapists contributing to the realization of this gospel mandate?"

The answer to this question is by no means self evident. There are contemporary writers, of whom Christopher Lasch (1978) was one, who would argue that insofar as that religious vision is an inherently social and collective one, the work of psychotherapy is a privatized, narcissistic retreat from the pursuit of a genuinely common good. This may be recognized as a version of a now familiar, often highly ideological argument against "the culture of psychology." These positions are not without a corrective merit, but ultimately I believe they are overdrawn and themselves fracture the interpersonal and intrapsychic from the social and cultural. I lack the room to develop the full argument, but I have come to believe that only when individuals come to a level of greater intimacy with what they genuinely feel and achieve a sense of the authority of their own critically appropriated experience or "felt sense" do they have a basis for standing on the margins and "unmasking" the abuses of society and culture (Gendlin, 1987). The point to be retrieved from the critiques is that ultimately persons cannot stand alone. Like the tree grown from the mustard seed in which "all the birds of the air find rest" (Matt 13:31–32), the Kingdom of God, whatever it means, intends a reality which is greater and more inclusive than any single person. Thus I see groups such as the one described in my article and perhaps countless other such groups, whether self-directed or professionally facilitated, as potential cells of spiritual insurgency against the hegemony of any social order that would diminish, exclude, or oppress any of its members. They, like all of our social constructions, including our church communities, are always "on the way," never quite home, or, as John Carter put it, "pilgrims in the land of Oz."

REFERENCES

Carter, J. D. (1994). An invitation to grace and truth from the margins: Commentary on "Group psychotherapy as spiritual discipline: From Oz to the Kingdom of God." *Journal of Psychology and Theology, 22,* 300–301.

Gendlin, E. (1987). A philosophical critique of the concept of narcissism: The significance of the awareness movement. In D. Levin (Ed.), *Pathologies of the modern self: Post modern studies on narcissism, schizophrenia, and depression.* New York: New York University Press.

Hopcke, R. (1989). *Jung, Jungians and homosexuality.* Boston: Shambhala Press.

Lasch, C. (1978). *The culture of narcissism: American life in an age of diminishing expectations.* New York: Norton.

McDargh, J. (1994). Group psychotherapy as spiritual discipline: From Oz to the Kingdom of God. *Journal of Psychology and Theology, 22,* 290–299.

Ulanov, A. (1971). *The feminine in Jungian psychology and Christian theology.* Evanston: Northwestern University Press.

Section III

Characteristics of Religious Development

The Book of Her Life
("The Four Waters")

Teresa of Avila

CHAPTER 11

Tells of the reason for the failure to reach the perfect love of God in a short time. Begins to explain through a comparison four degrees of prayer. Goes on to deal here with the first degree. The doctrine is very beneficial for beginners and for those who do not have consolations in prayer.

1.   Well, let us speak now of those who are beginning to be servants of love. This doesn't seem to me to mean anything else than to follow resolutely by means of this path of prayer Him who has loved us so much. To be a servant of love is a dignity so great that it delights me in a wonderful way to think about it. For servile fear soon passes away if in this first state we proceed as we ought. O Lord of my soul and my good! When a soul is determined to love You by doing what it can to leave all and occupy itself better in this divine love, why don't You desire that it enjoy soon the ascent to the possession of perfect love? I have poorly expressed myself. I should have mentioned and complained that we ourselves do not desire this. The whole fault is ours if we don't soon reach the enjoyment of a dignity so great, for the perfect attainment of this true love of God brings with it every blessing. We are so miserly and so slow in giving ourselves entirely to God that since His Majesty does not desire that we enjoy something as precious as this without paying a high price, we do not fully prepare ourselves.

6.   I shall have to make use of some comparison, although I should like to excuse myself from this since I am a woman and write simply what they ordered me to write. But these spiritual matters for anyone who like myself has not gone through studies are so difficult to explain. I shall have to find some mode of explaining myself, and it may be less often that I hit upon a good comparison. Seeing so much stupidity will provide some recreation for your Reverence.

It seems now to me that I read or heard of this comparison— for since I have a bad memory, I don't know where or for what reason it was used; but it will be all right for my purposes. The beginner must realize that in order to give delight to the Lord he is starting to cultivate a garden on very barren soil, full of abominable weeds. His Majesty pulls up the weeds and plants good seed. Now let us keep in mind that all of this is already done by the time a soul is determined to practice prayer and has begun to make use of it. And with the help of God we must strive like good gardeners to get these plants to grow and take pains to water them so that they don't wither but come to bud and flower and give forth a most pleasant fragrance to provide refreshment for this Lord of ours. Then He will often come to take delight in this garden and find His joy among these virtues.

7.   But let us see now how it must be watered so that we may understand what we have to do, the labor this will cost us, whether the labor is greater than the gain, and for how long it must last. It seems to me the garden can be watered in four ways. You may draw water from a well (which is for us a lot of work). Or you may get it by means of a water wheel and aqueducts in such a way that it is obtained by turning the crank of the water wheel. (I have drawn it this way sometimes—the method involves less work than the other, and you get more water.) Or it may flow from a river or a stream. (The garden is watered much better by this means because the ground is more fully soaked, and there is no need to water so frequently—and much less work for the gardener.) Or the water may be provided by a great deal of rain. (For the Lord waters the garden without any work on our part—and this way is incomparably better than all the others mentioned.)

8.   Now, then, these four ways of drawing water in order to maintain this garden—because without water it will die—are

what are important to me and have seemed applicable in explaining the four degrees of prayer in which the Lord in His goodness has sometimes placed my soul. May it please His goodness that I manage to speak about them in a way beneficial for one of the persons who ordered me to write this, because within four months the Lord has brought him further than I got in seventeen years. This person has prepared himself better, and so without any labor of his own the flower garden is watered with all these four waters, although the last is still not given except in drops. But he is advancing in such a way that soon he will be immersed in it, with the help of the Lord. And I shall be pleased if you laugh should this way of explaining the matter appear foolish.

9   Beginners in prayer, we can say, are those who draw water from the well. This involves a lot of work on their own part, as I have said. They must tire themselves in trying to recollect their senses. Since they are accustomed to being distracted, this recollection requires much effort. They need to get accustomed to caring nothing at all about seeing or hearing, to practicing the hours of prayer, and thus to solitude and withdrawal—and to thinking on their past life. Although these beginners and the others as well must often reflect upon their past, the extent to which they must do so varies, as I shall say afterward. In the beginning such reflection is even painful, for they do not fully understand whether or not they are repentant of their sins. If they are, they are then determined to serve God earnestly. They must strive to consider the life of Christ—and the intellect grows weary in doing this.

These are the things we can do of ourselves, with the understanding that we do so by the help of God, for without this help as is already known we cannot have so much as a good thought. These things make up the beginning of fetching water from the well, and please God that it may be found. At least we are doing our part, for we are already drawing it out and doing what we can to water these flowers. God is so good that when for reason His Majesty knows—perhaps for our greater benefit—the well is dry and we, like good gardeners, do what lies in our power, He sustains the garden without water and makes the virtues grow. Here by "water" I am referring to tears and when there are no tears to interior tenderness and feelings of devotion.

10. But what will he do here who sees that after many days there is nothing but dryness, distaste, vapidness, and very little desire to come draw water? So little is the desire to do this that if he doesn't recall that doing so serves and gives pleasure to the Lord of the garden, and if he isn't careful to preserve the merits acquired in this service (and even what he hopes to gain from the tedious work of often letting the pail down into the well and pulling it back up without any water), he will abandon everything. It will frequently happen to him that he will even be unable to lift his arms for this work and unable to get a good thought. This discursive work with the intellect is what is meant by fetching water from the well.

But, as I am saying, what will the gardener do here? He will rejoice and be consoled and consider it the greatest favor to be able to work in the garden of so great an Emperor! Since he knows that this pleases the Lord and his intention must be not to please himself but to please the Lord, he gives the Lord much praise. For the Master has confidence in the gardener because he sees that without any pay he is so very careful about what he was told to do. This gardener helps Christ carry the cross and reflects that the Lord lived with it all during His life. He doesn't desire the Lord's kingdom here below or ever abandon prayer. And so he is determined, even though this dryness may last for his whole life, not to let Christ fall with the cross. The time will come when the Lord will repay him all at once. He doesn't fear that the labor is being wasted. He is serving a good Master whose eyes are upon him. He doesn't pay any attention to bad thoughts. He considers that the devil also represented them to St. Jerome in the desert.

11.   These labors take their toll. Being myself one who endured them for many years (for when I got a drop of water from this sacred well I thought God was granting me a favor), I know that they are extraordinary. It seems to me more courage is necessary for them than for many other labors of this world. But I have seen clearly that God does not leave one, even in this life, without a large reward; because it is certainly true that one of those hours in which the Lord afterward bestowed on me a taste of Himself repaid, it seems to me, all the anguish I suffered in persevering for a long time in prayer.

I am of the opinion that to some in the beginning and to

others afterward the Lord often desires to give those torments and the many other temptations that occur in order to try His lovers and know whether they will be able to drink the chalice and help Him carry the cross before He lays great treasures within them. I believe His Majesty desires to bring us along this way for our own good so that we may understand well what little we amount to. The Favors that come afterward are of such great worth that He desires first that before He gives them to us we see by experience our own worthlessness so that what happened to Lucifer will not happen to us.

12. My Lord, what do You do but that which is for the greater good of the soul You understand now to be Yours and which places itself in Your power so as to follow You wherever You go, even to death on the cross, and is determined to help You bear it and not leave You alone with it?

Whoever sees in himself this determination has no reason, no reason whatsoever, to fear. Spiritual persons, you have no reason to be afflicted. Once you are placed in so high a degree as to desire to commune in solitude with God and abandon the pastimes of the world, the most has been done. Praise His Majesty for that and trust in His goodness who never fails His friends. Conceal from your eyes the thought about why He gives devotion to one after such a few days and not to me after so many years. Let us believe that all is for our own greater good. Let His Majesty lead the way along the path He desires. We belong no longer to ourselves but to Him. He grants us a great favor in wanting us to desire to dig in His garden and be in the presence of its Lord who certainly is present with us. Should He desire that for some these plants and flowers grow by the water they draw, which He gives from this well, and for others without it, what difference does that make to me? Do, Lord, what You desire. May I not offend You. Don't let the virtues be lost, if You only out of Your goodness have already given me some. I desire to suffer, Lord, since You suffered. Let Your will be done in me in every way, and may it not please Your Majesty that something as precious as Your love be given to anyone who serves you only for the sake of consolations.

13. It should be carefully noted—and I say this because I know it through experience—that the soul that begins to walk

along this path of mental prayer with determination and that can succeed in paying little attention to whether this delight and tenderness is lacking or whether the Lord gives it (or to whether it has much consolation or no consolation) has travelled a great part of the way. However much it stumbles, it should not fear that it will turn back, because the building has been started on a solid foundation. This is true because the love of God does not consist in tears or in this delight and tenderness, which for the greater part we desire and find consolation in; but it consists in serving with justice and fortitude of soul and in humility. Without such service it seems to me we would be receiving everything and giving nothing.

14.   In the case of a poor little woman like myself, weak and with hardly any fortitude, it seems to me fitting that God lead me with gifts, as He now does, so that I might be able to suffer some trials He has desired me to bear. But when I see servants of God, men of prominence, learning, and high intelligence make so much fuss because God doesn't give them devotion, it annoys me to hear them. I do not mean that they shouldn't accept it if God gives it, and esteem it, because then His Majesty sees that this is appropriate. But when they don't have devotion, they shouldn't weary themselves. They should understand that since His Majesty doesn't give it, it isn't necessary; and they should be masters of themselves. They should believe that their desire for consolation is a fault. I have experienced and seen this. They should believe it denotes imperfection together with lack of freedom of spirit and the courage to accomplish something.

15.   Although I lay great stress on this because it is very important that beginners have such freedom and determination, I am not saying it so much for beginners as for others. For there are many who begin, yet they never reach the end. I believe this is due mainly to a failure to embrace the cross from the beginning; thinking they are doing nothing, they become afflicted. When the intellect ceases to work, they cannot bear it. But it is then perhaps that their will is being strengthened and fortified, although they may not be aware of this.

We should think that the Lord is not concerned about these inabilities. Even though they seem to us to be faults, they are not. His Majesty already knows our misery and our wretched nature better than we do ourselves, and He knows that these souls now desire to think of Him and love Him always. This determination is what He desires. The other affliction that we bring upon ourselves serves for nothing else than to disquiet the soul, and if it was incapable before of engaging in prayer for one hour, it will be so now for four. Very often this incapacity comes from some bodily disorder. I have a great deal of experience in this matter, and I know what I say is true because I have considered it carefully and discussed it afterward with spiritual persons. We are so miserable that our poor little imprisoned souls share in the miseries of the body; the changes in the weather and the rotating of the bodily humors often have the result that without their fault souls cannot do what they desire, but suffer in every way. If they seek to force themselves more during these times, the bad condition becomes worse and lasts longer. They should use discernment to observe when these bodily disorders may be the cause, and not smother the poor soul. They should understand that they are sick. The hour of prayer ought to be changed, and often this change will have to continue for some days. Let them suffer this exile as best they can. It is a great misfortune to a soul that loves God to see that it lives in this misery and cannot do what it desires because it has as wretched a guest as is this body.

16.   I have said they should use discernment because sometimes the devil is the cause. And so it isn't always good to abandon prayer when there is great distraction and disturbance in the intellect just as it isn't always good to torture the soul into doing what it cannot do.

There are other exterior things like works of charity and spiritual reading, although at times it will not even be fit for these. Let it then serve the body out of love of God—because many other times the body serves the soul—and engage in some spiritual pastimes such as holy conversations, provided they are truly so, or going to the country, as the confessor might counsel. Experience is a great help in all, for it teaches what is suitable for us; and God can be served in everything. His yoke is easy, and it is very helpful not to drag the soul along, as they say, but to lead it gently for the sake of its greater advantage.

17.   So I return to the advice—and even if I repeat it many times this doesn't matter—that it is very important that no one be

distressed or afflicted over dryness or noisy and distracting thoughts. If a person wishes to gain freedom of spirit and not be always troubled, let him begin by not being frightened by the cross, and he will see how the Lord also helps him carry it and he will gain satisfaction and profit from everything. For, clearly, if the well is dry, we cannot put water into it. True, we must not become neglectful; when there is water we should draw it out because then the Lord desires to multiply the virtues by this means.

CHAPTER 13

14.   The beginner needs counsel so as to see what helps him most. For this reason a master is very necessary providing he has experience. If he doesn't, he can be greatly mistaken and lead a soul without understanding it nor allowing it to understand itself. For since it sees that there is great merit in being subject to a master, it doesn't dare depart from what he commands it. I have come upon souls intimidated and afflicted for whom I felt great pity because the one who taught them had no experience; and there was one person who didn't know what to do with herself. Since they do not understand spiritual things, these masters afflict soul and body and obstruct progress. One of these souls spoke to me about a master who held her bound for eight years and wouldn't let her go beyond self knowledge; the Lord had already brought her to the prayer of quiet, and so she suffered much tribulation.

15.   This path of self knowledge must never be abandoned, nor is there on this journey a soul so much a giant that it has no need to return often to the stage of an infant and a suckling. And this should never be forgotten. Perhaps I shall speak of it more often because it is very important. There is no stage of prayer so sublime that it isn't necessary to return often to the beginning. Along this path of prayer, self knowledge and the thought of one's sins is the bread with which all palates must be fed no matter how delicate they may be; they cannot be sustained without this bread. It must be eaten within bounds, nonetheless. Once a soul sees that it is now submissive and understands clearly that it has noth-

ing good of itself and is aware both of being ashamed before so great a King and of repaying so little of the great amount it owes Him—what need is there to waste time here? We must go on to other things that the Lord places before us; and there is no reason to leave them aside, for His Majesty knows better than we what is fitting for us to eat.

22.   I have wandered greatly from the subject I began to speak about. But everything is a subject for beginners that their journey on so lofty a road might begin on the true road. Now returning to what I was saying about Christ bound at the pillar: it is good to reflect awhile and think about the pains He suffered there, and why, and who He is, and the love with which He suffered them. But one should not always weary oneself in seeking these reflections but just remain there in His presence with the intellect quiet. And if a person is able he should occupy himself in looking at Christ who is looking at him, and he should speak, and petition, and humble himself, and delight in the Lord's presence, and remember that he is unworthy of being there. When he can do this, even though it may be at the beginning of prayer, he will derive great benefit; and this manner of prayer has many advantages—at least my soul derived them.

I don't know if I have been successful in speaking about this. Your Reverence will be the judge. May it please the Lord that I succeed in always giving Him pleasure, amen.

CHAPTER 14

Begins to explain the second degree of prayer in which the Lord now starts to give the soul a more special kind of consolation. Explains how this experience is supernatural. This matter is worth noting.

1.   It has been explained now how the garden is watered by labor and the use of one's arms, drawing the water up from the well. Let us speak now of the second manner, ordained by the Lord of the garden, for getting water; that is, by turning the crank of a water wheel and by aqueducts, the gardener obtains more

water with less labor; and he can rest without having to work constantly. Well, this method applied to what they call the prayer of quiet is what I now want to discuss.

2.   Here the soul begins to be recollected and comes upon something supernatural because in no way can it acquire this prayer through any efforts it may make. True, at one time it seemingly got tired turning the crank, and working with the intellect, and filling the aqueducts. But here the water is higher, and so the labor is much less than that required in pulling it up from the well. I mean that the water is closer because grace is more clearly manifest to the soul.

In this prayer the faculties are gathered within so as to enjoy that satisfaction with greater delight. But they are not lost, nor do they sleep. Only the will is occupied in such a way that, without knowing how, it becomes captive; it merely consents to God allowing Him to imprison it as one who well knows how to be the captive of its lover. O Jesus and my Lord! How valuable is Your love to us here! It holds our love so bound that it doesn't allow it the freedom during that time to love anything else but You.

3.   The other two faculties help the will to be capable of enjoying so much good—although sometimes it happens that even though the will is united, they are very unhelpful. But then it shouldn't pay any attention to them; rather it should remain in its joy and quietude. Because if the will desires to gather in these faculties, they both get lost. They are like doves that are dissatisfied with the food the owner of the dovecot gives them without their having to work. They go to look for food elsewhere, but they find it so scarce that they return. And thus these faculties go away and then come back to see if the will might give them what it enjoys. If the Lord desires to throw them some food, they stop; and if not, they return to their search. And they must think they are benefitting the will; and sometimes in desiring the memory or imagination to represent to the will what they're enjoying, they do the will harm. Well, then, be advised to behave toward them as I shall explain.

4.   All this that takes place here brings with it the greatest consolation and with so little labor that prayer does not tire one, even though it lasts for a long while. The intellect's work here is very slow paced, and it obtains a lot more water than it pulled out

of the well. The tears God gives are now accompanied by joy; however, although they are experienced, there is no striving for them.

5. This water of great blessings and favors that the Lord gives here makes the virtues grow incomparably better than in the previous degree of prayer, for the soul is now ascending above its misery and receiving a little knowledge of the delights of glory. This water I believe makes the virtues grow better and also brings the soul much closer to the true Virtue, which is God, from whence come all the virtues. His Majesty is beginning to communicate Himself to this soul, and He wants it to experience how He is doing so.

In arriving here it begins soon to lose its craving for earthly things—and little wonder! It sees clearly that one moment of the enjoyment of glory cannot be experienced here below, neither are there riches, or sovereignties, or honors, or delights that are able to provide a brief moment of that happiness, for it is a true happiness that, it is seen, satisfies us. In earthly things it would seem to me a marvel were we ever to understand just where we can find this satisfaction, for there is never lacking in these earthly things both the "yes" and the "no." During the time of this prayer, everything is "yes." The "no" comes afterward upon seeing that the delight is ended and that one cannot recover it nor does one know how. Were someone to crush himself with penances and prayer and all the rest, it would profit him little if the Lord did not desire to give this delight. God in His greatness desires that this soul understand that He is so close it no longer needs to send Him messengers but can speak with Him itself and not by shouting since He is so near that when it merely moves its lips, He understands it.

6. It seems impertinent to say this since we know that God always understands us and is with us. There is no doubt about this understanding and presence. But our Emperor and Lord desires that in this prayer we know that He understands us, and what His presence does, and that He wants to begin to work in the soul in a special way. All of this that the Lord desires is manifest in the great interior and exterior satisfaction He gives the soul and in the difference there is, as I said, between this delight and happiness and the delights of earth, for this delight seems to fill the void that

through our sins we have caused in the soul. This satisfaction takes place in its very intimate depths, and the soul doesn't know where the satisfaction comes from or how, nor frequently does it know what to do or what to desire or what to ask for. It seems it has found everything at once and doesn't know what it has found.

Nor do I know how to explain this experience because for so many things learning is necessary. Here it would be helpful to explain well the difference between a general and a particular grace—for there are many who are ignorant of this difference—and how the Lord desires that the soul in this prayer almost see with its own eyes, as they say, this particular grace. Learning is also required to explain many other things, which I perhaps did not express correctly. But since what I say is going to be checked by persons who will recognize any error, I'm not worrying about it. In matters of theology as well as in those of the spirit I know that I can be mistaken; yet, since this account will end in good hands, these learned men will understand and remove what is erroneous.

CHAPTER 15

Continues on the same subject and gives some advice about how to act in this prayer of quiet. Discusses the fact that many souls reach this prayer but few pass beyond. Knowledge of the things touched on here is very necessary and beneficial.

1.   Now let's return to the subject. This quietude and recollection is something that is clearly felt through the satisfaction and peace bestowed on the soul, along with great contentment and calm and a very gentle delight in the faculties. It seems to the soul, since it hasn't gone further, that there's nothing left to desire and that it should willingly say with St. Peter that it will make its dwelling there. It dares not move or stir, for it seems that good will slip through its hands—nor would it even want to breathe sometimes. The poor little thing doesn't understand that since by its own efforts it can do nothing to draw that good to itself, so much less will it be able to keep it for longer than the Lord desires.

I have already mentioned that in this first recollection and quiet the soul's faculties do not cease functioning. But the soul is so satisfied with God that as long as the recollection lasts, the quiet and calm are not lost since the will is united with God even though the two faculties are distracted; in fact, little by little the will brings the intellect and the memory back to recollection. Because even though the will may not be totally absorbed, it is so well occupied, without knowing how, that no matter what efforts the other two faculties make, they cannot take away its contentment and joy. But rather with hardly any effort the will is gradually helped so that this little spark of love of God may not go out.

2. May it please His Majesty to give me grace to explain this state well because there are many, many souls who reach it but few that pass beyond; and I don't know whose fault it is. Most surely God does not fail, for once His Majesty has granted a soul the favor of reaching this stage, I don't believe He will fail to grant it many more favors unless through its own fault.

It is very important that the soul reaching this stage realize the great dignity of its state and the great favor the Lord has bestowed on it and how with good reason it must not belong to the earth because it now seems His goodness will make it a citizen of heaven, provided it doesn't stop through its own fault; and unhappy it will be if it turns back. I think turning back would mean falling to the bottom, as I was doing, if the mercy of the Lord hadn't rescued me. For the most part, in my opinion, this turning back will come through serious faults; nor is it possible to leave so much good without the blindness caused by much evil.

3. Thus, for the love of the Lord, I beg those whom His Majesty has so highly favored in the attainment of this state that they understand it and esteem it with a humble and holy confidence so as not to return to the fleshpots of Egypt. If through weakness and wickedness and a miserable nature they should fall, as I did, let them keep ever in mind the good they have lost and be suspicious and walk with the fear—for they are right in doing so—that if they don't return to prayer, they will go from bad to worse. What I call a true fall is abhorrence of the path by which one gained so much good; and to these souls I am speaking. For I am not saying that they should never offend God or fall into sin, although it would be right for anyone who has begun to receive

these favors to be very much on guard against sinning; but we are miserable creatures. What I advise strongly is not to abandon prayer, for in prayer a person will understand what he is doing and win repentance from the Lord and fortitude to lift himself up. And you must believe that if you give up prayer, you are, in my opinion, courting danger. I don't know if I understand what I'm saying because, as I said, I'm judging by myself.

4.   This prayer, then, is a little spark of the Lord's true love which He begins to enkindle in the soul; and He desires that the soul grow in the understanding of what this love accompanied by delight is. For anyone who has experience, it is impossible not to understand soon that this little spark cannot be acquired. Yet, this nature of ours is so eager for delights that it tries everything; but it is quickly left cold because however much it may desire to light the fire and obtain this delight, it doesn't seem to be doing anything else than throwing water on it and killing it. If this quietude and recollection and little spark is from God's spirit and not a delight given by the devil or procured by ourselves, it will be noticed no matter how small it is. And if a person doesn't extinguish it through his own fault, it is what will begin to enkindle the large fire that (as I shall mention in its place) throws forth flames of the greatest love of God which His Majesty gives to perfect souls.

6.   What the soul must do during these times of quiet amounts to no more than proceeding gently and noiselessly. What I call noise is running about with the intellect looking for many words and reflections so as to give thanks for this gift and piling up one's sins and faults in order to see that the gift is unmerited. Everything is motion here; the intellect is representing, and the memory hurrying about. For certainly these faculties tire me out from time to time; and although I have a poor memory, I cannot subdue it. The will calmly and wisely must understand that one does not deal well with God by force and that our efforts are like the careless use of large pieces of wood which smother this little spark. One should realize this and humbly say: "Lord, what am I capable of here? What has the servant to do with the Lord—or earth with heaven?" Or other words that at this time come to mind out of love and well grounded in the

knowledge that what is said is the truth. And one should pay no attention to the intellect, for it is a grinding mill. The will may desire to share what it enjoys or may work to recollect the intellect, for often it will find itself in this union and calm while the intellect wanders about aimlessly. It is better that the will leave the intellect alone than go after it, and that it remain like a wise bee in the recollection and in enjoyment of that gift. For if no bee were to enter the beehive and each were employed in going after the other, no honey could be made.

14. In the progress they observe in themselves they will know that the devil is not the cause if, even though they fall again, there remains a sign that the Lord was present in their prayer; and it is that they rise again quickly. There are other signs as well which I shall now mention. When the prayer comes from God's spirit, there is no need to go dredging up things in order to derive some humility and shame because the Lord Himself gives this prayer in a manner very different from that which we gain through our nice little reasonings. For such humility is nothing in comparison with the true humility the Lord with His light here teaches and which causes an embarrassment that undoes one. It is well known that God gives a knowledge that makes us realize we have no good of ourselves; and the greater the favors, the greater is this knowledge. He bestows a strong desire to advance in prayer and not abandon it no matter what trial may come upon one. The soul offers itself up in all things. It feels sure, while still being humble and fearing, that it will be saved. He casts out from it all servile fear and grants a more mature trusting fear. It is aware of the beginning of a love of God that has much less self-interest. It desires periods of solitude in order to enjoy that good more.

CHAPTER 16

Treats of the third degree of prayer. Explains sublime matters and what the soul that reaches this stage can do and the effects produced by these great favors of the Lord. This prayer lifts the soul up in the praises of God and brings wonderful consolation to whoever attains it.

1. Let us come now to speak of the third water by which this garden is irrigated, that is, the water flowing from a river or spring. By this means the garden is irrigated with much less labor, although some labor is required to direct the flow of the water. The Lord so desires to help the gardener here that He Himself becomes practically the gardener and the one who does everything.

This prayer is a sleep of the faculties: the faculties neither fail entirely to function nor understand how they function. The consolation, the sweetness, and the delight are incomparably greater than that experienced in the previous prayer. The water of grace rises up to the throat of this soul since it can no longer move forward; nor does it know how; nor can it move backward. It would desire to enjoy the greatest glory. It is like a person who already has the candle in his hand and for whom little time is left before dying the death he desires: he is rejoicing in that agony with the greatest delight describable. This experience doesn't seem to me to be anything else than an almost complete death to all earthly things and an enjoyment of God.

I don't know any other terms for describing it or how to explain it. Nor does the soul then know what to do because it doesn't know whether to speak or to be silent, whether to laugh or to weep. This prayer is a glorious foolishness, a heavenly madness where the true wisdom is learned; and it is for the soul a most delightful way of enjoying.

2. In fact five or even six years ago the Lord often gave me this prayer in abundance, and I didn't understand it; nor did I know how to speak of it. Thus it was my intention, at this point, to say very little or nothing at all. I did understand clearly that it was not a complete union of all the faculties and that this type of prayer was more excellent than the previous one. But I confess that I couldn't discern or understand where the difference lay. I believe that on account of the humility your Reverence has shown in desiring to be helped by as simple-minded a person as myself, the Lord today after Communion granted me this prayer; and interrupting my thanksgiving, He put before me these comparisons, taught me the manner of explaining it, and what the soul must do here. Certainly I was startled and I understood at once. Often I had been as though bewildered and inebriated in this love, and never was I able to understand its nature. I understood

clearly that it was God's work, but I couldn't understand how He was working in this stage. For the truth of the matter is that the faculties are almost totally united with God but not so absorbed as not to function. I am extremely pleased that I now understand it. Blessed be the Lord who so favored me!

CHAPTER 18

Discusses the fourth degree of prayer. Begins to offer an excellent explanation of the great dignity the Lord bestows upon the soul in this state. Gives much encouragement to those who engage in prayer that they might strive to attain so high a stage since it can be reached on earth, although not by merit but through God's goodness. This should be read attentively, for the explanation is presented in a very subtle way and there are many noteworthy things.

1.   May the Lord teach me the words necessary for explaining something about the fourth water. Clearly His favor is necessary, even more so than for what was explained previously. In the previous prayer, since the soul was conscious of the world, it did not feel that it was totally dead—for we can speak of this last prayer in such a way. But, as I said, the soul has its senses by which it feels its solitude and understands that it is in the world; and it uses exterior things to make known what it feels, even though this may be through signs.

In all the prayer and modes of prayer that were explained, the gardener does some work, even though in these latter modes the work is accompanied by so much glory and consolation for the soul that it would never want to abandon this prayer. As a result, the prayer is not experienced as work but as glory. In this fourth water the soul isn't in possession of its senses, but it rejoices without understanding what it is rejoicing in. It understands that it is enjoying a good in which are gathered together all goods, but this good is incomprehensible. All the senses are occupied in this joy in such a way that none is free to be taken up with any other exterior or interior thing.

In the previous degrees, the senses are given freedom to

show some signs of the great joy they feel. Here in this fourth water the soul rejoices incomparably more; but it can show much less since no power remains in the body, nor does the soul have any power to communicate its joy. At such a time, everything would be a great obstacle and a torment and a hindrance to its repose. And I say that if this prayer is the union of all the faculties, the soul is unable to communicate its joy even though it may desire to do so—I mean while being in the prayer. And if it were able, then this wouldn't be union.

2.   How this prayer they call union comes about and what it is, I don't know how to explain. These matters are expounded in mystical theology; I wouldn't know the proper vocabulary. Neither do I understand what the mind is; nor do I know how it differs from the soul or the spirit. It all seems to be the same thing to me, although the soul sometimes goes forth from itself. The way this happens is comparable to what happens when a fire is burning and flaming, and it sometimes becomes a forceful blaze. The flame then shoots very high above the fire, but the flame is not by that reason something different from the fire but the same flame that is in the fire. Your Reverence with your learning will understand this, for I don't know what else to say.

3.   What I'm attempting to explain is what the soul feels when it is in this divine union. What union is we already know since it means that two separate things become one. O my Lord, how good You are! May You be blessed forever! May all things praise You, my God, for You have so loved us that we can truthfully speak of this communication which You engage in with souls even in our exile! And even in the case of those who are good, this still shows great generosity and magnanimity. In fact, it is Your communication, my Lord; and You give it in the manner of who You are. O infinite Largess, how magnificent are Your works! It frightens one whose intellect is not occupied with things of the earth that he has no intellect by which he can understand divine truths. That you bestow such sovereign favors on souls that have offended You so much certainly brings my intellect to a halt; and when I begin to think about this, I'm unable to continue. Where can the intellect go that would not be a turning back since it doesn't know how to give you thanks for such great favors? Sometimes I find it a remedy to speak absurdities.

Signs of Transition in
The Ascent of Mount Carmel

John of the Cross

BOOK II

Chapter 13: The signs of recognizing in spiritual persons when they should discontinue discursive meditation and pass on to the state of contemplation.

1. To avoid obscurity in this doctrine it will be opportune to point out in this chapter when one ought to discontinue discursive meditation (work through images, forms, and figures) so that the practice will not be abandoned sooner or later than required by the spirit. Just as it is fit to abandon it at the proper time that it may not be a hindrance in the journey to God, it is also necessary not to abandon this imaginative meditation before the due time so that there be no regression. For though the apprehensions of these faculties are not a proximate means toward union for proficients, they are a remote means for beginners. By these sensitive means beginners dispose their spirit and habituate it to spiritual things, and at the same time they void their senses of all other base, temporal, secular, and natural forms and images.

Hence we shall delineate some signs and indications by which one can judge whether or not it is the opportune time for the spiritual person to discontinue meditation.

2. The first is the realization that one cannot make discursive meditation or receive satisfaction from it as before. Dryness is now the outcome of fixing the senses upon subjects which

formerly provided satisfaction. As long as one can, however, make discursive meditation and draw out satisfaction, one must not abandon this method. Meditation must only be discontinued when the soul is placed in that peace and quietude to be spoken of in the third sign.

3. The second sign is an awareness of a disinclination to fix the imagination or sense faculties upon other particular objects, exterior or interior. I am not affirming that the imagination will cease to come and go (even in deep recollection it usually wanders freely), but that the person is disinclined to fix it purposely upon extraneous things.

4. The third and surest sign is that a person likes to remain alone in loving awareness of God, without particular consider-ations, in interior peace and quiet and repose, and without the acts and exercises (at least discursive, those in which one pro-gresses from point to point) of the intellect, memory and will; and that he prefers to remain only in the general, loving awareness and knowledge we mentioned, without any particular knowledge or understanding.

5. To leave safely the state of meditation and sense and enter that of contemplation and spirit, the spiritual person must observe within himself at least these three signs together.

6. It is insufficient to possess the first without the second. It could be that the inability to imagine and meditate derives from one's dissipation and lack of diligence. The second sign, the disin-clination and absence of desire to think about extraneous things, must be present. When this inability to concentrate the imagina-tion and sense faculties upon the things of God proceeds from dissipation and tepidity, there is then a yearning to dwell upon other things and an inclination to give up the meditation.

Neither is the realization of the first and second sign suffi-cient, if the third sign is not observed together with them. When one is incapable of making discursive meditation upon the things of God and disinclined to consider subjects extraneous to God, the cause could be melancholia or some other kind of humor in the heart or brain capable of producing a certain stupefaction and suspension of the sense faculties. This anomaly would be the explanation for want of thought or of desire and inclination for thought. It would foster in a person the desire to remain in that delightful ravishment.

Because of this danger, the third sign, the loving knowledge and awareness in peace, etc., is necessary.

7.   Actually, at the beginning of this state the loving knowledge is almost unnoticeable. There are two reasons for this: first, ordinarily the incipient loving knowledge is extremely subtle and delicate, and almost imperceptible; second, a person who is habituated to the exercise of meditation, which is wholly sensible, hardly perceives or feels this new insensible, purely spiritual experience. This is especially so when through failure to understand it he does not permit himself any quietude, but strives after the other more sensory experience. Although the interior peace is more abundant, the individual allows no room for its experience and enjoyment.

But the more habituated he becomes to this calm, the deeper his experience of the general, loving knowledge of God will grow. This knowledge is more enjoyable than all other things, because without the soul's labor it affords peace, rest, savor, and delight.

The Dark Night

John of the Cross

BOOK I

Chapter 9: Signs for discerning whether a spiritual person is treading the path of this sensory night and purgation.

1. Because the origin of these aridities may not be the sensory night and purgation, but sin and imperfection, or weakness and lukewarmness, or some bad humor or bodily indisposition, I will give some signs here for discerning whether the dryness is the result of this purgation or of one of these other defects. I find there are three principal signs for knowing this.

2. The *first* is that as these souls do not get satisfaction or consolation from the things of God, they do not get any out of creatures either. Since God puts a soul in this dark night in order to dry up and purge its sensory appetite, He does not allow it to find sweetness or delight in anything.

Through this sign it can in all likelihood be inferred that this dryness and distaste is not the outcome of newly committed sins and imperfections. If this were so, some inclination or propensity to look for satisfaction in something other than the things of God would be felt in the sensory part. For when the appetite is allowed indulgence in some imperfection, the soul immediately feels an inclination toward it, little or great in proportion to the degree of its satisfaction and attachment.

Yet, because the want of satisfaction in earthly or heavenly things could be the product of some indisposition or melancholic humor, which frequently prevents one from being satisfied with anything, the second sign or condition is necessary.

3. *The second sign* for the discernment of this purgation is that the memory ordinarily turns to God solicitously and with painful care, and the soul thinks it is not serving God but turning back, because it is aware of this distaste for the things of God. Hence it is obvious that this aversion and dryness is not the fruit of laxity and tepidity, for a lukewarm person does not care much for the things of God nor is he inwardly solicitous about them.

There is, consequently, a notable difference between dryness and lukewarmness. A lukewarm person is very lax and remiss in his will and spirit, and has no solicitude about serving God; a person suffering the purgative dryness is ordinarily solicitous, concerned, and pained about not serving God. Even though the dryness may be furthered by melancholia or some other humor—as it often is—it does not thereby fail to produce its purgative effect in the appetite, for the soul will be deprived of every satisfaction and concerned only about God. If this humor is the entire cause, everything ends in disgust and does harm to one's nature, and there are none of these desires to serve God which accompany the purgative dryness. Even though, in this purgative dryness, the sensory part of the soul is very cast down, slack, and feeble in its actions, because of the little satisfaction it finds, the spirit is ready and strong.

4. The reason for this dryness is that God transfers His goods and strength from sense to spirit. Since the sensory part of the soul is incapable of the goods of spirit, it remains deprived, dry and empty, and thus, while the spirit is tasting, the flesh tastes nothing at all and becomes weak in its work. But the spirit through this nourishment grows stronger and more alert, and becomes more solicitous than before about not failing God. If in the beginning the soul does not experience this spiritual savor and delight, but dryness and distaste, it is because of the novelty involved in this exchange. Since its palate is accustomed to these other sensory tastes, the soul still sets its eyes on them. And since, also, its spiritual palate is neither purged nor accommodated for so subtle a taste, it is unable to experience the spiritual savor and good until gradually prepared by means of this dark and obscure

night; the soul rather experiences dryness and distaste because of a lack of the gratification it formerly enjoyed so readily.

5. Those whom God begins to lead into these desert solitudes are like the children of Israel; when God began giving them the heavenly food which contained in itself all savors and, as is there mentioned, changed to whatever taste each one hungered after [Wis. 16:20, 21], they nonetheless felt a craving for the tastes of the flesh-meats and onions they had eaten in Egypt, for their palate was accustomed and attracted to them more than to the delicate sweetness of the angelic manna. And in the midst of that heavenly food, they wept and sighed for fleshmeat. [Nm. 11:4–6] The baseness of our appetite is such that it makes us long for our own miserable goods and feel aversion for the incommunicable heavenly good.

Yet, as I say, when these aridities are the outcome of the purgative way of the sensory appetite, the spirit feels the strength and energy to work, which is obtained from the substance of that interior food, even though in the beginning, for the reason just mentioned, it may not experience the savor. This food is the beginning of a contemplation that is dark and dry to the senses. Ordinarily this contemplation, which is secret and hidden from the very one who receives it, imparts to the soul, together with the dryness and emptiness it produces in the senses, an inclination to remain alone and in quietude. And the soul will be unable to dwell upon any particular thought, nor will it have the desire to do so.

If those in whom this occurs know how to remain quiet, without care or solicitude about any interior or exterior work, they will soon in that unconcern and idleness delicately experience the interior nourishment. This reflection is so delicate that usually if the soul desires or tries to experience it, it cannot. For, as I say, this contemplation is active while the soul is in idleness and unconcern. It is like air that escapes when one tries to grasp it in one's hand.

7. In this sense we can interpret what the Spouse said to the bride in the Canticle: *Turn your eyes from me, because they make me fly away.* [Ct. 6:4] God conducts the soul along so different a path, and so puts it in this state, that a desire to work with the faculties would hinder rather than help His work; whereas in the beginning of the spiritual life everything is quite the contrary.

The reason is that now in this state of contemplation, when the soul has left discursive meditation and entered the state of proficients, it is God who works in it. He therefore binds the interior faculties and leaves no support in the intellect, nor satisfaction in the will, nor remembrance in the memory. At this time a person's own efforts are of no avail, but an obstacle to the interior peace and work God is producing in the spirit through that dryness of sense. Since this peace is something spiritual and delicate, its fruit is quiet, delicate, solitary, satisfying, and peaceful, and far removed from all these other gratifications of beginners, which are very palpable and sensory. For this is the peace that David says God speaks in the soul in order to make it spiritual. [Ps. 84:9] The third sign follows from this one.

8.   The *third sign* for the discernment of this purgation of the senses is the powerlessness, in spite of one's efforts, to meditate and make use of the imagination, the interior sense, as was one's previous custom. At this time God does not communicate Himself through the senses as He did before, by means of the discursive analysis and synthesis of ideas, but begins to communicate Himself through pure spirit by an act of simple contemplation, in which there is no discursive succession of thought. The exterior and interior senses of the lower part of the soul cannot attain to this contemplation. As a result the imaginative power and phantasy can no longer rest in any consideration nor find support in it.

9.   From the third sign it can be deduced that this dissatisfaction of the faculties is not the fruit of any bad humor. For if it were, a person would be able with a little care to return to his former exercises and find support for his faculties when that humor passed away, for it is by its nature changeable. In the purgation of the appetite this return is not possible, because upon entering it the powerlessness to meditate always continues. It is true, though, that at times in the beginning the purgation of some souls is not continuous in such a way that they are always deprived of sensory satisfaction and the ability to meditate. Perhaps, because of their weakness, they cannot be weaned all at once. Nevertheless, if they are to advance, they will ever enter further into the purgation and leave further behind their work of the senses. Those who do not walk the road of contemplation act very differently. This night of

the aridity of the senses is not so continuous in them, for sometimes they experience the aridities and at other times not, and sometimes they can meditate and at other times they cannot. God places them in this night solely to exercise and humble them, and reform their appetite lest in their spiritual life they foster a harmful attraction toward sweetness. But He does not do so in order to lead them to the life of the spirit, which is contemplation. For God does not bring to contemplation all those who purposely exercise themselves in the way of the spirit, nor even half. Why? He best knows. As a result He never completely weans their senses from the breasts of considerations and discursive meditations, except for some short periods and at certain seasons, as we said.

Rules for the Discernment of Spirits, from the Spiritual Exercises

Ignatius Loyola

[313]. RULES TO HELP PERSONS GET IN TOUCH WITH AND UNDERSTAND IN SOME MANNER THE DIVERSE MOTIONS WHICH ARE PROMPTED IN THEM, SO THAT THEY MAY RECEIVE THE GOOD ONES AND EXPEL THE EVIL ONES. THESE RULES ARE MORE APPROPRIATE TO THE FIRST WEEK.[1]

[314]. Rule 1. In the case of those persons who go from mortal sin to mortal sin, the customary tactic of the enemy is to put before them illusory gratifications, prompting them to imagine sensual delights and pleasures, the better to hold them and make them grow in their vices and sins. With such persons, the good spirit employs a contrary tactic, through their rational power of moral judgment causing pain and remorse in their consciences.

[315]. Rule 2. As for those persons who are intensely concerned with purging away their sins and ascending from good to better in the service of God our Lord, the mode of acting on them is contrary to that [described] in the first rule. For then it is connatural to the evil spirit to gnaw at them, to sadden them, to thrust obstacles in their way, disquieting them with false reasons for the sake of impeding progress. It is connatural to the good spirit to give courage and active energy, consolations, tears, inspirations and a quiet mind, giving ease of action and taking away obstacles for the sake of progress in doing good.

[316]. Rule 3. Concerning spiritual consolation. I name it [spiritual] consolation when some inner motion is prompted in the person,[2] of such a kind that he begins to be aflame with love of his Creator and Lord, and, consequently, when he cannot love any created thing on the face of the earth in itself but only in the Creator of them all. Likewise [I call it consolation] when a person pours out tears moving to love of his Lord, whether it be for sorrow over his sins, or over the passion of Christ our Lord, or over other things directly ordered to his service and praise. Finally, I call [spiritual] consolation every increase of hope, faith, and charity, and every inward gladness which calls and attracts to heavenly things and to one's personal salvation, bringing repose and peace in his Creator and Lord.

[317]. Rule 4. Concerning spiritual desolation. I call [spiritual] desolation everything the contrary of [what is described in] the third rule, for example, gloominess of soul, confusion, a movement to contemptible earthly things, disquiet from various commotions and temptations, [all this] tending toward distrust, without hope, without love; finding oneself thoroughly indolent, tepid, sad, and as if separated from one's Creator and Lord. For just as [spiritual] consolation is contrary to [spiritual] desolation, in the same way the thoughts which spring from [spiritual] consolation are contrary to the thoughts which spring from [spiritual] desolation.

[318]. Rule 5. The time of [spiritual] desolation is no time at all to change purposes and decisions with which one was content the day before such desolation, or the decision with which one was content during the previous consolation. It is, rather, a time to remain firm and constant in these. For just as in [spiritual] consolation the good spirit generally leads and counsels us, so in [spiritual] desolation does the evil spirit. By the latter's counsels we cannot find the way to a right decision.

[319]. Rule 6. Granted that in [spiritual] desolation we ought not to change our previous purposes, it helps greatly to change ourselves intensely in ways contrary to the aforesaid desolation,

for instance, by insisting more on prayer, on meditation, on much examination, and on extending ourselves to do penance in some fitting manner.

[320]. Rule 7. Let one who is in [spiritual] desolation consider how the Lord has left him to his natural powers, so that he may prove himself while resisting the disturbances and temptations of the enemy. He is, indeed, able to do so with the divine aid, which always remains with him even though he does not clearly perceive it. For, although the Lord has withdrawn from him his bubbling ardor, surging love, and intense grace, nevertheless, he leaves enough grace to go on toward eternal salvation.

[321]. Rule 8. Let him who is in [spiritual] desolation work at holding on in patience, which goes contrary to the harassments that come on him; and, while taking unremitting action against such desolation, as said in the sixth rule, let him keep in mind that he will soon be consoled.

[322]. Rule 9. There are three principal causes which explain why we find ourselves [spiritually] desolate. The first is that we are tepid, indolent, or negligent in our spiritual exercises; and, as a result of our own failings, [spiritual] consolation departs from us. The second is that it serves to put our worth to the test, showing how much we will extend ourselves in serving and praising God without so much pay in consolations and increased graces. The third is this: spiritual desolation serves to give us a true recognition and understanding, grounding an inward experiential perception of the fact that we cannot ourselves attain to or maintain surging devotion, intense love, tears, or any other spiritual consolation, but rather that all is gift and grace from God our Lord. So, we do not build a nest on another's property, elevating our mind in a certain pride or vain-glory, giving ourselves credit for devotion or other constituents of spiritual consolation.

[323]. Rule 10. Let him who is in consolation think how he will bear himself in the desolation which will follow, gathering energy anew for that time.

[324]. Rule 11. Let him who is [spiritually] consoled set about humbling and lowering himself as much as he can, reflecting on how pusillanimous he is in the time of [spiritual] desolation without God's grace or consolation. On the other hand, let him who is in [spiritual] desolation keep in mind that, drawing strength from his Creator and Lord, he has with divine grace sufficiently great power to resist all his enemies.

[325]. Rule 12. The enemy acts like a shrewish woman, being weak and willful;[3] for it is connatural to such a woman in a quarrel with some man to back off when he boldly confronts her; and on the contrary when, losing courage, he begins to retreat, the anger vengeance, and ferocity of the woman swell beyond measure. In like manner, it is connatural to the enemy to fall back and lose courage, with his temptations fading out, when the person performing spiritual exercises presents a bold front against the temptations of the enemy, by doing what is diametrically the opposite. If, on the contrary, the person engaged in spiritual exercises begins to be fearful and to lose courage while suffering temptations, there is no beast on the face of the earth so fierce as is the enemy of human kind in prosecuting his wicked intention with such swelling malice.

[326]. Rule 13. Likewise he behaves as a seducer in seeking to carry on a clandestine affair and not be exposed. When such a frivolous fellow makes dishonourable advances to the daughter of a good father or the wife of a good husband, he wants his words and seductions to be secret. On the contrary, he is greatly displeased when the daughter discovers to her father or the wife to her husband his fraudulent talk and lewd design; for he readily gathers that he will not be able to carry out the undertaking he has initiated. In like manner, when the enemy of human kind insinuates into the faithful person his wiles and seductions, he intensely desires that they be received in secret and kept secret. It dispirits him greatly when one discloses them to a good confessor or to another spiritual person who is acquainted with his trickery and malice; for when his evident trickery is brought to light, he gets the idea that he will not be able to realize the evil plan he has set in motion.

[327]. Rule 14. So also, in order to conquer and plunder what he desires, the enemy of human kind acts like a caudillo. For, just as a military commander-in-chief pitching camp and exploring what the forces of a stronghold are and how they are disposed, attacks the weaker side, in like manner, the enemy of human kind roves around and makes a tour of inspection of all our virtues, theological and cardinal and moral. Where he finds us weaker and more in need of reinforcement for the sake of our eternal salvation, there he attacks us and strives to take us by storm.

[Set II]

[328]. RULES FOR THE SAME PURPOSE [AS THE FIRST SET], WITH MORE ACCURATE WAYS OF DISCERNING SPIRITS. THESE RULES ARE MORE SUITED FOR USE IN THE SECOND WEEK.[4]

[329]. Rule 1. It is connatural for God and his angels, when they prompt interior motions, to give genuine gladness and spiritual joy, eliminating all sadness and confusion which the enemy brings on. It is connatural for the latter to fight against such gladness and spiritual consolation by proposing specious arguments, subtle and persistently fallacious.

[330]. Rule 2. To give a person consolation without preceding cause is for God our Lord alone to do; for it is distinctive of the Creator in relation to the created person to come in and to leave, to move the person interiorly, drawing him or her totally into love of his Divine Majesty. I say without [preceding][5] cause, that is, without any previous perception or understanding of any object such that through it consolation of this sort would come by the mediation of the person's own acts of understanding and will.

[331]. Rule 3. With a [preceding] cause, an angel, good or evil, can console a person. In doing so, the good and evil angels have contrary purposes. The purpose of the good angel is the person's progress, that he may ascend from good to better. The

purpose of the evil angel is the contrary—and thereafter, to draw the person on to his damned intent and cunning trap.

[332]. Rule 4. It is characteristic of the evil spirit to take on the appearance of an angel of light, so that he can begin by going the way of a devout person and end with that person going his own way. By that I mean that he first prompts thoughts which are good and holy, harmonious with such a faithful person, and then manages, little by little, to step out of his act and lead the person to his hidden falsehoods and perverse designs.

[333]. Rule 5. We ought to pay close attention to the progression of thoughts. If the beginning, middle, and end of it are altogether good and tend entirely to what is right, that is a sign of the good angel's influence. It is, however, a clear sign that the line of thought originates from the influence of the evil spirit, the enemy of our spiritual progress and eternal salvation, if the thoughts which he prompts end up in something evil or distracting or less good than what the person had previously proposed to do, or if they weaken, disquiet, or confuse him, doing away with the peace, tranquility, and quiet experienced beforehand.

[334]. Rule 6. When the enemy of human nature has been perceived and recognized by his telltale train of thoughts terminating in the evil to which he leads, it is useful for the person who was tempted by him to look immediately at the course of good thoughts which were prompted in him, noting how they began and how, little by little, the evil spirit contrived to make him fall away from the earlier sweetness and spiritual joy until he led him to what his [the spirit's] own corrupt mind intended. The purpose is that observing such an experience and taking mental note of it will be a safeguard for the future against these customary hoaxes of the evil spirit.

[335]. Rule 7. Persons who are going from good to better the good angel touches sweetly, lightly, gently, as when a drop of water soaks into a sponge, while the evil spirit touches them sharply, with noise and disturbance, as when the drop of water

falls on a rock. Those who are going from bad to worse the aforesaid spirits touch in a way contrary to the way they touch those going from good to better. The cause of this contrariety is that the disposition of the one touched is either contrary to or concordant with each of the said angels. For when it is contrary, the angels enter perceptibly, with clamor and observable signs; when it is concordant, they come in quietly, as one comes into his own house through an open door.

[336]. Rule 8. Granted that when consolation is without [preceding] cause, it has no deception in it, since, as has been said, such consolation is from God our Lord alone; nevertheless, a spiritual person to whom God gives such consolation should, with great alertness and attention, examine his experience to discern the precise time of the actual consolation [without preceding cause] as distinct from the following time, in which the person is still glowing and still graced by the residue of [actual] consolation that is now over with. The reason for making this distinction is that frequently in this second period, either through one's own reasoning about the relations of concepts and judgments and the conclusions to be drawn from them, or through the influence of a good spirit or of an evil spirit, various purposes and opinions take shape which are not given immediately by God our Lord. Inasmuch as that is the case, these purposes and opinions are in need of prolonged and careful examination before full assent is given to them or they are put into execution.

NOTES

1. The *Spiritual Exercises* are divided into four periods called "weeks," but these are not understood as periods of seven days. The distinction between the First and the Second Week is not to the point here; it will be taken up in discussing the difference of the second set of rules from the first.

2. The Spanish is *en el ánima*. Here, as in *SpEx*, [313], and also in other occurrences in these rules where the context warrants, I translate Ignatius' *ánima* by "person" rather than "soul." Ignatius did not have a

Platonic or Cartesian notion of man; he uses *ánima* merely in the figurative sense of taking the part for the whole (synechdoche). Important for understanding rightly Ignatius' use of *ánima* is the following commentary of George E. Ganss, S.J., in his translation of St. Ignatius' *Constitutions of the Society of Jesus* (St. Louis, 1970), hereafter abbreviated as (*ConsSJComm*), p. 77: ". . . *ánima* in Ignatius' Spanish, here means the persons, the men considered as their entire selves. This was a frequent meaning of the word for 'soul' in all the languages of Christendom, as it was of the Latin *ánima* in classical times (e.g., *Aeneid,* xi, 24; Horace, *Satires,* i, 5, 41) and in Christian writers too. Ignatius also uses *ánima,* soul, in contrast to *cuerpo,* the body, e.g., in *Cons,* [312–814].

"The use of the Latin *anima* and Spanish *ánima* to mean the living man, the self, the person, is scriptural and occurs very frequently in the Latin Vulgate, especially in texts frequently quoted such as Matt. 16:26; Mark 3:48, 8:36 (Cf., e.g., Gen 2:7, 12:5, 49:6, Exod. 1:5; Acts 2:41; 1 Cor. 15:45). Hence this usage was common in all the languages of Christian Europe throughout the Middle Ages (see, e.g., Blaise, *Dictionnaire . . . des auteurs chrétiens,* s.v. 'anima', 4; also, Peter Lombard's *Sentences* II, 1, no. 8). Awareness of this usage is a key necessary for accurate interpretation of virtually all Christian writers on spirituality. Because of their heritage of Greek philosophy, medieval theologians and later spiritual writers regarded this, more frequently than modern scriptural scholars, as the figure of synecdoche by which the part (*anima*) was taken for the whole, the living man (*homo.*) Even this synecdoche, however, has a scriptural basis (Wisd. 3:1, 8:19–20). In the Spanish of the 1500's (as we gather s.v. from the *Tesoro* [A.D. 1611] of Covarrubias, who refers to Gen. 12:5 and 14:21), *ánima* and its synonym *alma* have among their meanings 'that by which we live' and are 'often used for the persons.' Ignatius' use of *ánima* rather than *hombre* or *homo* has occasionally been taken as evidence of exaggerated dualism or even of Neoplatonism in his thought. In the light of the pervading influence of the Latin Vulgate and its use of *anima* throughout the Middle Ages, this interpretation appears to be farfetched and groundless."

3. My version perhaps takes a slight liberty with the text, translating Ignatius' *mujer* by "shrewish woman" (which in this context is clearly his meaning) rather than merely by "woman." The text, I think, as well as Ignatius' respect for and friendship with women, calls for such a qualification.

4. See note 1 above.

5. Careful reading of the text shows that "without cause" is simply a contraction of "without preceding cause." First, the Vulgate version

and both the *Prima Versio* texts always speak of a cause that precedes. Secondly, in the autograph version of Rule II:2, where Ignatius first makes the shift, he writes, "*I say,* without cause," (emphasis mine) obviously referring back to the phrase "without preceding cause." He then adds a phrase to explain "without cause": "without any *previous* perception or understanding of any object such . . ." (italics mine).

The Spiritual Exercises of St. Ignatius Loyola. A New Inclusive Language Translation

Elisabeth Tetlow

313. RULES FOR THE DISCERNMENT OF SPIRITS IN THE FIRST WEEK

Rules for perceiving and understanding to some degree the different movements which occur in the soul: the good, that they may be accepted, and the bad that they may be rejected. These rules are most suitable for the first week of the Exercises.

314. First Rule. In the case of those who go from one mortal sin to another, the enemy ordinarily is accustomed to propose apparent pleasures, filling their imagination with sensual gratifications and pleasures, the more effectively to hold them fast and increase their attachment to their vices and sins.

With such persons the good spirit uses a method which is the reverse of the above: awakening their consciences to be consumed with remorse through their own moral judgment.

315. Second Rule. In the case of persons who strive earnestly to purify their lives from sin and who seek to advance from good to better in the service of God, the method used here is the opposite of that described in the first rule. In this case it is characteristic of the evil spirit to harass with anxiety, afflict with sadness, raise obstacles based on false reasoning that disturb the soul, preventing it from progressing.

It is characteristic of the good spirit, however, to give courage and strength, consolation, tears, inspiration and peace, making things easier and removing obstacles, in order that the person may make further progress in doing the good.

316. Third Rule. Spiritual Consolation. Consolation is when a person is aroused by an interior movement in the soul which causes it to catch fire with love for its Creator and God, and, as a result, it can love no created thing on the face of the earth in itself, but only in the Creator of all. It is likewise consolation when one sheds tears, moved by love for God, whether it be because of sorrow for sins, or because of the sufferings of Christ our Lord, or for any other reason immediately directed to the service and praise of God. Finally, consolation includes every increase of faith, hope, and love, and all interior joy which call and attract the soul to that which is of God and to salvation by filling it with tranquility and peace in its Creator and Sovereign.

317. Fourth Rule. Spiritual Desolation. Desolation is that which is completely the opposite of what was described in the third rule, such as darkness of soul, turmoil of spirit, attraction to what is base and worldly, and restlessness caused by many disturbances and temptations, all of which can lead to lack of faith, hope and love. The retreatant may find him or herself completely apathetic, lukewarm, and unhappy, as if separated from God. Just as consolation is the opposite of desolation, so in the same way, thoughts which come out of consolation are the opposite of those which come out of desolation.

318. Fifth Rule. In time of desolation, never make any change, but remain firm and constant in the resolution and decision which were manifest before the time of desolation, or in the decision which was made in the preceding consolation. For just as in consolation it is the good spirit which guides and counsels us, so in desolation it is the evil one which guides and counsels. Following the counsels of the evil one, we can never find the way to a right decision.

319. Sixth Rule. Though in desolation we should never change former resolutions, it may be very profitable to make important

changes in ourselves by insisting on more prayer, more meditation, and more self-examination, and by increasing our penance
in some appropriate way.

320. Seventh Rule. When we are in desolation, we should reflect
that God has left us to our own natural faculties to resist the
different agitations and temptations of the enemy as a test. We
can resist with the help of God, which is always available, although we may not clearly perceive it. For even when it seems
that God has taken away the former abundance of fervor, ardent
love and intense grace, nevertheless God always leaves sufficient
grace to reach eternal salvation.

321. Eighth Rule. When we are in desolation, we should work on
being patient. This is contrary to the turmoil which disquiets us.
We should also reflect that consolation will soon return, and in
the meantime, we should diligently use the means against desolation given in the sixth rule.

322. Ninth Rule. There are three principal reasons why we find
ourselves in desolation. The first is because we have been lukewarm, lazy or negligent in our spiritual exercises, and so through
our own fault consolation has been withdrawn from us. The second reason is because God sometimes wishes to test us, to see how
much we are worth, and how much we will progress in God's service and praise when left without the reward of consolation and
special graces. The third reason is that God wishes to give us a true
knowledge and understanding of ourselves, so that we may experience internally that it is not within our power to acquire or retain
great feelings of devotion, ardent love, tears, or any other spiritual
consolation; but that all these are the gratuitous gift and grace of
God. Finally, God does not want our egos to become inflated with
pride or vainglory, falsely attributing to ourselves feelings of devotion or other elements of spiritual consolation.

323. Tenth Rule. When we are in consolation it is good to reflect
how we will act during a future time of desolation, and store up
new strengths for that time.

324. Eleventh Rule. One who is in consolation should as humble and self-abasing as possible. The person should recall how little is possible in time of desolation without grace or consolation. On the other hand, one who is in desolation should remember that since sufficient grace is always offered, he or she can do much to withstand the enemy, taking strength from God.

325. Twelfth Rule. The enemy behaves like a cowardly bully, seeming strong in the face of weakness, but proving to be weak when faced with strength. When involved in a fight with someone, such a bully will prove to be a coward and run away if his or her opponent shows much courage. On the other hand, if the opponent loses courage and tries to run away, the rage, spite and ferocity of the enemy increase and know no bounds.

In the same way, when one experienced in spiritual things faces the enemy's temptations boldly, doing exactly the opposite of what the enemy suggests, then the enemy characteristically will reveal its weakness and turn to flight along with its temptations. However, if the one making spiritual exercises begins to show fear and lose heart while undergoing temptations, there is no wild animal on the face of the earth so fierce as the enemy of human nature in carrying out its evil plans with ever increasing malice.

326. Thirteenth Rule. The enemy may also act like a seducer, seeking to remain hidden and undetected. Such a false "lover" seeks with evil intent to seduce a faithful and virtuous spouse or child, desiring that all insidious words and solicitations be kept secret. Such a seducer is greatly displeased if his or her deceitful suggestions and dishonorable intentions are revealed by the object of such misguided lust to another person, such as a righteous spouse or parent. From that moment on, the seducer knows that the project will not be successful.

In the same way, when the enemy of human nature tempts a righteous person with its wiles and seductions, it earnestly desires that they be received secretly and kept secret. But if the person reveals them to a good confessor or some other spiritual person who has understanding of such deceptions and malicious intentions, the evil one will be quite vexed, knowing that it will be impossible to succeed in this evil undertaking once its manifest deceptions have been revealed.

327. Fourteenth Rule. The conduct of the enemy may also be compared to the tactics of a military strategist intent upon conquering and seizing a desired objective. Such a strategist will set up his or her camp and prepare a plan by investigating the strength of the opposing forces and their deployment, and then he or she will attack at the weakest point.

In the same way, the enemy of human nature explores around us from every side, probing our virtues of faith, hope, and love, justice, righteousness, and morality. Where it finds our defenses weakest and most deficient in regard to eternal salvation, it is at that point that the enemy will storm in to attack and defeat us.

328.   RULES FOR THE DISCERNMENT OF SPIRITS IN THE SECOND WEEK

Rules for understanding the different movements in the soul for a more subtle discernment of spirits in the second week.

329. First Rule. It is characteristic of God and the good angels, when they act upon the soul, to give true happiness and spiritual joy, taking away all the sadness and turmoil caused by the enemy.

It is characteristic of the evil one to fight against such happiness and spiritual consolation by suggesting false reasonings, full of subtleties and persistent fallacies.

330. Second Rule. God alone can give consolation to the soul without previous cause. It is the prerogative of God alone to enter into a soul, depart from it, evoke spiritual movements within it and draw it totally toward divine love. Without previous cause means without any previous feeling or experience of anything by means of which such consolation might come to the soul through the person's own acts of intellect or will.

331. Third Rule. When there is a cause, consolation can come from either the good spirit or the evil one, but for quite different purposes. The good spirit consoles so that the person may progress, growing and advancing from what is good to what is better. The evil one consoles for the opposite purpose, so that later it may draw the soul toward its own malicious intentions and toward evil.

332. Fourth Rule. It is characteristic of the evil one to assume the appearance of a good angel. It begins by suggesting thoughts appropriate for a devout soul and ends by suggesting its own. Then, little by little, it will move out, drawing the soul into its hidden deceptions and evil plans.

333. Fifth Rule. We should carefully observe the whole course of our thoughts. If the beginning, middle and end of the thoughts are wholly good and oriented to all that is good, it is a sign that they are from the good spirit. But if the end of the course of thought suggested to us is something evil or distracting or less good than what the person previously had proposed to do, or if it weakens or disturbs the person or causes turmoil in the soul, destroying the peace, tranquility and quiet it had before, this is a clear sign that these thoughts are coming from the evil one, the enemy of our spiritual growth and eternal salvation.

334. Sixth Rule. When the enemy of human nature has been detected and recognized by the trail of evil which marks its course and by the evil end to which it leads us, it will be profitable for one who has been tempted immediately to review the whole course of the temptation. One should recall when the good thoughts began and how the evil one little by little drew the person away from the state of spiritual joy and consolation, and toward its own evil plans. The purpose of this review is that once such an experience has been understood and carefully noted, in the future one may be better able to guard against these customary deceptions of the enemy.

335. Seventh Rule. In persons who are progressing from good to better, the good spirit is delicate, gentle and light, like a drop of water falling onto a sponge. The evil one enters the soul violently, with noise and disturbance, like a drop of water falling on a stone.

In the case of those who are going from bad to worse, the action of the spirits mentioned above is just the opposite. The reason for this is the disposition of the soul, whether in harmony with or in opposition to the spirits. When the person's disposition is contrary to the spirit, it will enter with noise and commotion which are easily perceived. When the disposition is in harmony with the spirit, it will enter silently, as one enters one's own house when the door is open.

336. Eighth Rule. When consolation is without previous cause, there can be no deception in it since it can come only from God. But the spiritual person, to whom God has given such consolation, should examine the experience very attentively and cautiously, to distinguish the actual time of the consolation from the period after it, when the soul is still fervent and filled with the grace and memories of the consolation. In this second period, we often act according to our own reason and judgment, or under the influence of the good or evil spirit. Thus we can make various resolutions or plans which are not directly inspired by God. Therefore, any decisions we make at such a time should be carefully examined before they are fully accepted or put into action.

Letters of Spiritual Direction

Jane de Chantal

LETTERS TO THE VISITATION 1616–1618

The Visitation of Holy Mary was founded in 1610 as a small, quasi-monastic contemplative community. The concerns that occupied its first Superior, Jane de Chantal, were for the most part particular to the first house and its few residents. For the first five or six years of its existence, the Visitation was in the process of acquiring its own self-identity and Jane was learning to govern and to instill in her daughters the particular Salesian spirit. But by 1616 things had changed.

A new phase of Jane de Chantal's life had begun. She had just returned from Lyons and founding the first monastery after Annecy. She had left the very young Marie Jacqueline Favre as superior, and continued to guide her as she took her first steps under fire. The Archbishop of Lyons did not quite understand Francis de Sales's ideal of a community of women consecrated to a life of prayer, without solemn vows, bound only by their love for God which also defined their cloister. Marie Jacqueline was in the delicate position of not offending her bishop, yet remaining faithful to the lifestyle established by Francis at Annecy. Jane suggested how she should act when the archbishop proposed unacceptable changes in the Rule. Mother Jeanne Charlotte de Brechard, although a much more mature woman, was, like Marie Jacqueline, superior of a new foundation, in this case at Moulins. These were the first two offshoots of the Annecy community. She let both these and other new superiors and novice mistresses act freely, but skillfully reinforced the spirit with which they should carry out their work.

From the superiors of the order she expected an attitude of motherly attentiveness toward all the Visitandines, the kind of care and solicitude for each entrant that a mother might show her own child. While it was required that faults be noted and that advancement in virtue be cultivated, such guidance must never become judgmental and so cause discouragement or intimidation. Sustaining all this maternal caretaking was the very real belief that this most attractive of methods would suit best to draw the sisters into a loving relationship with God. They were to be drawn, attracted to this vocation in a manner that had less to do with rational arguments than with affective response.

To Mother Marie-Jacqueline Favre, Superior at Lyons

Live + Jesus!

Annecy, 9 February 1616[1]

What a surprise! M. de Boisy just told me that if I want to write you, my darling, now is a good time because someone will be leaving before dawn; so here I am, before dawn, writing you this quick note. First of all, I must tell you that all your letters delight and please me very much. I can see that God, by His grace and fatherly care, is leading you by the hand and that all you have to do is trust Him, cling to Him, and, under His protection, journey on as humbly and simply as possible. See to it that your little flock advances faithfully, for this is how you can show God your own fidelity. This is why, as I'm always telling you, my very dearest daughter, you must free yourself from too much activity so that, insofar as your duties allow, you can be with your Sisters whenever they are together, to instruct them and encourage them in the performance of their duties, as much by your example as by precept. I find our good and worthy Archbishop's wish on this subject very fair. He is right, believe me, Sister, when he says you have to be both Superior and Mistress. Nevertheless, it is well that you are training our little *cadette* [Sister Marie-Aimée de Blonay] for she has a good mind, though she is a little too reserved in expressing herself, and she is somewhat lazy and given to following her natural inclinations.[2] Still, I hope that with God's help, she will inspire those dear novices more and more every day, both by her good example and by what she has to say as she opens up. She will be a great help to you since you will often be called away. [. . .]

Be at peace about our dearest Péronne-Marie. I never gave a thought to what others said to you, but do not, on that account, hesitate to have the Sisters trained to do the housework, for certainly, we are obliged, in charity, to let Sister get a good rest after she has set the house in order and trained others to do the work.

Dearest, I have such compassion for poor Sister Anne-Marie; undoubtedly, her imagination plays a part in the trouble. If the Archbishop and her confessor show some disapproval of and trim down to size all that she is puffed up about, they should help to cure her. I'll write to her, as to the others, as soon as I have time. Take good care of dear Sister Jeanne-Françoise; try to keep her as happy and busy as possible, and see to it that she eats well and gets enough sleep, for ordinarily an unstable mind is easily carried away by imaginary temptations. So, for that reason, dear Sister, be extremely compassionate, loving, and patient with her. God and time will reveal to us what this is all about.

Day is dawning; I can't think of anything that requires a prompt answer, except to say that, certainly, my darling, God has blessed you in giving you these two great and worthy prelates as fathers. Their remarkable piety is pleasing to God and everyone. I can't tell you how encouraged I am to see how God has united these two men. I believe that this friendship will bring more glory to our Lord than we, with our small minds, can possibly grasp. I feel very satisfied and I praise God for this with all my heart. For a long time now I have prayed that in His goodness, God would bring it about, for I could see clearly that it would benefit everyone, and especially that the Archbishop would receive from it the joy and consolation he so deserves and needs. Our Bishop [Francis de Sales] has high regard for him.

I shall write as much as I can to those dear daughters of mine at my first opportunity. For now, I send them my most affectionate greetings. May our good Jesus fill them with His gentleness, simplicity, and innocence! My respectful and warm remembrance to the Archbishop; best regards also to Father Phillippe, Father de St. Nizier, to your chaplain, and to anyone else you can think of. Don't ever say again to the President [M. Favre] that you never receive letters from me! I never fail to write you whenever I can. Remember me very especially to your dear companions, my daughters and most dear Sisters.

Good morning, dearest love. May Jesus be our all. Amen. Amen.

To Sister Péronne-Marie de Châtel at Lyons

[Annecy, 9 February 1616][3]

At last, my dearest daughter, I have your letter before me to answer as best I can. May God inspire me to say what is for His glory and your consolation.

In my judgment, all your reluctance to speak to me, all your aversions and difficulties are for your greater good; so much so that you have an obligation not to act upon such feelings. Every day you should resolve to resist them and fight them. However, should you fall even fifty times a day, never, on any account, should that surprise or worry you. Instead, ever so gently set your heart back in the right direction and practice the opposite virtue, my darling Péronne, all the time speaking words of love and trust to our Lord after you have committed a thousand faults, as much as if you had committed only one. Try to remember what I have so often said to you on this subject, put it into practice for love of God, and know that out of this weakness of yours He will draw forth both His glory and your perfection. Never doubt this. No matter what happens, be gentle and patient with yourself. Once in a while, if you feel particularly weak, without courage, without confidence, force yourself to make affirmations which are the opposite of your feelings. Say with conviction: "My Savior, my All, despite my feelings of misery and distrust, I place all my confidence in You; You are strength for the weak, refuge for the miserable, wealth for the poor; You are indeed my Savior who has always loved sinners." But, dearest, say these or similar words resolutely, without self-pity or tears; then turn your attention to something else. The Almighty will never let you slip from His arms, for He holds you firmly. Don't you see how very gently He comes to your rescue?

I beg you, never forget the teachings you received here and put them into practice wherever and whenever you have occasion to do so. Write to me whenever you like. I shall always answer you promptly from this heart of mine which is all yours. Take care to set a good example, and remember that in order to do this, you should be exact in following the observances, mindful that a well-ordered exterior results from an awareness of God's presence. As far as possible, ask to be relieved of household duties. I've already suggested this to Sister [Favre] who, I think, likes the idea. If she doesn't, then don't ask for this, but it would be well if you could be training those whom you will be assigning to these tasks.

Certainly, my darling love, I am very happy and pleased with the dearly loved Mother there. Everyone tells me how well she is getting along. I am especially happy with all you tell me about her for I know you speak very sincerely. I hope that someday she will be a great servant of God who will do good to many persons. She will have deepened in humility and abandonment: help her, according to your lights, and tell her forthrightly, in all sincerity, whatever seems good both for her and for the community. I know her heart—God knows how much I love her—and I know she will be grateful to you for whatever your conscience prompts you to tell her. I know well, personally, the great help my *coadjutrix* gives me.[4] A coadjutrix is a tremendous help to a Superior who, because she is preoccupied with so many affairs, cannot pay much attention to minor things which, nevertheless, should be corrected.

So, my darling Péronne, once again I am asking you to cheer up our dear Sister and to keep an eye on her health. Without nagging her, do tell her frankly what she should do to stay well. See to it that she follows through on what you tell her. She should yield to your request in this, just as you should obey her quite simply when she orders what she considers necessary for your health. You may correct her humbly, but in such a manner that she will not lose confidence in you and be unhappy; it is better to be too lenient than to work her too hard. And don't be overly anxious about your own problems. Do whatever you can to get well, for it is only your nerves.

I am closing now because I do not feel well. A thousand million greetings to all our darling sisters. I certainly love that little flock with all my heart. I want them to be ever attentive to their Spouse and to live in His presence like pure, sweet, simple and chaste doves. In spirit I embrace them all lovingly and tenderly—everyone, young and old, but, above all the others, my precious beloved Péronne-Marie. Our Bishop sends greetings and loves you tenderly also. Live Jesus!

LETTERS TO THE VISITATION 1623–1641

As foundations spread swiftly, Jane continued her ministry to superiors, novice mistresses and other Sisters. Her situation changed dramatically after the death of Francis de Sales in 1622. She began to shoulder alone the full responsibility for the rapidly growing order. Her prime concern was its consolidation. Juridical status had been acquired in 1618 when the new congregation was erected into a religious order. But she felt it necessary, in 1624, to call a meeting of the first Mothers and Sisters who had known Francis personally, to establish the rules and customs on a solid basis. And the means of maintaining union and conformity among the monasteries would haunt her until her death.

For her Sisters the hopeful foundress painted an ideal representation of a Visitation community: the superiors, perfectly surrendered to the spirit of the Institute as expressed in its Rules, with great sisterly affection and maternal attentiveness would lead and guide a household of women likewise united in heart and mind in a spirit of abundant "douceur." In practice, the historical record often resembles more a canvas in progress than a finished work. Yet Jane de Chantal had a genius for spiritual direction which made that continuing work a viable and commendable one.

In her more mature years Jane counseled superiors and Sisters with the same affection—although sometimes there is less spontaneity in its expression—understanding and firmness. Her letters frequently betray her fatigue. But nothing quells her ardent quest for God for herself and those confided to her care.

To Sister Anne-Marie Rosset, Assistant and Novice Mistress at Dijon

Live + Jesus!

[Annecy, 1623]⁵

God knows the pain I feel in my heart over the misunderstanding that exists in your house. I ask Him to take it in hand. In the end, if a reconciliation doesn't occur, you will have to find a way of sending away the sister who is the cause of it all. No good ever comes from the sisters' wanting to control the Superior; if they were humble and submissive, all would go well. Indeed, my very dear Sister, she who governs there has done so very successfully elsewhere, and this ought to keep the Sisters at peace. Help them to understand this as far as you can so that there may be humble and cordial submission in the house. Help Sister N*** to unite herself to her Superior and to be sincerely open with her. Oh! is this behavior the way to honor the memory of him who so often recommended to us peace and union! What a dangerous temptation! May God, in His goodness, straighten this out! And we shall do what we can, with His help, to remedy the situation.

Now back to you. For my part, I would have no problem in professing Sister A.M., for she shows good will, and fails only through forgetfulness. I can't get over how that sister dares to harass her; what nerve! Would to God she were somewhere else. I think that from now on the Sisters should be asked to give their opinion only after they have left the novitiate.

To be sure, I am convinced, and experience has taught me, that nothing so wins souls as gentleness and cordiality. I beg you, dearest, follow this method, for it is the spirit of our blessed Father. Curtness in words or actions only hardens hearts and depresses them, whereas gentleness encourages them and makes them receptive. I think that in no way should the time planned for the reception of young women be changed; you should wait a year or so for the little niece of Sister de Vigny, though you may go on instructing her. But I shall be seeing her, and I think she is so reasonable that she will make the adjustment.

To return now to the question of Sister N***. I don't say that she should be treated with affection, but cordially and gently; by that I mean without coldness in words or actions. I suggest the same, and even more strongly, in the case of Sister Anne Jacqueline who has to be handled playfully. She is still very much a child and wouldn't have the stomach for eating solid meat, so to speak, and whoever would give her some would ruin her. She has to be led slowly and tenderly, and be brought to observe silence and other obediences, but not as yet to perform penances and mortifications. You see, my dear, we have to cultivate in these young, delicate souls lots of vigor, cheerfulness, and joy, and thus bring them to want those things they would fear or dread if they were led in any other manner.

Dearest, you must be faithful to ask for relief, and be more frank, warm, open and sincere with Mother, speaking to her with an open heart about everything, quite freely. In this way, my dear, and for love of God, you will be giving to our blessed Father the glory of seeing you live according to his spirit of gentleness and trust, even as you bring others to do the same.[6]

Pray for me, and relieve my heart by telling me there is perfect mutual understanding among you. It is under such circumstances that we witness to the purity of our love and serve God according to His liking, practicing virtues for His glory and not our satisfaction.

You know that I am yours unreservedly.

God be praised!

To the Superior at Digne

Annecy, 1625[7]

My very dear daughter,

In the name of our Divine Savior, I beg you, and urge you, to govern according to His Spirit and that of our vocation, which is a humble, gentle spirit, supportive and considerate of all. In order to govern in this manner, my dear, you must not act according to the willfulness of your own nature, nor according to your inclination to austerity. What we are asking of you, my dearest daughter, and without further delay, please, is to be most gentle in spirit, word and action, and to treat your own body and those of your Sisters better than you have been doing.

What good will it do to put bread on the table when they don't have teeth to chew it or stomachs to digest it? So, I urge you once again not to let us hear any more talk about your harshness and severity with the Sisters and yourself. Your minds and bodies will be wrecked if you stubbornly refuse to accept humbly what we are saying and begging you to do in the name of God and of our blessed Father. He greatly feared such harshness in his Institute, which he established for those who are delicate and where he wanted a spirit of humility and gentleness to reign. This is what he so recommended everywhere.

Sister, the sincere affection I have for you prompts me to write to you in this way for I am confident that you will not ignore my request nor the humble lessons I have given you before God and in His name. I beg Him to help all of you accomplish what I tell you. I am all yours, and I send greetings to all the Sisters and earnestly ask for their prayers.

God be praised!

To Sister Anne-Catherine de Sautereau, Novice Mistress to Grenoble

Annecy, c. 12 December 1626[8]

My dearest daughter,

As you wished, and in God's presence, I shall tell you what His goodness will inspire me to say to you, for I ask Him to help me. First of all, it seems to me, my dear Sister, that you should try to make your own devotion, and that of your novices, generous, noble, straightforward, and sincere. Try to foster that spirit in all those whom God will ever commit to your care—a spirit founded on that deep humility which results in sincere obedience, sweet charity which supports and excuses all, and an innocent, guileless simplicity which makes us even-tempered and friendly toward everyone.

From there, my dearest daughter, move on to a total surrender of yourself into the hands of our good God, so that, insofar as you can, you may help your own dear soul and those you are guiding, to be free of all that is not God. May these souls have such a pure, upright intention that they do not waste time worrying about created things—their friends, their appearance, their speech. Without stopping at such considerations or at any other obstacle they may meet along the way, may they go forward on the road to perfection by the exact observances of the Institute, seeing in all things only the sacred face of God, that is, His good pleasure. This way is very narrow, my dear Sister, but it is solid, short, simple and sure, and soon leads the soul to its goal: total union with God. Let us follow this way faithfully. It certainly precludes multiplicity and leads us to that unity which alone is necessary. I know you are drawn to this happiness, so pursue it, and rest quietly on the breast of divine Providence. Those souls who have put aside all ambition except that of pleasing God alone should remain peaceful in this holy tabernacle.

My dearest Sister, Abraham (how I love this patriarch!) left his country and his family in order to obey God; but the only Son of God accomplished the will of His heavenly Father by working in the country of His birth. So be content, dear, to imitate the Lord, for nothing can equal His perfection. Don't look elsewhere, but carefully try to accomplish lovingly and with good heart all the tasks that Providence and obedience place in your hands. The principal exercises of the novitiate are mortification and prayer.

This is enough—and perhaps too much—for me to be telling a soul who is already enlightened and led by God. I beg Him in His goodness to guide you to perfection in His most pure love. My soul cherishes yours more than I can say; be absolutely assured of this, and pray for her who is yours unreservedly.

God be praised! Amen.

To Sister Anne-Marie de Lage de Puylaurens, Assistant and Novice Mistress at Bourges

[Annecy, 1626][9]

My very dear daughter,

God has certainly blessed you by giving you the light and the strength to pull away from the dangerous temptation you have had against your very fine, virtuous Mother. The evil spirit did that; he would like to upset both of you by this disunion. May God who set you free from this evil be praised! Be on your guard, dearest, never to fall into it again. Keep yourself ever and invariably united both to your written Rule and to the living one who is your Superior. Even if someday God should permit that you have a very imperfect Superior, remain steadfast. You will find the Spirit of God in her, so do not look for anything else. Surely you will never lose Him if you follow this way and remain faithful to your duty.

True, my very dear Sister, your timidity stems from self-love.

Try, for the love of God, to overcome your inclinations and live, as your Rule recommends, according to reason and the will of God. If you don't decide to do this yourself, no one can help you; others may tell you what to do, but nobody can do it for you. Courage then, darling. God asks this of you and calls you to a high perfection. Correspond faithfully by the exact observance of your Institute, for this is your true way and the only one by which you can reach such perfection. Do all this with the holy fervor of a most humble, gentle and simple spirit.

I am pleased to know that you are cutting back on all your self-scrutiny and that you are more peaceful about your desire to make progress. Such eagerness comes from self-love. Always be on your guard against this, I beg you, and in order to unite yourself to God, get into the habit of seeking His will in all things.

Nothing has changed in the Ceremonial. You may take from the Custom Book and the Spiritual Directory whatever you think fit for your novices whom I greet very affectionately. As for you whom my heart loves with a special, warm affection, I encourage you to be kind and generous.

To a Superior

Annecy, after 1623[10]

Take care, dearest daughter, not to dismiss the novice with the pulmonary disorder. What would our blessed Father say? "But she will die!" you reply. Well, wouldn't she die in the world, and wouldn't she be happy to die as a spouse of Jesus Christ? There is a postulant here at Annecy with the same illness, but she certainly is not being sent away because of that. "It's flesh and blood that gives such advice," our blessed Father used to say. He never wanted candidates to be sent away because of any physical infirmity unless they had a contagious disease. So let us be unyielding in this matter, holding on to what we have received from our holy Founder. I know this is what you really want to do.

I promise you, I do not choose the most capable or most virtuous Sisters to be superiors, but rather those who I see have the God-given talent of governing well. I have put to the test those who are intelligent, attractive in the eyes of the world, and devout, as well as those who are genuinely holy. I found that neither kind was successful unless they knew how to govern or had the true humility, prudence, and sincerity that the Institute calls for. But if they had these virtues, even if they had other imperfections which I saw they were trying to overcome, I didn't hesitate to put them in charge. This is what our holy Father did, with the hope that God would bless them. Still, he did look at the external talents of those whom we thought of making superiors, so that, as he put it, they might satisfy and attract secular persons.

Your answer to the Archbishop is fine, except that instead of submitting to an infringement of this point in the Constitution if he ordered it, you should have asked him very humbly to let you continue the practice which obliges you to show your accounts to the ecclesiastical superior every year when he asks to see them, or to the one making the visitation, but not to anyone else. This is an obligation of the Rule.

My dearest Sister, we must, in all humility, resolve to maintain our observances; otherwise, if we break down on one point, then all the rest will be dissipated. Let us be obedient toward our ecclesiastical superiors in everything that they ask as long as it is not contrary to our Institute; but let us always be faithful to our Founder's recommendations. Our ecclesiastical superiors are there only to see that we observe our Rule, not to destroy it. What would happen if each one of these superiors wanted to make changes? What would happen to the Visitation? It would soon look very different. Dearest, let us be constant in our fidelity; once small irregularities creep in, the big ones follow. Our holy Founder so often advised us not to fail in any detail or soon we would lose everything.

I am writing to our houses to encourage them to persevere in and maintain their holy union. I am doing and saying what my conscience dictates and what I know or feel to be the intention of our blessed Father. Beyond that, I leave the care of it all to Divine Providence. As for people making fun of us—that won't last, for I'm not worthy of such suffering. But we should be careful not to bring on ridicule ourselves.

I greet all your dear daughters, but especially the older Sisters. May God keep each of us according to His heart. Yours, etc. . . .

To Mother Marie-Adrienne Fichet, Superior at Rumilly

[Annecy, 1627][11]

(The first lines are illegible) . . . As for your temptations, pay no attention to them, and do whatever is necessary to keep your mind off them. These efforts, though forceful, must reflect moderation. You see, dear, the way by which you are being led is at once mild yet strong and solid. God hides the prize of eternal glory in our mortifications and the victory over ourselves which we always strive for with gentleness. Otherwise, your impulsiveness would cause you, and others, to suffer. In the end, *gentleness plays a large part in the way we govern.* Every day I notice that kindness, gentleness, and support, as well as generosity, can do so much for souls. You know that God has given me a very special love for your house, and it seems to me that it is like a dormitory or annex of Annecy.

So people are talking, are they, saying that your house is unlucky because you've had so much misfortune.[12] That's the language of the world! God speaks quite a different one. It is a great mark of His blessing when a house is stricken with some tribulation or other which does not offend Him, for instance, the death of the Sisters. On the contrary, He is glorified by this sorrow because these dear souls have gone to heaven to praise Him forever.

Furthermore, be more and more careful that your corrections are not too harsh, for that would be neither beneficial nor useful. Those who are responsible for others cannot always say with St. Paul [sic]: "I am innocent of your blood," that is, of the faults his people were committing. But we, on the other hand, are usually guilty, as much for the faults of others as for our own, either because we over-corrected or tolerated too much, or else, corrected too harshly or neglected to correct; or because we failed to include in our correction the sweetness of holy charity.

Dearest, here is the money for the new habit which you sent me, and please, send me back the one which our Sisters kept. There is nothing that bothers me more than their attachment to these external signs of imaginary holiness in me. These are traps which the devil puts in my way to make me stumble into the bottomless pit of pride. I am already weak enough, and enough of a stumbling-block to myself, without anyone adding another. So I beg all of you not to be an occasion of such temptation for me. If anyone has anything belonging to me, do me the kindness of burning it. If only our Sisters would treat me as I deserve to be treated before God, then I would have some hope of becoming, through these humiliations, what they imagine me to be. But to be presenting me with continual temptations to vanity is intolerable. This brings sadness to my heart and tears to my eyes as I tell it to you.

Dear N. and N. seem to be happy to have to bear so many external humiliations. For this, I love them even more and believe them to be even greater in the sight of God whose judgment is so different from ours. Yours. . . .

To a Visitandine

[no date][13]

My very dear daughter,

Although I have never met you, I know you and love you very much. Your letter showed me very clearly the state of your soul and the source of its pain and perplexity, which is your over-eagerness to attain the true happiness you desire, and your lack of patience and docility to the will of Him who alone can grant it to you. Therefore, if you really want to acquire the spirit of your vocation, you will have to correct this overeagerness. Do everything you are taught in a spirit of gentleness and fidelity in order to reach the goal toward which you are being guided, cutting short all thought of attaining it except in God's good time. It seems to me that you are not satisfied with doing those acts required for your perfection, but that you want to feel and know that you are doing them. You must put an end to that and be content with telling God, without any feeling, "Lord, with all my heart I desire to practice such and such virtue just to please You." Then, set to work, although without feeling, and lovingly resolve to serve God in this way, desiring nothing more. If you do this, you will soon find yourself in that state of tranquility and peace which is so necessary for souls who wish to live virtuously, according to the spirit, and not according to their own inclinations and judgments.

This is what I see to be necessary for your peace of mind and spiritual advancement. May God fill each one of us with Himself, and may He grant you the grace of putting into practice all that she who has the obligation to guide you will advise. I am yours with love.

To Mother Marie-Aimée de Rabutin, Superior at Thonon

[Annecy] 26 June 1641[14]

My very dear daughter,

I bless God who gives you the courage to bear your burden cheerfully, despite the aversion you feel. It becomes clearer all the time that our Lord has destined you to be there for the good and happiness of that house. [. . .]

Do well what I advised you some time ago: help souls along very gently by word and deed and good example, without worrying so much about those who don't seem to profit from your efforts. There is nothing you can do about that. God's interest in these Sisters is greater than yours and He will, in His tender mercy, touch their hearts when He wishes.

Be careful not to put too much stock in what the Sisters say about each other, for often they can be mistaken. [. . .] My dear, you mustn't be so disturbed about the Sisters who resist your leadership. Always tell them what you think is for their good, but do so calmly, without raising your voice. If they follow your advice, praise God! If they don't, remain at peace, pray for them, and turn your attention to the other Sisters. Don't show annoyance or a desire to keep them under control.

This is how God, who is Master and has power to do whatever He wants, deals with us. Don't listen to those Sisters whom you see not acting out of pure charity, and urge all of them to cut back on all gossip, speaking only when charity or necessity requires it.

I see, my darling, that your soul still agonizes when you feel without grace or when you commit some fault that comes from the rigor with which you would like to make progress in a purity that is not to be found in this life. Your failings are not worth bothering about. I still think that the best thing is to stop examining yourself and to remain wide open in a holy confidence and joy, avoiding tension as much as possible.

I'm waiting for your articles in order to answer them. To this end, may God inspire me to say what He wills! Pray for me who am so intimately yours. . . .

To a Visitandine

[no date][15]

I return your greeting and also wish you a "forever," not of this perishable life, but of a blessed eternity which will be yours to claim after you've led a long, holy life of service to God through a faithful observance of your Rule. Our blessed Father used to say that the best means of grasping the spirit of our vocation was to put into practice the instructions found in our Rules. And you know that the principal ones are humility, self-effacement, and a holy simplicity which of itself does away with all kinds of vanity, self-seeking and self-satisfaction. If you put these virtues into practice, it will become apparent in all that you say, do, and write. Now it is this very simplicity that I especially want for you because it is the distinctive quality of the daughters of the Visitation.

Your indulgent heart, which I love most sincerely, gives me confidence to mention something in passing that I think you won't mind hearing. I find your letter very well written, but, it seems to me, it contains too many expressions that lack simplicity. That's why I hope that the virtues I have just spoken of will be seen in your thoughts, words and deeds, and that there will be nothing in your manner of speaking or writing that smacks of affectation. In truth, I would rather have us appear unskilled in letter-writing than be considered affected. [. . .]

I beg you, my dearest daughter, to pray to God for me. I wish you the attainment of a most holy perfection.

To a Superior

[no date][16]

My dearest daughter,

[. . .] If it appears that a Sister has done something that could lessen the mutual love and confidence that should exist among us, I prefer that before taking the rumor seriously and talking about it, you write to her quite candidly, not as if you believed what was being spread, but to learn the truth from her directly and to believe her.

I beg you, my dear Sister, govern your community with great expansiveness of heart: give the Sisters a holy liberty of spirit, and banish from your mind and theirs a servile spirit of constraint. If a Sister seems to lack confidence in you, don't for that reason show her the least coldness, but gain her trust through love and kindness. Don't entertain thoughts against any one of the Sisters, but treat them all equally. Lead them, not with a bustling, anxious kind of concern, but with a care that is genuine, loving, and gentle. I know there is no better way to succeed in leading souls. The more solicitous, open, and supportive you are with them, the more you will win their hearts. This is the best way of helping them advance toward the perfection of their vocation. So be present at the community exercises as often as you can, and let the Sisters know how much you enjoy being with them.

You tell me that you can no longer stand the burden of being Superior. Oh, Sister! please, don't ever let me hear you say that again! Do you want to bury your talents and render useless all the gifts God has lavished upon you? He has given you the graces so that His glory may be increased in whatever houses He confides to your governance. So look beyond your timid, fearful hesitations. Trample them underfoot, my dearest daughter, and keep your eye on God's good pleasure and His eternal plan for you. Surrender all the remaining days of your life to Him and let Him use them for such activities and services as please Him, and not yourself. Finally, place in His hands all your consolations, and believe that I am

Always your, etc. . . .

NOTES

1. *Sa Vie et ses oeuvres*, IV, 55–57: Letter XXXVII.
2. "Cadette" in French is a tender, affectionate term, almost a diminutive or nickname often given to a youngest child. In the Visitation M. Aimée de Blonay was often referred to in this way.
3. *Sa Vie et ses oeuvres*, IV, 78–81: Letter XLVII.

4. A *coadjutrix* was a sister who acted as an unofficial advisor to the Superior in personal and spiritual matters.

5. *Sa Vie et ses oeuvres,* V, 175–77: Letter CDLXIX.

6. "Blessed Father" refers to Francis de Sales. He died in December 1622.

7. *Sa Vie et ses oeuvres,* V, 513–14: Letter DCLXXII.

8. *Sa Vie et ses oeuvres,* V, 546–47: Letter DCXCI.

9. *Sa Vie et ses oeuvres,* V, 633–34: Letter DCCXXXVIII.

10. *Sa Vie et ses oeuvres,* VI, 47–49: Letter DCCLXXXIV.

11. *Sa Vie et ses oeuvres,* VI, 49–51: Letter DCCLXXXV.

12. At this time, 1627, many sisters in the young, struggling community of Rumilly (founded on September 29, 1625) were stricken by long, dangerous illnesses. Some townspeople who were against the foundation were saying that all this bad luck was a sign of God's displeasure.

13. *Sa Vie et ses oeuvres,* VIII, 432–34: Letter MDCCXC.

14. *Sa Vie et ses oeuvres,* VIII, 452–54: Letter MDCCCIV.

15. *Sa Vie et ses oeuvres,* VIII, 542: Letter MDCCLXIV. *[To a Visitandine]*

16. *Sa Vie et ses oeuvres,* VIII, 556–57: Letter MDCCCLXXII. *[To a Superior]*

A Developmental View
of Salesian Spirituality

Joann Wolski Conn

My ministry of doing spiritual direction and teaching it has led me to examine carefully how St. Francis de Sales (1567–1622) and St. Jane de Chantal (1572–1641) carried out this ministry. Reading their *Letters of Spiritual Direction*[1] and becoming familiar with the story of their lives has been giving me an ever deeper appreciation for their consummate skill as spiritual directors. Desiring a Salesian perspective on the classical theme of "self-knowledge and self-acceptance" in this ministry, I decided on an approach that was new for me: What would I notice about self-knowledge if I read the letters from the perspective of developmental psychology? This approach has reinforced my original conviction about their artistry as spiritual guides.

Let me share my enthusiasm by means of a two-part treatment. First, I will outline the kind of developmental psychology that I bring to the *Letters of Spiritual Direction* and show how it clarifies what we mean by "self" in the phrase "self-knowledge and self-acceptance." Second, I will use this as a lens for seeing more sharply not only the way Francis and Jane know and accept themselves, but also—primarily—the way they know and accept their directees. For it is through being deeply known and accepted that we can know and accept ourselves honestly—that is, humbly—and simply and lovingly. The goal of my presentation is such self-knowledge because all the great spiritual teachers declare that self-knowledge is the foundation of contemplative life and love, no matter what our ministry or particular vocation.

"SELF" IN DEVELOPMENTAL PSYCHOLOGY

In January 1615, when Jane set out for Lyons to make the first Visitation foundation from Annecy, Francis gave to her traveling companion a little packet of notes, one of which she was to give Jane every evening when they reached the inn where they were to spend the night. One note begins with a series of blessings: "These are the blessings which Jacob called down upon himself when he set out for Bethel, and I wish them to my own self. . . ."[2] Here "my own self" refers to Jane, whom Francis loves and feels is so united with him, in Christ, in deep human friendship that she is inseparable from his very own person. Thus, self means one's own deepest personal identity and one's way of understanding and valuing others. In other words, self is not only what I mean when I say "me," but also how I know and feel my relationship to others.

This identity changed and developed in both Jane and Francis so that self was understood differently at different times in their lives. For example, as a young student of the Jesuits in Paris, Francis experienced a profound transformation of his understanding of himself. This experience, described by Jane, who knew him better than anyone else in the world, was one of knowing himself as doomed to hell and then, after about six weeks of anguish, as transformed when his troubles fell away and he knew himself to be deeply loved by God. Eventually this love led him to pastoral ministry as priest and bishop, as promoter of spirituality for the laity, and as cofounder of the Visitation order.[3] Jane's self-knowledge also changed dramatically, but over a longer time. She understood herself, at one time, as completely identified with her husband, then gradually experienced a profound transformation into her identity as a widow, then as Visitandine foundress and as a spiritual director. This evolution in the way one makes the meaning of oneself is the focus of the developmental psychology that I bring to the appreciation of Jane and Francis as spiritual directors.

SELF FROM A STRUCTURAL PERSPECTIVE

First, let me distinguish the approach to development I will use here from "life-span development" made famous by Erik Erikson. Erikson explains how each era of biological life brings a crisis, such as the adolescent crisis of identity. We each meet this crisis with the uniqueness of our personality and the particular expectations of our culture. Whether or not we successfully resolve this crisis of identity, life continues to bring the subsequent developmental task, such as intimacy or generativity. Development, in this perspective, concentrates on how we resolve life's inevitable tasks; "ready or not," we have to meet the next phase of development.

In contrast, from a structural perspective, development does not happen necessarily or inevitably. A next phase or stage may never happen. We can support or inhibit development, but we cannot directly make it happen. Our own experience, as well as research, surely verifies the fact that we cannot make ourselves grow into selves who are completely loving and full of self-knowledge and generosity. Development is a wonderfully complex process that involves much more than our own effort, although our own cooperation is surely necessary.

Notice that I have just identified human development with greater love and self-knowledge. I have made these gospel ideals synonymous with psychological maturity because the developmental perspective I use makes human maturity and Christian spiritual maturity completely compatible, even identical in some ways. In my book *Spirituality and Personal Maturity*,[4] I fully explain this conclusion, but here, for the sake of brevity and focus, I must presume this conclusion. As I present the outline of how the self develops, it will be evident that the more mature person is characterized by freer love and more realistic self-knowledge and self-acceptance.

In the following outline of development, I will be using Elizabeth Liebert's *Changing Life Patterns: Adult Development in Spiritual Direction*[5] as well as my own work. Remember in all of this that any description of developmental stages is like stopping a movie at different parts of the story. It allows the contrast between characters' attitudes at different times to stand out, but it obscures the complexity of the transition between these stages. Also, of course, we must remind ourselves that no one fully exemplifies the characteristics of any stage. The value of this developmental outline is its ability to help us empathize with our own struggles and those of others; it helps us appreciate the mysterious working of grace within nature, and it suggests ways to support development.

WHY AND HOW THE SELF DEVELOPS

A person's natural condition is a state of dynamic poise, something like Francis de Sales's image of the heart's tranquillity resulting from steady, continuous, balanced movement. This movement is one of assimilating what takes place in our environment and thus changing, if ever so slightly, to accommodate the new reality. Often we unconsciously absorb new data into our current assumptions about reality, but we also often overlook or misperceive what is too unexpected or what we have no language for. A new experience "is Greek to me," we say. If we repeatedly accommodate ourselves to the new reality we see or read or hear or feel, we are likely to lose equilibrium, the sense of stability and balance we originally had. For example, we may meet Lutherans or Presbyterians whose faith in the presence of Christ in the Eucharist may undo our convictions about the clear distinction between Catholic and Protestant faith, or, finding ourselves misunderstood for some reason, we may question our own identity or our value as a person. When that happens a stage, or a balanced movement, gives way to a transition, which is that disorienting, very uncomfortable period between balances. Eventually a more complex view of "the way things are" *may* open up to us and give us a more inclusive sense of my "self" and "my relationship to others."

Elizabeth Liebert images development as an expanse of tiered rice paddies at the edge of a river.[6] The spring flood will fill the lowest field, but only when it has saturated all the ground at this level will it begin to rise to the next level. It cannot rise to level three without reaching the saturation point of the earlier levels. In other words, we may or may not eventually reorganize the meaning of ourselves and others in terms of a new sense of "the way things are"; if we do, this new perspective enables us to understand how people feel when they think the way we did at an earlier stage. What is the work of each stage? Let me outline this work in a few sentences, then outline the way to support this developmental work, and finally expand on these with more detail and with examples from Francis and Jane.

OUTLINE OF DEVELOPMENT

Each phase of development is a balancing of the two basic human longings for independence and attachment. Like chicks we "hatch out" of shells that enclose meanings of ourselves in our relation with others that have become too confining. For example, as children we eventually "hatch out" of the sphere of our family into a bigger world. At each phase, the balancing movement tilts either toward autonomy or relationship as we seek more independence for the sake of richer relationships. We have to become an independent self precisely so that we can freely give our self in love to others. Without this self-identity, what appears to be self-identity, what appears to be self-sacrifice or self-surrender may be compulsion (unfreedom), or simply conformity to roles (mother, "man for others," "servant of all") that others tell us we "should be." Remember, in this perspective, autonomy and relationship are inseparable at every stage. It is not a matter of either-or, but of *how* the balance that includes both will tilt. It is impossible to develop a more inclusive sense of self while bypassing the continuing development of relationships. Likewise, the understanding of groups "pulls along with it" the realization of the self as individual.[7]

HOW TO SUPPORT A DEVELOPING SELF

Most development occurs without much conscious awareness or action on our part. However, if we look at what studies uncover about these natural dynamics, we can learn to provide, in our various relationships, the "helpful pressures" that enable people to change and grow. These "helpful pressures" are three Cs:

confirming, contradicting, and *continuing.* We can first confirm persons as individuals and support them in whatever helps them at their stage of growth. Second, we can contradict what prevents growth at that stage and thus really encourage a new level of independence for the sake of deeper and more inclusive relationships. Third, we can continue our presence; we need to "stay around" while people struggle to find a new sense of self and of us; we can continue to be with them while they are often angry and unsure and vulnerable. Clearly, interpersonal relationships provide the most crucial context for supporting development. The power of friends, family, and spiritual directors to challenge one's assumptions about reality and one's place in it can be extremely important developmental stimuli, as we will notice now with Jane and Francis.[8]

Knowing just *how* to confirm, contradict, and continue will depend on knowing *how* persons tend to think and feel at each developmental stage. The three stages where adults cluster most can be described as *conformist, conscientious,* and *interindividual.*[9] Looking at the strengths and weaknesses of persons in these stages will help us appreciate how Francis and Jane supported the growth of such persons.

SUPPORTING THE DEVELOPMENT OF A CONFORMIST SELF

As the word conformist suggests, the strength of this stage comes from investing the meaning of one's self in persons and institutions outside oneself. For example, Jane de Chantal, before she met Francis de Sales, was completely invested in a spiritual-direction relationship that demanded complete secrecy and interminable prayers. This burdened her conscience and created aversion and anxiety. Nevertheless, for two and a half years she battled on under this discipline and obedience to an external authority, and did not break under the burden.[10] This strength is simultaneously its weakness. The self here is so fused with others that one lacks an inner, self-chosen identity. For example, if I make the meaning of myself this way, what I want is really what I want as part of all my fused relationships. That is, I want what my family wants, what my spiritual director wants, what a friend or spouse wants, what the church wants. When these different people turn out to want different things, then I feel torn apart. I feel this way because these various relationships are not something I *have;* they are what I *am.* For example, if my spiritual director teaches spiritual liberty and my parish community lives in conformity to an authoritarian image of the church, I can feel profoundly threatened, or anxious, or depressed. I face conflict I do not know how to handle. I do not have my own psychic space in which to negotiate the conflict. Virtues of this stage include generosity, loyalty to the group, niceness. Temptations include limiting growth by repressing negative feelings like anger, literal interpretations of rules and relationships, prejudice against others perceived as different, harsh judgments on self and others for breaking rules, succumbing to shame for personal failures. Francis's early letters to Jane reveal that she was struggling with this type of shame and self-condemnation.

Transition out of this stage requires the seeker to decide whether to explore the implications of unruly emotions. For example, Jane had to be willing to examine her anxiety and her dissatisfaction with her domineering director in order to see what these negative emotions were teaching her about herself and what she really desired. Also, for example, one must choose to reflect on the implications of conflicting themes such as the different interpretations of good spiritual direction given by Francis de Sales and Jane's previous director. Some persons begin to notice these conflicts and choose to keep life artificially simple and clear, thus foreclosing the possibility of development. They resist developing or refuse to develop a more complex, more mature balance of autonomy that would lead to deeper and richer relationships. Those who choose to do the work of development slowly achieve greater self-awareness and face the challenge of developing a consistent, secure, enduring self-concept with which to anchor transformed relationships. This is often a long transition, especially for women, in which panic and self-doubt alternate with a joyful sense of rebirth.[11]

Jane was experiencing this transition when she met Francis, and her willingness to deal with her unruly emotions reveals her choice to accept herself, with all discomfort that involved, and to do the work of spiritual development demanded at this stage. Francis's response to Jane demonstrates not only his acceptance of her, but also his awareness of how to confirm, contradict, and continue in such a way that authentic spiritual development becomes possible for a person like Jane at that stage.

Francis confirms Jane's "conforming self" in all that is good about this stage of her development: loving relationships that will expand her horizons; honesty about her strengths and weaknesses; awareness of her interior thoughts and feelings. In 1604, at the beginning of their relationship, Francis says, "Write to me, I beg you, as often as you can and with complete trust; in my great concern for your advancement, I shall be distressed if I do not know how things are going with you . . . never stop hoping for further opportunities to advance. Such longings are the blossoms on the tree of your desire; the leaves are the frequent admissions of your weakness, which keeps both your good works and your desires in a healthy condition" (124–125).

Special wisdom is needed to know how to contradict lovingly what is harmful for the growth of a "conformist self" like Jane at that stage. Here Francis is wonderful. Jane's kind of self needs to be contradicted when she avoids taking responsibility for her own preferences and decisions. In order to have an authentic self that one can give to God and others, the conformist self must grow in adult independence. Here is how Francis contradicts Jane's avoidance and promotes her mature self-direction: ". . . make use of some devout meditation similar to the one of which I am enclosing a copy. . . . Nevertheless, do not tie yourself down to this . . . use it only if you really prefer it, for in everything and at all times I want you to have a holy liberty of spirit in the means you take to attain perfection" (124–125). Beginning to trust one's own discernment can feel frightening, and so Francis says, "Guard against anxiety, depression, and scruples. You would never . . . want to offend God; that is reason enough to live joyously" (129). "The choice you have made gives every indication of being a good and legitimate one; so, please, have no further doubt about this" (130). Francis invites Jane to consider using the discipline (a small rope whip) as an ascetical practice and assumes Jane will make the decision whether or not to do this. Francis writes, "But this . . . must be taken in moderation, depending on the good it achieves, as you will know after trying it out for a few days" (134). Then he gives one of his famous spiritual maxims: "Do all through love [that is, freely chosen response to one's attraction], nothing through constraint" (134).

Not only does Francis give Jane wise confirmation and contradiction, but he assures her that he will continue to be present to her no matter what the future brings. ". . . I have never understood that there was any bond between us carrying with it any obligation but that of charity and true Christian friendship, . . . 'the bond of perfection'. . . . All other bonds are temporal, . . . which can be broken through death or other circumstances; but the bond of love grows and gets even stronger with time" (127). Francis's bold affirmations of affection for Jane and pledges of fidelity to her are beautiful examples of his own self-knowledge and self-acceptance of a male identity that need not shrink from candid acknowledgment of his growing love for Jane and awareness of its delightful effects on his prayer and ministry and life.

SUPPORTING THE DEVELOPMENT OF A CONSCIENTIOUS SELF

The transition I have described above may result in someone's becoming a conscientious self. Here the balancing motion of humanity's basic longings for both autonomy and attachment tilts toward autonomy, since the previous balance was tilted toward attachment. Here one has stronger ego boundaries and therefore can more freely *have* relationships instead of *being* relationships. Virtues of this person include inner moral standards, integrity, understanding and empathy, altruism. Temptations include avoiding the responsibility entailed in self-chosen standards; this avoiding shows up as alienation, cyncism, or activism. One is also tempted toward self-examination; excluding oneself from the scope of one's care; getting sidetracked into a search for inner religious experiences; seeking to control others, judging them by one's own norms.

How did Jane and Francis support the development of this kind of self? How did they confirm, contradict, and continue with these persons? Notice how Jane *confirmed* Noel Brulart, an aristocrat who, after years of immersion in the vanities and power of the French court, underwent a conversion, which was then nurtured by Jane's spiritual direction. She praises the strength of this kind of self: his candor and unpretentiousness, his initiative as a generous "guardian angel of our Congregation," his apostolic work (186–190). Most noticeable, however, is the way Jane's letters are filled with gentle *contradictions* focused precisely on the temptations attracting a conscientious self to stay in control or in self-absorption. She advises Brulart to "yield lovingly to this divine will when it allows you to fail to perform some good deed or to commit some fault. Resign yourself to not being able to resign yourself as completely and utterly as you would like, or as you think our Lord would like" (188). Aware of how competent persons are tempted to impatience with their inability to make themselves grow, Jane advises Brulart, "Have only a pure, simple, peaceful longing to please God, and . . . this will lead you to act without such impetuosity and overeagerness, but with peace and gentleness" (189).

Using this lens of developmental psychology, I am struck by Jane's very wise advice to a conscientious Visitandine superior: ". . . help souls along very gently by word and deed and good example, without worrying so much about those who don't seem to profit from your efforts. There is nothing you can do about that. God's interest in these sisters is greater than yours and he will, in his tender mercy, touch their hearts when he wishes." Jane knows that development cannot be rushed or directly produced. "Always tell [the sisters] what you think is for their good, but do so calmly, without raising your voice. . . . Don't show annoyance or a desire to keep them under control." The primary reason for accepting people as they are, not as they meet our interpretation of holiness, is that God accepts us as we are: "This is how God, who is Master and has power to do whatever he wants, deals with us" (263).

Because the conscientious self has struggled so long and hard to gain interior freedom from mere conformity, she has strong ego boundaries. Jane realizes, from personal experience, that this strong interiority can also be a problem. To this same Visitandine superior, Jane says, "I see, my darling, that your soul still agonizes when you feel without grace or when you commit some fault that comes from the rigor with which you would like to make progress in a purity that is not to be found in this life. Your failings are not worth bothering about. I still think that the best thing is to stop examining yourself and to remain wide open in a holy confidence and joy, avoiding tension as much as possible" (263). How is Jane's advice to "stop examining yourself" compatible with the whole spiritual tradition's emphasis on self-knowledge as a constant necessity? It is consistent, I believe, if we recall that Jane is speaking to a person with strong ego boundaries, to one tempted to self-examination that is hypercritical. This is not advice to a "conformist self" that needs to get in touch with what she really feels and wants. In this case of a conscientious self, the danger is that self-examination will subtly result in the illusion that we are "doing it," we are making ourselves grow in holiness, and we will lose sight of the reality that our life is a *relationship* to God and others who are freely relating to us in ways that we cannot control.

SUPPORTING THE DEVELOPMENT OF THE INTERINDIVIDUAL SELF

Transition out of this controlling self occurs here through the dark night of experiencing the limitations of the goodness of being conscientious. For example, moral values open out into greater awareness of inner conflict and toleration of paradox and contradiction. Feelings and needs can be vividly conveyed, and opposite needs may coexist at the same moment. For example, only after secure self boundaries are developed in spiritual liberty may one also appropriately affirm the opposite need—to be "dissolved" in God. Notice this toleration of paradox and contradiction in Jane's letter to a Visitandine: "You tell me, dear, that you experience God's infinite goodness so intimately present in your soul that you are scarcely aware of yourself. . . . This is a great grace. . . . How blessed are the souls who are so lost in God, for they can truly say . . . I live now, no longer I, but Jesus Christ lives in me!' But, you tell me, it's only your soul that attains this intimate union and that you have to do violence to yourself to get your other faculties to move in that direction. Don't be surprised at this. . . . God himself will calm them when it is expedient to do so" (257).

The typical conflict at this stage of development is between personal freedom and interpersonal responsibility. The challenge here is to allow others to be responsible individuals, finding their own way and making their own mistakes. Meeting this challenge creates the possibility for authentic intimacy and mutuality. Here is Jane's wise advice to a Visitation community: "Never be astonished at the faults of the community or of any individual sister, for to be shocked at our sisters' faults . . . to get all upset about them is the sign of a narrow-mindedness which has no insight into human frailty and very little charity or forbearance" (261).

When persons, such as Jane and Francis, involve themselves in the joys and pains of this phase of development, they experience the strengths and weaknesses of the interindividual stage. Strengths include a vision and commitment beyond the self, but including self as an integrated component of the vision; increased tolerance for other's autonomy, including one's own unconscious self and God. The weakness consists in the dividedness that results from one's inevitable participation in structures and institutions whose values differ from one's own and which stubbornly refuse to respond to individual action. Here I think first of modern women's struggle with the male-centered structures of the church and the suffering of the poor caused by unjust structures of our selfish global economy. Even within the smaller world of the Visitation communities, Jane's inclusive, interindividual self realized her inevitable participation in sinful social structure when she reminds a superior: "We . . . are usually guilty, as much for the faults of others as for our own, either because we overcorrected or tolerated too much, or else corrected too harshly or neglected to correct; or because we failed to include in our correction the sweetness of holy charity" (254).

Virtues of this mature stage include increasing intimacy with self, others, and God; a sense of cocreating with God; commitment to social concerns unrestricted by one's own boundaries of gender, race, or class; greater consistency between inner life and outer action. The temptation of this phase of development sounds familiar to all who know the spiritual classics of Salesian spirituality, or of Carmelite or Franciscan or Ignatian spirituality. It is the enticement to avoid the self-emptying necessary for granting others adult autonomy, the self-denial needed for building relationships of authentic mutuality and appropriate intimacy and even for confronting the sinful realities in which one can now see oneself inevitably embedded. The energy given to becoming a true self is needed to give that self away in partnership with God and others for the good of all in the cosmos. Francis supported Jane in this phase of her maturity by continuing to assure her of his faithful friendship even as he confirmed her desire to surrender all to God, including her connection to Francis himself. During her retreat of 1616, he wrote, "I agree that you should continue your exercise of complete self-renunciation, leaving yourself to our Lord and to me. . . . Furthermore . . . you must not keep any sort of nurse, but as you see, you must give up even the nurse [that is, Francis] who will nevertheless still be there. . . . May God make me all his for ever. Amen. For I am his here and also where I am in you, most completely, as you know; for we are inseparable except in the exercise and practice of our complete self-renunciation for God's sake."[12]

Having noticed how Francis and Jane accept themselves and know themselves and others at each phase of development, we can appreciate how their spiritual direction was so sensitively focused on just what each person needed. Beginners who made the meaning of themselves through fusion with others were encouraged to discern for themselves, to have spiritual liberty. In the 17th century this was, of course, understood within a different religious culture from ours. The boundaries of 17th-century social consciousness did not extend as far as the 20th century in awareness of gender, race, and class domination and restriction. Nevertheless, Francis and Jane did contradict conformity and confirm free, responsible discernment of one's own unique experience of God's direction in one's life. We can learn from them that the people in our lives are in different stages of development and therefore need different kinds of confirmation, contradiction, and continuation. We learn from Jane and Francis to wait before stressing complete self-abandonment until a person has struggled to find her or his own true self. Then, and only then, when one has a conscientious, freely self-directed kind of self, is one capable of spending one's life joyously, and gently doing, as Francis and Jane did, "all through love, nothing through constraint" (134).

NOTES

1. Francis de Sales, Jane de Chantal, *Letters of Spiritual Direction*, trans. Peronne Marie Thibert VHM, selected and introd. Wendy M. Wright and Joseph F. Power OSFS (New York: Paulist, 1988). Hereafter page references to this book will be given in parentheses after the quotation.

2. St. Francis de Sales, *Selected Letters*, trans. and introd. Elisabeth Stopp (New York: Harper, 1960), p. 226.

3. Michael J. Buckley, "Seventeenth-Century French Spirituality: Three Figures," in *Christian Spirituality: Post-Reformation and Modern*, ed. Louis Dupré and Don E. Saliers (New York: Crossroad, 1989), pp. 32–41.

4. Joann Wolski Conn, *Spirituality and Personal Maturity* (New York: Paulist, 1989; Lanham, Md.: University Press of America, 1994).

5. Elizabeth Liebert, *Changing Life Patterns* (New York: Paulist, 1992).

6. Ibid. p. 59.

7. Conn, *Spirituality*, pp. 50–57.

8. This outline is expanded in Conn, *Spirituality*, pp. 57–90.

9. The strengths and weaknesses of these are synthesized below primarily from Liebert, *Changing*, pp. 84–125. Applications to Francis and Jane are my own.

10. Elisabeth Stopp, *Madame de Chantal* (Westminster, Md.: Newman Press, 1963), pp. 47–48.

11. Liebert, *Changing*, p. 92–101.

12. de Sales, *Selected Letters*, pp. 243–244.

The Passion of My God

Rowan Williams

Christian faith has its beginnings in an experience of profound contradictoriness, an experience which so questioned the
religious categories of its time that the resulting organization of
religious language was a centuries-long task. At one level, indeed,
it is a task which every generation has to undertake again. And if
"spirituality" can be given any coherent meaning, perhaps it is to
be understood in terms of this task: each believer making his or
her own that engagement with the questioning at the heart of faith
which is so evident in the classical documents of Christian belief.
This is *not,* it must be said, to recommend any of the currently
fashionable varieties of relativism or to romanticize a wistful
"half-belief." The questioning involved here is not our interrogation of the data, but its interrogation of us. It is the intractable
strangeness of the ground of belief that must constantly be allowed to challenge the fixed assumptions of religiosity; it is a
given, whose question to each succeeding age is fundamentally
one and the same. And the greatness of the great Christian saints
lies in their readiness to be questioned, judged, stripped naked
and left speechless by that which lies at the centre of their faith.

The problem was, is and always will be the Christian attitude
to the historical order, the human past. By affirming that all "meaning," every assertion about the significance of life and reality, must
be judged by reference to a brief succession of contingent events in
Palestine, Christianity—almost without realizing it—closed off
the path to "timeless truth." That is to say, it becomes increasingly
difficult in the Christian world to see the ultimately important

human experience as an escape into the transcendent, a flight out of history and the flesh. Even when Christian writers use language suggesting such a picture, there are strong forces pulling in an opposite direction, demanding the affirmation of history, and thus of human change and growth, as significant. If the heart of "meaning" is a human story, a story of growth, conflict and death, every human story, with all its oddity and ambivalence, becomes open to interpretation in terms of God's saving work. Once we have stopped drawing a distinction between "compromising" activities and spheres (the family, the state, the individual body or psyche) and "pure" realities (the soul, the intelligible world), the spiritual life becomes a much more complex, demanding and far-reaching matter. "Spirituality" becomes far more than a science of interpreting exceptional private experiences; it must now touch every area of human experience, the public and social, the painful, negative, even pathological byways of the mind, the moral and relational world. And the goal of a Christian life becomes not enlightenment but wholeness—an acceptance of this complicated and muddled bundle of experiences as a possible theatre for God's creative work.

The pages which follow are meant as an introduction to the ways in which a succession of Christian saints attempted to articulate their vision of the Christian calling, the diverse ways in which they responded to the call toward wholeness. In the life and work of each of them, we may see the conflict and puzzlement which follow inevitably from the nature of their data. But it is a conflict supported and made bearable by one thing: every Christian thinker, if he or she at all merits the designation, begins from the experience of being reconciled, being accepted, being held (however precariously) in the grace of God. And this is mediated in the objective form of a shared life and language, a public and historical community of men and women, gathering to read certain texts and perform certain acts. That which transmits God's question from generation to generation is the Church (perhaps the Church can be defined only in some such way, as the bearer of that question; and, conversely, it might be said that whatever bears that question is, or is within, the Church); in this vastly diverse community, extending so widely in time and space, are the first resources for each person to live with the question. The failure of *every*

Christian to grasp and express the fullness of God's act in history can itself be a sustaining, even a heartening witness to our own particular doubts. The sense of common enterprise, *shared* speech, may help to save the individual, if only by reminding him or her that the focus of meaning is not private and particular, but a reality which incorporates and gives an identity and a structure to individual experience, and is never reducible to its limited terms. The study of the Christian past should properly be an exercise in living more seriously *in* the Church and *into* the historical corporateness of its tradition—not passively or uncritically, but with enough commitment to find in it nourishment and hope.

The first question, then, must be about the nature of our datum itself, the nature of God's alleged presence and work in Palestine. More specifically still, we must turn our attention to that aspect of the story of God-in-Christ which most sharply focuses the problems posed here for religious language. The final control and measure and irritant in Christian speech remains the cross: the execution of Jesus of Nazareth. Christianity is born out of struggle because it is born from men and women faced with the paradox of God's purpose made flesh in a dead and condemned man. Those who first believed in Jesus of Nazareth as God's herald and delegate had to find some way of dealing with the fact that the promised representative of God's restoration of his people had been rejected by those who claimed to speak for God's people, and had died a ritually contaminating death at the hands of the enemies of God's people. If the new age had dawned, it was with the slaughter of the Anointed at the instigation of those who controlled the religious "constructions of meaning" in Judea, and with the triumph of the kings of the Gentiles over the faithful of Israel. The early believers had to confront the possibility that the actual administration of law and covenant in Israel as a political entity had become incapable of either securing or recognizing true obedience to the purpose of God: an intimidatingly disorienting thought, which, within a generation, had already led some to postulate that the "old" covenant was itself a delusion.

The New Testament obstinately refuses this shortcut. It is often deeply marked by a fierce animus against Israel as it now exists, an animus that has helped to nourish and justify the appalling history of Christian antisemitism. There is no way of condoning or softening this aspect of so many strands of the Christian scriptures. But part of the anger and bewilderment shown in this arises precisely from an unwillingness to cut the cord connecting the new community with Israel. To make a bid to be the "real" Israel at least involves the trust that the same God is at work *through* the events of conflict and rupture, through the crisis of accessible religious meanings, clustered around the execution of Jesus. Jesus, in his ministry and in his death, had been seen as setting up models of the purpose of God and the involvement of human beings in this purpose that subverted important aspects of how the official religiousness of Israel understood these things in the special circumstances of the Second Temple period and the Roman occupation. The Christian agenda was set largely, at first, in terms of making sense of this perception against the background of the whole history of Jewishness. If God's herald and God's people appeared to come into open and fatal conflict, the "sameness" of the God involved needed to be thought through. The identity of the God of Christians could be neither exactly that of the God of the Jewish people, nor yet something other than or supplanting that prior identity defined by Israel's history. If God is to be seen at work here, he is indeed a strange God, a hidden God, who does not uncover his will in a straight line of development, but fully enters into a world of confusion and ambiguity and works in contradictions—the new covenant which both fulfills and radically alters the old, the Messianic age made real amid the suffering and failure of the present time.

NEW TESTAMENT FOUNDATIONS

It is the experience of these tensions which underlies most of the writings of the New Testament. In one way or another, practically all the writers are attempting to come to terms with the devastating finality of the life and death of Jesus: a finality which, on the one hand, means that attitudes to the law and the chosen people cannot ever be the same again, and, on the other, leaves the believer with all the problems of living in a visibly untransformed world. Yet the finality is inescapable. The believer now lives in and from the life of Jesus crucified and *risen*. The dead Jesus has been vindicated by his Father: the resurrection is that which *points to* the crucified as God's decisive manifestation. He is "designated Son of God in power according to the Spirit of holiness by his resurrection from the dead" (Rom 1:4); "God has highly exalted him and bestowed on him the name which is above every name" (Phil 2:9). Now that he is risen, the reconciliation he brings is made available for all men in all times and places (Mt 28:18–20; Lk 24:45–48; Jn 20:21–23). He is no longer limited by his historical particularity (no longer known "from a human point of view," "after the flesh"—2 Cor 5:16), though he never ceases to be particular—the man executed under Pontius Pilate, and no other. He does not belong to a finished and determined past, not even physically, as the stories of the empty grave impress upon us. He is "Lord." All things, all conditions, are now to be referred to him, to the pattern set by his story. And it is in this sense that Jesus alters the past of Jewish history as well as the present of the believer. The resurrection, which sets free the mission of the Church to reconcile, which *creates* reconciled lives, directs us to Calvary as an event which uncovers the truth, the resilient, inexhaustible, demanding objectivity of what God and God's work is like. From now on, all that can be said of God's action in the past or the present must pass under the judgment of this fact.

One immediate and disturbing implication of this is that God provokes crisis and division. Even during his ministry, Jesus had regularly spoken of the tragically divisive nature of his work (Mt 10:34–39 and parallels, 23:37–39 and parallels and, most starkly, 26:24 and parallels): the Fourth Gospel makes this a major literary theme, employing unparalleled subtlety in underlining the inexorable ironies of salvation and condemnation united in a single story. But it is Paul, especially in Romans and 2 Corinthians, who makes perhaps the most serious attempt in the New Testament to face and understand this. The ninth to the eleventh chapters of Romans painfully confront the question, of such personal urgency to Paul himself, of God's fidelity and consistency. Has the word of God failed? Is God unjust? Has he rejected his people? These queries send the reader back to the bleakest pages of the Old Testament—Lamentations, Job, the terrible eighty-ninth Psalm: God is the one who rejects and destroys, not only the one who elects and loves. He *drives* his people into turning their backs upon him; there are echoes of that hard Johannine saying, "If I had not come and spoken to them, they would not have sin" (Jn 15:22). The rejection of Jesus by men is at the same time the rejection of men by God, and it is acted out among the particular people whose privilege and burden it is to understand the intimacy of election to the full. Paul is here pointing to the single but enormous fact which forced Christianity out of its Jewish milieu, which made, and makes, Christian belief distinctively itself. It is not an ascription of "importance" to Jesus, not even a recognition of him as a supreme directive teacher or example. It is the acknowledgment of God as a God who is present in and works in human failure and helplessness—so much so that it can be said that he "forces" people into a decision to acknowledge or not to acknowledge their failure, in the events of Jesus' life and death.

For Paul, God had revealed the inadequacy of "Law" in the death of Jesus. This can mislead the modern reader into thinking Paul is committed to some kind of libertarian optimism, an opposition to "rules and regulations." Paul, however, treats "Law" as if it meant, fundamentally, *self-dependence*. To live by "Law" is to live by the accumulation of patterns of behavior, plans and projects and organizations of our human life. It is true that we cannot live without these things: law was given to Israel as a *gift*, as the possibility of a pattern of behavior honoring God in every detail of individual and corporate life; but where this has turned into a matter of abstract demand, whose satisfaction can justify a sense of "claim" upon God's favor, it has become a means of oppressing self and others. It is possible to build up a secure reality for ourselves resting on tangible achievement by individuals; to erect a system that allows no authentically positive role for dependence, belonging. Jesus had been remembered as defining the conditions for entering God's Kingdom in terms of the readiness to belong and to trust—to be a "child" (Mk 10:15), to make a simple commitment to Jesus himself (Mk 10:17–31), and so on. Insofar as this stands in clear opposition to the principle of systematic self-dependence—whether in the form of individual legalism, the elitism of the pious or the religious power system of the Jerusalem priesthood of the day—it can be said that Jesus stands against "Law." It is abundantly plain that he never preached a programmatic disregard for the Torah as such; but his recorded preaching sets a different sort of standard for probity before God from most of those currently recognizable. And to the extent that his proclamation was interpreted as a threat to the political administration of a Palestine governed by tacit alliance between occupying power and native clergy, it is possible to say that "Law," in Paul's sense, is responsible for the death of Jesus. A monopolistic and oppressive pattern of religious control is not capable of coexisting with the project of a society in which the readiness to trust is the sole determining factor in whether one does or does not count as a participant.

To believe in Jesus' God, the God of unconditional accessibility and even-handed compassion, to believe in an anarchic mercy that ignores order, rank and merit, is to accept that our projects and patterns are the mark of failure, of illusion, of the infantile belief that we can dictate truth and reality. Because it is menacing and painful to be confronted with the knowledge that our constructions of controlled sense are liable to be empty self-serving, we readily turn to violence against the bearers of such knowledge: in Johannine terms, we have decided we want to stay blind when the light is there before us, claiming we can see perfectly well (Jn 8:41). And the New Testament (especially the Fourth Gospel) suggests that only when such a naked collision of interest occurs can the uncompromising reality of God over against our patterns of "religious control" become clear. God provokes crisis to destroy our self-deceiving reliance on "Law," our dependence on what we as individuals can make and sustain, or what we as societies can administer for our own unchallenged interest. Self-dependence is revealed as a mechanism of self-destruction; to cling to it in the face of God's invitation to trust is a thinly veiled self-hatred.

"God has consigned all men to disobedience, that he may have mercy upon all" (Rom 11:32), writes Paul; and, "the scripture consigned all things to sin, that what was promised to faith in Jesus Christ might be given to those who believe" (Gal 3:22). The continuity and unity of God's work is, for Paul, manifest in these extraordinary reversals; and of course it is not easy for Paul, any more than for any believer, to assimilate this. At the conclusion of all the involved rabbinical disputation of Romans 9 to 11, he can do no more than cry out his wonder at the ways of God. It is a wonder not entirely new in Scripture; by some providential accident, it is Psalm 89, with its agonized protests, which concludes the third book of the Psalter and so ends with the doxology, "Blessed be the Lord forever! Amen and Amen." But Paul has been compelled to examine the logic of the greatest rejection of all, to strive for a reconciliation of his most basic commitments. He believes in God's election of Israel; in Israel as the paradigmatic recipient of grace; in God's self-consistency and faithfulness to his promises; and in God's decisive presence and work in the crucified Jesus, and his election of those baptized into Jesus. A God who can be the object of such commitment is a God who saves by fire. Conversion and repentance—those words which Christians of all persuasions have come to use so glibly—involve going down into the chaotic waters of Christ's death, so that the Spirit can move to make "new creation," being unmade to be remade.

It is part of the whole logic of this argument that the new life is not simply infused in all-conquering fullness in a single moment. It does not become a new Law, a new fixed pattern or possession, but a new state of affairs, the new "position" in which the believer can address the Father as Jesus had done, as "Abba" (Rom 8:15; Gal 4:6), a new state above all of *liberty* (2 Cor 3:17), but never a state possessed, always one *to be* realized. The Spirit is given as pledge, "advance payment" (2 Cor 5:5), as the ground of hope; and life in the Spirit is a "straining forward to what lies ahead" (Phil 3:13). The Spirit's work is to make the believer like Christ, and being like Christ means *living through* certain kinds of human experience—not once, but daily. The second letter to the Corinthians is Paul's most passionate meditation on this. Here he speaks of the daily affliction, the daily rejection, the daily dying by which the Spirit works, transforming us "from one degree of glory to another" (3:18). The veil of the Law is removed, illusion is stripped away; but only slowly does this penetrate every area of human living. And it penetrates by means of the pervasive and inexorable experience of failure, by the "wasting away" (4:16) of the instincts which look for clarity, ease and effectiveness and the acceptance of the hiddenness of God's working. God's servants, writes Paul with a delighted irony, have to "commend them-

selves" by their disasters, "in ill repute and good repute," acknowledging the flat paradoxicality of the believer's life in the
eyes of the world (6:3–10). And although the later chapters of this
epistle most probably come from a different document, it was a
sound instinct which united them with the beginning. For here
Paul in grief and anger and bitterness spreads out his apostolic
credentials to the skeptical: a catalogue of wretchedness, concluding with the humiliating memory of his ignominious escape from
Damascus (1 Cor 1:32–33). Here is the transfiguration from glory
to glory, realized daily in the absurd, the bitter, even the comical;
this is, surprisingly, what it is to live in the Messianic age and be
conformed to the pattern of the Messiah. When the future breaks
into the present order, it shows itself in Paul's "folly" for Christ,
in the stupid incongruities of this curious life in two worlds.

The new life is not a possession. It is, simply, new *life*—that
is to say, a new world of possibilities, a new future which is to be
constructed day by day. Life, after all, implies movement and
growth. And perhaps this rather banal and obvious point is an
indicator of what must be central for any adequate understanding
of Christian spirituality. It is worth noting how much stress not
only Paul but other writers lay upon the themes of the call to
maturity and the risks of regression: salvation is to be realized in
growth, and not to grow is to fall away. The opening chapters of 1
Corinthians remind a community of self-satisfied and fractious
converts that they are chosen in the first place for their weakness
(1:26–31) and that their calling is to an ever greater identification
with the weakness and hiddenness of God's action in Christ
(1:17–25; 2:1–9); and this (2:6) is their maturity and their
wisdom—a maturity which their various self-assertions amply
show them not to possess (3:1–4). They believe themselves to
have entered securely upon an inheritance; and Paul expends
some of his heaviest sarcasm upon this confidence (4:8–13). They
are confident of their spiritual riches, they measure their growth
in terms of tangible spiritual acquisition; but God marks out his
servants by their constant humiliations, "as the refuse of the
world, the offscouring of all things" (4:13). As much as in 2 Corinthians, Paul is struggling against a view which sees growth as
achievement, a "thing" acquired; for this has nothing to do with

his own sense of being daily grasped in his helplessness by a totally demanding and transforming fact, the death, and life past death, of Jesus the Messiah.

So much is this a whole and finished reality over against him that he has small interest in the imitation of Jesus' life. It would be wholly wrong to say that he has no "imitation" spirituality; but what is involved, what is to be followed, is the single great fact of obedience and self-emptying—Christ who "though he was rich, yet for your sake . . . became poor, so that by his poverty you might become rich" (2 Cor 8:9). And as the significance of Christ grows more and more plain, and the language of preexistence and cosmic lordship begins to appear, so, proportionately, does the sense of wonder at the scale of humility and poverty involved in Jesus' life and death. The greatest statement of this is, of course, the Christological hymn of Philippians 2, with its eloquent echoes of the gospel's concern with the redeemer as servant or slave of all.

But this is not the only response to the event of Christ's death among the early writers. The writer to the Hebrews is no less concerned than Paul with maturity and regression (Heb 5:11–6:12; 10:32–35; 12:1–11, etc.); but for him the appeal is to Christ as the sufferer and victor, the man who undergoes the harshest temptations and inner struggles in accepting his calling. Christ is the model for the *tempted* Christian: he has gone before into the dark places of doubt and fear and weakness, and endured to death. Our attention is drawn less to the "finished" reality of Paul's thought, more to the fragmented and uncertain human history behind that reality. The experience of weakness, failure, self-despair of which Paul has so much to say is in Hebrews treated less "programmatically," more pastorally. We are enabled to interpret and so to bear our doubt and pain by the knowledge that our salvation is won by the doubt and pain of Christ. "Although he was a Son, he learned obedience through what he suffered; and being made perfect he became the source of eternal life to all who obey him" (Heb 5:8–9). Our healing lies in obedient acceptance of God's will; but this is no bland resignation. It is a change wrought by anguish, darkness and stripping. If we believe we can experience our healing without deepening our hurt, we have understood nothing of the roots of our faith; Jesus' obedience in the circumstances of his earthly life, in temptation and fear, "with loud cries and tears" (5:7), is what opens the long-closed door between God and our hearts, and although that door is now decisively open, all must still pass through it to make the reconciliation their own. They must now "obey" *Christ*, surrender to the pattern of his sacrificial torment and death—not in some kind of constructed self-immolation, but in response to the trials encountered simply in living as a believer, living in the insecurities of faith, "the conviction of things not seen." It is an acceptance of the hidden God and his strange work, the God who is only attained through stripping and the purgation of his "consuming fire" (12:27). We go to him, as did the saints of the old convenant, by going out: out of the camp, out of the city (13:12–14), beyond the settled and the ordered, to the place where Jesus died in his night, his desert.

> The desire to be in God's image without attaining Christ's image is a desire for immediacy, which wants everything without detour and without self-actualization, a narcissistic desire of the ego to settle down in God, immortal and almighty, that doesn't find it necessary "to let its life be crucified" and to experience the night of pain.

Thus Dorothee Sölle, in her passionate and moving book *Suffering* (p. 131), reiterates the New Testament's protest against a "spirituality" without conflict, against the illusion that God is to be found apart from Jesus crucified. But at the same time it is one of the great strengths of her study that she consistently refuses to identify the *acceptance* of pain with passivity in the face of it, a passivity which is, in fact, hardening and dehumanizing. The Christian meets pain in acceptance and *hope;* he or she confronts it, identifies with those experiencing it, and then struggles through it to grow into a new humanness, "more capable both of pain and of love" (p. 134). In suffering, the believer's self-protection and isolation are broken: the heart is broken so as to make space for others, for compassion. Pain is borne in hope of a new and more compassionate humanity; returning to the New Testament, we may speak again of the Holy Spirit's work. The Spirit is "pledge," the Spirit is that which more and more conforms to Christ; and so the Spirit is that which impels us forward, which creates hope out of our cries of protest in the present. We protest because we have tasted the reality of new life, God's life, already, the life of self-gift and self-forgetting, so that we know that our present pain is not the whole of reality, that behind it is a more final fact, God's vulnerable love drawing us forward. For God is in our pain and our protest: the Spirit, says Paul, is "bearing witness with our spirit" (Rom 8:16) to our destiny and our hope, and prays in us "with sighs too deep for words" (8:26). The crying and longing of the homesick creation is the Spirit's crying. It is in and by the Spirit that we call on God as "Abba!" in his Gethsemane, at the depth of his fear and doubt. The cry to God as Father in the New Testament is not a calm acknowledgement of a universal truth about God's abstract "fatherhood," it is the child's cry out of nightmare. It is the cry of outrage, fear, shrinking away, when faced with the horror of the world—yet not simply or exclusively protest, but trust as well. "Abba, Father, all things are possible to thee" (Mk 14:36). From the middle of the night, we recognize the finality of God's mercy and acceptance. Even when there is no comfort given, there may still be hope: "not what I will, but what thou wilt" (ibid.). Hope is in trusting whatever God may will; and this is preeminently the gift of the Spirit. "Christ . . . through the eternal Spirit, offered himself without blemish to God" (Heb 9:14). Our pain is conformed to the pattern of his by the presence of that same Spirit of protest, trust and hope.

The presence of this hope is what makes us alive with "newness of life" (Rom 6:4), in the sharing of Christ's *risen* life. Christ's risen life is a life *free* from the threat of death and annihilation ("Christ being raised from the dead will never die again"— Rom 6:9), the "threatenedness" that is part of the condition of human sin and distance from God. In sharing this life, we share his freedom from "threatenedness," it is never—as is perfectly clear in all Paul's epistles—a freedom from exposure to suffering or from fear, but it is a decisive transition to that new level of existence where God is the only ultimate horizon—not death or nothingness. "From now on, therefore, we regard no one from a human point of view; even though we once regarded Christ from a human point of view, we regard him thus no longer" (2 Cor 5:16): the "human point of view," for which death is the final horizon, is put away, so that we are free with Christ's freedom. We have, in John's terms, "passed out of death into life" (Jn 3:14).

For Paul and John equally, the sign of this passage is a new capacity for love. "We *know* that we have passed out of death into life, because we love the brethren." It is a reflection of Jesus' synopsis of the Law and of the parable of the Great Assize (Mt 25:31–46). It is not that (as some recent writers on the ethics of the New Testament seem to suggest) love is presented as an impossible ideal, to be realized only by grace in the new age; rather the simple assertion that where love is, the Kingdom is, and that reconciliation with the Father is at work, even when unrecognized. The "unselfing" involved in union with Christ's death is made real in the public and social world; the displacing of the ego becomes a giving "place" to others, as God has given "place" to all in his Son. We love because we are loved (1 Jn 4:7–11), because our "place" with the Father is secured by Jesus (Jn 14:2–3). We know ourselves accepted without qualification, and so have no need of the self-assertive struggle to win a place, a status, a justification. We have understood that the final security is God's gift, and therefore that others will equally find their security in gift—in our humility and "emptiness" in service to them. "Love does not insist on its own way," as Paul has it in his great hymn in 1 Corinthians 13 (v. 5); or, in the more comprehensive rendering of the Authorized Version, "seeketh not her own." This, as Paul and John agree, is the most clear and enduring mark of Christian identity: not (as, again, it has become fashionable in some quarters to suppose) a benevolence toward all and a generalized wish for their welfare, but an entirely costly *disponibilité,* availability in service which gives no room to the superficial interests of the ego. And it is, once again, something evolving. We have "put away childish things" in the painful maturity of love, and we move from darkness and enigma in our understanding towards the light of day (1 Cor 13:11–12). We already have our adoption, our "place" as children of God, but we cannot begin to imagine the final realization; we know only that it will be seeing God as he is and, in that seeing, being fully conformed to his likeness (1 Jn 3:2). The end of the believer's life is knowledge of God in conformity to God. Knowledge of God is not a subject's conceptual grasp of an object, it is sharing what God is—more boldly, you might say, sharing God's "experience." God is known in and by the exercise of crucifying compassion; if we are like him in that, we know him. And we know "as we are known," "as I have been fully understood" (1 Cor 13:12), since God knows the human condition in loving it. This knowledge by identification, loving union, is imaged in the appropriating of marital imagery (in 2 Cor 11:2; Eph 5 and the final chapters of Revelation) to describe the union of Christ with the believing community, as it had once described God's union with Israel. The Messianic feast at the end of all things is, as in Jesus' parables (Mt 22:1–10; 25:1–13), a marriage supper; and the longing of the Church and the protesting and struggling Spirit in the Church is the bride's longing for her husband. "The Spirit and the Bride say, 'Come' " (Rev 22:17).

REFERENCES

Among general guides to the development of Christian spirituality, the following are of particular value: *The Study of Spirituality,* eds. Cheslyn Jones, Geoffrey Wainwright and Edward Yarnold, SJ (London, 1986), especially good on patristic and Eastern sources; *A Dictionary of Christian Spirituality,* ed. Gordon Wakefield (London, 1983); *Mysterion. Du mystère à la mystique* by Louis Bouyer (Paris, 1986), which studies the biblical and patristic origins of the vocabulary of mysticism, locating the whole discussion in the context of a general account of revelation and humanity in the purposes of God; *The Origins of the Christian Mystical Tradition* by Andrew Louth (London, 1981), probably the best and most reliable book in English on the appropriation and transformation by Christians of the Platonic world of reference; *Asking the Fathers* by Aelred Squire (London, 1973); *Ways of Imperfection* by Simon Tugwell (London, 1984); *Christian Spirituality I. Origins to the Twelfth Century,* eds. B. McGinn and J. Meyendorff (London, 1986).
Three books in particular have shaped a great deal of this chapter: *The Religious Imagination and the Sense of God* by John Bowker (Cambridge, 1978); *The Crucified Is No Stranger* by Sebastian Moore (London, 1977); *Suffering* by Dorothee Sölle (London, 1976).
Among works on New Testament scholarship, I owe a particular debt to the writings of Professor C. F. D. Moule: most recently, *The Origin*

of Christology (Cambridge, 1977). On the complex question of Jesus' relation to Israel and the Law, my earlier and very much over-simplified account has been revised in the light of more recent work, notably *Jesus and Judaism* by E. P. Sanders (London, 1985). And, although many of its conclusions are overturned by Sanders, the earlier work of John Riches, *Jesus and the Transformation of Judaism* (London, 1980), still has insights of great value.

Stages of Faith

James Fowler

Stage 1 Intuitive-Projective faith is the fantasy-filled, imitative phase in which the child can be powerfully and permanently influenced by example, moods, actions and stories of the visible faith of primally related adults.

The stage most typical of the child of three to seven, it is marked by a relative fluidity of thought patterns. The child is continually encountering novelties for which no stable operations of knowing have been formed. The imaginative processes underlying fantasy are unrestrained and uninhibited by logical thought. In league with forms of knowing dominated by perception, imagination in this stage is extremely productive of long-lasting images and feelings (positive and negative) that later, more stable and self-reflective valuing and thinking will have to order and sort out. This is the stage of first self-awareness. The "self-aware" child is egocentric as regards the perspectives of others. Here we find first awarenesses of death and sex and of the strong taboos by which cultures and families insulate those powerful areas.

The gift of emergent strength of this stage is the birth of imagination, the ability to unify and grasp the experience-world in powerful images and as presented in stories that register the child's intuitive understandings and feelings toward the ultimate conditions of existence.

The dangers in this stage arise from the possible "possession" of the child's imagination by unrestrained images of terror and destructiveness, or from the witting or unwitting exploitation of her or his imagination in the reinforcement of taboos and moral or doctrinal expectations.

The main factor precipitating transition to the next stage is the emergence of concrete operational thinking. Affectively, the resolution of Oedipal issues or their submersion in latency are important accompanying factors. At the heart of the transition is the child's growing concern to know how things are and to clarify for him- or herself the bases of distinctions between what is real and what only seems to be.

Stage 2 Mythic-Literal faith is the stage in which the person begins to take on for him- or herself the stories, beliefs and observances that symbolize belonging to his or her community. Beliefs are appropriated with literal interpretations, as are moral rules and attitudes. Symbols are taken as one-dimensional and literal in meaning. In this stage the rise of concrete operations leads to the curbing and ordering of the previous stage's imaginative composing of the world. The episodic quality of Intuitive-Projective faith gives way to a more linear, narrative construction of coherence and meaning. Story becomes the major way of giving unity and value to experience. This is the faith stage of the school child (though we sometimes find the structures dominant in adolescents and in adults). Marked by increased accuracy in taking the perspective of other persons, those in Stage 2 compose a world based on reciprocal fairness and an immanent justice based on reciprocity. The actors in their cosmic stories are anthropomorphic. They can be affected deeply and powerfully by symbolic and dramatic materials and can describe in endlessly detailed narrative what has occurred. They do not, however, step back from the flow of stories to formulate reflective, conceptual meanings. For this stage the meaning is both carried and "trapped" in the narrative.

The new capacity or strength in this stage is the rise of narrative and the emergence of story, drama and myth as ways of finding and giving coherence to experience.

The limitations of literalness and an excessive reliance upon reciprocity as a principle for constructing an ultimate environment can result either in an overcontrolling, stilted perfectionism or "works righteousness" or in their opposite, an abasing sense of badness embraced because of mistreatment, neglect or the apparent disfavor of significant others.

A factor initiating transition to Stage 3 is the implicit clash or contradictions in stories that leads to reflection on meanings. The transition to formal operational thought makes such reflection possible and necessary. Previous literalism breaks down; new "cognitive conceit" (Elkind) leads to disillusionment with previous teachers and teachings. Conflicts between authoritative stories (Genesis on creation versus evolutionary theory) must be faced. The emergence of mutual interpersonal perspective taking ("I see you seeing me; I see me as you see me; I see you seeing me seeing you.") creates the need for a more personal relationship with the unifying power of the ultimate environment.

In Stage 3 Synthetic-Conventional faith, a person's experience of the world now extends beyond the family. A number of spheres demand attention: family, school or work, peers, street society and media, and perhaps religion. Faith must provide a coherent orientation in the midst of that more complex and diverse range of involvements. Faith must synthesize values and information; it must provide a basis for identity and outlook.

Stage 3 typically has its rise and ascendancy in adolescence, but for many adults it becomes a permanent place of equilibrium. It structures the ultimate environment in interpersonal terms. Its images of unifying value and power derive from the extension of qualities experienced in personal relationships. It is a "conformist" stage in the sense that it is acutely tuned to the expectations and judgments of significant others and as yet does not have a sure enough grasp on its own identity and autonomous judgment to construct and maintain an independent perspective. While beliefs and values are deeply felt, they typically are tacitly held—the person "dwells" in them and in the meaning world they mediate. But there has not been occasion to step outside them to reflect on or examine them explicitly or systematically. At Stage 3 a person has an "ideology," a more or less consistent clustering of values and beliefs, but he or she has not objectified it for examination and in a sense is unaware of having it. Differences of outlook with others are experienced as differences in "kind" of person. Authority is located in the incumbents of traditional authority roles (if perceived as personally worthy) or in the consensus of a valued, face-to-face group.

The emergent capacity of this stage is the forming of a personal myth—the myth of one's own becoming in identity and faith, incorporating one's past and anticipated future in an image of the ultimate environment unified by characteristics of personality.

The dangers or deficiencies in this stage are twofold. The expectations and evaluations of others can be so compellingly internalized (and sacralized) that later autonomy of judgment and action can be jeopardized; or interpersonal betrayals can give rise either to nihilistic despair about a personal principle of ultimate being or to a compensatory intimacy with God unrelated to mundane relations.

Factors contributing to the breakdown of Stage 3 and to readiness for transition may include: serious clashes or contradictions between valued authority sources; marked changes, by officially sanctioned leaders, or policies or practices previously deemed sacred and unbreachable (for example, in the Catholic church changing the mass from Latin to the vernacular, or no longer requiring abstinence from meat on Friday); the encounter with experiences or perspectives that lead to critical reflection on how one's beliefs and values have formed and changed, and how "relative" they are to one's particular group or background. Frequently the experience of "leaving home"—emotionally or physically, or both—precipitates the kind of examination of self, background, and lifeguiding values that gives rise to stage transition at this point.

The movement from Stage 3 to Stage 4 Individuative-Reflective faith is particularly critical for it is in this transition that the late adolescent or adult must begin to take seriously the burden of responsibility for his or her own commitments, lifestyle, beliefs and attitudes. Where genuine movement toward stage 4 is underway the person must face certain unavoidable *tensions:* individuality versus being defined by a group or group membership; subjectivity and the power of one's strongly felt but unexamined feelings versus objectivity and the requirement of critical reflection; self-fulfillment or self-actualization as a primary concern versus service to and being for others; the question of being committed to the relative versus struggle with the possibility of an absolute.

Stage 4 most appropriately takes form in young adulthood (but let us remember that many adults do not construct it and that

for a significant group it emerges only in the mid-thirties or forties). This stage is marked by a double development. The self,
previously sustained in its identity and faith compositions by an
interpersonal circle of significant others, now claims an identity
no longer defined by the composite of one's roles or meanings to
others. To sustain that new identity it composes a meaning frame
conscious of its own boundaries and inner connections and aware
of itself as a "world view." Self (identity) and outlook (world
view) are differentiated from those of others and become acknowledged factors in the reactions, interpretations and judgments one
makes on the actions of the self and others. It expresses its intuitions of coherence in an ultimate environment in terms of an
explicit system of meanings. This is a "demythologizing" stage. It
is likely to attend minimally to unconscious factors influencing its
judgments and behavior.

Stage 4's ascendant strength has to do with its capacity for
critical reflection on identity (self) and outlook (ideology). Its
dangers inhere in its strengths: an excessive confidence in the
conscious mind and in critical thought and a kind of second narcissism in which the now clearly bounded, reflective self over-
assimilates "reality" and the perspectives of others into its own
world view.

Restless with the self-images and outlook maintained by
Stage 4, the person ready for transition finds him- or herself attending to what may feel like anarchic and disturbing inner
voices. Elements from a childish past, images and energies from a
deeper self, a gnawing sense of the sterility and flatness of the
meanings one serves—any or all of these may signal readiness for
something new. Stories, symbols, myths and paradoxes from
one's own or other traditions may insist on breaking in upon the
neatness of the previous faith. Disillusionment with one's compromises and recognition that life is more complex than Stage 4's
logic of clear distinctions and abstract concepts can comprehend,
press one toward a more dialectical and multileveled approach to
life truth.

Stage 5 Conjunctive faith involves the integration into self
and outlook of much that was suppressed or unrecognized in the
interest of Stage 4's self-certainty and conscious cognitive and
affective adaptation to reality. This stage develops a "second

naïveté" (Ricoeur) in which symbolic power is reunited with conceptual meanings. Here there must also be a new reclaiming and reworking of one's past. There must be an opening to the voices of one's "deeper self." Importantly, this involves a critical recognition of one's social unconscious—the myths, ideal images and prejudices built deeply into the self-system by virtue of one's nurture within a particular social class, religious tradition, ethnic group or the like.

Unusual before mid-life, Stage 5 knows the sacrament of defeat and the reality of irrevocable commitments and acts. What the previous stage struggled to clarify, in terms of the boundaries of self and outlook, this stage now makes porous and permeable. Alive to paradox and the truth in apparent contradictions, this stage strives to unify opposites in mind and experience. It generates and maintains vulnerability to the strange truths of those who are "other." Ready for closeness to that which is different and threatening to self and outlook (including new depths of experience in spirituality and religious revelation), this stage's commitment to justice is freed from the confines of tribe, class, religious community or nation. And with the seriousness that can arise when life is more than half over, this stage is ready to spend and be spent for the cause of conserving and cultivating the possibility of others' generating identity and meaning.

The new strength of this stage comes in the rise of the ironic imagination—a capacity to see and be in one's or one's group's most powerful meanings, while simultaneously recognizing that they are relative, partial and inevitably distorting apprehensions of transcendent reality. Its danger lies in the direction of a paralyzing passivity or inaction, giving rise to complacency or cynical withdrawal, due to its paradoxical understanding of truth.

Stage 5 can appreciate symbols, myths and rituals (its own and others') because it has been grasped, in some measure, by the depth of reality to which they refer. It also sees the divisions of the human family vividly because it has been apprehended by the possibility (and imperative) of an inclusive community of being. But this stage remains divided. It lives and acts between an untransformed world and a transforming vision and loyalties. In some few cases this division yields to the call of the radical actualization that we call Stage 6.

Stage 6 is exceedingly rare. The persons best described by it have generated faith compositions in which their felt sense of an ultimate environment is inclusive of all being. They have become incarnators and actualizers of the spirit of an inclusive and fulfilled human community.

They are "contagious" in the sense that they create zones of liberation from the social, political, economic and ideological shackles we place and endure on human futurity. Living with felt participation in a power that unifies and transforms the world, Universalizers are often experienced as subversive of the structures (including religious structures) by which we sustain our individual and corporate survival, security and significance. Many persons in this stage die at the hands of those whom they hope to change. Universalizers are often more honored and revered after death than during their lives. The rare persons who may be described by this stage have a special grace that makes them seem more lucid, more simple, and yet somehow more fully human than the rest of us. Their community is universal in extent. Particularities are cherished because they are vessels of the universal, and thereby valuable apart from any utilitarian considerations. Life is both loved and held to loosely. Such persons are ready for fellowship with persons at any of the other stages and from any other faith tradition.

Changing Life Patterns

Elizabeth Liebert

INTERPERSONAL STYLE OF A CONFORMIST PERSON

The Conformist's desire to belong obviously influences interpersonal style in significant ways. First, the scope of social interaction remains relatively concrete and "close-in" at this stage.
Conformist persons feel trust and warmth from and extend cooperation and helpfulness to groups "like me," such as immediate or extended family, one's religious congregation, parish or
denomination, one's colleagues at a particular workplace or in a
certain profession, even one's fellow-citizens. Yet two significant
limitations characterize the Conformist interpersonal style. First,
awareness of mutuality, the ability to participate equally in relationships, is still limited to conscious participation; a grasp of
unconscious motivation has yet to occur spontaneously. Second,
a broad and inclusive social worldview is developmentally beyond the Conformist person; it becomes ascendant only at the
Interindividual stage. Consequently, amid the niceness and loving concern for one's own, malignant or thoughtless prejudices
to out-groups can coexist. This developmental constraint helps
explain why some religious groups, typically those who attract
large numbers of Conformist persons, can be among the most
prejudiced in our society—for such persons, being outside the
pale should merit *God's* judgment.[1]

Another stage-specific Conformist characteristic involves understanding relationships in terms of action rather than of still
relatively inaccessible feelings and motives. Thus, for Conformist

349

persons, friends are people you do things with. In a sense, inter-personal style is *the* significant dimension of the Conformist stage. Interpersonal relationships, though tacitly held, comprise the chief focus of identity formation.

What issues arise for the spiritual director? First, interpersonal mutuality can extend to God, as well as to the valued members of one's self-chosen groups. To a more significant degree than possible at earlier developmental levels, God can be a separate person with whom one can have an increasingly deep relationship. The somewhat prepersonal anthropomorphic conceptions of God typical of earlier stages may now become intensely personal, though still concrete and anthropomorphic. The hierarchical, authoritarian and dualistic conception of parent-child relationships which also characterize this stage may carry over into the conception of God, encouraging a power-oriented, exploitatively dependent attitude.[2] Thus, in a malevolent turn of the same dynamics, some individuals may experience God as a personal judge or strict parent who haunts their every infraction of the rules.

Being a valued member of a congregation, religion, or religious community can assume central importance in identity formation. Seeking, "God's will," whether through denominational leaders, clergy, formation personnel or spiritual directors, through "God's Word" in scripture, or through religiously sanctioned behavior, can serve as crucial behavioral motivators. However, "God's will" will most likely be understood in behavioral terms rather than in attitudinal or motivational terms.

A delicate issue arises around the spiritual director's participation in Conformist dynamics. It is clearly important to encourage growth of a personal relationship with God. But, because directors will necessarily have to respond concretely to Conformist persons, they may also tend to become more "directive." To the extent that seekers perceive spiritual directors as valued authorities, directors may unwittingly collude in confirming and even strengthening a Conformist orientation past its usefulness. Sanctions by valued religious authorities, especially within the context of a one-to-one continuous relationship, can have tremendous power. On the other hand, spiritual directors may also lose sight of the fact that the Conformist orientation can be valuable in its own right if it is an authentic expression of one's life and call at that moment. As James Fowler says:

> For persons in a given stage at the right time *for their lives*, the task is the full realization and integration of the strengths and graces of that stage rather than rushing on to the next stage. Each stage has the potential for wholeness, grace and integrity and for strengths sufficient for either life's blows or blessings.[3]

RECAPITULATION

The *strength* of the Conformist stage comes from investing in persons and institutions outside oneself. Socialization into groups and communal norms readily occurs. But the strength of one stage simultaneously comprises its weakness with respect to subsequent constructions. At the Conformist stage, individuals remain submerged within the various groups to which they belong. The lack of an inner, self-chosen identity allows Conformist persons to take on various identities—to be different persons—as dictated by the diverse groups to which they have committed themselves.

In somewhat more theological language, the *virtues* of the Conformist stage include generosity, consistency, niceness, helpfulness. Conformist persons will actively promote the goals of the groups with which they identify; certainly they will not "rock the boat." They are capable of a new level of trust and interpersonal relations, including a personal relationship with God. Prayer will be action-oriented and concrete (but with so-called affective prayer still beyond their comfort range). Corresponding *temptations* include an outright return to impulsive behavior, resisted by limiting one's negative feelings; literal and concrete interpretations of rules, texts and relationships (including the relationship with God); prejudice against others perceived as different; authoritarianism; rigidity; harsh judgments on self and others for infractions of rules; and succumbing to shame for personal failures.

Some spiritual directors will find Conformist directees frustrating and challenging. To the degree that directors assume that seekers will come with and will grow in self-awareness, self-identity and self-responsibility before others and before God, they may be puzzled and irritated by the apparent inability of Conformist persons to take life into their own hands, to work "inside," or to pray affectively. They may feel that they have to be more directive with such individuals and to assume more responsibility for their spiritual life than they would like. Therefore, they may fall into a parental style without confirming and enhancing the strengths of this developmental type.

SIGNS OF TRANSITION

Although it is impossible to point out any one time or behavior as the actual stage change, some situations and experiences tend to precipitate transition. At this point in the developmental continuum, those issues and experiences include realizing that respected authorities disagree, and that the various groups to which one belongs demand contradictory commitments or behaviors. Possibly, too, an individual may have experienced "failures" to live up to the idealized portrait set by social norms. For example, a person may work assiduously to earn recognition or advancement but be passed over without notice. Another person may be ashamed that less desirable drives and their attendant feelings surface, despite attempts to keep such unruly aspects of personality out of conscious awareness.

The beginning of the transition out of Conformity presents the seeker and the spiritual director alike with a crisis—though not one that can be settled once and for all. The seeker must decide whether to explore the implications of unruly emotions or conflicting stories, despite the painful disorientation which may result from the undoing of one's worldview. Some persons will foreclose the possibility of change or even regress to an earlier dualistic level. Such persons, who have in some sense "chosen" to keep life artificially simple and clear, will present a particular challenge to spiritual directors.

For their part, directors must decide what to confirm: the "old" view of the world, the confusion of the present experience, or the possibility of a new self which as yet may be only a hope. Furthermore, what constitutes hope at this juncture? Who is God for the directee now? How can or must the relationship between the director and the directee change?

Transition may happen so gradually that one only recognizes it in retrospect. And, in fact, a transition itself may make sufficient sense of inner and outer challenges that it becomes a quasi-permanent reality construction in its own right.

INTERPERSONAL STYLE OF A CONSCIENTIOUS PERSON

The turn to the inner life characteristic of the Conscientious person simultaneously allows broadening and deepening of all other relationships. Developmental readiness for intimacy appears at this stage, resulting in increased potential for mutual, intense relationships. A sense of responsibility for others and a concern for communication, especially of differentiated feelings, sustains these relationships.

Reconstructing the sense of self-in-relationship has tremendous implications for spiritual direction. First, one's conception of self in relation to self changes. Persons become truly reflexive, not as an occasional insight, but as a characteristic way of seeing. Directees can recognize strengths and weaknesses in their relationships, personality traits and responses.

Second, self-objectivity extends to objectivity with others, the prerequisite for deepened reciprocity and intimacy in interpersonal relations. However, spiritual directors also receive the breakdown or frustration of this turn to mutuality. When directees do not experience themselves treated as unique individuals within significant relationships, such as when judicatory boards or religious congregations resort to filling slots, when authority appears depersonalizing, or when one's spouse does not share an interest in inner life, the resulting crisis can even challenge basic vocational choices. This dilemma might be expressed as "I don't see how I can keep growing any more; there's no support for my inner life any longer," or "There's no way we can communicate on the level of feelings and values and what's important to me." When Conscientious persons make this kind of statement, they imply that other persons or institutions should somehow accommodate their newly forged self-identity; when Interindividual persons say something similar, it may function simply as a statement of fact and serve as a launching pad for constructing a new sense of self in the midst of the resulting tension.

In another twist to the possibilities and problematics of the Conscientious frame of reference, individuals may expend themselves out of a deepened sense of ideals, relationships between persons and systems and an enhanced sense of self. There is, in a sense, more of oneself to give than at prior developmental positions. The limitation that Conscientious persons labor under, however, makes it appear to them that caring for others is antithetical to caring for themselves. Hence, directees may resist suggestions that they include themselves in their own caring, or feel guilty when they do quit constantly pouring themselves out for others. Although Conscientious individuals can learn strategies to prevent their own burnout, the ultimate resolution of this dilemma awaits a reframing of the possibilities of care to include oneself within its scope.[4]

Increased potential for interpersonal relationships also extends to relationship with God. The locus for meeting God moves *inside* the person; God can now be "my God," rather than the God of one's parents, church or society. The desire and concern for communication and the differentiated range of feelings can extend to one's relationship with God and others. Prayer, perhaps for the first time, can be truly affective. The question: "Have you expressed how you feel about that to God?" will make sense to Conscientious persons, even though they may not be in the habit of so doing. Some persons may find it relatively easy to express "positive" emotions, but communicating sexual, aggressive, or angry feelings toward God or others may be another matter. Directors can again profitably underscore the person's emotional responses, encouraging directees to express their broadened range of feelings directly to God.

RECAPITULATION

The *strengths* of the Conscientious stage, then, include the emergence of adult conscience with the concomitant abilities to grasp long-term, self-evaluated, self-chosen goals, and the reflexivity and psychological-mindedness which accompany a developed and differentiated inner life. Its *limitations* include the possibility of losing one's moorings for the short or long term through confronting a more relativistic world; idiosyncratic self-centered and subjective judgments about self and others; and excessive confidence in one's own assessments and critical reflections. Sometimes behaviors toward strangers may be as exclusive as those of Conformist persons, but organized around a different understanding of "the way things are."

The characteristic *virtues* of Conscientious persons include inner moral standards, integrity, truthfulness, understanding, empathy, altruism, even a kind of humor which persists through successive developmental transformations. Its characteristic *temptations* include: avoiding—through alienation, cynicism, or activism—the responsibility entailed in self-appropriated standards; hypercritical self-examination; excluding oneself in the scope of care; getting sidetracked into a search for inner religious experiences or ideological formulations; and seeking to control others, judging them by one's own norms.

The traits and abilities which make either spiritual direction or any insight-oriented psychotherapy possible exist as a matter of structure in the Conscientious person: reflexive awareness of one's inner life, self-chosen standards and goals, extended vision about goals and commitments, adult moral conscience. Indeed, prior to this stage persons may not spontaneously seek out formal spiritual direction. But to the degree that spiritual directors expect all directees to respond like Conscientious persons, they may find themselves disappointed with directees who are not, and may never be at the Conscientious stage.

INTERPERSONAL STYLE OF
INTER-INDIVIDUAL PERSON

As the sense of autonomy within oneself develops, so does the reality of one's irrevocable commitments. Recognizing that autonomy is mutual leads inevitably to interdependence in one's interpersonal relationships. Further, recognizing the legitimacy of perspectives other than one's own raises the issue of interdependence with groups or structures whose values and goals may be antithetical. Hence the ability to learn from different viewpoints, so significant in ecumenical and intercultural discourse, becomes structurally ascendant at the Interindividual stage.

Two spin-offs which may appear in spiritual direction include incorporating the self in care and freeing God to be God. Since one's self was the touchstone for evaluating and assessing reality throughout the Conscientious stage, one could not step outside its limits and include self in the group to whom one responded with care. When Conscientious persons do include themselves in care, it forms a special case, but Interindividual persons reframe the entire issue of care and care-giving in a way that dissolves the apparent contradiction between "selfishness" and "responsibility." Thus, Carol Gilligan speaks of an ethic of care "which reflects a cumulative knowledge of human relationships, [and] evolves around a central insight, that self and other are interdependent."[5] This issue is not confined to women, but represents one of "the paradoxical truths of human experience—that we know ourselves as separate only insofar as we live in connection with others, and that we experience relationship only insofar as we differentiate other from self."[6] Only at the Interindividual stage does sufficient complexity and depth exist for reframing and therefore resolving the issue of self-care as a matter of the way one views reality.

Second, seekers may now experience God as autonomous, as Other, to an entirely new degree. To the extent that images of God rely on images of self, God-images fall away, inadequate to this new relationship with self and God. The phenomenological experience often consists in darkness and obscurity about who God is while simultaneously being drawn into the darkness to meet this Other One in paradoxically deepened intimacy. John of the Cross' wisdom about what he calls the "dark night of the spirit" appears to address a death to self in some respects similar to that occurring when the Interindividual stage challenges the Conscientious stage's secure, solid ego.

As persons live more and more out of an Interindividual framework, spiritual directors may need simply to accompany seekers in their own processes. Two reasons lie behind this judgment. Growing autonomy extends to spiritual life as well as other aspects of human existence. Directees assume greater responsibility as individuals before a God who, to speak metaphorically, is also more autonomous. In addition, the spiritual director's own level of ego development may neither have reached the Interindividual stage, nor have transcended it. Thus, in a very real sense, the spiritual director can only act as a fellow-traveler at this complexity of ego integration.

RECAPITULATION

The *strengths* of the Interindividual stage entail the following: a vision and commitment beyond the self, but which still includes self as an integrated and valued component of the vision; increased tolerance for the autonomy of others, including one's own unconscious self and God. The *weakness* of the Interindividual stage is that, at root, one remains divided. The locus of the division resides in one's inevitable participation in structures and institutions whose goals and values differ from one's own and which stubbornly refuse to respond to individual action.

The *virtues* of the Interindividual stage include increasing intimacy with self, others and God; a sense of cocreating with God; commitment to social concerns unrestricted by the boundaries of one's own social group, class, religion or nation; and integrity resulting from enhanced congruity between inner life and outer actions, between moral principles and behavior. The *temptation:* avoiding the self-emptying required for granting others autonomy, for building relationships of authentic mutuality and appropriate intimacy, or even more significantly, for confronting the sinful realities of the structures in which one can now see oneself inevitably embedded.

The Integrated Stage

Since this stage is rarely found, it is difficult to study empirically. Furthermore, the more complex the stage, the more likely it is to be skewed by the psychologist's own perceptions of an "ideal person." For these reasons, Loevinger describes this stage only in broad strokes. Its essence involves transcending and coping with the conflicts and differentiations of the Interindividual stage, reconciling the unattainable where necessary. The struggle for personal identity unifies a spectrum of life activities. Intimacy and mutuality combine with agency in a singularly unified personality. Integrated persons also manifest a broad range of social and cultural concerns.[7]

Neither James Fowler nor Daniel Helminiak manifest Loevinger's reticence about describing the end-point of the developmental continuum. Each of them sketches an "ideal person" to culminate his developmental theory. Fowler bases his description of maturity on Christian theological concepts. Persons who live out Fowler's universalizing faith are incarnational and disciplined; they are activists who make tangible the imperatives of love and justice. They are heedless of their own self-preservation as they redefine the usual criteria of normality and subvert limited and limiting social structures. Their communities and their compassion are universal in extent.[8]

Helminiak relies on Bernard Lonergan's philosophical system to "project a theoretical account of the ideal perfection" of the final stage. Helminiak's Cosmic persons continually manifest a process of integration and authentic self-transcendence. They are open to all that is and willing to change as circumstances demand. They are alive to the present moment and in touch with the very depths of themselves, living a deep harmony between themselves and all that is.[9] Loevinger, it seems, describes a few real people, while Fowler and Helminiak draw pictures of the normative persons whom they assume would evolve in an ideal developmental situation.

We now have sufficient context to address a troubling issue implied in the very developmental categories themselves. A theory which postulates a developing ego implies that ego or self becomes stronger, more autonomous and more differentiated as one progresses through the stages. The classic literature of spirituality, however, is filled with images of self-emptying, self-denial and asceticism. Are not these two sets of images antithetical to each other? Does not the ascetical tradition, through a simplistic or even destructive anthropology, betray modern critical views of the human person? On the other hand, could the pursuit of self and development simply mask our capitulation to the basically anti-ascetical lure of hedonism and narcissism?

From the perspective of the entire developmental continuum, we can see that *every* transition requires, quite literally, a self-transcendence, a death to a self that makes a particular kind of meaning.[10] The Conscientious stage's blindness lies in assessing everything by the norm of the individual self—here the temptation to make self-fulfillment the ultimate goal can be particularly attractive. But the Interindividual and Integrated stages reveal the limit of this reality construction; true fulfillment arises from handing oneself over to a larger vision and purpose. The Interindividual and Integrated stages each require dethroning self as the norm of reality. But the language of emptying and discipline speaks its deepest challenge when, in fact, there is a self to hand over, and when there exists a cause, a value, a vision or a Person of sufficient transcendence to be caught up with. Perhaps only from the perspective of a self-composed self can one hand oneself over without self-annihilation. Thus, the developmental continuum itself reveals that images of growth, development, self, abnegation, discipline, and death to self undergo transformation of their meanings.[11]

Therefore, developmentally astute spiritual directors recognize that the guises which clothe the call to death to self vary by stage, and at times they will ally themselves with a seeker's fragile and newly emerging sense of self. We must also be aware that these images vary in their relationship to sex, class, culture—all of these realities individualize ego development and make concrete God's workings in the lives of directees. But the theory of ego development itself reveals that a bigger, stronger, more independent ego is neither the simple and predictable end result of the developmental continuum nor the enemy of self-denial.

Two other important caveats bear repetition as we leave this discussion of spiritual direction with persons at various developmental levels. First, we must place these successive transformations of motive which we have called ego development in a wider framework of God and God's activity. That is, God is not only the God who can most readily be apprehended by the Conformist or the Conscientious or even the Integrated meaning constructions. As we become aware of the deconstruction which inevitably attends each stage, one may be less apt to assume that God is "like that." It is, I submit, the spiritual director's most basic role simultaneously to stand for the transcendent God and to facilitate the seeker's experience of this God in ways which he or she is most capable of apprehending.

Second, the implications for spiritual direction raised in this discussion are only typical and suggestive of the issues which might appear. Individual experiences and the particular tone of these events cannot be specified by a structural theory, which by its nature stresses *form* over *contents*. Furthermore, to the extent that spiritual directors force these stage descriptions onto conversations, or see individuals as "stages," they are guilty of misplaced concreteness in the use of the theory. Persons are not reducible to stages—even though a stage-concept may be useful for grasping why a person sees something a certain way. The two are vastly different.

NOTES

1. See Richard L. Gorsuch and Daniel Aleshire, "Christian Faith and Ethnic Prejudice: A Review and Interpretation of Research," *Journal for the Scientific Study of Religion* 13 (June 1974):281–307. The authors note that people who are extrinsic in their orientation and accept stereotyped Christian beliefs are the most prejudiced subgroups (p. 284). These findings imply that to the extent that a particular style of denominational leadership, doctrinal interpretation, and closed society encourages Conformity as the average expected level of development among large numbers of its members, prejudicial, negative or rigid attitudes toward groups perceived as different, bad or wrong may also periodically surface.

2. Loevinger, "Measuring Personality Patterns of Women," *Genetic Psychology Monographs* 65 (1962), p. 113. Loevinger attributes to Adorno the suggestion about extending one's view of family to God.

3. *Stages of Faith*, p. 275, italics his. Despite Fowler's assertion of the value of each stage, he leaves open the possibility that stages may have outlived their usefulness. The pastor or spiritual director may have a privileged opportunity to ally with an emergent self, just as a therapist may have the same opportunity in another context.

4. Gilligan, *In a Different Voice*, describes the particular difficulty

that caring for others at the expense of caring for oneself can be for women. Sharon Parks, *The Critical Years,* pp. 57–58, places the resolution of this dilemma earlier than I do, at her equivalent to the Conscientious Stage. My experience suggests, however, that women who have been strongly socialized toward the "virtues" of humility and selflessness, also have imbibed a particularly strong bias against care for self that makes it seem selfish. Perhaps women who have not internalized such a deep proscription against selfishness, can, in fact, resolve this dilemma earlier. Or, perhaps the discrepancy between Parks and me on this point is more one of initial versus habitual resolution of this dilemma. I favor the thesis that there are several styles of resolving this dilemma, the most complete occurring at the Interindividual stage or the transition into it. See Loevinger, *Ego Development,* p. 23.

    5. *In a Different Voice,* p. 74.

    6. Ibid., p. 63.

    7. Loevinger, *Ego Development,* p. 26; "The Relation of Adjustment," p. 168; Young-Eisendrath, "Ego Development," p. 330.

    8. Fowler, *Stages of Faith,* pp. 199–211.

    9. Helminiak, *Spiritual Development,* pp. 87–89.

    10. See Bridges, *Transitions,* especially Ch. 4.

    11. Joann Wolski Conn and Walter Conn, "Developmental Psychology: From Moral Theology to Spirituality," in *Proceedings of the Fortieth Annual Convention,* ed. George Gilcourse (San Francisco: The Catholic Theological Society of America, 1985), p. 171, note that Kegan's theory is especially useful regarding the tension between autonomy and self-emptying because it traces successive poles of emphasis which find their ultimate reconciliation at the Interindividual stage.

Section IV

Revisioning the Tradition of Christian Spirituality

Remembering Creator Spirit

Elizabeth A. Johnson

GOD WHO ARRIVES

Within a Trinitarian framework the "person" of the Spirit refers primarily to God present and active in the world. Early Christian theology illustrated this by a series of natural metaphors that remain helpful in their illuminating power. If the great, unknowable mystery of God is pictured as the glowing sun, and God incarnate as a ray of that same light streaming to the earth (Christ the sunbeam), then Spirit is the point of light that actually arrives and affects the earth with warmth and energy. And it is all the one light. Again, the transcendent God is like an upwelling spring of water, and a river that flows outward from this source, and the irrigation channel where the water meets and moistens the earth (Spirit). And it is all the one water. Yet again, the triune God is like a plant with its root, shoot, and fruit: deep, invisible root, green stem reaching into the world, and flower that opens to spread beauty and fragrance and to fructify the earth with fruit and seed (Spirit). And it is all the one living plant.[1]

The point for our pondering is that speaking about the Spirit signifies the presence of the living God active in this historical world. The Spirit is God who actually arrives in every moment, God drawing near and passing by in vivifying power in the midst of historical struggle. So profoundly is this the case that whenever people speak in a generic way of "God," of their experience of God or of God's doing something in the world, more often than not they are referring to the Spirit, if a triune prism be introduced.

Of all the activities that theology attributes to the Spirit, the most significant is this: the Spirit is the creative origin of all life. In the words of the Nicene Creed, the Spirit is *vivificantem,* vivifier or life-giver. This designation refers to creation not just at the beginning of time but continuously: the Spirit is the unceasing, dynamic flow of divine power that sustains the universe, bringing forth life. From this primordial religious intuition, three other insights reverberate.

First, as the continuous creative origin of life the Creator Spirit is immanent in the historical world. "Where can I go from your presence," sings the psalmist, "and from your Spirit where can I flee?" The Spirit is in the highest sky, the deepest hole, the darkest night, farther east than the sunrise, over every next horizon (Ps 139:7–12). The Spirit fills the world and is in all things. Since the Spirit is also transcendent over the world, divine indwelling circles round to embrace the whole world, which thereby dwells within the sphere of the divine. Technically this is known as panentheism, or the existence of all things in God. Distinct from classical theism which separates God and the world, and also different from pantheism which merges God and the world, panentheism holds that the universe, both matter and spirit, is encompassed by the Matrix of the living God in an encircling that generates freedom, self-transcendence, and the future, all in the context of the interconnected whole. The relationship created by this mutual indwelling, while non-hierarchical and reciprocal, is not strictly symmetrical, for the world is dependent on God in a way that God is not on the world. Yet the Spirit's encircling indwelling weaves a genuine solidarity among all creatures and between God and the world.

Second, when things get broken, which can happen so easily, this divine creative power assumes the shape of a rejuvenating energy that renews the face of the earth (Ps 104:30). The damaged earth, violent and unjust social structures, the lonely and broken heart—all cry out for a fresh start. In the midst of this suffering the Creator Spirit, through the mediation of created powers, comes, as the Pentecost sequence sings, to wash what is unclean; to pour water upon what is drought-stricken; to heal what is hurt; to loosen up what is rigid; to warm what is freezing; to straighten out what is crooked and bent.[2] When Jesus reads from the scroll of Isaiah in the Nazareth synagogue, he highlights this point with explicit examples. The Spirit who was upon him had sent him to bring good news to the poor, to proclaim release to captives, sight to the blind, and liberty to the oppressed (Lk 4:16–20). The resurrection of Jesus from the dead into the new life of glory is but the most surprising revelation of this characteristic of the Creator Spirit. Precisely as the giver of life the creative Spirit cherishes what has been made and renews it in myriad ways.

Third, the continuous changing of historical life reveals that the Spirit *moves*. From the beginning of the cosmos, when the Spirit moves over the waters (Gen 1:2), to the end, when God will make all things new (Rev 21:5), standing still is an unknown stance. The long and unfinished development known as evolution testifies to just how much novelty, just how much surprise, the universe is capable of spawning out of pre-given order or chaos. In every instance the living Spirit empowers, lures, prods, dances on ahead. Throughout the process, the Spirit characteristically sets up bonds of kinship among all creatures, human and non-human alike, all of whom are energized by this one Source. A Christian liturgical greeting expresses this very beautifully: "The grace of our Lord Jesus Christ, and the love of God, and the fellowship of the Holy Spirit be with you all." Fellowship, community, *koinonia* is the primordial design of existence, as all creatures are connected through the indwelling, renewing, moving Creator Spirit.

The fundamental insight that the Spirit is the giver of life with its three corollaries of the Spirit's renewing, indwelling, and moving power cry out for concrete, imaginative expression. How shall we speak of Creator Spirit? If we search the scriptures with our major thesis in mind, we find a small collection of cosmic and female symbols of the Spirit, most of which are marginalized by a patriarchal imagination. Remembering these texts can give us the beginnings of a vocabulary for an ecological ethic and spirituality.

COSMIC SYMBOLS

Among the elements of the natural world that biblical writers deem to have an affinity with the Spirit, the most important are wind, fire, and water.[3] In Hebrew the word for spirit, *ruah,* means moving air or wind. The term encompasses all the movements of wind, from the small, gentle breeze caressing our cheek to the mighty storm gale that reshapes the landscape. The Spirit is like this invisible, natural force, a power that declares itself in the movement of the wind. Jesus spoke of this symbol in a beautifully allusive way: the wind blows where it chooses; you hear the sound of it, but you do not see where it comes from nor where it is going. But you know it is passing by when you see its effects. So it is with the Spirit of God (Jn 3:8).

The Spirit can be likened to the wind and can be discerned as actively present in dramatic, windblown events. Think of the strong wind that blows back the Reed Sea so the escaping slaves can run free (Ex 14:21); and of the wind that blows through the valley of the dry bones, breathing life into the vast multitude (Ez 37:1–14); and of the mighty Pentecost wind that shakes the house where Jesus' disciples, women and men alike, are praying, impelling them to public witness of the good news (Acts 1:13–14; 2:1–4). But the blowing Spirit can also be discerned in mundane events, none the less wondrous for being so regular. The warm breezes of spring melt the winter ice, producing flowing waters that green the earth (Ps 147:18).

Wind is connected with wings. The symbol of the bird and her wings signified female deity in ancient Near East religions. In Greek mythology, as Ann Belford Ulanov points out, the dove is the emblem of Aphrodite, goddess of love. Doves were even cultically protected, with towers erected for them and a steady supply of food provided. The figure of the dove in the gospels and in Christian art thus links the Holy Spirit with the broad pre-Christian tradition of divine female power: "Iconographically the dove is a messenger of the goddess and of the Holy Spirit."[4] Whether hovering like a nesting mother bird over the egg of primordial chaos in the beginning (Gen 1:2); or sheltering those in difficulty under the protective shadow of her wings (Pss 17:8; 36:7; 57:1; 61:4; 91:1,4; Is 31:5); or bearing the enslaved up on her great wings toward freedom (Ex 19:4; Deut 32:11–12); or resting on Jesus to grace and mission him during his baptism (Lk 3:22), the Spirit's activity is evoked with allusion to femaleness.

Ruah, finally, is linked with the breath in the throats of both animals and people. Its presence gives life (Gen 2:7; 7:15); its withdrawal means death (Ps 104:29–30). It makes words, especially prophetic ones (Zech 7:12). Here the primary analogue for Creator Spirit is the distinctive vitality, creativity, and mystery of the human spirit itself.

Drawn by the evocative power of the wind, Meinrad Craighead, artist and religious thinker, muses that "Perhaps it is the wind's infinity which excites that vertiginous desire for edgelessness. It is a longing to be inside the rhythm and duration of the Spirit's inhalation and exhalation, prolonged into the void, east of the sun and west of the moon."[5] Likening this symbol of Creator Spirit to the Native American indwelling spirit named Old Wind Woman, she continues:

> The dark wind of my Mother expands and contracts, winding to and from the hub of the spinning wheel, which is everywhere. She spirals, uncoiling and recoiling, leaving and returning to her source; her spirit evolving, involving the entire universe.[6]

Signifying the Spirit of God with the symbol of wind already begins to transcend the hard dualism of spirit and matter played out in divine unrelatedness to the world. The whole community of creation is sustained by the breath, the Spirit of God, who "rides on the wings of the wind" (Ps 104:3) in profound, if free, connection.

Fire is another cosmic symbol of the Spirit. There is no definite shape to fire, and its every-changing form signifies something that is unto itself, mysterious. It is a dangerous element that sears if you touch it and that can easily escape human control. At the same time, the light and heat that emanate from fire are indispensable to human well-being. It points to the greater fires in the universe, the glowing sun and stars, and the fierce lightning storms. All are powerful biblical symbols of the presence of God. A bush burns but is not consumed as Moses hears the compassionate message of deliverance from slavery (Ex 3:1–12). Tongues of fire, streams of ardent heat, are seen above the heads of the women and men who will bring the good news of the risen Christ to the whole world (Acts 2:1–3). To borrow the analogy of a fourth century theologian, if fire passing through a mass of iron

makes the whole of it glow, so that what was cold becomes burning and what was black is made bright, so too does the power of
the Spirit transform hearts and minds, and indeed the clay of
creation itself.[7] Perhaps no one has captured the evocative power
of this symbol better than Hildegard of Bingen when she writes of
the Spirit:

> I, the highest and fiery power, have kindled every living spark
> and I have breathed out nothing that can die. . . . I flame
> above the beauty of the fields; I shine in the waters; in the sun,
> the moon and the stars, I burn. And by means of the airy
> wind, I stir everything into quickness with a certain invisible
> life which sustains all. . . . I, the fiery power, lie hidden in
> these things and they blaze from me.[8]

Contemporary scientific theory about the origin of the universe in
a primeval explosion, inelegantly named the Big Bang, releases
yet another layer of meaning from this symbol. The act of creation is already a Pentecost, a first and permanent outpouring of
the fiery Spirit of life.

Water is elemental, absolutely essential for life as we know it,
although like fire it too can kill. On this planet life began in the
primeval seas, and human and other mammalian life continues to
originate in the water of the womb. Sap in the tree, dew on the
grass, blood in the veins, wine in the vessel, rain on the earth,
water outpoured: all bespeak the active presence of God. As a
symbol of the Spirit, water points to the bottomless wellspring of
the source of life and to the refreshment and gladness that result
from deep immersion in this mystery.

Scripture is replete with instances where water symbolizes
the Spirit of life. Speaking through the prophet Ezekiel, God
promises that the people will find their true heart: "I will sprinkle
clean water upon you . . . and a new spirit I will put within you;
and I will remove from your body the heart of stone and give you
a heart of flesh" (Ez 36:25–26). In Isaiah's vision, justice and
peace in the human world and the natural world are the gifts that
result when the Spirit, like a cascade of water from a vessel, is
poured out (Is 32:15–18). For Joel, sons and daughters will proph-
esy and even the old will dream again when drenched with this

Spirit poured out on all flesh (Jl 2:28–29). This same Spirit is the living water Jesus promised to the Samaritan woman, a spring of love welling up at the core of creation (Jn 4:7–15). As Paul points out to the Romans, God overflows in the depth of the divine being and from there "the love of God is poured into our hearts by the Holy Spirit given to us" (Rom 5:5).

The poetry of water and the Spirit enticed some early Christian theologians to flights of rhetoric. The second century bishop Irenaeus, for example, describing the life of his community, wrote:

> Just as dry wheat cannot be shaped into a cohesive lump of dough or a loaf held together without moisture, so in the same way we many could not become one . . . without the water that comes from heaven. As dry earth bears no fruit unless it receives moisture, so we also were originally dry wood and could never have borne the fruit of life without the rain freely given from above . . . . [we] have received it through the Spirit.[9]

With an eye on the natural world Cyril of Jerusalem observed:

> Why did he [Christ] call the grace of the Spirit water? Because by water all things subsist; because water brings forth grass and living things; because the water of the showers comes down from heaven; because it comes down in one form but works in many forms . . . it becomes white in the lily, red in the rose, purple in violets and hyacinths, different and varied in each species. It is one thing in the palm tree, yet another in the vine, and yet all in all things.[10]

To sum up: the Spirit is life that gives life. She is radiant life energy that like wind, fire, and water awakens and enlivens all things. Each of these symbols has a numinous quality that evokes better than abstract words the presence of the Creator Spirit in the world, moving over the void, breathing into the chaos, pouring out, informing, quickening, warming, setting free, blessing, dancing in mutual immanence with the world.

In the course of her visionary work on Christian doctrine Hildegaard spun out variations on these images that bring home the Spirit's vivifying movement in a lustrous way. The Spirit, she writes, is the life of the life of all creatures; the way in which everything is penetrated with connectedness and relatedness; a burning fire who sparks, ignites, inflames, kindles hearts; a guide in the fog; a balm for wounds; a shining serenity; an overflowing fountain that spreads to all sides. The Spirit is life, movement, color, radiance, restorative stillness in the din. She pours the juice of contrition into hardened hearts. Her power makes dry twigs and withered souls green again with the juice of life. She purifies, absolves, strengthens, heals, gathers the perplexed, seeks the lost. She plays music in the soul, being herself the melody of praise and joy. She awakens mighty hope, blowing everywhere the winds of renewal in creation.[11] Hildegaard's rhetoric puts me in mind of the encouragement offered in the fourth century by Basil of Caesarea in his great work on the Spirit. Let us not be afraid of being too extravagant in what we say about the Holy Spirit, he writes; our thoughts will always fall short.[12]

FEMALE SYMBOLS

It is an interesting point, and one of the saving graces of the religious patriarchal tradition, that in addition to the natural world women's reality is also thought suitable to image the Spirit. The most extended biblical instance of female imagery of the Spirit occurs in the wisdom literature where the Spirit's functions are depicted as acts of Woman Wisdom. The female figure of Wisdom is the most acutely developed personification of God's presence and activity in the Hebrew scriptures. Not only is the grammatical gender of the word for wisdom feminine (*hokmah* in Hebrew, *sophia* in Greek), but the biblical portrait of Wisdom is consistently female, casting her as sister, mother, female beloved, chef and hostess, teacher, preacher, maker of justice, and a host of other women's roles. In every instance Wisdom symbolizes transcendent power pervading and ordering the world, both nature and human beings, interacting with them all to lure them into the path of life.[13]

Early in the book of Wisdom this female figure is identified with spirit, a people-loving spirit: "Wisdom is a kindly spirit"

(1:6). In a subsequent passage the metaphor shifts slightly to say that Wisdom has a spirit. Her spirit is then described in glorious vocabulary with twenty-one attributes, or three times the perfect number seven. She is:

> intelligent, holy, unique, manifold, subtle, mobile, clear, unpolluted, distinct, invulnerable, loving the good, keen, irresistible, beneficent, humane, steadfast, sure, free from anxiety, all-powerful, overseeing all, and penetrating through all other intelligent spirits (7:22–23).

Poetic parallelism clinches the Wisdom-Spirit equivalence: "Who has learned thy counsel, unless you have given Wisdom, and sent your Holy Spirit from on high?" (Wis 9:17). These and other allusive wisdom texts point to the fittingness of speaking about the Spirit in female imagery, given Sophia's undoubted female symbolization.

Understanding this equivalence, we read the wisdom texts and find magnificent renderings of creation and redemption themes in female symbols. As the Nicene Creed would later say of the Spirit, these texts say of Wisdom that she is the giver of life, she is a tree of life, "she is your life" (Prov 4:13). So intimately is the divine blessing of life associated with her that she can proclaim "whoever finds me finds life" (Prov 8:35). All life is a gift and Woman Wisdom, a personification of the Creator Spirit, gives that gift. She is the "fashioner of all things" (Wis 7:22), responsible for their existence and therefore knowing their inmost secrets. She knows the solstices and changes of the seasons, the constellations of the stars, the natures of animals and the tempers of wild beasts, the variety of plants and the virtues of roots, and the ways of human reasoning (Wis 7:17–22). This passage from the book of Wisdom contains a poignant aside. Solomon, while rejoicing to learn about these things from Wisdom, admits "but I did not know that she was their mother" (Wis 7:12).

It is not just individual creatures who are the subject of Spirit-Sophia's life-giving knowledge, but the world as a whole is shaped harmoniously by her guidance: "She reaches mightily from one end of the earth to the other, and she orders all things well" (Wis 8:1). This ordering is a righteous one, inimical to exploitation and oppression. Sophia hates the ways of arrogance and evil but works to establish just governance on the earth: "By me kings reign, and rulers decree what is just" (Prov 8:15). Indeed, the echoes of the prophetic promise of shalom sound in her self-description: "I walk in the way of righteousness, in the paths of justice" (Prov 8:20).

Spirit-Sophia's presence fills the world: "For Wisdom is more mobile than any motion; because of her pureness she pervades and penetrates all things" (Wis 7:24). This is the same divine presence spoken about in the Jewish rabbinic tradition of the *shekinah,* the female symbol of God's indwelling, the weighty radiance that flashes out in unexpected ways in the midst of the broken world. Most significant is her work of accompaniment, for "Wherever the righteous go, the Shekinah goes with them.[14] No place is too hostile. She accompanies the people through the post-slavery wilderness, and hundreds of years later into exile again, through all the byways of rough times. "Come and see how beloved are the Israelites before God, for withersoever they journeyed in their captivity the Shekinah journeyed with them."[15] In other words, God's indwelling Spirit was with them and this accompaniment gave rise to hope in their suffering.

Virtually every aspect of the Creator Spirit's activity in the world, as delineated in doctrine and theology, is depicted in the wisdom literature in female symbolism. When things become damaged, the power to refresh them pours out from her: "while remaining in herself, she renews all things" (Wis 7:27). This renewing energy profoundly affects human beings in their relation to divine mystery and the rest of the world, weaving them round with a web of kinship: "in every generation she passes into holy souls and makes them friends of God, and prophets" (Wis 7:27). One aspect of Wisdom has not been seriously appropriated by Christian doctrine of the Spirit, but its time may be coming. The great creation poem of Proverbs shows us creative Wisdom actually playing in the newly minted world, delighting in it all, especially in those intelligent creatures called human (8:22–31).

In addition to the texts about Wisdom, biblical books hold a constellation of maternal images that delineate the Spirit's work in the world. Jesus' conversation with Nicodemus, for example, carries a clear presentation of God the Spirit as mother. A person must be born anew in order to enter the reign of God, Jesus insists, to which Nicodemus queries, "How can anyone be born after having grown old? Can one enter a second time into the mother's womb and be born?" (Jn 3:4). Jesus' reply keeps the metaphor of physical birth and amplifies it to speak of Spirit: "No one can enter the reign of God without being born of water and the Spirit. What is born of the flesh is flesh, and what is born of the Spirit is spirit" (3:5–6). Creator Spirit is here likened to a woman giving birth to offspring who are henceforth truly identified as "born of God."[16]

Other fragments of women's experience of mothering also provide biblical writers symbolic material for Creator Spirit. Like a woman with her knitting needles she knits together the new life in a mother's womb (Ps 139:13); like a woman in childbirth she labors and pants to bring about the birth of justice (Is 42:14); like a midwife she works deftly with a woman in pain to deliver the new creation (Ps 22:9–10); like a washerwoman she scrubs away at bloody stains till the people be like new (Is 4:4; Ps 51:7).

The early Christian centuries carried forward explicit use of female imagery to characterize God's Spirit. In Syriac Christianity, for example, the Spirit's image was consistently that of the brooding or hovering mother bird tending to her chicks. This symbolism of the motherhood of the Spirit fostered a spirituality characterized by warmth which expressed itself in private and public prayer. In one prayer the believer meditates:

> As the wings of doves over their nestlings,
> And the mouths of their nestlings toward their mouths,
> So also are the wings of the Spirit over my heart.[17]

In another prayer spoken in the context of liturgy the community implores the Spirit:

> The world considers you a merciful mother. Bring with you calm and peace, and spread your wings over our sinful times.[18]

In time most of this maternal imagery migrated away from the Spirit and accrued to the church, called Holy Mother the Church, or to Mary the mother of Jesus, venerated as mother of the faithful as well. The symbol of the maternity of the Spirit was virtually forgotten, along with the capacity of images of Wisdom and Shekinah to evoke divine presence and activity in female form. But this resonance abides in the texts of scripture and tradition, and can be retrieved.

Looked at against the background of hierarchical dualism, female and cosmic symbols of the Creator Spirit and the insights to which they give rise have unique potential to heal divided consciousness. The One who blows the wild wind of life, who fires the blaze of being, who gives birth to the world, or who midwifes it into existence does not stand over against it or rule it hierarchically from afar but dwells in intimate, quickening relationship with humanity and the life of the earth. The female symbols in particular dramatize that being women and being fertile is not a dangerous, polluted state but a participation in the fecundity of the Creator Spirit and, conversely, a sign of her presence. Enfolding and unfolding the universe, the Spirit is holy mystery "over all and through all and in all" (Eph 4:6). Remembering Creator Spirit this way dismantles the theological dualism that sets God apart from the universe, thus removing one of the pillars of support for dualism within the human community and between human beings and the earth. We are all woven into the fabric of the one cosmic community. Indeed, God is not far from any one of us, for in her we live and move and have our being, as some of our poets now say (cf. Acts 17:28).

DIVINE RELATION TO THE WORLD

Using cosmic and female images for the Spirit's presence and action in the world enables our minds to attend to the pattern of divine relation to the world in ways that are ecologically helpful. The Spirit is the great, creative Matrix who grounds and sustains the cosmos and attracts it toward the future. Throughout the vast sweep of cosmic and biological evolution she embraces the material root of existence and its endless new potential, empowering the cosmic process from within. The universe, in turn, is self-organizing and self-transcending, corresponding from the spiraling galaxies to the double helix of the DNA molecule to the dance of her quickening power. The Spirit's action does not supplant that of creatures but works cooperatively in and through the created action, random, ordered, or free. Nor does the Spirit's dynamic power arrive as an intervention from "outside," but is immanent in the world that is becoming. In keeping with this view, the scientist and religious thinker Arthur Peacocke suggests that a fitting image for the Creator Spirit would be that of a choreographer of an unfinished dance, ingeniously improvising steps for a piece that requires the creativity of the dancers to complete.[19] The relation is not one of dominating or commanding power over, but one of reverent, empowering love.

This does not exclude the enormous amounts of violence, entropy, and suffering that exist throughout the cosmos. Stars are born and die, species appear and disappear due to natural catastrophe, individuals know debilitating pain. We may well wonder how Love could be empowering such a messy and at times tragic arrangement, made more so by the advent of conscious human beings with our historical propensity to sin, to hurt others. I have thought about this all my life, and have read what many wise minds have said, and the bottom line is that nobody knows. What can be ventured is that it has something to do with the nature of love. Love grants autonomy to the beloved and respects this, all the while participating in the joy and pain of the other's destiny. It vigorously cares and works for and urges the beloved toward his or her own well-being, but never forces.

In an open-ended, evolutionary universe death often becomes the matrix for the birth of the new: earth from an exploding star, mushrooms from a rotting tree trunk, a new community from the cross of Jesus. At other times there is no obvious productive outcome, simply the disastrous surd of evil. In either case, the Love who is the Creator Spirit participates in the world's destiny. She can be grieved (Eph 4:30); she can even be quenched (1 Thes 5:19). When creation groans in labor pains and we do too (Rom 8:22–23), the Spirit is in the groaning and in the midwifing that breathes rhythmically along and cooperates in the birth. In other words, in the midst of the agony and delight of the world the Creator Spirit has the character of compassion. In multifaceted relationships she resists, reconciles, accompanies, sympathizes, liberates, comforts, plays, delights, befriends, strengthens, suffers with, vivifies, renews, endures, challenges, participates, all the while moving the world toward its destiny. Moved by this Spirit, human beings are similarly configured to compassion, taught to be co-creators who enter the lists on behalf of those who suffer, to resist and creatively transform the powers that destroy.

A theology of the Creator Spirit overcomes the dualism of spirit and matter with all of its ramifications, and leads to the realization of the sacredness of the earth. The Spirit of God dwelling in the world with quickening power deconstructs dualism and draws in its place a circle of mutuality and inclusiveness. Instead of matter being divorced from spirit and consigned to a realm separate from the holy, it is an intrinsic part of the cosmic community, vivified, indwelt, and renewed by the Creator Spirit. The Spirit creates matter. Matter bears the mark of the sacred and has itself a spiritual radiance. Hence the world is holy, nature is holy, bodies are holy, women's bodies are holy. For the Spirit creates what is physical—worlds, bodies, senses, sexuality, passions— and moves in these every bit as much as in minds and ideas. About the Creator Spirit this can be said: loves bodies, loves to dance. The whole complex, material universe is pervaded and signed by her graceful vigor.

NOTES

1. These images are suggested by Tertullian, *Adversus Praxeas* 8. See Brian Gaybba, *The Spirit of Love* (London: Chapman, 1987) for a history of the doctrine of the Spirit.

2. Metaphors from the hymn "Veni Sancte Spiritus," Sequence for the feast of Pentecost. See also Karl Rahner, "The Spirit That Is Over All Life," *Theological Investigations,* Vol. 7 (NY: Herder & Herder, 1971) 193–201; and José Comblin, *The Holy Spirit and Liberation* (Maryknoll, NY: Orbis, 1989).

3. The biblical view is delineated by Eduard Schweizer, *The Holy Spirit* (Philadelphia: Fortress, 1980); natural images described in Paul Newman, *A Spirit Christology* (Lanham, MD: University Press of America, 1987) 69–74.

4. Ann Belford Ulanov, *The Feminine: In Jungian Psychology and in Christian Theology* (Evanston: Northwestern University Press, 1971) 325.

5. Meinrad Craighead, *The Mother's Songs: Images of God the Mother* (NY: Paulist, 1986) 65.

6. Ibid.

7. Cyril of Jerusalem, *Catechetical Lectures* 17.13, in *The Holy Spirit,* J. Patout Burns and Gerald Fagin, eds. (Wilmington, DE: Glazier, 1984) 34–35.

8. From *Hildegard of Bingen: Mystical Writings,* Fiona Bowie & Oliver Davies, eds. (NY: Crossroad, 1990) 91–93.

9. Irenaeus, *Adversus Haereses* Book 3, chap. 17.2; in Burns and Fagin, 34–35.

10. Cyril of Jerusalem, *Catechetical Lectures,* 16.12, in Burns and Fagin, 94.

11. Hildegaard of Bingen, *Scivias,* trans. Mother Columba Hart and Jane Bishop (NY: Paulist, 1990) 190 and passim. Here I render only the metaphors and not the full Hart/Bishop translation, which articulates the Spirit as "it."

12. Basil of Caesarea, *On the Holy Spirit,* chap. 19.49, in Burns and Fagin, 126.

13. See Johnson, *SHE WHO IS,* 86–100.

14. Genesis *Rabbah* 86:6, cited in Dale Moody, "Shekinah," *Interpreter's Dictionary of the Bible* (Nashville: Abingdon, 1962) 4:317–19.

15. *Bar. Meg.* 29a, cited in Moody, ibid.

16. Sandra Schneiders, *Women and the Word* (NY: Paulist, 1986) 38.

17. Cited in Robert Murray, "Holy Spirit as Mother," in *Symbols of Church and Kingdom* (London: Cambridge University, 1975) 315.

18. Cited in E. Pataq-Siman, *L'Expérience de l'Esprit de'après la tradition syrienne d'Antioche* (Théologie historique 15, Paris: 1971) 155.

19. Arthur Peacocke, critically discussed in Ian Barbour, *Religion in an Age of Science* (San Francisco: Harper & Row, 1990) 177–78.

On the Open Road to Galilee

Elisabeth Schüssler Fiorenza

I have argued for a redefinition of the concept of patriarchy to mean not simply the rule of men over women but rather a complex social pyramid of graduated dominations and subordinations.[1] Because feminist discourses continue to use the term "patriarchy" in the sense of gender dualism, I introduced in *But She Said* the neologism "kyriarchy," meaning the rule of the emperor/master/lord/father/husband over his subordinates. With this term I mean to indicate that not all men dominate and exploit all women without difference and that elite Western educated propertied Euro-American men have articulated and benefited from women's and other "nonpersons' " exploitation.[2] As a consequence, the hermeneutical center of a critical feminist theology of liberation cannot simply be women. Rather, it must be constituted and determined by the interests of women who live at the bottom of the kyriarchal pyramid and who struggle against multiplicative forms of oppression. The term "kyriocentric," in turn, refers to ideological articulations that validate and are sustained by kyriarchal relations of domination. Since kyriocentrism replaces the category of androcentrism, it is best understood as an intellectual framework and cultural ideology that legitimates and is legitimated by kyriarchal social structures and systems of domination.

The "dangerous memory" of the young woman and teenage mother Miriam of Nazareth, probably not more than twelve or thirteen years old, pregnant, frightened, and single, who sought help from another woman, can subvert the tales of mariological fantasy and cultural femininity. In the center of the Christian story stands not the lovely "white lady" of artistic and popular imagination, kneeling in adoration before her son. Rather it is the young pregnant woman, living in occupied territory and struggling against victimization and for survival and dignity. It is she who holds out the offer of untold possibilities for a different christology and theology.

IN PLACE OF A CONCLUSION:
ON THE OPEN ROAD TO GALILEE

The chapters of this book have not been concerned with establishing "definite" closed readings of biblical texts nor with providing closure to debated issues in feminist christology. Rather they have sought critically to engage biblical and feminist discourses on Jesus, Miriam's child and Sophia's prophet, and to position them symbolically on the "road to Galilee." Against the allurement of literalist certainty and the enticement of playful excess, I have argued that the road of a critical feminist christological inquiry must be variegated, inclusive, and open-ended but still remain engaged and committed.

Like the women of the resurrection narratives on the way to the tomb, I was particularly concerned with how to remove the "common-sense" stone that closes and contains potentially transformative readings within the preconstructed frame/tomb of the kyriarchal sex/gender system. I have argued that the very early, still open-ended Jesus' traditions might be helpful for articulating feminist interreligious christological discourses today. These traditions understand John and Jesus as standing in a long line of messengers and prophets whom Divine Wisdom sent to announce "good news" not only to men but also to women, not to those who have made it but to those who are poor, hungry, and weeping now. Like John the Baptizer and Jesus the Galilean, or like Elizabeth of Ain Karim and Miriam of Nazareth, feminist theologians today continue the long line of Sophia's prophets and messengers that spans the centuries and points to an open-ended future.

Like the women of the infancy narratives, the women disciples, Mary of Magdala, and the women around her enunciate the open-endedness of the journey. They proclaim that the executed Jesus is believed to be the Resurrected One. The Living One goes ahead of them and enables the disciples of the *basileia* to continue the tradition and vision of Sophia's messengers by announcing the good news of G*d's new "world order" of justice and well-being for every wo/man without exception. The Living One is present wherever the disciples of the *basileia* practice the inclusive discipleship of equals, making it a present reality among poor, hungry, abused, and alienated wo/men. As Katie G. Cannon has underscored, central for struggling communities such as the Black Church are three things: the notion of *imago dei,* justice and love, and last but not least solidarity in community.[3]

Instead of assuming that a "feminine" style of thinking or a mode of theologizing from "the woman's perspective" promotes liberationist christological discourses in the interest of wo/men, I have argued that we need to explore critically how even such discourses can perpetrate kyriarchal mind-sets. In addition, we have to inquire whether and to what degree the textualized wo/men characters of the Christian Testament communicate kyriarchal values and visions. We must also consider that women, sometimes even more than men, have internalized cultural-religious feminine values and hence are in danger of reproducing the preconstructed kyriarchal politics of either womanly submission or feminine glorification in their own speaking and writing. Feminist theological discourses have to position themselves in such a way that they are "crossing" the "double cross" of the preconstructed kyriarchal sex/gender frame of meaning that is especially determinative of christology.

Consequently, I have insisted, the category of "woman" must be critically assessed rather than presupposed or idealized as a special source of christological insight. It must be shown for what it is, the "common-sense" construct of the cultural-religious sex/gender system that serves kyriarchal interests.[4] Fortunately today, more and more diverse and resistant discourses of emerging feminist movements around the world are interrupting those discourses of middle-class academic gender or women's studies that have conceptualized feminist inquiry in terms of reading or speaking *as a woman.* These feminist discourses challenge universalistic kyriarchal claims that all women have a feminine nature in common that defines them as "others" or as "subordinates" to men.

If feminist christology is to displace the politics of meaning that is determined by the preconstructed kyriarchal sex/gender system, feminist theologians must no longer articulate wo/men's identity in essentialist universalistic terms. Instead they must carefully analyze their own assumptions as well as those of malestream christological discourses to determine how much they take into account the diverse cultural-religious contexts, the historically shaped subjectivity, and the diverse voices of wo/men. By so doing, feminist theologies can unravel the unitary exclusive conceptualizations of christological and other cultural-religious discourses that define woman as the "naturalized" or "revealed" Other of men, an Otherness that is in reality that of *elite Woman to elite Man*. The insights into the collusion of theological discourses with the kyriarchal structures of race, class, heterosexuality, and colonialist oppression compel us not to duplicate or multiply those white malestream christological discourses that are drawn upon the preconstructed rock of the cultural sex/gender system.

Instead, feminist scholars in religion must firmly situate their theological discourses within the emancipatory movements of wo/men around the globe. Biblically based women's liberation movements have their historical roots in the liberation from slavery and oppression announced by Miriam, in the repentance preached by John, and in the *basileia* vision proclaimed by Jesus. Those wo/men who have been engaged in such emancipatory *basileia* movements have sought through the centuries again and again to realize the *basileia* of G*d not only as a power for abolishing kyriarchal domination and exploitation but also as a force for establishing the salvation and well-being of all, which Mary announced in the Magnificat. At the same time this Christian vision of the discipleship praxis of equals realizes that the *basileia* is not yet here, not yet an accomplished reality. Wo/men still have to struggle and hope for the liberation and well-being of all, a vision still to be realized by G*d in the future. Nevertheless, like Mary, feminist liberation theologians proclaim that the *basileia,* that is, G*d's different world and renewed creation symbolized in the abundant table set by Divine Wisdom, is promised especially to wo/men suffering from multiple oppressions and dehumanizations.

For that reason I have argued here that G*d-language, discourses about Jesus Christ, and Marian symbolism must remain embedded in feminist liberation movements and practices of transformation. They are to be contextualized in the praxis of the discipleship of equals, which provides the fecund ground and theological matrix in which new symbols, images, songs, hymns, prayers, rituals, and feast days are growing. A critical feminist discourse on Jesus and Mary will be able to bring about the transformation of patriarchal church and kyriarchal society for the liberation of all only if it does not limit itself to intellectual theological speculations and emotional devotional piety. Instead it must engage in an uncompromising liberationist practice that consciously seeks to transcend its kyriarchal predicaments, locations, and limitations.

We have arrived at the end of our arduous journey through the mountainous country of christological discourses. The meeting and conversation between Elizabeth and Mary, which is supposed to have taken place in Ain Karim, have provided the imaginative space for our critical feminist conversations. The "visitation" celebrated here is between two women of Wisdom. I hope they have become a symbolic paradigm of wo/men coming together for theological reflection in their struggles for liberation. Jesus, Miriam's child and Sophia's prophet, goes ahead of us on the open-road to Galilee signifying the beginnings of the still-to-be-realized *basileia* discipleship of equals.

NOTES

1. "Patriarchy" is generally either understood in the sense of sexism and gender dualism or used as an undefined label. The term in the "narrow sense" is best understood as "father-right and father-might." However, this translation overlooks that the father as the head of household was in antiquity also lord, master, and husband. Consequently, "patriarchy" connotes a complex system of subordination and domination. Moreover, the patriarchal system of the household was the paradigm for the order of society and state. For a review of the common feminist understanding of patriarchy see V. Beechey, "On Patriarchy," *Feminist Review* 3 (1979): 66–82; G. Lerner, *The Creation of Patriarchy* (New York: Oxford University Press, 1986), 231–41; Christine Schaumberger,

"Patriarchat als feministischer Begriff," in *Wörterbuch der feministischen Theologie* (Gütersloh: Mohn, 1991), 321–23, with literature.

2. See my article "The Politics of Otherness: Biblical Interpretation as a Critical Praxis for Liberation," in Marc H. Ellis and Otto Maduro, *The Future of Liberation Theology: Essays in Honor of Gustavo Gutiérrez* (Maryknoll, N.Y.: Orbis Books, 1989), 311–25.

3. Katie Geneva Cannon, *Black Womanist Ethics* (Atlanta: Scholars Press, 1988).

4. Christiane Schmerl and Ruth Grossmass, " 'Nur im Streit wird die Wahrheit geboren' . . . Gedanken zu einer prozessbezogenen feministischen Methodologie," in Christiane Schmerl and Ruth Grossmass, eds., *Feministicher Kompass, patriarchales Gepäck: Kritik konservativer Anteile in neueren feministichen Theorien* (New York, Frankfurt: Campus Verlag, 1989).

Feminist View of Christian Anthropology

Anne Carr

Here I raise one of the deepest issues in feminist theology—
the question of what it means to be human in a Christian theological framework of understanding. I argue that the "nature" of
being human is in human hands and that human being is changing
because of the reflection of women on their own experience.

Contemporary theology is widely characterized by its concern with human experience in all its variety. Theologians such as
Tillich and Rahner have argued for the need to correlate the
kerygma with the "situation" in theology, the need today to
search for "the connections by correspondence" between revelation and experience.[1] David Tracy has reformulated Tillich's
method as "the critical correlation of the meaning and the truth of
the interpreted Christian fact (. . . the texts, symbols, witnesses,
and tradition of the past and present) and the meaning and truth
of the interpreted contemporary situation."[2] This concern with
the pluralism of experience of the human situation is apparent in
the focus of political and liberation theologies on the experience
of the poor under oppressive social and economic systems, and in
the radical grounding of theological discussion in the specific contexts of the particular experiences that characterize the Latin
American or the black communities.

Christian feminist theology, too, has explored the implications of the gospel and the Christian tradition in relation to the
experience of women as a subordinate class in both church and
society. Feminist theologians have criticized theological perspectives and institutional structures that place women in secondary

status and have been concerned to reformulate Christian theology and to restructure the church's institutional life in a manner consonant with both their own new experience and with the gospel, particularly in its message of equality: "there are no more distinctions between Jew and Greek, slave and free, male and female, but all of you are one in Christ Jesus" (Galatians 3:28).

One part of this critical and revisionist work of feminist theology has focused on the meaningfulness of traditional theological categories in relation to the experience of women, sometimes suggesting the harmfulness of certain masculine theological perspectives and sometimes offering alternative approaches. This essay explores aspects of this recent discussion as it touches on fundamental issues of Christian theological anthropology and thus affects the church's theology, preaching, patterns of pastoral care, and its liturgical and institutional life generally.

THE EXPERIENCE OF WOMEN

Where does the theologian locate the experience of women as a source for theological reflection? Here the significance of Tracy's notion of the *interpreted* meaning of the contemporary situation becomes clear. The theologian studies interpretations of various sorts: reflections on personal and collective experience, cultural creations, social scientific studies, and other religious and theological interpretations of women's experience. In the large body of feminist literature, secular and religious, which has accumulated in recent decades, there is broad agreement about the situation of women as subordinate in the context of patriarchy and sexism, both in the private and the societal dimensions of human life. Feminists are united in efforts to analyze the fundamental injustice in this situation and in discussion of strategies for overcoming it.

In this search for the meaning and truth of the contemporary experience of women, however, a particular problem arises. It is difficult to universalize this experience, for women are as uniquely individual as men. Because of the variety of female experience, especially in different cultures and classes, one must be wary of absolutizing any particular set of experiences or any single interpretation as *the* experience of women.

Thus, Judith Plaskow indicates that her description of the experience of women refers to white, middle-class, Western women as disclosed in contemporary novels about women and women's fundamental problem of autonomy or self-actualization.[3] The temptation or "sin" of such women, she argues, is that of not acquiring a strong sense of self, of failing to assume responsibility, to make reasoned and free decisions, to take hold of their lives. She concludes that theological formulations that view sin primarily as prideful self-assertion and grace as self-sacrificial love fail to speak to the experience of women who have sacrificed too much of their selves. It is clear that while this discussion has powerful meaning for some women, it may not be appropriate to women in other cultural situations or to some women within the white, Western middle class. Like the pluralism that characterizes theology generally today, there is pluralism in the experience of women and so in feminist theology as well. Women theologians are not of a single mind with regard to all issues or strategies. This pluralism, moreover, is partly due to radically different interpretations of the experience of women in our culture.

An enduringly valuable analysis of some of these diverse interpretations is provided by Aquin O'Neill in an article from the midseventies that describes contemporary secular feminism in its three "faces."[4] In a survey of the then current literature, she discerned three fundamental interpretations of the experience of women with regard to the sources of sexism and its remedies. The first group explains the cause of women's subordination simply as male supremacy; men are the agents of oppression. In this view, male domination is the oldest and primary form of exploitation, and all other oppressions are its extensions. The strategy proposed by this form of feminism, both in cool analytical terms and in rhetorical challenge, is radical separatism, celibacy. Men must be forced to change. None of the blame can be placed on women themselves. The second face of feminism is quite opposite. In this view, women are to blame for their current situation of inferiority and powerlessness. They are unwilling to grow up, to assume responsibility for themselves and to make the decisions demanded of them by rapid social change. Victims of their own self-hatred, women are accused of a failure of nerve in which they have not dared to claim their own freedom. This form of feminism does not question the character of the greater liberty that men enjoy, but urges women to assume it for themselves. The third face of contemporary feminism is critically directed toward social structures and reigning cultural mythologies about women. Elizabeth Janeway, for example, argues that two myths about women undergird the age-old division of "man's world, woman's place"—myths of female weakness and female power. "The first, which is older . . . holds the second at bay" and constitutes a strong pressure for keeping women in a defined, secondary position in society.[5] This traditional notion of a single, defined "place," however, runs counter to the whole trend of Western civilization (and, one might add, Christian views) that stress the freedom, responsibility, and transcendence of the human person. Women long to be treated as complete persons, and the way for this to come about is through concerted critique of myths about women and change of societal structures. Such change would mean that men as well as women would have wider choices in a less rigidly gender-based social system. These feminists propose specific changes in social policy to free women and men, and society itself, from patriarchy and sexism.

Another set of fundamental differences within feminist thought concerns the cultural and religious valuation of female sexual power and the traditional relation of women to natural processes and to nature itself in contrast with the valuation of the male and the masculine relationship to culture. Much feminist analysis recognizes some form of dualism as the basis or consequence of this difference in valuation and as the source of the asymmetry in interpretation of the masculine/feminine distinction in Western urbanized society.[6] Rosemary Radford Ruether, for example, argues persuasively that, while in tribal and pre-urban cultures the close relation of the entire community to nature and natural process is commonly celebrated in myth and symbol by both women and men, a sharp split occurs between nature and culture in the transition to urban and then to industrial society.[7] Males celebrate freedom and transcendence of nature in cultural creativity, while the realm of nature and natural bodily processes becomes the domain of women. However, feminist theorists take several positions on the issue of dualism.

Some accept the dualism, celebrate the uniqueness of female spiritual experience, and insist that there is a transformative power in women's close relationship to nature and natural process. This power may derive from women's own bodily and spiritual makeup or may simply be the result of centuries of historical and cultural conditioning. While these writers recognize that women's roles of childbearing and nurture of the young often have been oppressive, they believe that a legacy of oppression can be turned into a source of vision and power. Carol Christ's method of literary analysis is a striking example of this form of feminism. She explores the unique dimensions of women's spiritual quests, using Erich Neumann's psychological theory about female knowing as primarily a mode of participation and identification, whereas the male mode is differentiation. In religious terms, "participation and union of a nonpersonal core of the self with the whole" would be the most typical, though not the only, form of female religious experience, as contrasted to "confrontation or encounter" as the primary form of male religious insight.[8] This position is viewed with some nervousness by other feminists who are conscious of the danger of stereotypical thinking that such a celebration of male/female difference can encourage.

A second position on this question accepts the male/female differentiation and views the transcendent, cultural pole as more highly valued than the immanent, natural side. Women are therefore urged to assume their place on the transcendent side of the duality. Though not a widespread view, it is the position taken by Shulamith Firestone in her controversial manifesto *The Dialectic of Sex*.[9] She envisions a future when technology will free women from their bodily ties to reproduction and thus to nature. Artificial reproduction would mean not only the liberation of women but also a situation in which there would be no significant distinction between male and female; women would in fact become like men. The experience of women, in this view, is so alienated that women seeking equality would give up completely their natural and biological positions as bearers and nurturers of the young in order to participate equally in male liberty. Firestone dedicates her book to

Simone de Beauvoir who, though she does not accept the male/female dualism, nevertheless accepts a transcendence/immanence polarity, a body/mind dualism that is inherently conflictual.

For de Beauvoir, the male/female dualism is a mythology to be overcome. The experience of women in oppressive immanence, "the eternal feminine," is richly documented in her feminist classic *The Second Sex*.[10] She describes the experience of women as one of longing for participation in transcendence and liberty. Arguing that there are no eternal essences of male and female, she envisions a world where women are welcomed into full "brotherhood" with men. Since de Beauvoir's groundbreaking work, feminist analysis has more commonly taken a position that also recognizes the dualism of male/female, culture/nature as culturally imposed and created ideologies that are destructive of human wholeness. Dualism issues in stereotypes that are as harmful for men as for women. Women's experience is one of deep dissatisfaction with relegation simply to the private realm of immanence, of home and family, though its values are not ones they wish to forego. Rather, women look for participation in the public world as well, and for the incorporation of traditional, so-called feminine values into that world. This feminism urges that women (and men) must assume their place in the fullness of both dimensions of human experience. Ruether argues that rejection of the traditional identification of women with nature would be to "buy into that very polarization of which we have been the primary victims."[11] And Plaskow criticizes the dualism of culture and nature as it finds expression in theological views that stress the conflict between transcendence and creatureliness rather than their harmony. She claims that "immersion in and transcendence of nature" are "two scarcely separable moments of experience."[12]

While the first approach to the nature/culture dualism focuses on it as the source of the unequal situation of women and develops strategies for overcoming it, the second is concerned with women's experience of identification with nature and its consequent significance for their experience. In both approaches, however, it is evident that "experience" is an elastic term. It includes the past, both personal and historical, the present, however variously interpreted, and the anticipated future: a variety of hopes, longings, desires are clearly a major part of women's experience. Further,

neither approach signifies airtight categories. Feminist theorists
stress one or other way of viewing the experience of women depending on the problem being addressed. But all are one in asserting the
historical and contemporary oppression of women as a class, whatever variations in experience arise from the particular conditions of
women's universal subordination.

THE NATURE OF WOMEN

It is not surprising that similar versions of the experience of
women appear in recent Catholic discussions of theological anthropology in which distinct positions on human nature or the nature of
women emerge again. It was O'Neill who first suggested that three
basic "visions of humanity" arise from the chorus of voices that
comprise contemporary feminism. In her first type she sees a new
expression of the traditional view that the division of female and
male involves a polarity in which each sex embodies different possibilities of being human, possibilities from which the other sex is
excluded. Derivations are made, in this view, from the biological to
the psychological, social, and spiritual planes in determining the
characteristics of male and female. The emphasis here is on difference and complementarity. This position, she points out, is fraught
with problems, the chief of which is that defining male and female
polarities (activity/passivity, reason/intuition, emotion/will, etc.)
denies the wholeness of human experience and the hopes of
women themselves. In this vision of humanity, the activities of each
sex are rigidly limited, as is the scope of human freedom, judgment, and responsibility over nature. It is a version of "anatomy is
destiny" that ignores the impact of cultural conditioning and expectations. "Neither sex can embody the fullness of humanity, nor can
a person of one sex serve as a model for the other."[13] In O'Neill's
second vision of humanity, the goal of human life is androgynous
existence. In this view, sexual differences are seen as purely biological, affecting only the reproductive roles of human beings. Men
and women are free to adopt styles of being that include the best of
traditional masculine and feminine characteristics—both strength
and sensitivity, rationality and gentleness—in the search for the
fullness of humanity. In this view, emphasis is placed on the similari-

ties rather than the differences between men and women. While it is an attractive vision, it has problems as well, for it ignores the importance of human embodiment so emphasized, for example, in recent phenomenology. And it presents the specter of a single human ideal, which may be destructive of the variety and difference in human beings. O'Neill's third type envisions a unisex goal for humanity. And though one could imagine that sex being female, in fact the proponents of this vision call for assimilation of the female to the male model of humanity. Firestone's arguments for freeing women from the oppression of bodily tyranny seem to indicate a stage of female alienation where male characteristics are so highly valued that all real differences between the sexes should be obliterated. Nevertheless, the unisex goal may have a rhetorical power that serves to jolt society into awareness of the seriousness of the marginalized position of women and thus encourage less radical steps toward genuine equality.

O'Neill concludes by pointing to the challenge of feminism to Christian theological anthropology: what vision of humanity, what goal for human life is proposed in Christian revelation? Is it the same for both men and women? Would it be sinful to cultivate certain ways of being human? How does salvation in Christ relate to the traditional dominance of men in Western society? And what does such salvation offer to women? Two theological studies have attempted some answers to these questions.

The issue of the "nature of women" is considered in the 1978 *Research Report* of the Catholic Theological Society of America (CTSA), which studied official theological argumentation about the question of the ordination of women.[14] In one of its sections, the *Report* notes the difference in anthropological presuppositions in such arguments. Using a simplified typology, it suggests that arguments against the ordination of women imply a two-nature or dual anthropology in which a complementary duality between the sexes is seen as inherent in nature (the "order of creation") and therefore part of the divine plan. This duality "is the ordering principle for complementary roles, functions and activities of women and men." On the other hand, arguments in favor of the ordination of women generally presuppose a one-nature or single anthropology in which "there are no preordained roles or functions, beyond the biological, for either men or women since the appropriate activities of the individual are extrapolated from spiritual and personal characteristics."[15] As the *Report* indicates, fundamental theological differences are entailed in each view.

While there are no longer assertions of the inferiority of women in Christian ecclesiastical or theological discourse, many official Catholic documents affirm a dual anthropology, the complementarity or "different but equal" status of men and women as inherent in nature, in the created order, and therefore as part of the divine plan. This is the basis from which the complementary roles and functions of the sexes are determined. Beyond the biologically determined psychological and sociological characteristics and the limited scope of human freedom already noted, the *Report* states that this view finds a central analogy between "nature" and the economy of salvation. This is often expressed in the marriage symbolism of the relation of Christ to the church (activity-passivity) as a relation of husband to wife (male to female). The dual anthropology emphasizes the unchanging structures of nature and views revelation, tradition, theology and ethics as past-oriented: what is, has been given in nature by God and must not be changed. New knowledge of the human person, derived from the biological and human sciences, is irrelevant to theological discussion since the goal of theology is to preserve the past order as natural, as the order of creation, and therefore as revealed by God.

The single anthropology is radically opposite. Besides its negation of rigidly defined roles for men or women beyond the biological, the *Report* observes that this anthropology puts emphasis on history and the data of experience rather than on "nature," and so affirms the importance of the human sciences for theological reflection. Greater scope is given to human freedom and responsibility, since past social patterns are more likely to be construed as human products rather than as God-given permanent structures. The emphasis on history, whose changing patterns are seen as the responsibility of human agency, entails views of revelation, tradition, theology, and ethics as sourced in present experience as well as the past.

In evaluating the two models, the CTSA *Report* notes that while the single anthropology may be criticized for its neglect of the significance of human bodiliness and sexuality and of the results of centuries of social and cultural conditioning on the "nature" of women, it is nevertheless the sounder basis for theological discussion. Thus contemporary biology, as it indicates the active and not merely passive role of women in sexual relations and procreation, for example, cautions against the use of biological dualism as male activity and female passivity in theological argument. Contemporary psychology discredits unproven assumptions about "feminine psychology" and distinctive feminine characteristics or virtues. Historical studies demonstrate the variety of leadership roles that women have assumed in the past, showing that stereotyped notions of women's nature, place, or role are not universal or unchanging.[16] Sociology and anthropology analyze the position of women in patriarchal cultures, so as to caution against arguments that the nature of women can be determined from particular past societal patterns.

Moreover, the authors of this *Report* point to the Second Vatican Council's affirmation of the importance of history, of revelation as historical, personal, and ongoing as well as past, and of the increased centrality of human responsibility in relation to the structures of church and society, all signaled in the phrase, "the signs of the times." The importance of these themes argue against the assumption of a dual anthropology or of a one-sided emphasis on established structures as natural, the order of creation, the divine choice. Noting recent Vatican statements recognizing the women's movement as a necessary and positive effort for the achievement of equality for women in society, the *Report* concludes that "the assumption of a dual anthropology, derived from cultural and religious situations which assumed the inferiority and subordination of women as a class, is unsound."[17] It urges the need for the church's self-criticism with regard to institutional and ideological forms that perpetuate and legitimize unequal views of women and asserts that a dual anthropology means an uncritical acceptance of patriarchal structures as "normal" and so willed by God rather than as historically conditioned human products. The feminist critique of cultural and religious stereotypes about women as passive, emotional, and dependent must confront theological arguments that invoke "feminine psychology," the "headship of the male," and the "complementarity of the sexes"—all of which can be understood as rationalizations for the subordination of women.

When the CTSA met the following year for discussion of "The Meaning of the Human," the question of theological anthropology and the feminist critique was picked up once again by Mary Buckley. Using a form of the critical correlational method, she analyzed the experience of women, especially as reflected in the social sciences, in the light of biblical revelation and Christian faith.

In Buckley's view, a third vision of humankind is struggling into existence today, a "transformative, person-centered model." She sees both the dual and single anthropologies as inadequate because they reflect society as it was and as it is. Further, these models place the impetus for change simply on individual efforts. Her third, transformative model is both personal and public; it transforms the old gender stereotypes at the same time that it aims to transform the social and cultural structures that are their inseparable context in human life. She argues that this transformative model receives its impetus from changes that have begun to take place in society and from the Christian faith as it calls all persons to likeness to the God of Jesus in "love, compassion, mercy, peace, service, care and community."[18] Both men and women are called to this likeness, not the half-person-hood of complementarity that often conceals a hidden domination, but to an equality that breaks the confines of sex and race and class.

But how, in fact, is this model different from the single anthropology of the CTSA *Report* with its expressed aim of an androgynous goal for all humanity in which "either sex can and should develop those qualities traditionally associated with the other" and in which "greater scope is given to human agency and responsibility in changing . . . the structures of human life?" It is different, according to Buckley, because of its more explicit acknowledgement that anthropological models are not merely formal, individualistic concepts but rather are embedded in particular social contexts. Thus the dual anthropology corresponds to a hierarchic-elitist model of society. It is a model present in clearest form since the rise of the state and the development of political ruling classes, although it was broken in principle by the English, American, and French revolutions.

On the other hand, the one-nature model corresponds to the "one-dimensional" society, a product of the modern period, and is associated with the revolutions' ideals of freedom, equality, brotherhood, and democracy. Despite the inspiring ideals of this vision, experience has proved that "under the cloak of democracy, the real ruling groups have been hidden."[19] In America, for example, blacks, Indians, newly arrived immigrants—and women—must struggle to have a voice; the upper elite is really the paradigm for all people, and thus women and minorities must conform to the single (male, white, Protestant) norm.

Buckley adds that, in order for this transformative vision of a new society to come to pass, a critical task must be performed that probes deeply into the distorted social systems in which we live. This is an arduous task that calls for courage, knowledge, independence, initiative, and responsibility, the ability to challenge and to struggle—qualities traditionally associated with male humanity. Hence, she argues, both "feminine" and "masculine" qualities are needed by both women and men. And in religious terms, repentance and conversion are needed not only by individuals but also at the institutional levels of church and society. The transformative vision may appear utopian, but such is the liberating vision of the reign of God in which the personal and the public are joined.

THEOLOGICAL REFLECTION

This experience of women, in its plural contemporary expressions, surely demands the attention of the church in its theology, preaching, and pastoral care, its liturgical and institutional life. Here, some initial theological appraisal of that experience is suggested through a dual critique. What does the experience of women have to say to the church? And what does the church's gospel message offer to the experience of women? Finally, a perspective will be sketched on the relation of experience to the question of human nature.

There are important dimensions of truth in each expression of the feminist experience we have described. The first "face" of feminism, which expresses anger toward men and appears to entail a reverse sexism, can be a necessary stage in the experience of

Christian women. Feminists have long recognized the significance
of women's anger as a first step toward greater self-determination.
The church can sensitively deal with the anger women sometimes
feel, their need for a period or place of separation in which to
discover, affirm, and strengthen their own powers. Such separation, in which women find support and challenge from one another,
may be a temporary or ongoing but partial dimension of an authentically Christian experience, particularly in the shedding of false
forms of innocence and in the assumption of adult responsibility.
There is a legitimate anger on the part of women toward those
structures (more often than individuals) or traditions that have
demanded and expected less than full personhood of them. Nevertheless, the ultimate goal of any Christian perspective demands a
wider, indeed universal, vision of the community and solidarity of
all persons. In the light of gospel values, then, a "separatist" position cannot be a final one for Christians: the ultimate goal is an
inclusive mutuality: "all one in Jesus Christ."[20]

A similar Christian critique relates to the second "face" of
feminism, which claims that women themselves are to blame for
failing to assume responsibility for their lives. Placing blame, either
on men or women, can only be a provisional moment in the process
of coming to full adulthood. And while blaming, either of oneself
or another, may be an important step, too much blame is finally
destructive. The church can reflect on Jesus's word about loving
the neighbor as the self; the message of love, not hatred of self, is
an important Christian word for women to hear. A moment of self-
blame can be significant to the extent that women are content to
hide behind myths of dependency, fail to decide about their own
lives, drift into decision according to familial or societal expectation. The feminist critique, however, plays back upon Christian
interpretations that keep women in a "place" that prevents their
equal and responsible participation and upon a church that fails to
challenge women to full adult freedom and responsibility.

The face of feminism that focuses on social structures and the
underlying myths that support them is one that the whole church
needs to reflect on seriously. While such myths and structures are
not the entire truth about the human person from a Christian perspective, they do condition the scope of human freedom. While
affirming individual freedom, the church can aid women in coming

to full personhood by applying its gospel principles in critical scrutiny of the culture in which women's self-understanding and range of choices are formed. The message of human dignity and equality before God differs radically from cultural and religious myths about women as moral paragons or temptresses, superwomen or helpless housewives. Such myths deserve not only feminist but Christian criticism as well. Images in the media, for example, are powerful symbols that work on the imagination to shape notions of value, meaning, success. What image of authentic human life does the church present to women, and to the whole Christian community, about women? Is the perspective of its preaching on the situation of women (whether single, married, divorced, working inside or outside the home, professional) one that aids the authentic discovery of self and God in contemporary culture? If the church fails to speak to the experience of women, perhaps feminist criticism ought to be a regular part of sermon preparation. The church's critique of the culture that produces *Cosmopolitan, Playboy* and *Penthouse* must at the same time heed the feminist critique of its own institutional forms and traditional myths about women if it is to speak to the heart of the matter for women today.

Feminists who celebrate women's special relation to nature have an important insight, born of centuries of historical experience, to offer to an over-mechanized culture faced with ecological and nuclear crisis and to a church whose institutional life often appears bureaucratically structured, rigid, sexist. If such women leave Christianity to find their spiritual homes in the new feminist religions, what response does the church offer? While it may offer critique of the separatist tendencies of some feminist spirituality, its word will not be seriously heard until it integrates women and their experience more fully into its own structures, practical life, and worship in genuine solidarity.

So too with the opposite feminist experience that places absolute value on the transcendent, cultural pole of the traditional male/female division. If the church is to address contemporary women's desire to participate in the full range of cultural, societal, and public life with a meaningful Christian perspective, it will have to see that its own institutional life offers opportunity for that full participation as well. Then its gospel critique of this position—the values of home and family; the inherent limitations of all human choice, sin, finitude, suffering, and lack of human fulfillment as abiding human problems and not simply the result of patriarchy—will be a wisdom that can be welcomed by contemporary women.

The more common feminist experience that values both sides of the traditional dualism relates most closely to gospel norms. For the nature/culture polarity can readily be transposed to biblical and theological ideas of the limitations of human creaturehood or finitude and the transcendence of human freedom and spirit. Both are dimensions of human personhood, experience, and action. While the church focuses its critique on social and political forms that fail to reverence both poles (natural life *and* human agency or responsibility), the feminist critique must be heard in the church as well, with its insistence that neither pole is more fully embodied in either sex. Nature and culture are the responsibility of both men and women as human beings. The integration of this biblical and theological anthropology would be truly revolutionary in both church and society, changing the dual, gender-based character of the separation between private and public life. The gospel vision of the integrity of human creatureliness and transcendence has something important to teach the culture and women. But the feminist experience has something to teach the church as well.

What is the relation of the plurality of women's experience to the question of human nature? Karl Rahner's theological anthropology is helpful at this point. Rahner argued that the idea of nature as a static essence is false. He criticized that concept in traditional theology as one based on an uncritical, external observation of merely factual continuities in individual and society. These continuities are always in need of scrutiny lest they become rationalizations of given, but historically relative, social institutions. Rahner points, rather, to the importance of the creativity of human freedom, decision, and praxis as these play back into the elaboration of a never-finished concept of human nature. In Rahner's view, the unchangeable aspects of human beings are consciousness (or knowledge) and freedom in a worldly, historical context, the very conditions of possibility within which persons shape themselves before God in time and history. It is within this fundamental framework that the Christian message of sin and grace should be placed in a theological anthropology.[21]

Thus Rahner emphasizes the importance of human self-creation, and of human freedom and decision-making in the determination of what human being is and will become. It is the choice of persons themselves. Therefore, he argues, Christian women themselves will have to determine their future position in a society and in the church largely out of their own experience, and this precisely within the contemporary pluralistic situation. Rahner referred to "the church of women" as central in this new determination of human nature.

> While it may be true that human nature as constituted by the distinction of the sexes may endure throughout as a metaphysical reality, still the actual mode in which this one nature is objectively realized in the concrete is stamped and conditioned by the specific circumstances of history which correspond to the plurality of types and situations justifiably existing in the church.[22]

While Rahner recognized that societal situations may severely limit human freedom in its self-determination, it is the political and liberation theologians who above all have stressed even further the depth and persuasiveness of societal conditioning on freedom and responsibility as these provide the very basis and precondition for human and religious response to God.

These themes are helpful in appraising the variety of views of human nature or the nature of women, especially as they emphasize past, present, or future perspectives. While the dual anthropology conforms at least partially to the past experience of women, the single anthropology corresponds in part to women's present experience and aspiration. The transformative model indicates especially the future hopes of women for both the individual and social dimensions of human life. The single anthropology and the transformative model also indicate the element of radical human freedom in determining what human nature will become: humankind will choose whatever future human beings will be. The dual anthropology, though adequate to the historical past, clearly proves inadequate to the experience and aspiration of women and many men today and to the gospel message of quality. The single anthropology is more adequate, but fails if it capitulates to an individualistic, or single male or female model; all the virtues of the gospel are needed by all persons and must inform public, ecclesial, and societal structures as well. The transformative model is more adequate to a fully social vision of the future as it preserves awareness of the historical conditioning of the past and recognizes the struggle for equality and authentic transformation on the part of feminist women and men in the present.

Women's recent reflection on their own experience in all its variety and women's efforts to develop corresponding models of humanity is an important development in theological anthropology. Far from a merely speculative enterprise, it is a necessary exploration of past and present experience that has now become focused on the question of the future: what will humankind become? For if human persons have the power to determine, in part at least, what the human future will be, then indeed the experience of women must be heeded. How will the perspectives of the gospel, with its message of sin and liberation in Christ, be integrated into that future for both women and men? The church needs to pay critical attention to the changes in human nature that are occurring in the experience of women and in the "church of women" or "womenchurch" today.[23]

NOTES

1. Paul Tillich, *Systematic Theology* (Chicago: University of Chicago, 1951), I:3–5; Karl Rahner, *Theological Investigations,* trans. Graham Harrison (New York: Herder and Herder, 1973), IX:28–45.

2. David Tracy, "Particular Questions within General Consensus," *Consensus in Theology?* ed. Leonard Swidler (Philadelphia: Westminster Press, 1980), 34; *The Analogical Imagination: Christian Theology and the Culture of Pluralism* (New York: Crossroad, 1980), 230–40.

3. Judith Plaskow, *Sex, Sin and Grace,* 6, 9–50.

4. Mary Aquin O'Neill, "Toward a Renewed Anthropology," *Theological Studies* 36:4 (December 1975): 725–36.

5. Elizabeth Janeway, *Man's World, Women's Place,* 51–57, cited in O'Neill, 732.

6. See Sherry B. Ortner, "Is Female to Male as Nature Is to Culture?" *Women, Culture, and Society,* ed. Michelle Zimbalist Rosaldo and Louise Lamphere (Stanford, CA: Stanford University Press, 1974), 67–87.

7. Rosemary Radford Ruether, *New Woman/New Earth,* 3–23. See her *Sexism and God-Talk,* 47–54.

8. Carol Christ, "Margaret Atwood: The Surfacing of Women's Spiritual Quest and Vision," *Signs* 2:2 (Winter 1976): 327.

9. Shulamith Firestone, *The Dialectic of Sex* (New York: William Morrow, 1971).

10. Simone de Beauvoir, *The Second Sex,* trans. H. M. Parshley (New York: Vintage Books, 1974).

11. Rosemary Radford Ruether, "Motherearth and the Megamachine: A Theology of Liberation in a Feminine, Somatic and Ecological Perspective," *Womanspirit Rising,* ed. Carol Christ and Judith Plaskow, 51.

12. Judith Plaskow, "On Carol Christ: Some Theological Reflections," *Signs* 2:2 (Winter 1976): 336.

13. O'Neill, 735.

14. *Research Report: Women in Church and Society,* ed. Sara Butler (Mahwah, NJ: Catholic Theological Society of America, 1978).

15. Ibid., 37.

16. Historical study has also demonstrated that patriarchy is an historical creation. See Gerda Lerner, *The Creation of Patriarchy.*

17. *Research Report,* 39.

18. Mary Buckley, "The Rising of the Woman is the Rising of the Race," *Proceedings of the Catholic Theological Society of America* 34 (1979), 48–63.

19. Ibid., 59.

20. See Carolyn Osiek, *Beyond Anger: On Being A Feminist in the Church* (New York: Paulist, 1986).

21. See, for example, Karl Rahner, "The Experiment with Man," and "The Problem of Genetic Manipulation," *Theological Investigations* IX:205–24, 225–52.

22. Karl Rahner, "The Position of Women in the New Situation in Which the Church Finds Herself," *Theological Investigations,* VIII:75; see p. 88 for reference to "the church of women."

23. See the essays in *Women: Invisible in Church and Theology,* Concilium 182, eds. Elisabeth Schüssler Fiorenza and Mary Collins (Edinburgh: T. and T. Clark, 1985); Rosemary Radford Ruether, *Women-Church: Theology and Practice* (San Francisco: Harper & Row, 1986).

Women and the Spirituality
of Hope and Fear

Rosemary Haughton

Fear is the appropriate reaction to evil. That fear may sometimes give place to rage—the rising energy of a fierce determination to destroy the evil thing—but fear is the trigger. However, if
the thing that threatens is experienced as a real threat—whether
to oneself or to others—then it is only an idea and doesn't rouse
us to respond. Theologians can discuss the nature of evil and
wonder how it could exist in a universe created by a loving God,
they can define its operations in humans and categorize those
operations, but no emotion is stirred by such a study, useful as it
can be, and it does not of itself motivate us to confront the actual
evils we encounter.

The actual experience of evil is different, whether it be direct
or indirect. It may be encountered through the experience of
seeing TV news footage about famine, or reading about torture
and disappearance in South American countries, or it may be the
result of volunteering in a soup kitchen and seeing a little of the
everyday misery around us, or, more personally, it may be found
in the discovery that a son or daughter is taking drugs, or the
experience of personal betrayal, abuse or abandonment, or hearing first-hand the story of an abused woman. It may be the sudden
recognition of what world economic systems and our own government are deliberately doing to the poor and marginal, or it may
be the realization of the way the regular outpouring of brilliantly
crafted commercials exploits ignorance. Evil may be recognized
by reading with imagination the statistics for prison construction

or watching bulldozers smash yet another neighborhood to build roads or malls.

Whatever form the evil takes, the symptoms experienced on encountering it are those of fear: there is perhaps a kind of coldness, nausea or a feeling like a lump in the stomach, a tightness of the face, clenching of the hands, a feeling of dizziness, faintness, a light sweat. These are the same symptoms that may occur if we hear a step behind us in a dark street, or stand on the high diving board for the first time, receive a threatening letter, or get bad news from the doctor. These are the symptoms of fear.

We don't always think of them as symptoms of fear because we don't expect to feel fear in relation to situations that don't threaten us directly, but it helps to recognize that fear is what we feel, because fear tells us we are in the presence of evil. And until we can identify evil emotionally and not merely notionally we cannot rouse the rage—and the courage—to confront it effectively.

But we also need hope. Without hope fear paralyzes us. We feel trapped and helpless; the response is denial or depression or despair.

Hope breaks the paralysis, when even at some instinctive and barely conscious level we can believe the evil that threatens can be confronted, can be overcome. Whether the action is that of refugees fleeing or the organization of a protest or the confrontation in any degree of the evil, it is fear that makes action necessary and hope that makes it possible.

I wanted to clarify all this, not least for myself, in order to understand why fear is so important—not a shameful but an essential and spiritually significant emotion—and also how it relates to evil and to hope. All this naturally applies to men and women equally. However there is a particular way of experiencing fear and hope which women are often obliged to understand, if only instinctively, and which engages them in living by what only can be called a kind of spirituality. It is not peculiar to women, nor do all women deal with life in this way, but it is a very common female experience, since it concerns the care of others who are loved and for whom one is responsible.

About a year ago, I had dinner with some friends and I asked the little group for their thoughts about evil and hope and fear, and one of them, a Lutheran minister and a sensitive, wise and compassionate man, began to talk about fear as an important personal challenge, as an emotion that must not be avoided by denial or rationalization, but faced. We must also allow ourselves to feel that fear, to face it and go on, he said. Fear is a way to grow in courage and faithfulness. Even as he spoke I experienced an uneasiness, but it was not until later that I began to recognize why the description did not seem adequate. I wondered why my own experience of fear did not fit what he was saying, even though he seemed to be describing an important spiritual strategy.

In the end I began to recognize that for women fear is generally not so much a personal spiritual challenge as a basic condition of living in relationship with fidelity and humility. It is not too much to say that, at least once they are grown-up, women live their lives with that relational kind of fear. The fears of childhood and adolescence are personal, even egocentric, concerned with real or fantasy threats to security, fear of the loss of nurturing adults, of the unknown and uncontrollable world outside. I remember a niece of mine who had lost her own mother as a baby, and at the age of nine her grandmother who had raised her also died. Her immediate response to the news was: "What will happen to me?" The personal fear comes first; the grief—real grief—comes afterward. Children, too, can show great courage in facing their fears if they have hope, and terrible despair when they lack it. But the fear of an adult woman is a fear that embraces those she loves—partners, children, close friends or others who are hers to care for. The price of the creation of those bonds of love is the pressure of fear, for to love is to know herself vulnerable to danger—not danger to herself but to those who are loved.

There is no escape, there are no guarantees, there is no end except death. No precautions can ensure that the ones she cares for will be safe. Illness, accident, alienation, loss of a job, just or unjust accusation of law-breaking—the list goes on. At any time the precarious creation can crack, and that creation includes the woman herself as the one who seems responsible for holding it all in being. Such fears can become exaggerated—fear is like that—but the risks are real and practical and inevitable. Accidents *do* happen, children *are* vulnerable, people *do* die, instantly or slowly, partners *can* change their affections, mothers *do* get sick, families *do* lose their homes. This awareness and the fear that goes with it are the condition of the bonds of love and compassion.

Women don't have all this in their conscious minds all the time, because as well as the fear there is hope, a hope that both motivates the actions of caring and nurturing and is fed by them. The balance is different in each life but, for all, there are the moments, and even long periods, of confidence and happiness when the fears are pushed away from consciousness. The work that goes into making a welcoming, nurturing home is the work of hope, and hope paints the lovely picture of what life can be like, and sometimes is. But the hope itself is there because of the fear, it is the energy that responds to fear, and motivates the never-ending work. When something bad does happen, the embracing fear has known it and the hope is ready to respond—with incredible energy, dogged patience, towering rage when it is appropriate—and to work at rebuilding what has been broken.

All this doesn't mean that women don't experience personal fears—the fear of attack in the street, or cancer, for instance. Yet even then, mixed with it, is the fear of what one's own injury or death will do to the community of relationships. For women dying of AIDS, for instance, the biggest preoccupation is usually what will happen to their children—the prospect of their own pain and death is secondary. This is not because they are unusually heroic and selfless; this is what fear is like for most women, it is how they are.

So, how is all this spiritual? It is spiritual because it is the operation of the human spirit. To a reductionist mind it can be referred simply to the female protective instinct, and that is where it begins, but the operation of this kind of fear and hope is, being human, a matter of choices.

The conscious spirituality of hope and fear is involved in making choices about how to respond to the images created by fear and by hope. Those who are loved, and whose vulnerability creates the embracing fear, are not possessions; even from infancy they are human beings with their own spiritual destiny to work out. How much to protect? How much to risk? When does protection become imprisonment? When does the desire for a child's adult security and success become the pressure to achievement that cripples personality? The choices are hard, and none carries guarantees of rightness. Every parent must live with the consequences of choices that seemed right, but in the event were destructive. Every parent who deals with a child's death or injury suffers the guilt and the questions; if only I had kept him indoors, if only I had taught her better. Every man or woman who loses a partner to divorce and desertion goes over past choices with agonized care—Did I take enough trouble? Did I expect too much? Did I miss signals of something wrong? But women are generally more liable to take the blame when disaster strikes—they have been socialized that way, it's true, but also they have usually more of a history of what I call the embracing fear, the fear as the condition of relationship.

Because of the awareness of choices whose outcome is never certain, the spirituality of fear and hope develops traditionally stressed virtues—humility, and the willingness to accept pain. Humility recognizes the limits of power and is willing to accept the pain of letting go. The toddler becomes the schoolchild who goes out of the gate and out of reach. However careful the choice of schools, doctors, baby-sitters, and later on travels and colleges and careers, the literal truth is that anything can happen. It is necessary to accept the fear and not let it become a ravening beast that seeks to control, that blames and questions. The partner or friend, however beloved, has a life outside, a life inside the mind; it is necessary to let go, to *decide* not to probe, not to manipulate with neediness, not to give way to the fear or exaggerate the hope until it becomes a demand impossible to satisfy. Humility acknowledges the limits of the power to protect the creation of love; it accepts the risks of the gift of freedom and the pain that goes with it, which is the pain of fear.

The spirituality of hope and fear is about dealing with evil as a reality that will not go away, that must be lived with but must not dictate decisions. It knows that fear is the condition of caring but that hope is the guide and humility the discipline. In Catholic cultures the mother of God has been an important symbol of this for women. Women in poverty, burdened and with little power, light their candles before the throned statue, recognizing another woman who herself experienced fear and hope and made decisions and suffered failure. When clergy, and even the savior on the cross, might not understand, she—above the candles but part of the circle of women's lives—will understand and encourage.

The spirituality of hope and fear is a spirituality of the bleak truth that the earth will continue quite well without humans—better, quite possibly. But if we hope, not unnaturally, for a human future, then we have to recognize that the evils we face are human evils. Even what we call "natural disasters" only seem disastrous to us because they hurt human beings—otherwise they are merely geological or biological adjustments. The fear we have to live with is fear for the human community, but the fear releases our hope, drives our work for one another, binds us together, calls us to humility and heroism and rewards us with the joy of companionship. It may be true that fear, rightly faced, enhances personal holiness, but more importantly it is the condition of our bonding as people of God committed to the struggle against evil, in whatever form. Fear is the true indication of the reality of evil, and we must be willing to live with that fear, in hope, so that love and courage may carry on the struggle, however great the odds. If we cease to be afraid, that means that evil has numbed us, we have accepted it, we have given up the struggle. That is why fear is not the enemy but the condition of our work for the kingdom for which, in spite of all, we still hope.

Impasse and Dark Night

Constance FitzGerald

A number of issues in contemporary Christian spirituality underpin and influence the theological interpretation developed in this chapter. Today our spirituality is rooted in experience and in story: the experience and story of women (poor women, black women, white women, exploited women, Asian women, Native American women, etc.); the experience of the poor and oppressed of the world; the experience of the aging; the experience of the fear of nuclear holocaust and the far-reaching evils of nuclear buildup for the sake of national security, power, and domination; the experience of the woundedness of the earth and the environment.

This experience is nourished with meaning by history. It values, therefore, the interpretation of and dialogue with classical sources, with the story of the tradition. Within this framework, Christian spirituality remains attentive to the centrality of the self—to stages of faith development, to passages, to crises of growth—in one's search for God and human wholeness. It reaches, moreover, with particular urgency in our own time for the integration of contemplation and social commitment.

Against this background, I hope to interpret John of the Cross' concept and symbolism of "dark night" (including his classical signs concerning the passage from meditation to contemplation) to show what new understanding it brings to the contemporary experience of what I would call impasse, which insinuates itself inescapably and uninvited into one's inner life and growth and into one's relationships.[1] What is even more significant today is that many of our *societal* experiences open into profound impasse, for which we are not educated, particularly as Americans.

This brings me to two assumptions. First, our experience of God and our spirituality must emerge from our concrete, historical situation and must return to that situation to feed it and enliven it. Second, I find a great number of dark night or impasse experiences, personal and societal, that cry out for meaning. There is not only the so-called dark night of the soul but the dark night of the world. What if, by chance, our time in evolution is a dark-night time—a time of crisis and transition that must be understood if it is to be part of learning a new vision and harmony for the human species and the planet?

To discover meaning, there is value in bringing contemporary impasse into dialogue with the classical text of John.[2] In unfolding the mystery of dark night and unpacking its symbolism in response to the experience of impasse, I would hope to help others understand, name, and claim this experience of God and thereby direct their own creative and affective energy.

IMPASSE

By impasse, I mean that there is no way out of, no way around, no rational escape from, what imprisons one, no possibilities in the situation. In a true impasse, every normal manner of acting is brought to a standstill, and ironically, impasse is experienced not only in the problem itself but also in any solution rationally attempted. Every logical solution remains unsatisfying, at the very least. The whole life situation suffers a depletion, has the word *limits* written upon it. Dorothée Soelle describes it as "unavoidable suffering," an apt symbol of which is physical imprisonment, with its experience of being squeezed into a confined space. Any movement out, any next step, is canceled, and the most dangerous temptation is to give up, to quit, to surrender to cynicism and despair, in the face of the disappointment, disenchantment, hopelessness, and loss of meaning that encompass one.

It is not difficult to imagine how such attitudes affect self-image and sense of worth and turn back on the person or group to engender a sense of failure, to reinforce a realization—not always exact—that their own mistakes have contributed to the ambiguity.

Moreover, intrinsic to the experience of impasse is the impression and feeling of rejection and lack of assurance from those on whom one counts. At the deepest levels of impasse, one sees the support systems on which one has depended pulled out from under one and asks if anything, if anyone, is trustworthy. Powerlessness overtakes the person or group caught in impasse and opens into the awareness that no understandable defense is possible. This is how impasse looks to those who are imprisoned within it. It is the experience of disintegration, of deprivation of worth, and it has many faces, personal and societal.

There is, however, another dimension of impasse that philosophers and psychologists, sociologists and theologians, poets and mystics, have reflected upon from their particular perspectives. Belden Lane, director of historical theology at Saint Louis University, indicates it in his article, *Spirituality and Political Commitment:*

> . . . in a genuine impasse one's accustomed way of acting and living is brought to a standstill. The left side of the brain, with its usual application of linear, analytical, conventional thinking is ground to a halt. The impasse forces us to start all over again, driving us to contemplation. On the other hand, the impasse provides a challenge and a concrete focus for contemplation. . . . It forces the right side of the brain into gear, seeking intuitive, symbolic, unconventional answers, so that action can be renewed eventually with greater purpose.[3]

The negative situation constitutes a reverse pressure on imagination so that imagination is the only way to move more deeply into the experience. It is this "imaginative shock," or striking awareness that our categories do not fit our experience, that throws the intuitive, unconscious self into gear in quest of what the possibilities really are.

Paradoxically, a situation of no potential is loaded with potential, and impasse becomes the place for the reconstitution of the intuitive self. This means the situation of being helpless can be efficacious, not merely self-denying and demanding of passivity.

While nothing seems to be moving forward, one is, in fact, on a homeward exile—*if* one can yield in the right way, responding with *full consciousness* of one's suffering in the impasse yet daring to believe that new possibilities, beyond immediate vision, can be given.

It must be stressed, writes Dorothée Soelle, that insofar as the experience of impasse, or suffering, is repressed, "there is a corresponding disappearance of passion for life and of the strength and intensity of its joys" and insights.[4] The person caught in impasse must find a way to identify, face, live with, and express this suffering. If one cannot speak about one's affliction in anguish, anger, pain, lament—at least to the God within—one will be destroyed by it or swallowed up by apathy. Every attempt to humanize impasse must begin with this phenomenon of experienced, acknowledged powerlessness, which can then activate creative forces that enable one to overcome the feeling that one is without power.[5]

A genuine impasse situation is such that the more action one applies to escape it, the worse it gets. The principles of "first order change"—reason, logic, analysis, planning—do not work, as studies by three Stanford psychiatrists try to show. Thoroughgoing impasse forces one, therefore, to end one's habitual methods of acting by a radical breaking out of the conceptual blocks that normally limit one's thinking.

Genuine change occurs through a "second order" response, "one which rethinks the solution previously tried and suggests something altogether unexpected. The quality of paradox is at the heart of 'second order change.' "[6] It implies that the unexpected, the alternative, the new vision, is not given on demand but is beyond conscious, rational control. It is the fruit of unconscious processes in which the situation of impasse itself becomes the focus of contemplative reflection.[7]

The psychologists and the theologians, the poets and the mystics, assure us that impasse can be the condition for creative growth and transformation *if* the experience of impasse is fully appropriated within one's heart and flesh with consciousness and consent; *if* the limitations of one's humanity and human condition are squarely faced and the sorrow of finitude allowed to invade the human spirit with real, existential powerlessness; *if* the ego does not demand understanding in the name of control and predictability but is willing to admit the mystery of its own being and surrender itself to this mystery; *if* the path into the unknown, into the uncontrolled and unpredictable margins of life, is freely taken when the path of deadly clarity fades.

DARK NIGHT IN JOHN OF THE CROSS

When I am able to situate a person's experience of impasse within the interpretive framework of dark night, that person is reassured and energized to live, even though she feels she is dying. The impasse is opened to meaning precisely because it can be redescribed.

In order to understand dark night, it is important to realize that John of the Cross begins and ends with love and desire in his poems and prose writings.[8] He is intent on showing what kind of affective education is carried on by the Holy Spirit over a lifetime. He delineates, therefore, the movement from a desire, or love, that is possessive, entangled, complex, selfish, and unfree to a desire that is fulfilled with union with Jesus Christ and others. In the process of affective redemption, desire is not suppressed or destroyed but gradually transferred, purified, transformed, set on fire. We go *through* the struggles and ambiguities of human desire to integration and personal wholeness.

This means there is a dark side to human desire, and the experience of dark night is the way that desire is purified and freed.[9] What is important to realize is that it is *in* the very experience of darkness and joylessness, in the suffering and withdrawal of accustomed pleasure, that this transformation is taking place. Transfiguration does not happen at the end of the road; it is in the making now. If we could see the underside of this death, we would realize it is already resurrection. Since we are not educated for darkness, however, we see this experience, because of the shape it takes, as a sign of *death*. Dark night is instead a sign of *life*, of growth, of development in our relationship with God, in our best human relationships, and in our societal life. It is a sign to move on in hope to a new vision, a new experience.

Night in John of the Cross, which symbolically moves from

twilight to midnight to dawn, is the progressive purification and transformation of the human person *through* what we cherish or desire and through what gives us security and support.[10] We are affected by darkness, therefore, where we are mostly deeply involved and committed, and in what we love and care for most. Love makes us vulnerable, and it is love itself and its development that precipitate darkness in oneself and in the "other."

Only when love has grown to a certain point of depth and commitment can its limitations be experienced. Our senses are carried to deeper perception, as it were, by exhaustion. A fullness in one way of being and relating makes one touch its limits. This is not a question of disgust, as it often appears and feels like, but of a movement through sensual pleasure and joy to deeper, stronger faithfulness and to the experience of a love and a commitment, a hope and a vision, unimagined and unexpected on this side of darkness.

We all need some satisfaction of our desire in order to begin and go on in prayer, relationship, or ministry, but it is the withdrawal of pleasure and the confrontation with limitation (our own and others') that signals the transition or growth crisis of the dark night. The test is whether we can, in the last analysis, maintain the direction or momentum of our life without either glancing off permanently into another direction to escape, or succumbing to the darkness of total despair.[11]

Love (romance!) makes us hunger for the unambivalent situation. Yet it is in the very light of love that we encounter the opaqueness of our own humanness and experience the destructiveness within ourselves and the "other." Ambiguity arises, on the one hand, from human inadequacy; it arises, on the other hand, from the Spirit of God calling us beyond ourselves, beyond where we are, into transcendence. We are being challenged to make the passage from loving, serving, "being with," because of the pleasure and joy it gives us, to loving and serving regardless of the cost. We are being challenged to a reacceptance of the "other."[12]

Every God relationship, every significant human love, every marriage, every ministry, every relationship between a person and a community, and perhaps every human group and every nation will come to this point of impasse, with its intrinsic demands for and promise of a new vision, a new experience of God, a quieter, deeper, freer, more committed love. And it will come precisely when imagination seems paralyzed, when intimacy seems eroded, and when desire feels dead.

This brings us to John of the Cross' signs for discerning the genuineness of the dark night purification. Traditionally, they have been recognized as theological signs of the passage in prayer from discursive meditation to contemplation and are, therefore, descriptive of one's spiritual development, one's intrapersonal life. A careful reading of John of the Cross, integrated with concrete human experience, would seem to indicate, however, that the interpretation of these signs must be extended to one's inter-personal life as well, and perhaps even to one's societal life. I submit that a societal interpretation of these signs, and dark night in general, throws considerable light on the contemporary experience of societal impasse.

Although John seems to delineate a smooth transition, his developmental model includes breakdown and failure. This is why the signs speak to us of death, even though they are in reality signs of development and growth. There are two sets of signs, one in the second book of the *Ascent of Mount Carmel* (chap. 13, nos. 2–4); the other in the first book of the *Dark Night* (chap. 9, nos. 2–8). Although the perspective is different in each (the *Ascent* signs are given from the side of the person's faith response, the *Dark Night* signs from God's side), the signs are the same and can be correlated.

The first set of signs underlines one's powerlessness to pray with one's reason or rational mind "since God does not communicate himself through the senses as he did before, by means of the discursive analysis and synthesis of ideas, but begins to communicate himself through pure spirit by an act of simple contemplation in which there is no discursive succession of thought." The senses cannot attain to this contemplation, and dryness results.[13]

Basic to the experience of disintegration or dark night is an apparent breakdown of communication and a powerlessness to do anything about it. One's usual way of functioning, or relating, provides no satisfaction and does not work. What formerly was essential for growth and fidelity (e.g., an active choice and decision for Christ in reasoned meditation) now hinders growth.[14] Nothing happens in meditation. One cannot relate to the loved one as before. The system on which one depends breaks down. Certainty and pleasure give way to ambiguity, misunderstanding, and dryness or boredom.

It is difficult to realize, except by hindsight, that a new kind of love and deeper level of communication, transcending the former love, is developing and is already operative (contemplation). Accustomed to receiving love and insight in one way, one perceives this communication and situation as darkness. What is, in fact, a call to a new vision and to deeper, more genuine intimacy with God, with the "other," and with the world, is experienced as less commitment and less love, precisely because the call comes when intimacy seems to be falling apart and limitation looms large. There seems no possibility of movement backward or forward but only imprisonment, lack of vision, and failure of imagination. "Everything seems to be functioning in reverse," writes John, in this forced passage from rational, analytical, linear thinking to intuitive, metaphorical, symbolic consciousness.[15]

In his probing article "Atheism and Contemplation," Michael J. Buckley shows that John of the Cross, like Feuerbach, is very "sensitive to the humanization consciousness works on its God." John is acutely aware, with Freud, that the religious movement toward God can emerge either from the desire for satisfaction or from the drive for reassurance.[16] In other words, John is conscious of the tendency of religion to become projection and is always subtly asking the question What is the focus of your desire, of your religious awareness and its commitment? "He takes the theological dictum, 'Whatever is received is received according to the mode of the one receiving it,' and he applies it to a person's conceptions and images of God."[17]

> Because in the initial stages of the spiritual life, and even in the more advanced ones, the sensory part of the soul is imperfect, it frequently receives God's spirit with this very imperfection.[18]

We make our God, or gods, in our own image. "Our understanding and our loves are limited by what we are. What we grasp and what we long for is very much shaped and determined by our own nature and personality-set," writes Buckley. If this is not changed by the Spirit of Jesus gradually permeating individual experiences and influencing patterns of development and growth, "there is no possibility of [the] contemplation of anything but our own projections."[19] John of the Cross is at pains to show how our images of God are progressively and of necessity changed and shattered by life experience. The very experience of dark night does, in fact, critique our present images of God. As Buckley says,

> The continual contemplative purification of the human person is a progressive hermeneutic of the nature of God. The self-disclosure of God . . . is finally only possible within the experience of the contradiction of finite concepts and human expectations. The darkness and its pain are here, but there are finely dialectical movements in which the human is purified from projection by a "no" which is most radically a "yes." The disclosures of God contradict the programs and expectations of human beings in order to fulfill human desire and human freedom at a much deeper level than subjectivity would have measured out its projections.[20]

When, in the first sign, we reflect on the breakdown of communication and relationship, therefore, we are assuming also a change and a shattering of one's images. This causes confusion and a sense of loss and meaninglessness.

This is not a defense of Christian masochism, as Dorothée Soelle calls it, nor a sadistic understanding of God, but rather a recognition of the ongoing process of self-acceptance and re-acceptance of the "other" that is necessary for real, enduring love and progressive, mutual insight and creativity. This process presupposes that, in every significant relationship, we come to the experience of limitation, our own and others'. We come to the point where we must withdraw and reclaim our projections of God, of friend, of ministry, of community, and let the "others" be who and what they are: mystery.

The emphasis in the second set of signs is on emptiness in life experience and deadness of desire. Not only is prayer dry, but life is dry, relationship is dry, ministry is dry.

> Souls do not get satisfaction or consolation from the things of God [and] they do not get any out of creatures either. Since

God puts a soul in this dark night in order to dry up and purge its sensory appetite, he does not allow it to find sweetness or delight in anything.[21]

John assures us the time must come in our development when neither God, nor the "other," nor one's life project satisfy, but only disappoint, disillusion, and shatter one's naive hope.

Because desire seems dead, because there is no inclination to do anything about the situation, because one really ceases to care, the temptation to quit, to walk away, becomes overpowering. Hopelessness and worthlessness invade one's perception and one's psyche. It is in the throes of this crisis that people abandon God and prayer, a marriage, a friend, a ministry, a community, a church, and forfeit forever the new vision, the genuine hope, the maturity of love and loyalty, dedication and mutuality, that is on the other side of darkness and hopelessness. Darkness is the place where egoism dies and true unselfish love for the "other" is set free. Moreover, it is the birthplace of a vision and a hope that cannot be imagined this side of darkness.

John can write about self-knowledge as a primary effect of the dark night for two reasons. First, the light and development of contemplative love show up one's limitations, Second, the withdrawal of accustomed pleasure in life, and the consequent frustration of desire, trigger one's seemingly destructive tendencies and move them into action on a level that is beyond conscious control.[22]

What must be remembered at all costs is that desire is not destroyed. Rather, right in this situation of unassuaged emptiness and apparent deadness of desire, in the very area of life in which one is most involved and therefore most vulnerable, desire is being purified, transformed, and carried into deeper, more integrated passion. Dark night mediates the transfiguration of affectivity, and obstacles conceal within themselves untold, hidden energy.

Here we sense what powerful symbolism dark night is. It is an image of productivity and speaks of life buried in its opposite: life concealed, life invisible, life unseen in death.

Thus the third set of signs has two different moments, moving from painful anxiety about culpability to a new and deeper level of appreciation of God and/or the "other" in a quiet, loving attentiveness. John describes the suffering side of this experience when he writes,

> The memory ordinarily turns to God solicitously and with painful care, and the soul thinks it is not serving God but turning back, because it is aware of this distaste for the things of God.[23]

Here it is a question of being obsessed with the problem. How much easier it would be to bear the darkness were one not conscious of one's failures and mistakes. The most confusing and damnable part of the dark night is the suspicion and fear that much of the darkness is of one's own making. Since dark night is a limit experience, and since it does expose human fragility, brokenness, neurotic dependence, and lack of integration, it is understandable that it undermines a person's self-esteem and activates anxious self-analysis.

The only way to break out of this desperate circle of insoluble self-questioning is to surrender in faith and trust to the unfathomable. Mystery that beckons onward and inward beyond calculation, order, self-justification, and fear. John continues, therefore:

> The third and surest sign is that a person likes to remain alone in loving awareness of God, without particular considerations, in interior peace and quiet and repose. . . .
> If those in whom this occurs know how to remain quiet, without care and solicitude about any interior or exterior work, they will soon in that unconcern and idleness delicately experience the interior nourishment.[24]

It is precisely as broken, poor, and powerless that one opens oneself to the dark mystery of God in loving, peaceful waiting. When the pain of human finitude is appropriated with consciousness and consent and handed over in one's own person to the influence of Jesus' spirit in the contemplative process, the new and deeper experience gradually takes over, the new vision slowly breaks through, and the new understanding and mutuality are progressively experienced.

At the deepest levels of night, in a way one could not have

imagined it could happen, one sees the withdrawal of all one has been certain of and depended upon for reassurance and affirmation. Now it is a question, not of satisfaction, but of support systems that give life meaning: concepts, systems of meaning, symbolic structures, relationships, institutions. All supports seem to fail one, and only the experience of emptiness, confusion, isolation, weakness, loneliness, and abandonment remains. In the frantic search for reassurance, one wonders if anyone—friend or spouse or God—is really "for me," is trustworthy. But no answer is given to the question.[25]

The realization that there is *no* option but faith triggers a deep, silent, overpowering panic that, like a mighty underground river, threatens chaos and collapse. This "scream of suffering contains all the despair of which a person is capable, and in this sense every scream is a scream for God," writes Soelle.[26] In this experience of the cross of Jesus, what the "soul feels most," John explains, "is that God has rejected it and with abhorrence cast it into darkness."[27] And Soelle continues:

> All extreme suffering evokes the experience of being forsaken by God. In the depth of suffering people see themselves as abandoned and forsaken by everyone. That which gave life its meaning has become empty and void: it turned out to be an error, an illusion that is shattered, a guilt that cannot be rectified, a void. The paths that lead to this experience of nothingness are diverse, but the experience of annihilation that occurs is the same.[28]

Yet it is the experience of this abandonment and rejection that is transforming the human person in love. This is a possession, a redemption, an actualizing and affirmation of the person that is not understood at the time. Its symbolic expression is dispossession and death.[29]

John seems to say that one leaves the world of rejection and worthlessness by giving away one's powerlessness and poverty to the inspiration of the Spirit and one moves into a world of self-esteem, affirmation, compassion, and solidarity. Only an experience like this, coming out of the soul's night, brings about the kind of solidarity and compassion that changes the "I" into a "we," enabling one to say, "we poor," "we oppressed," "we exploited." The poor are objects until we are poor, too. This kind of identification with God's people, with the "other," is the fruit of dark night.[30]

Some years ago it became evident to me that in our most significant human relationships we go through precisely the kind of suffering John describes concerning the soul's journey to God. In our ministries, moreover, we inevitably come to personal impasse. John's signs of passage and development, refashioned for the present time, should be a valuable tool for discernment. They relate to the breakdown of marriages, to departures from priesthood and religious life, and to the contemporary phenomenon of burnout, among other things.

SOCIETAL IMPASSE

I want to bring together dark night and societal impasse because, as I said, our experience of God and our spirituality must emerge from our concrete historical situation and because our time and place in history bring us face to face with profound societal impasse. Here God makes demands for conversion, healing, justice, love, compassion, solidarity, and communion. Here the face of God appears, a God who dies in human beings and rises in human freedom and dignity.

We close off the breaking in of God into our lives if we cannot admit into consciousness the situations of profound impasse we face personally and societally. If we deal with personal impasse only in the way our society teaches us—by illusion, minimization, repression, denial, apathy—we will deal with societal impasse in the same way. The "no way out" trials of our personal lives are but a part of the far more frightening situations of national and international impasse that have been formed by the social, economic, and political forces in our time.

We are citizens of a dominant nation, and I think that as a nation we have come to an experience of deep impasse and profound limitation. On the other side of all our technology, we have come to poverty and to dark night. We can find no escape from the world we have built, where the poor and oppressed cry out, where the earth and the environment cry out, and where the specter of nuclear waste already haunts future generations. We can find no way out of the horror of nuclear stockpiles but more sophisticated and deadly weapons systems.

As Americans we are not educated for impasse, for the experience of human limitation and darkness that will not yield to hard work, studies, statistics, rational analysis, and well-planned programs. We stand helpless, confused, and guilty before the insurmountable problems of our world. We dare not let the full import of the impasse even come to complete consciousness. It is just too painful and too destructive of national self-esteem. We cannot bear to let ourselves be totally challenged by the poor, the elderly, the unemployed, refugees, the oppressed; by the unjust, unequal situation of women in a patriarchal, sexist culture; by those tortured and imprisoned and murdered in the name of national security; by the possibility of the destruction of humanity.

We see only signs of death. Because we do not know how to read these kinds of signs in our own inner lives and interpersonal relationships, we do not understand them in our societal or national life, either. Is it possible these insoluble crises are signs of passage or transition in our national development and in the evolution of humanity? Is it possible we are going through a fundamental evolutionary change and transcendence, and crisis is the birthplace and learning process for a new consciousness and harmony?

Let us examine the signs. Our impasses do not yield to hard, generous work, to the logical solutions of the past, to the knowledge and skills acquired in our educational institutions. The most farsighted economists said some years ago that the economic solutions of past decades do not fit the present economic crisis in the world. It is argued that the whole economic, social, and political system would collapse were we to feed the poor with surplus crops and stop the wars, the exploitation, the oppression, in which we are involved. Not only God and the loved one fail us, our institutions fail us.

We are obsessed with the problem and with the need for new insight and breakthrough; we are disillusioned with a political system that contributes to international oppression, violence, and darkness. Is it any wonder we witness the effects of impasse among us—anger, confusion, violence—since real impasse or dark night highlights destructive tendencies? Frustrated desire fights back.

Recently, a Jesuit on our local Peace and Justice Commission described the stance of a prominent Roman Catholic theologian, a layman, at a meeting of theologians, bishops, and others on the nuclear question. It was the focused awareness, the incredible logic and rationality, of this man who favored nuclear superiority and denied that a nuclear freeze was a good idea that made such a negative impression on pro-freeze participants. Reason, left to itself, moved to a basically destructive position, unrecognized and unacknowledged in the speaker.

Dark night shows up the "shadow," the dark side of desire. If we refuse to read the signs of dark night in our society and avoid appropriating the impasse, we see cold reason, devoid of imagination, heading with deadly logic toward violence, hardness in the face of misery, a sense of inevitability, war, and death. And we witness the projection of our national shadow on others, "the inevitable shadow of over-rational planning," as Irene de Castillejo calls it.[31]

Today, instead of realizing that the impasse provides a challenge and concrete focus for prayer and drives us to contemplation, we give in to a passive sense of inevitability, and imagination dies. We do not really believe that if we surrender these situations of world impasse to contemplative prayer that new solutions, new visions of peace and equality, will emerge in our world. We dare not believe that a creative re-visioning of our world is possible. Everything is just too complex, too beyond our reach. Yet it is only in the process of bringing the impasse to prayer, to the perspective of the God who loves us, that our society will be freed, healed, changed, brought to paradoxical new visions, and freed for nonviolent, selfless, liberating action, freed, therefore, for community on this planet earth. Death is involved here—a dying in order to see how to be and to act on behalf of God in the world.[32]

This development suggests two questions: Do we really expect anything at all of the contemplative process of prayer in our world today? And how does the failure of imagination and creativity in our national life relate to the breakdown of the contemplative process of prayer and transformation in people's lives? With these questions concerning the intersection of impasse and contemplation, I move into my concluding reflection, on women's religious experience today.

FEMININE IMPASSE

I submit that the feminine experience of dark night, if we read it, interpret it, understand it, and live it through, is in itself a critique of religious consciousness and, therefore, ultimately of Christianity, with its roots in a sexist, patriarchal culture. It is not my intention simply to apply a Christian theme, dark night, to a contemporary issue, women. Rather, I am probing a resource within the theological-mystical tradition in order to understand the contemporary feminist experience of God and to see if John of the Cross' dark night can function in the struggle of women for liberation and equality.[33]

Behind every new spirituality and any creative re-visioning of the world—at the root of any real theology—is an experience of God. Yet every religious experience comes from a meeting with a new and challenging face of God in one's own time and social situation. I suspect that although it is imperative, for example, for feminist theologians to develop new interpretive paradigms that function to liberate people, only women's *experience* of God can alter or renew our God images and perhaps our doctrine of God. I want, therefore, to examine the feminist experience of God in impasse, because this is where many women in the Church, and in the world, find themselves. "We have only begun to experience the depth of women's alienation from Christian belief systems and from the existing Churches," writes Elisabeth Schüssler Fiorenza.[34]

Today feminists struggle with the Judeo-Christian image of a male God and a male Church. Just as Marxism sees religion as the opiate of the people and Christianity's doctrine of God as a support of oppression and misery, so the feminists see a patriarchal system that visualizes God, and consequently Church, in almost exclusively patriarchal terms as basically destructive. The masculine image of God is experienced as unsatisfying and confusing because it serves to reinforce male domination, a patriarchal value system, and an entire male world view.

This is an impasse for women, since their past religious experience has come to them through these images and this inherited symbol system, which does not function for women now as it did before. There is no going back to what was—what gave comfort and clarity and brought feminists to their present stage of religious development and commitment—but there is no satisfactory going forward either. There seems to be no way out of this God-less situation because no genuine evolution of God images has really occurred. We touch this in Alice Walker's latest novel, *The Color Purple,* a story of a black women, Celie, who moves from being oppressed and brutalized to self-actualization and religious transformation. What is significant is that Celie's transcendence requires or coincides with a radical redefinition of God. "The author's choice of the genre of the epistolary novel, in this case composed entirely of letters for which there is no direct response," places the whole story in a prayer context.[35] In the first fifty-five letters Celie writes the story of her life to God, because she is ashamed to talk to him about it. Abused by the man she thought to be her father and deprived by him of the children she consequently bore, dehumanized by her husband and deprived by him of any knowledge of or communication with her sister, she is loved by one woman, Shug Avery. Aware finally, under the influence of Shug's love and affirmation, of the extent of her exploitation, Celie rebels not only against men but against God and can no longer write to *him.* She writes instead to her sister:

What God do for me? I ast. . . . He give me a lynched daddy, a crazy mama, a lowdown dog of a step pa and a sister I probably won't ever see again. Anyhow, I say, the God I been praying and writing to is a man. And act just like all the mens I know. Trifling, forgitful and lowdown. . . .

All my life I never care what people thought bout nothing I did, I say. But deep in my heart I care about God. What he going to think. And come to find out, he don't think. Just sit up there glorying in being deef, I reckon. But it ain't easy, trying to do without God. Even if you know he ain't there, trying to do without him is a strain.

When Shug asks what her God looks like, Celie senses the incongruity of her image but replies:

He big and old and tall and graybearded and white. He wear white robes and go barefooted.
Blue eyes? she ast.
Sort of bluish gray. Cool. Big though, White lashes, I say. . . . Ain't no way to read the bible and not think God white, she say. Then she sigh. When I found out I thought God was white, and a man, I lost interest. You mad cause he don't seem to listen to your prayers. Humph! Do the mayor listen to anything the colored say? . . . Here's the thing, say Shug. The thing I believe. God is inside you and inside everybody else. You come into the world with God. But only them that search for *it* inside find it. And sometimes it just manifest itself even if you not looking, or don't know what you looking for. Trouble do it for most folks, I think.
. . . [U]s talk and talk about God, but I'm still adrift. Trying to chase that old man out of my head. I been so busy thinking bout him I never truly notice nothing God make. Not a blade of corn (how it do that?) not the color purple (where it come from?) Not the little wildflowers. Nothing.
Man corrupt everything, say Shug. He on your box of grits, in your head and all over your radio. He try to make you think he everywhere. Soon as you think he everywhere, you think he God. But he ain't. Whenever you trying to pray, and man plop himself on the other end of it, tell him to git lost, say Shug. Conjure up flowers, wind, water, a big rock.
But this is hard work, let me tell you. He been there so long, he don't want to budge. He threaten lightening, floods and earthquakes. Us fight. I hardly pray at all. Every time I conjure up a rock, I throw it. Amen.[36]

Thus feminists, unable to communicate with the God of patriarchy, are imprisoned in a night of broken symbols. They ask how the idea of God undergoes transformation.

Is it by changing our religious language? By feminizing God, uncovering feminine images and attributes of God in the Scriptures? Is it by the desexualization of God and a move toward deism? Or is it by contemplation? (A step in the criticism of Marxism is implied here. Can experience really be altered simply by changing language?) What our programs to eliminate sexist language in our theological, devotional, and liturgical life have shown us is that our solutions are unsatisfactory and confusing. We find impasse not only in the problems but even in the solutions.

So-called postpatriarchal theologians and philosophers have suspected this for some time and in consequence have moved beyond Judeo-Christian religion. These radical feminist thinkers claim feminine consciousness and Christian faith are contradictions in terms. Aware, like John of the Cross, of the tendency of religion to become projection, they have rejected the Christian God that patriarchy projects. But is this the only option? Here the advance of postpatriarchy intersects with the development of contemplation. If one admits that religious belief and desire can be analyzed into episodes of projection, does the force of this discovery indicate a movement toward the total rejection of the God of patriarchy, or can it equally indicate that faith and desire must move into contemplation, one movement of which is apophatic? Is the alternative either to deny the reality of the God of Christianity or to insist that the evolution of faith and desire must pass through the darkness and the cross, in which the meaning of the night is found? It is imperative to emphasize, as Buckley observes,

> that apophatic theology is not primarily one which does or does not make statements about God. It is primarily an experiential *process,* a process of entering into the infinite mystery that is God, so that gradually one is transformed by grace and this grace moves through the intense experience of darkness [impasse] into the *vision* of the incomprehensible God [the God who transcends present images and symbols]. Apophatic theology involves both interpretation and criticism, conceptualization and theological argument. But all of these are descriptive of *a process in which one is engaged,* a process in which *one must be engaged* in order to grasp its interpretation in any depth.[37]

If the impasse in which feminists find themselves *is* dark night, then a new experience of God, transformative of alienating symbols, is already breaking through even though it is not comprehensible yet, and impasse is a call to development, transcendence, new life, and understanding. Ultimately, therefore, impasse is a challenge to feminists to be mystics who, when human concepts disillusion, symbols break, and meanings fail, will let their "faith . . . relocate everything known within a new horizon in which it is radically reinterpreted and transvaluated."[38] Feminists need to realize that the gap that exists between human, patriarchal concepts of God and what is internalized by them in impasse is exactly what promises religious development and is the seed of a new experience of God, a new spirituality, and a new order—what Elizabeth Janeway calls the "Great Myth, as yet unborn," to which Madonna Kolbenschlag refers in her article, "Feminists, the Frog Princess, and the New Frontier of Spirituality."[39]

I believe there is no alternative for feminists except contemplation, if they are to avoid the trivialization of their own religious experience in dark night. The experience of God in impasse is the crucible in which our God images and language will be transformed and a feminine value system and social fabric generated. All the signs (of dark night) indicate this is the next step in any positive, creative re-visioning of the future, in any genuinely feminine generativity. Theology is dependent on this experience, which cannot be created by theological reflection alone. Dark night is, as was stated before, "a progressive hermeneutic of the nature of God." If this passage is not recognized and traversed, a certain kind of atheism and permanent cynicism are inevitable.

The contemplative love experience, which is beyond conscious control and is not given on demand, is concerned not for the image of God, as political theologians are, but with God, who does in the end transcend our images and expectations. What is critical to see is that one has to *allow* the experience to take place through a love that is gradually welling up from the ground of one's being and that serves as a basis for contemplation. Only this experience can give to theology the insight it needs "to search out a new doctrine of God which is related to the intellectual, practical, and ethical concerns of the present situation of women and which suggests transformation or emancipative possibilities for the future."[40]

Contemplation, and ultimately liberation, demand the handing over of one's powerlessness and "outsider-ness" to the inspiration and power of God's Spirit. How imperative it is that women take possession of their pain and confusion; actively appropriate their experience of domination, exploitation, and oppression; consent to their time in history; and hold this impasse in their bodies and their hearts before the inner God they reach for in the dark of shattered symbols. Although the God of the dark night seems silent, this God is not a mute God who silences human desire, pain, and feeling, and women need to realize that the experience of anger, rage, depression, and abandonment is a constitutive part of the transformation and purification of the dark night. This very rage and anger purify the "abused consciousness" of women in the sexism they have internalized.[41]

If there is, as we suggest, an incipient experience of God, this presence of God will necessarily throw light on woman's "shadow" and reveal her to herself with all the destructive power she has and all the repressed possibilities or "lost alternatives" that cry within her for a voice. It is in the experience of this kind of night, when women put all the power of their desire, not in ideology, but here before the inner God, that the real bonding of women takes place, and purified of violence, they are readied for communion with their God, for sisterhood, equality, liberation, and mutuality.

Impasse internalizes the option for the poor and effects an identification with and compassion for all "women whose cry for liberation is so basic and unmistakable that it shouts out for all of us in our common quest for equality."[42] In one's own womanhood, one holds every woman before God, women of the present and women of the past. This is an experience, not a theory! Though one lives in Baltimore or Atlanta or California or Washington, one's life is lived within the bleeding borders of El Salvador and Guatemala, Lebanon and South Africa, Afghanistan and Cambodia. Though one lives at the end of the twentieth century, the voiceless sorrow of women long dead is felt as one's own. One senses this in Alice Walker's essay "In Search of Our Mother's Gardens":

When Jean Toomer walked through the South in the early twenties, she discovered a curious thing: Black women whose spirituality was so intense, so deep, so *unconscious,* that they themselves were unaware of the riches they held. They stumbled blindly through their lives: creatures so abused and mutilated in body, so dimmed and confused by pain, that they considered themselves unworthy even of hope. In the selfless abstractions their bodies became to the men who used them, they became more than "sexual objects," more even than mere women: they became Saints. Instead of being perceived as whole persons, their bodies became shrines: what was thought to be their minds became temples suitable for worship. These crazy "saints" stared out at the world, wildly, like lunatics—or quietly like suicides; and the "God" that was in their gaze was as mute as a great stone. . . .

. . . [T]hese grandmothers and mothers of ours were not "saints," but Artists: driven to a numb and bleeding madness by the springs of creativity in them for which there was no release. They were Creators who lived lives of spiritual waste, because they were so rich in spirituality—which is the basis for Art—that the strain of enduring their unused and unwanted talent drove them insane. Throwing away this spirituality was the pathetic attempt to lighten the soul to a weight the work-worn sexually abused bodies could bear.[43]

Such a time is past: the time of throwing away one's spirituality in order to survive.

It is regrettable that the possible liabilities of dark night theology cannot be dealt with in full here. Although some *interpretations* of dark night could reinforce passivity and women's internalized inferiority, subordination, lack of self-esteem and self-actualization, John of the Cross sings of the affirmation of the person by God within and of the redemption or transformation of affectivity that dark night effects. Dark contemplation is not a validation of things as they are or a ploy to keep women contented "outcasts of the [patriarchal] land"[44] but a constant questioning and restlessness that waits for and believes in the coming of a transformed vision of God; an affirmation of the self as woman that comes from deep inside and the consequent maturing to wholeness as a complete person; and a new and integrating spirituality capable of creating a new politics and generating new social structures.

Contemplation is what Dorothée Soelle calls revolutionary patience and is the epitome of passionate desire, activity, self-direction, autonomy, and bondedness.[45] It is a time bomb and will explode in new abilities and energy in women that cannot be conquered. Ultimately, it is the mystic, the contemplative woman, who will be reassured, affirmed, and loved, and who will see and love, and for whose sake the world will be given sight, language, reassurance, and love. And she will understand Celie's final epistle, a letter to God: "Dear God. Dear stars, dear trees, dear sky, dear peoples. Dear Everything. Dear God."

NOTES

1. See David Tracy, *The Analogical Imagination, Christian Theology and the Culture of Pluralism* (New York: Crossroads, 1981), chap. 3, "The Classic."

2. Not only Tracy has influenced my methodology, but also Thomas H. Groome, *Christian Religious Education* (San Francisco, Harper & Row, 1980), pp. 185–222, and John Shea, *Stories of Faith* (Chicago: Thomas More Press, 1980), pp. 76–90. These three studies are helpful in dealing with the dialogue between tradition and contemporary story or issues.

3. Belden C. Lane, "Spirituality and Political Commitment: Notes on a Liberation Theology of Nonviolence," *America*, March 14, 1981; see also Urban T. Holmes III, *Ministry and Imagination* (New York: Seabury, 1981), pp. 89–93, for a good treatment of right- and left-brain thinking. Holmes works out of the contributions of Jerome S. Bruner, *On Knowing: Essays for the Left Hand* (New York: Atheneum, 1971), and Robert E. Ornstein, *The Psychology of Consciousness* (New York: Viking, 1972), pp. 57–64.

4. Dorothée Soelle, *Suffering* (Philadelphia: Fortress, 1975), p. 36.

5. See ibid., p. 76, 11.

6. Lane, "Spirituality and Political Commitment," p. 198. Lane's discussion of the theory of Paul Witzalawick, John Weakland, and Richard Fisch in *Change: Principles of Problem Formation and Problem Resolution* (New York: Norton, 1974).

7. There are other models to explain and verify this experience:

e.g., the creative process as it is described by Ralph J. Hallman, "Aesthetic Pleasure and Creative Process," *Humanitas* 4 (1968), pp. 161–68, or *Journal of Humanistic Psychology* 6 (1966), pp. 141–47; the process of individuation developed by Carl Jung and described by John Welch, O. Carm., *Spiritual Pilgrims: Carl Jung and Teresa of Avila* (New York: Paulist Press, 1982), esp. pp. 136–37, 141–43, 151–62; the model of structure and anti-structure developed by Victor W. Turner, *The Forest of Symbols: Aspects of Ndembu Ritual* (Ithaca: Cornell University Press, 1967), pp. 93–101, *The Ritual Process: Structure and Anti-Structure* (Chicago: Aldine, 1969), *Dramas, Fields and Metaphors: Symbolic Action in Human Society* (Ithaca: Cornell University Press, 1974). See Holmes, *Ministry and Imagination,* pp. 119–36, for material on Turner's structure and anti-structure.

8. See John of the Cross, *The Collected Works of St. John of the Cross,* trans. Kieran Kavanaugh and Otilio Rodriguez (Washington, D. C.: Institute of Carmelite Studies, 1973), *Ascent of Mount Carmel,* Book I, chap. 13, no. 3; chap. 14, no. 2: poem, "The Dark Night," p. 296; poem, "The Spiritual Canticle," pp. 410–15; *The Dark Night,* Book II, chap. 9, no. 1; *The Living Flame,* stanza 3, nos. 1,3,7.

9. See John of the Cross, *CW, The Dark Night,* Book I, chaps. 1–8, for a view of the dark side of human desire. John calls this dark side the faults of beginners.

10. See Michael J. Buckley, "Atheism and Contemplation," *Theological Studies* 40 (1979), p. 696; see also John of the Cross, *CW, The Spiritual Canticle,* stanzas 3–7, to grasp how one moves through that which one cherishes—the self, the world, relationships—to deeper love for God.

11. See John of the Cross, *CW, The Dark Night,* Book I, chap. 7, no. 5; chap. 8, no. 3.

12. See ibid., Book I, chap. 9, no. 4.

13. For the first set of signs, see ibid., Book I, chap. 9, no. 8; *Ascent of Mount Carmel,* Book II, chap. 13, no. 2.

14. John, *CW, The Dark Night,* Book I, chap. 9, no. 7.

15. Ibid., Book I, chap. 8, no. 3.

16. Buckley, "Atheism and Contemplation," p. 694.

17. Ibid., p. 693, see also p. 690.

18. John, *CW, The Dark Night,* Book I, chap. 16, no. 2.

19. Buckley, "Atheism and Contemplation," p. 694.

20. Ibid., pp. 696–97.

21. See John, *CW, The Dark Night,* Book I, chap. 9, no. 2; for correlating signs, see also *Ascent of Mount Carmel,* Book II, chap. 13, no. 3.

22. See John, *CW, The Dark Night,* Book I, chap. 14, where he speaks of the spirit of fornication, blasphemy, and confusion *(spiritus vertiginis),* or what I would call frustrated desire. See also Welch, *Spiritual Pilgrims,* pp. 141–46.

23. John, *CW, The Dark Night,* Book I, chap. 9, no. 3.

24. John, *CW, Ascent of Mount Carmel,* Book II, chap. 13, no. 4; *The Dark Night,* Book I, chap. 6, no. 2.

25. See Welch, *Spiritual Pilgrims,* p. 145.

26. Soelle, *Suffering,* p. 85.

27. John, *CW, Ascent of Mount Carmel,* Book II, chap. 6, no. 2.

28. Soelle, *Suffering,* p. 85.

29. See Buckley, "Atheism and Contemplation," p. 696.

30. See Constance Fitzgerald, "Contemplative Life as Charismatic Presence," *Contemplative Review* II (1978), p. 45, or *Spiritual Life* 29 (1983), p. 28.

31. See Irene Claremont de Castillejo, *Knowing Woman: A Feminine Perspective* (New York: Harper & Row, 1974), pp. 32, 39; see also pp. 17–18 for a very interesting analysis of the different levels on which people discuss nuclear weapons.

32. See Holmes, *Ministry and Imagination,* p. 154. The entire chapter 6, "Dying to Image," pp. 137–164, is excellent supplementary reading to my development.

33. See Anne Carr, B.V.M., "Is a Christian Feminist Theology Possible?" *Theological Studies* 43 (1982), pp. 282, 292; Elisabeth Schüssler Fiorenza, "Toward a Feminist Biblical Hermeneutics: Biblical Interpretation and Liberation Theology," *The Challenge of Liberation Theology,* ed. Mahan, p. 109: "Theological interpretation must also critically reflect on the political presuppositions and implications of theological 'classics' and dogmatic or ethical systems. In other words, not only the content and traditioning process within the Bible, but the whole of Christian tradition should be scrutinized and judged as to whether or not it functions to oppress or liberate people."

34. Elisabeth Schüssler Fiorenza, "Sexism and Conversion," *Network* (May-June 1981), p. 21.

35. Sue E. Houchins, "I Found God in Myself/And I Loved Her/I Loved Her Fiercely: A Study of Suffering in the Archetypal Journey of Alice Walker's Female Heroes," a chapter of a dissertation in progress, p. 15.

36. Alice Walker, *The Color Purple* (New York: Harcourt Brace Jovanovich, 1982), 164–168.

37. Buckley, "Atheism and Contemplation," p. 690 (italics mine).

38. Ibid., p. 695.

39. Quoted by Madonna Kolbenschlag, "Feminists, The Frog Princess, and the New Frontier of Spirituality," *New Catholic World,* July-August 1982.

40. Carr, "Is a Christian Feminist Theology Possible?" p. 293.

41. Here I am addressing the call of Fiorenza for "a spirituality that understands anger, persecution, defamation, violence and suffering in political-theological terms." See "Sexism and Conversion," pp. 20–21.

42. Maureen Fiedler, "The Equal Rights Amendment and the Bonding of Women," *LCWR Newsletter* (1980), p. 5.

43. Alice Walker, "In Search of Our Mother's Gardens," in *Working It Out,* ed. Sara Rudick and Pamela Daniels (New York: Pantheon, 1977), p. 93.

44. Houchins, "I Found God in Myself," quoted from Anne Pratt, *Archetypal Patterns in Women's Fiction* (Bloomington, Ind.: Indiana University Press, 1981), 5.

45. Dorothée Soelle, *Revolutionary Patience* (Maryknoll, N.Y.: Orbis, 1977); see also Marianne Katoppo, *Compassionate and Free: An Asian Woman's Theology* (Maryknoll, N.Y.: Orbis, 1980), p. 21.

The Transformative Influence of Wisdom in John of the Cross

Constance FitzGerald

The intense interest over the past fifteen years in John of the Cross' Dark Night is certainly part of a much larger retrieval in contemporary theology of the mystical tradition and the classic spiritual texts of the past. More importantly, the current awareness of darkness and the affinity of so many for the dark night experience seem to be a sign of the rebirth and more public valuing of the experience of God in contemplative prayer. There is little doubt, moreover, that over the past twenty years the creative work of the Jesuits in reinterpreting and making available Ignatian prayer, particularly through the medium of the Exercises and directed retreats, has made a significant contribution to this movement toward contemplative prayer in people's lives. This may be why we are now witnessing an intersection of Ignatian and Carmelite spirituality at the present time, an intersection related to darkness. This may be why some people, practiced in Ignatian prayer and yet faced with the bewildering experience of darkness, dryness and loss of meaning in their own lives or in the lives of those they guide, find helpful the Dark Night teaching of John of the Cross. For John writes of a critical, contemplative phase of spiritual growth easily misunderstood and not specifically treated by Ignatius.

This intersection or complementarity of Ignatian and Carmelite spirituality reaches back to sixteenth century Spain when young Jesuits from Ignatius' newly founded Society of Jesus provided spiritual direction for Teresa of Avila as she attempted not only to understand her own disturbing mystical graces but also to reform the ancient Carmelite Order. Thomas H. Green, a loyal son of Ignatius, stands, therefore, within a long history of mutuality and respect when, in his second book on prayer, he turns to John of the Cross and Teresa to provide guidance on "prayer beyond the beginnings." For Green, John of the Cross' discussion on the Dark Night "is one of the most important passages in the whole literature of prayer."[1]

In this article, I hope to extend contemporary interpretation of the Dark Night in John of the Cross in two ways: first, by examining the transformative and subversive role of Wisdom (Sophia) in the Dark Night, which is a specifically Christological emphasis suggested by contemporary feminist theologians;[2] and second, by bringing out the meaning of the deeper experience of darkness, called by John of the Cross the Dark Night of the spirit.

WISDOM IN JOHN OF THE CROSS

John moves in the milieu of Wisdom from the beginning of the *Ascent of Mount Carmel* to the end of the *Living Flame of Love.*[3] An analysis of his major writings reveals that he is radically influenced by the Wisdom texts of pre-Christian Judaism. Particularly important for John in defining who Sophia is and what she does are the books of Wisdom (ch 7–9) and Proverbs (ch 8). Out of his own distinctive configuration of this Jewish wisdom literature emerge some of the most basic principles of his teaching. It fashions John's understanding of who Jesus is, who God is and how this God functions in the dynamic of human transformation. It suggests the place of Sophia in human suffering and hints at how the beloved of Sophia functions in the world.

It is clear that for John of the Cross, as for St. Paul and the writers of the Gospels of John and Matthew, Jesus Christ is divine Wisdom (Sophia), the Word, the Son of God. In the unitive experience of Jesus-Sophia the person is transformed, and in this Jesus the entire creation is gathered into the tender, unifying embrace of Sophia-God, who pervades and connects the entire cosmos and every form of life in it.

This means that John of the Cross appropriates not only

pre-Christian Judaism's understanding of a feminine gestalt of God, Sophia, but he seems to be completely at home with the identification made by New Testament writers of Jesus as Divine Sophia: *Jesus is Sophia incarnate.* To underpin his own cohesive Christology John uses most of the significant New Testament Wisdom texts and he does this in a context that frequently reveals his knowledge of their connection with the Wisdom texts of pre-Christian Judaism. The tradition of personified Wisdom which played a foundational role in the development of Christology in the early Church seems to have been singularly important to him, since some of his most profound Christological assertions are couched in its terms. The recognition of the central, critical function of Wisdom is therefore basic to an understanding of John's Christology. Furthermore, to explore the subversive and transformative function of Sophia in the Dark Night is to probe the role of Jesus Christ in the process of transformation.

THE ROLE OF JESUS CHRIST

In John's anthropology the human person is seen as an infinite capacity for God. As long as the great "caverns" of the mind, heart, memory and imagination are filled with human knowledge, loves, dreams and memories that seem or promise to satisfy completely, the person is unable to feel even or imagine the depths of the capacity that is there. Only when we become aware of our emptiness, in the face of the experience of the fragility and breakdown of what or whom we have staked our lives on, the limitation and failure of our life project and life love, the shattering of our dreams and meanings, can the depths of thirst and hunger that exist in the human person, the infinite capacity, really be felt (LF 3.19–22).[4]

Few people understand that John is actually addressing this infinite capacity when he urges them at the end of the first book of the *Ascent* to have an on-going desire to pattern their lives on Christ's.

Have habitual desire to imitate Christ in all your deeds by bringing your life into conformity with his. You must then study his life in order to know how to imitate him and behave in all things as he would behave. (IA 13.3)[5]

This means only one thing: desire to know Jesus Christ. Human desire is educated by an immersion in the Jesus of the Gospels. However, if you channel your desire toward knowing Jesus Christ, the one you will learn to know is loving Sophia who will slowly and secretly redirect and claim your desire and subvert your life. Desire is educated, therefore, by the companionship, the friendship, of Jesus-Sophia. This dynamic underlies John's whole philosophy of prayer and indicates how a conscious decision of the heart for Christ takes place, how a shift in the focus of desire and meaning begins in our lives.

But often the human person is not satisfied with the day-to-day fidelity to this companionship, nor with its slow, unpretentious, mysterious development. Too many people educated in our culture live with a consuming desire for novelty, excitement, change, new pleasures and extraordinary experiences. But John, appropriating both St. Paul and the Book of Wisdom in one of his most famous christological passages, affirms that we do not need unusual new revelations, visions or secret truths (IIA 22.5–7). We have everything we desire in the gospel and the unitive companionship of the human Jesus, in whom dwells for us the nearness and fullness, the compassionate kindness, of Sophia-God embracing and energizing from within the totality of the human situation.

In stressing the complete sufficiency and unlimited potential of Christ as divine Sophia, John of the Cross validates new possibilities for appropriating the inexhaustible meaning of Jesus. What will we unlock if *in prayer* we experience the life of Jesus in the light of Sophia, thereby transforming for our time the symbol of Christ and reclaiming Christ and christological doctrine in a new way?[6]

Fasten your eyes on him alone, because in him I have spoken and revealed all, and in him you will discover even more that you ask for and desire . . . For he is my entire locution and response, vision and revelation, which I have already spoken . . . to you . . . (IIA 22)

IMAGE OF JESUS CHRIST AND GROWTH IN WISDOM

It is in this walking with the human Jesus that Sophia becomes a lifegiving, indwelling image and one's primary focus of affective and cognitive meaning. This image is unique for each person, forming a basis for relationship, direction, love, purification and transformation. In fact, a gradual transference of desire occurs as the presence of loving Sophia takes shape within, influencing motivation and affecting imagination.

A principle fundamental to John's wisdom Christology is operative here: love will never reach the fullness of its possibilities, human desire will never stop yearning and aching, until the lovers are so alike that one is transfigured in the love and goodness of the other. This means that a transforming image of Jesus-Sophia is, in a way totally harmonious with human development, gradually etched within the human personality. As I know Jesus-Sophia, this knowledge subverts my life, shows me to myself as in a mirror and redirects and purifies my desire.

If I look long enough at one who truly loves me, I become what I see in the other's eyes. I am transfigured. The image of the loved one, the eyes of the beloved, are burnt into my heart and seen with my inner eye. We see this with remarkable clarity in the Spiritual Canticle poem:

> Reveal your presence,
> And may the vision of your beauty be my death;
> For the sickness of love
> Is not cured
> Except by *your very presence and image.*
> O spring like crystal!
> If only, on your silvered over face,
> You would suddenly form
> The eyes I have desired,
> Which I bear sketched deep within my heart. (SC st 11–12)

The soul experiences within herself a certain sketch of love . . . and she desires the completion of the sketch of this image, the image of her Bridegroom, the Word, the Son of God, who as St Paul says, 'is the splendor of [God's] glory and the image of [God's] substance,' (Heb. 1.3) for this is the image into which the soul desires to be transformed through love. (SC 11.11–12)

Because this is a fundamental experience for John, and not just a concept, it is important to understand the developmental and transformative function of this Wisdom image. Through it the whole creative aspect of Old Testament Sophia is brought to human transformation. If it is not valued relative to spiritual growth, the tender, careful, nurturing creativity of Sophia will be thwarted and we will "damage or lose the sublime image that God [is] painting within [us]."[7]

At first the developing image of Jesus-Sophia is a strength and consolation motivating one toward a generous, self-giving life influenced by the Jesus of the Gospels and sensitizing one to this Sophia presence in the world that energizes and connects all of reality.[8] As the intimacy with Christ matures, however, this image, within and without, begins to make deeper claims and there is a shift in the way Sophia operates within the depths of human personality.

DARK NIGHT AND THE CONTINUING ROLE OF SOPHIA

In time the presence of Sophia becomes afflictive. The image becomes too threatening. Jesus-Sophia subverts my own self-image and this marks the first aspect of subversion. I cannot accept the claims of Sophia upon me nor can I accept Wisdom as a life-vision in an unconditional commitment; Sophia is too revolutionary and seditious. Sophia turns life upside-down, challenges my most deeply held beliefs and values, undermines what I have learned, claims whom and what I possess, and highlights the limitations and oppressive character of what I depend on most for satisfaction and assurance.

This brings us to the relationship between the Dark Night and the presence of loving Wisdom.[9] John says very explicitly that Dark Night, infused contemplation, *is* the loving Wisdom of God.[10] It follows that if Jesus Christ *is* Divine Wisdom, Sophia, then *dark contemplation is the presence of Jesus Christ as Wisdom* and Dark Night is the time when the image of Jesus-Sophia takes on all the marks of crucifixion: suffering, isolation, failure, marginality, rejection, abandonment, hopelessness, meaninglessness, death. The image of the Crucified One, reflective of a seemingly silent, incomprehensible God, functions in the Dark Night as incomprehensible, secret, hidden and yet loving Wisdom-Sophia.[11] And this is the second aspect of subversion: not only has my self-image been subverted but now too the images of Christ and God. Therefore when John says that the Dark Night is an inflow of God, this inflow is of a God imparting a secret Wisdom who is Jesus Crucified, a secret, unitive, loving knowledge indicative of more intimate relationship (IDN 10.6). Dark Night is not primarily *some thing,* an impersonal darkness like a difficult situation or distressful psychological condition, but *someone,* a presence leaving an indelible imprint on the human spirit and consequently on one's entire life.

This image is the touch of God's hand marking, wounding, challenging, shaping, purifying and transforming human personality (LF 2.16). In the mirror of this broken, ambiguous image of suffering Wisdom, we see the miseries and hypocrisies of our lives. This crucified image is the living knowledge of human darkness, limitation, oppression and sinfulness which overpowers our shallow self-confidence, questions what we think we know about God, raises doubts about what we have accomplished and undercuts our entire affective life. In fact, this image subverts our whole individualistic perception of reality, that is, the way we experience not only other people, but also other species, the earth and even the cosmos. It is the language of God (Word) inviting and teaching the human mind and heart, calling us in our confusion and emptiness to pass over into the perspective of loving Sophia by an identification with Jesus Crucified.

It is at this point in development that the images of the poor, the oppressed, the exploited, the suffering, take on an overpowering clarity and significance. They are clearly a suffering extension of the inner image of Jesus-Sophia, and they make a claim. They are the darkness of humanity; they are *our* darkness. Just as the personal unconscious is revealed in the mirror of suffering Sophia, so too is the collective darkness, the shadow of humanity. The "poor" are recognized and embraced to the degree that the identification with suffering Sophia has taken place in our inner darkness. Thus Sophia, having subverted our images of ourselves and of God, now subverts our understanding of the world. This is the third aspect of subversion. In the secret, painful, unitive relationship with dark Sophia, a new participatory love-fired knowledge begins to take over human desire and consciousness and to express itself not only in the gradual repudiation of all kinds of personal and socio-cultural violence and oppression but also in an entry, albeit dark and unfinished, into the experience of mutuality, communion, connectedness and kinship with the earth that marks transformed or mystical consciousness.

Richard Tarnas suggests that a "participatory epistemology" that moves beyond the hierarchical dualism characteristic of the Cartesian-Kantian paradigm has been emerging in philosophy for over a century. Common to all its thinkers is an essential conviction that the relation of the human mind to the universe is ultimately not dualistic but participatory.[12] This participatory way of knowing reveals itself in the new paradigm proposed by Thomas Berry, Brian Swimme and many others. They challenge humanity to accept the limitation and death that will usher in the next evolutionary era, when the universe will be experienced not as a collection of objects for human use and mastery but rather as an intimate, interconnected and diverse communion of subjects.[13]

Integral to and one with this participatory way of knowing and understanding life on earth is the tremendous emergent power of the feminine in our culture. It arises out of the unitive energies at work in the universe and heralds the end of the fundamental masculine dominance of the western mind. It appears that we are truly at a highly critical stage of transformation in which the masculine (in all of us) must voluntarily transcend itself in its own dark night of death. This transformation will fit it to enter into a fundamentally new relationship of mutuality with the feminine in all its forms.

We observe in the last years of the twentieth century a massive breakdown of numerous structures, suggestive of the necessary deconstruction or death prior to new birth. We see this participatory vision break through on so many levels, in so many disciplines that it appears reflective of a deeper, powerful archetypal process impelled by forces beyond the merely human. This is where the experience of Crucified Sophia intersects and resonates with the current state of the collective psyche. The unitive relationship with Suffering Sophia can be so deep and, consequently, the solidarity with "the other" so profound, that not only does the person in this Dark Night carry and bring to consciousness the collective longings of humanity and energies of the cosmos, but brings to them in her very being this participatory, love-fired knowledge which Jesus-Sophia both gives and is. This contribution of mysticism to a broader transformation must not be overlooked by ecologists, creationists, geologists, scientists or philosophers.

Neither may we forget that this is the time to seek not the consolation and escape of other images or practices or relationships but "the living image of Christ Crucified within" (IIIA 35.5) and to stand open to this transforming imprint of suffering Sophia, which is actually experienced as "no image" but which nonetheless acknowledges, reflects and even accepts our personal and societal darkness. This is the blackest time of night when the last delicate shading of the image of Christ, crucified and abandoned, is being sketched within the human heart in total darkness and silence.

PURIFICATION OF SPIRIT

When the invisible, mute God of an abandoned Jesus seems to draw us into lonely introspection where prayer and relationships, as we have known them, are painful or gone; when loss, failure and hopelessness loom large; when all supports drop from one's consciousness and life's deepest meanings and symbol systems are empty and stale; when our inherited language and images no longer reveal the divine, then a dark Wisdom is operative, nurturing the human person with love and confirming values little prized in our society. John throws a stark light on the experience by showing *the whole person* deprived totally in her or his imaginative powers, intellectual intuitions and human sensitivities:

> God divests the faculties, affections and senses, both spiritual and sensory, interior and exterior. God leaves the intellect in darkness, the will in aridity, the memory in emptiness and the

affections in supreme affliction, bitterness and anguish by depriving the soul of the feeling and satisfaction it previously enjoyed from spiritual blessings . . . *For this privation is one of the conditions required that the spiritual form, [the image] which is the union of love, may be introduced into the spirit and united with it.* The Lord works all this in the soul by means of a pure and dark contemplation. (IIDN 3.3)

If in earlier times the Dark Night wove its way in and out of life bringing dryness, boredom and absence of satisfaction, this darker Night removes the very support systems that have structured our lives, given them meaning and value, and provided a source of affirmation and final assurance.[14]

But what precisely can John mean when he says the intellect is emptied and left in darkness? Perhaps he warns us that the time will come when our philosophy of life, our theology and our carefully constructed meanings fall apart before our eyes. All we have accumulated intellectually that has given us "God," "faith" and security loses its significance. Nothing makes any sense. The mind, while *full* on one level of a lifetime of knowledge, is in total darkness on another, the level of meaning. We feel as if we have been duped, and succumb to silence, afraid to shock others by the depth of our cynicism and unbelief.[15]

Our minds stumble over the concept of emptiness in the memory because we know that human memory is full of experience. But now the imagination can no longer connect life's memories to create meaning and hope. We can speak of emptiness in the memory, not because one remembers nothing, but because all that the memory holds which once provided motivation and security, which engendered trust and promise for the future, seems now an illusion and a mockery. Memories do not mean what one thought they did. The memory is indeed empty, possessing nothing but the scattered remains of cherished experiences and the crushing remembrance of personal failure and defeat (IIDN 5.5–6).

This kind of clarity about one's miseries generates the overwhelming feeling of being rejected and abandoned not only by one's friends but particularly by God. In fact, abandonment and the betrayal of trust are the hallmarks of this dark experience.

However it happens, what or whom one cherishes most in life is cut off, taken away. The worst thing about this "purification of the will" is that the loved one, the very focus of one's love and desire, becomes the cause of one's agony.[16] There is nothing so destructive of affirmation and worth as rejection by one who has loved you and on whom you have counted with complete assurance. It leaves one unable to grasp anything affectively. The destruction of mutuality, with its deep frustration of desire, leaves one without any strength of purpose, bereft of motivation and prone to bitterness. A transcendence in which one is not at home and against which one rebels is forced upon the person.

ALTERNATIVE VISION: FAITH, HOPE AND LOVE

We face a challenge in this night to throw into gear the kind of radical faith, hope and love that can endure the death-dealing "touch of God's hand," the imprint, which is emptying out our isolated self-sufficiency, on the one hand, and our unfree dependence and fear of transformation and evolution on the other. Activated by Sophia's dark presence, the theological virtues are our only option, presenting a very uncomfortable alternative vision. Because initially we do not feel faith, hope and love, maintaining this basic contemplative posture in our prayer and life is extremely difficult. It must overcome an anger, fear and rebellion that want to refuse these theological gifts rather than be left with "nothing." Yet the only way the deprivation of the Dark Night will open into a radical change of consciousness and affectivity is by the acceptance of this contemplative posture or vision whereby one actually passes over to the love perspective of Divine Wisdom (IIA 6.6, IIDN 21.11–12).

Faith, however, causes darkness in our very power to understand. Now it is at cross purposes with our ability to make logical sense out of life, death or eternity. When Jesus Christ recedes from consciousness, it is faith that moves us into the Mystery which is unimaginable, incomprehensible and uncontrollable. While we do not set out to empty the mind, imagination or memory, prayer development and life exacts this of us and then faith becomes an opening into a realm of significance far beyond human understanding.[17]

The hopelessness and emptiness of the Dark Night is precisely the condition that makes hope, in the strictly theological sense, possible. Hope comes into play when we are really radically at the end, unable to find any further resources to connect the memories, feelings, images and experiences of life in a meaningful pattern or a promising future. Then hope, forfeiting the struggle to press meaning out of loss, becomes a free, trustful commitment to the impossible, which cannot be built out of what one possesses.[18]

Estrangement and abandonment administer the final test of love. Love prevents us from forcing the loved one into the constraints of our needs and so takes the beloved as he or she is. In the face of seeming rejection and affective loss, theological love will not, in the end, surrender to hatred or violence nor forfeit belief in its own worth and lovability. Overcoming the will to die, this love lives honestly with the pain of its own woundedness and longing. It continues to serve others, often with great effectiveness, in spite of profound affective deprivation and loss.[19]

The contemplative posture of faith, hope and love slowly repatterns or transforms desire and consciousness and prepares the human person for the participatory love-driven knowledge Divine Wisdom is and gives. This subversive dynamic of beloved Sophia is set in motion when human suffering, loss and emptiness have reached such a pitch of consciousness, are such a reflection of Jesus silenced, rejected, abused, dismissed or abandoned, that the capacity of the human person is hollowed out for deeper knowing, deeper mutuality, a Wisdom presence and vision in the world. Then the image of Jesus-Sophia Dying, the image of all that is dying within and without, reaches completion.

[This is] the real imitation [imprinting] of the perfect life of the Son of God . . . [through which God] will bring her to the high perfection of union with the Son of God, her spouse, and transformation in Him through love. [Therefore,] When this . . . night (God's communication to the spirit, which usually occurs in extreme darkness of soul) has passed, a union with the Spouse, *Who is the Sophia of God,* then follows . . .

[and] love is perfect when the transformation of the soul in God is achieved. (SC 1.10; IA 2.4)[20]

The limits of this article on Dark Night preclude examining what it means in real life to be transfigured in Divine Sophia and to become a prophet of Sophia in the world.

IMPLICATIONS

First, if there is at the present time a participatory world-view crying out for paradigmatic significance, Sophia may well be the God-image that resonates with the current state of the collective psyche.[21] Sophia is the one clear, significant God emerging out of a long dark night of broken symbols. Thus we may see Jesus more and more taking on the marks of Sophia. This is where the tradition of Wisdom, so long muted and marginalized but embodied with such prophetic power in the mysticism of John of the Cross, will reassure us and enable theology to speak anew about Jesus Christ.

Second, there is a correlation between the intense interest in the Dark Night, the awareness of Sophia and the emergence of feminism, just as there was a correlation in the past between the muting of contemplation, the suppression of Sophia and the marginalization of women.

Third, feminists have long been conscious of the darkness of this dying time as they struggled to find meaning in the experience of impasse in their God images, in their churches and in their socio-political lives. But Richard Tarnas emphasizes that the crisis of modern man is essentially not a feminine but a masculine crisis. It is the dominance of the masculine in us that is dying and being called to transcend itself in the Dark Night experience of a Sophia-God. Perhaps now when this pervasive masculinity has become so apparent and when the feminine is welling up with such powerful energy, Sophia is the God-image capable of moving with humanity into the next evolutionary era.

Fourth, initially it seemed to me that transformation in Jesus-Sophia or Dark Night was subversive because it radically changed desire, consciousness and ultimately vision and behaviour, personal and societal. But perhaps it is subversive, above all, because it could change radically our theological discourse since it is, in fact, a hermeneutic of the very nature of God.

These are the questions that contemplative people may face today and those who pray with depth and seriousness under the guidance of St Ignatius may well face these contemporary problems of the Dark Night as they continue to grow in prayer.

NOTES

1. Thomas H. Green, *When the Well Runs Dry* (Notre Dame: Ave Maria Press, 1979), pp. 10 and 110. See pp. 110–133.

2. I am using the Greek *Sophia,* not only because feminists prefer it, but because the biblical depiction of Wisdom is invariably female, suggesting a person rather than a concept or an attribute. Biblical Wisdom is treated not as an "it" but as a summoning "I," as a "sister, mother, female beloved . . . and a myriad of other female roles . . . " See Elizabeth Johnson, *She Who Is* (New York: Crossroad, 1992), p. 87, whose analysis of Sophia has influenced my study, and Roland E. Murphy, *The Tree of Life: An Exploration of Biblical Wisdom Literature* (New York: Doubleday, 1990), pp 133–49, for a treatment of "Lady Wisdom."

3. The Institute of Carmelite Studies will publish in late 1995 *Education for Contemplation* in which a more extensive study of Wisdom in John of the Cross will appear. This article is part of that study.

4. Most references to John of the Cross are inserted in text. A=*Ascent of Mount Carmel,* DN=*Dark Night,* SC=*Spiritual Canticle,* LF=*Living Flame of Love.* Most quotations are from Kieran Kavanaugh and Otilio Rodriguez, *The Collected Works of John of the Cross* (Washington, DC: ICS Publications, 1991).

5. This is a fundamental text indicating the direction of affective transformation and interpreting all that precedes it concerning desire in Book I of the *Ascent.*

6. Elizabeth Johnson's work is a superb example of this. See also Sandra Schneiders, *The Revelatory Text: Interpreting the New Testament as Sacred Scripture* (San Francisco: Harper and Row, 1991), pp. 180–97, for an example not of Sophia's retrieval but of a feminist interpretation of the meaning of Jesus in John 4.

7. See LF 3.41–45 where John castigates those spiritual directors who do not understand the secret, loving wisdom of contemplative

prayer that is "the sublime anointings and shadings of the Holy Spirit," and therefore damage or destroy by poor direction the image God is painting within the human person. "Who will succeed," he says, "in repairing that delicate painting of the Holy Spirit once it is marred by a coarse hand?"

8. Here we intersect with John M. Staudenmaier's interpretation of the dynamic of the Second Week of the *Exercises* which "inculcates a form of personal intimacy with Jesus that opens out to intimacy with the larger world, an intimacy of affective engagement that leads to action in the world." See "To Fall in Love with the World," *Studies in the Spirituality of Jesuits 26* (May 1994).

9. When I wrote "Impasse and Dark Night" in *Living with Apocalypse,* ed. Tilden Edwards (San Francisco: Harper and Row, 1984), I did not address the significance of Jesus-Sophia in the Dark Night. This christological interpretation of the Dark Night is a necessary complement to the impasse experience.

10. See IIDN 5.1–2; IIDN 17; IIA 8.6 to study the equivalencies that John sets up.

11. Christ Crucified is seen as the unitive image or pattern of the Dark Night in IIA 7.

12. I draw heavily on the creative thought of Richard Tarnas regarding this "participatory epistemology." See *The Passion of the Western Mind* (New York: Harmony Books, 1991), pp. 433–445.

13. See Brian Swimme and Thomas Berry, *The Universe Story* (San Francisco: Harper, 1992), p. 243. "Existence itself is derived from and sustained by this intimacy of each being with every other being."

14. I first developed this interpretation in "A Discipleship of Equals: Voices from a Tradition" in *A Discipleship of Equals: Toward a Christian Feminist Spirituality,* ed. Francis A. Eigo (Villanova: Villanova University Press, 1988).

15. See IIDN 9.3; 5.3–5; IIA 4 & 8.

16. See IIDN 7; IIDN 9.3 & 7; IIIA 16 & 35.5; LF 1.23.

17. John writes in IIDN 21.11: "Faith darkens and empties the intellect of all its natural understanding and thereby prepares it for union with divine wisdom, who is the Word the Son of God." See also IIA 3 for John's teaching on faith and IIA 4.1–3; IIA 8 & 9; IIDN 16.8.2.

18. John explains in IIDN 21.11: "Hope empties and withdraws the memory from all creature possessions, for as St Paul says, hope is for what is not possessed. It withdraws the memory from what can be possessed and fixes it on that for which it hopes. Hence, only hope in God prepares the memory perfectly for union with Him." Karl Rahner has helped me interpret John's thought on hope and on the theological

virtues. See "On the Theology of Hope," *TI* X and "Theology of Death," *TI* XIII.

19. John explains in IIDN 21.11–12: "Charity empties and annihilates the affections and appetites of the will of whatever is not God and centers them on God alone. Thus charity prepares the will and unites it with God through love."

20. Elizabeth Johnson reminds us of a long-standing tradition of interpretation concerning martyrs, a tradition which Vatican II continues: "Martyrdom 'transforms' a disciple into an intense image of Christ, *imago Christi,* for the martyr 'perfects that image even to the shedding of blood.' " See *She Who Is,* p. 74 and *Lumen gentium* 42.

21. What Tarnas writes about paradigms is applicable to our God images: "The birth of every new paradigm begins the process of gestation, growth, crisis and revolution all over again. Each paradigm is a stage in an unfolding evolutionary sequence and when the paradigm has fulfilled its purpose, when it has been developed and exploited to its fullest extent, then it loses its luminosity . . . it becomes oppressive, limiting, opaque, something to be overcome . . . " (*op. cit.,* p. 439).

A Feminist View of Thérèse

Joann Wolski Conn

I wish I could have enjoyed more the film "Thérèse," winner of the Jury Prize at the 1986 Cannes film festival. During the second viewing I was able to suspend some of my disappointment with the superficial portrayal of Thérèse's personality and notice two scenes that hint at a deeper story: the prioress once explicitly addresses Thérèse as an adult, and Thérèse once demonstrates insight into the meaning of the spiritual darkness she suffered during the last eighteen months of her life. Nevertheless, I remain disappointed because the film perpetuates the one-dimensional image too often associated with this saint. Most of all I remain disappointed because my feminist concerns have led me to discover how this image is profoundly distorted.

This essay offers a more adequate vision of Thérèse, a resource for feminist spirituality. In order to accomplish this goal, I will proceed in three phases: (1) explain my feminist perspective and its consequent methodology for studying Thérèse; (2) review briefly the conclusions of two earlier stages of my project of recovering Thérèse for contemporary Christian feminist spirituality; (3) move to a new stage of the project and explain four ways in which Thérèse could be a resource for "a discipleship of equals."[1]

I should like to begin with a biographical sketch. Thérèse Martin, called Thérèse of Lisieux to distinguish her from the sixteenth century Spanish mystic and Doctor of the Church, Teresa of Avila, was born in Alençon, France, the youngest of five daughters (four children had died before Thérèse was born). Thérèse's mother, who ran a lacemaking business from her home, died

452

when Thérèse was four years old. Her father, whose life was centered on the church and his family, then moved the family to Lisieux in order to be near his wife's relatives. At age nine Thérèse lost her "second mother," Pauline, who entered the cloistered Carmelite monastery in Lisieux. This triggered six weeks of nervous illness in Thérèse. Four years later (1886) her oldest sister Marie entered the same Carmel. On Christmas Eve of that year Thérèse experienced what she called her "conversion," a transformation of her from a self-centered child into a person who is concerned about others. The next year she asked for special permission to enter Carmel (at age fourteen), not for any other reason but "for God alone." She was refused at first, but eventually given permission to enter in April, 1888. The next year her father, senile and disoriented, was committed to a mental hospital. Céline, the fourth daughter, stayed near to attend to him until his death, five years later. Then she, too, entered the same Carmel (1894). By this time Thérèse (a nun for six years) had been entrusted with the religious formation of new members, so that Thérèse became Céline's Novice Mistress. Léonie Martin, the only sister not in the Lisieux Carmel, also became a cloistered nun, but in a different order. The following year (1895) Thérèse offered herself formally as a "Victim of Holocaust to God's Merciful Love," and wrote the first of three autobiographical manuscripts. On Good Friday, 1896, she first coughed up blood, the first symptom of her death from tuberculosis, and within a few days she entered into the "thickest darkness" of a trial of faith. In September she wrote a letter to Marie describing her vocation to "be Love" in the heart of the Church (Manuscript B). In June, 1897, severely ill, she wrote more about her spiritual insights (Manuscript C). On September 30, 1897 she died at age twenty-four. All of her sisters lived into their seventies or older. Thérèse was canonized a·saint in 1925.[2]

FEMINIST PERSPECTIVE AND METHODOLOGY

I agree with the conclusion that "feminist perspective" is an ambiguous and unstable category and that the most productive method is to admit the illusion of "a consistent, coherent theory accepted by all feminists" and proceed to use the instability as a resource for thinking and practice.[3] Therefore, I will clarify, as best I can, what I want to say at the moment and acknowledge its limitations.

My feminist perspective includes the following convictions and goals. Feminism affirms and promotes women's equal value and possibilities in society and religious institutions. It requires a critical awareness of the history and effects of women's oppression, especially the story of how and why religion both oppressed and liberated women. I am committed to a "reformist" position in religion, namely to the "loyal opposition" in the Roman Catholic tradition which now seeks to recover a "usable past" for women and reconstruct a nonsexist Christian tradition and present practice. I seek hermeneutical categories and methods which allow me to approach classical texts, images, and persons in Christian spirituality with feminist questions and allow these texts, images, and persons to question me.

Among the most significant questions to address to the text (assume, also, the image or person) are these. Can this text promote equality of women and men? That is, can it promote the relationships of mutuality and non-domination that are essential to a "discipleship of equals?" Does this religious text reveal that women's spiritual development necessarily involves a struggle for autonomy and self-direction as much as a desire for relationship and loving union with God and others? Are the relationships characterized more by mutuality and reciprocity or by domination? What is recovered in this text when it is approached from a perspective that pays as much attention to women's experience as it does to men's? Or what is noticed when it is approached from a totally women-centered perspective? Does this text grasp women's experience as an agent as well as a subject of androcentric religious institutions? Some questions that the text could ask me include the following: "Why do you resist certain beliefs and images in this text and what does that tell you about your self and your relationship to the religious perspective of this text?" "Does the experience of God communicated in this text resemble your own?" "Do the religious desires of the person(s) in this text resemble your own?" Hermeneutics of a text involves a genuine dialogue, a two-way process of questioning.

All of these questions are part of my ongoing project of dialogue with the texts and images of Thérèse of Lisieux, but they are more comprehensive than the limited focus of this essay. Here I wish to focus simply on two issues: the process of spiritual development and the appropriate feminist method for studying it. Regarding the first, I am interested in whether the texts reveal that Thérèse attained a spiritual maturity which included autonomy and self-direction as well as relationships of mutuality rather than control or hierarchical status. Regarding the methodological issue, I wonder what is uncovered when Thérèse is approached from a feminist perspective, that is, one which pays as much attention to women's experience as it does to men's. A feminist perspective on these issues—method and spiritual development—deserves some further explanation.

Women's Spiritual Development

As I explain elsewhere[4] contemporary women's spiritual development is perplexing and difficult because Christian spirituality includes every dimension of human life. Once this view is accepted, women's spiritual development begins to be recognized as problematic for several reasons.

(1) For women, the possibilities for mature humanity/spirituality are restricted. Models of human development universally recognized that movement away from conformity and predetermined role expectations and toward greater autonomy (i.e., self-direction, self-affirmation, self-reliance) is necessary for maturity. Yet women's experience shows that too many women are arrested at the threshold of autonomy. To make matters worse, the most prevalent psychological models of human development assume that maturity aims at autonomy, at differentiation. Yet women's experience convinces them that maturity must include not only autonomy but also relationship; indeed it must value belonging as much as independence. Thus, women's experience makes them suspicious of autonomy as the goal of maturity even as they struggle against social pressure to reach that ambiguous goal.

(2) Christian teaching and practice, instead of promoting women's maturity, has significantly contributed to its restriction. Women have been taught to value primarily one type of religious development: self-denial and sacrifice of one's own needs and interests. While men have been taught to couple self-denial with courage to resist unjust authority, women have been taught to assume all legitimate authority is vested in males who determine the criteria of appropriate self-denial for women. A common criterion is, of course, that assertion of women's own desires is a sign of selfishness.

Recognizing these problems has led me to seek resources in Christian tradition that will assist women (and men) to correct these distortions of human and religious maturity. Thirteen years ago I began a long-term project to study whether Thérèse of Lisieux could be one of these resources for promoting religious and human development that takes account of the feminist issues described above.

Method

My Catholic theological perspective regarding grace and nature assumes that God's grace works in and through nature, that they can be distinguished theologically but cannot be, in concrete human life, separated. Everything is "graced." But everything cannot be "reduced" to grace, nor can anything be "reduced" to nature.[5] What this implies for the study of Thérèse is that I assume that human and religious maturity are mutually compatible. Indeed they must have the same general characteristics; otherwise, religion would be detrimental to one's mental and emotional health and, conversely, human maturity would prevent religious "perfection" or maturity.

There is no doubt that the primary characteristic of human and religious maturity is relationship. Religious maturity has always been described this way in biblical and systematic theology. Union with God and loving relationships with all are the two aspects of the one goal of Christian life. There is doubt, however, about whether autonomy or self-direction can be claimed as a characteristic of religious maturity. This looks, at first glance, too much like the classical description of sin, and it is particularly suspicious as a characteristic of a holy woman.

Yet every psychological model of adulthood has given primacy to having one's own identity, in the sense of directing one's own life independently of the wishes of others. That is until recently, when feminist psychologists (women and men) questioned this model of maturity for several reasons. It is rooted primarily in the experience of men. Its bias toward autonomy causes it to lose sight of the fact that adaptation is equally about integration and attachment. The result of this bias has been that differentiation (the stereotypical overemphasis of males) is favored with the language of growth and development, while attachment (the stereotypical female overemphasis) gets referred to in terms of dependency and immaturity. This doubt about the adequacy of most models of human maturity led me[6] to adopt the model developed by Robert Kegan.[7]

For the purposes of this essay it is sufficient to say that Kegan's model of human development is more compatible with study of religious development than other models I know for two reasons. First, it demonstrates that both attachment/relationship and independence/autonomy are integral to *every* state of development. Consequently, it defines maturity as the intimacy made possible by moving beyond autonomy to relationship rooted in differentiation-for-the-sake-of-relationship. This is characteristic of religious living. Second, it pays as much attention to women's experience as it does to men's in order to guard against the bias described above. I see this as a bias that not only favors men but also, inevitably, leads to suspicion of religion as "immature" because it gives primacy to attachment and relationship.

This essay will use Kegan's feminist model of development as a primary hermeneutical tool for examining how Thérèse struggled for autonomy and mutual relationships as necessary dimensions of her religious maturity.

Reliability of the Texts

In 1976, when I began my scholarly study of Thérèse, I was amused to learn that my devotional study of her, going back as far as 1947, had been based on unreliable sources. To paraphrase Patricia

O'Connor's summary of the situation,[8] when the first scholar to probe beneath the editions of Thérèse's autobiography that were published according to her sisters' wishes entered the Carmel Archives in 1945 he found Thérèse's original manuscripts in a shocking state. While correcting Thérèse's grammar, spelling, and style, Pauline had extensively edited and altered the manuscript.

In 1956 a completely reliable facsimile copy of Thérèse's three major autobiographical writings was published. In 1895, as an act of obedience to her sister, Pauline, who was prioress at that time, Thérèse filled a copybook with memories of her childhood and earliest years in Carmel (Manuscript A). During her private retreat in 1896, Thérèse wrote a letter to her sister Marie describing her current darkness and struggle of faith as well as her own unique vision of her religious vocation (Manuscript B). As she was dying in 1897, at the request of Mother Marie de Gonzague, her new prioress, Thérèse filled part of a small notebook with her spiritual insights until her hand was too weak to hold a pencil (Manuscript C). My references are to the Institute of Carmelite Studies English translation (1975) of this reliable manuscript.[9]

Thérèse's letters were withheld from publication by her sisters for many years. Then, under restrictive conditions, many letters were published in French (1948) and English (1949). In 1972–1973 all of Thérèse's letters were published in a two-volume critical French edition that also includes correspondence to Thérèse and about her. This is now available in English.[10]

Only retouched photographs of Thérèse were available until 1961 when François de Sainte-Marie published an album of authentic portraits. Thérèse's poetry has not yet been translated in a critical English edition. Neither of these sources is referred to in this essay.

Following a pious custom of some monasteries, Thérèse's sister Pauline kept a detailed account of Thérèse's last illness and of Thérèse's conversations with her and others during the final months of Thérèse's life. Clarke's English translation of these *Last Conversations* (1977), omits the controversy that surrounded them when they were published in French in 1971. As I explain in more detail in my review of this English translation,[11] the public dialogue of René Laurentin and Jean-François Six held at the Institut Catholique, Paris (1973), demonstrates divergent scholarly opinion about the reliability of Pauline's note-books.[12] As Pauline admitted, she edited these notebooks many times before publication, and, as evidence now reveals, she altered Thérèse's autobiographical manuscripts to suit her own image of Thérèse. Can she reliably transmit Thérèse's authentic spirituality? Laurentin answers definitively, yes, and Six strongly disagrees. I concur with Six and, therefore, make no references in this essay to these "last conversations."

In summary, I approach these texts from a feminist perspective. Seeking to find in Thérèse a resource for contemporary feminist spirituality, I needed, first, to demonstrate that she went beyond the conventional image and interpretation of her that I had inherited from my Catholic elementary school education. As I became sensitized to feminist issues I wanted to see if I could recover this young woman as a resource for Christian feminist spirituality.

THE BEGINNING OF A FEMINIST PERSPECTIVE ON THÉRÈSE: WAS SHE A CHILD OR A MATURE ADULT?

As I explain in an earlier article,[13] what most people remember about Thérèse, when they are alerted to feminist issues or to the characteristics of adult faith, makes them quite uncomfortable. She is imaged as the epitome of the simple, unquestioning, pious, sentimental, accepting "child-woman." People cannot envision Thérèse dealing with the struggle for adult autonomy as an integral aspect of what she called her "Little Way" to holiness. They can only imagine her from popular holy-cards and stories, where she is portrayed as the Pollyanna-type "good little Sister" who picked up pins for the love of God and let filthy laundry water splash in her face.

The Thérèse I have discovered is quite a different woman from the "Little Flower" I loved years ago. Studying Thérèse from a feminist perspective, I originally discovered two things: first, the central religious experience that Thérèse calls her "conversion" was, basically, a movement into adulthood that developed into deeper human and religious maturity; second, that Thérèse's holiness was the opposite of conventional conformity to the ideals of her family and her Carmelite monastery. On the contrary, Thérèse demonstrates a central feminist value: a developing appropriation of her own original vision of life.

Conversion in Thérèse of Lisieux

Using Bernard Lonergan's definition of conversion as a hermeneutical tool,[14] I noticed several aspects of Thérèse's religious experience. I discovered that the event which Thérèse calls "my complete conversion" is more accurately understood as a moral conversion rather than as a religious conversion, which is its common interpretation. Understanding Thérèse's conversion in this way demonstrates her development into religious and human adulthood; indeed it reveals a movement into authentic maturity. I will summarize my argument here since the appropriate texts are quoted and explained in detail in the earlier article.[15]

Nine years after the event she is describing, and only two years before her death, Thérèse narrates the story of what she calls "my complete conversion."[16] I believe the basic reason why she calls this a conversion is that a dramatic change happens, she says, "in an instant." This permanent change in direction is from being a girl of thirteen who "was really unbearable because of [her] extreme touchiness" to a "strong and courageous" young woman whose "source of tears was dried up and has since reopened rarely and with great difficulty," who "discovered once again the strength of soul which she had lost." She who "wasn't accustomed to doing things for [herself]" now experienced "the need to forget [herself] and to please others." She now had "a great desire to work for the conversion of sinners."

Because this dramatic change occurred after the Midnight Mass of Christmas, Thérèse uses the images and symbols of Christmas to explain the conversion's cause. The following underlining is that of the original text and follows Thérèse's literary device of frequent underlining for emotional emphasis. "Jesus, the gentle, *little* child of only one hour, changed the night of my soul into rays of light. On that *night* when he made himself subject to *weakness* and suffering for love of me, he made me *strong* and courageous, arming me with his weapons."[17]

Although Thérèse gives this conversion a religious interpretation, I believe it is more accurately understood as a moral conversion. This is not to deny genuine religious aspects of the event. Rather, it is to affirm that the basic change of direction described by Thérèse corresponds more closely, in three ways, to that of a moral conversion.

First, Thérèse speaks principally of a change in her criteria of decision from adherence to self-pity and an excessively sensitive desire for attention to an attitude of self-forgetfulness, to a desire to care for others, to convert sinners, and, thus, to do good. This change—from concern for self-satisfaction to desire for a life lived according to value—is the primary characteristic of moral conversion, according to Lonergan.

Second, moral conversion is an experience of more adult decision-making. Children are persuaded or compelled to do what is right. As one's knowledge of reality increases one discovers that one's choosing affects ourselves no less than the object which we choose or reject—we create ourselves through our choices. Thus, we must freely decide what we will be. This movement out of childhood is precisely the process that Thérèse identifies as most characteristic of her own conversion: "God would have to work a little miracle to make me *grow up* in an instant, and this miracle he performed on that unforgettable Christmas day."[18]

This change of direction away from childhood can be more or less independent of parental or social values, that is, more or less critical. Reading the full text one notices that the occasion for Thérèse's conversion, her "growing up," is her father's annoyance at her prolonging a childhood ritual of filling her shoes with Christmas presents. Jean-François Six emphasizes that here Thérèse realizes that, from now on, her father does not want to see her as a child but as an adult.[19] I emphasize that Thérèse stops crying out of a desire somehow to please her father, which would suggest that her conversion, at this time, was uncritical and, thus, typically adolescent. Yet I agree with Six that Thérèse later progresses in detachment from dependence on her father and in steadfast freedom from reliance upon the values of her "second mothers," her older sisters, Marie and Pauline.[20] That is, her Christmas conversion became more critical in the following years. A little further on the next section will present evidence of Thérèse's independent thinking and action.

Third, the qualities of strength and freedom of decision—characteristics of moral conversion and of adulthood—are singled out in Thérèse's later interpretation of this conversion. In a letter of 1896, Thérèse interprets her conversion as that of a woman whom St Teresa of Avila would acknowledge because Teresa wished her daughters to equal strong men.[21]

In summary, Thérèse describes her conversion as a dramatic entry into adulthood. She understands it as a change from selfishness to self-forgetfulness. It is a shift from self-satisfaction to a choice for value. Although this conversion demonstrates a movement into greater maturity it raises the question of adult autonomy. Is this experience of a young woman of thirteen part of a deeper movement that reaches authentic autonomy?

Thérèse's Struggle for Autonomy: An Original Vision of Life

Since automony is a category of contemporary psychology not that of Thérèse's nineteenth-century milieu, I have searched for the analogous experience in terms of Thérèse's originality.[22] Do the texts demonstrate that Thérèse was her own authority? That is, was she the author of her own distinctive vision of life?

How could Thérèse acquire an original vision of religious life while living according to the Carmelite Rule which values obedience and conformity to religious customs handed down from the sixteenth century? She does this in two ways. Principally, Thérèse trusts her own experience of God and her own insight. Thérèse calls herself an "explorer" into Scripture, discovering new insights that she is drawn to because they support her own prior experience of God. Second, she strengthens her original vision by attempts at expressing and sharing it with her sisters—three of whom are in the same Carmel. When she realizes that most often they misunderstand her, she makes a basic effort to clarify her ideas but does not pursue the explanation. She does, however, peacefully persevere in acting according to her own original vision. This originality demonstrates Thérèse's growth beyond the conventional to an autonomous, adult personality who can freely give a mature self to relationships to God and to others. I will explore Thérèse's relationships in the third section of this essay. But first it is necessary to demonstrate her independence in order to affirm that her relationships were more than conformity to role expectations authored by her family or her religious superiors.

In what ways is Thérèse original? One way has always been associated with her: in a Catholic milieu permeated by fear and rigorism Thérèse proclaimed her experience and conviction about a God who is full of tenderness, mercy, and love. There are, in addition, many other aspects of her originality that could only recently be recognized with the help of critical editions of her autobiography and letters, with more thorough studies of nineteenth-century French popular religion in general, and of French Carmelite monasteries in particular. This essay will summarize just one of the three aspects of Thérèse's vision explained in an earlier article:[23] the originality of her vision of spiritual development.

The Nature of Spiritual Development

Thérèse had several motives for communicating her vision of spiritual development with care and precision. First of all, during the first seven years of her religious life Thérèse wanted to share with her dearly-loved sister, Céline (who was at home caring for their sick father), all that she, Thérèse, was discovering about the spiritual life. She did this in letters which gradually reveal the younger sister, Thérèse, as the spiritual director of the older sister. These letters (1888–1894) cease when Céline enters the Lisieux Carmel where Thérèse is, by now, the acting directress of novices. Second, Thérèse's involvement with the religious formation of the novices from 1893 onward, naturally, prompted her meditation upon issues at the core of Christian spirituality. Lastly, during the final three years of her life Thérèse is told to write about her life, a task she interprets as an opportunity to review "the mercies of the Lord" in her life. These texts demonstrate that Thérèse is well aware of the fact that the vision of life she has developed is uncommon and even goes directly against methods for spiritual growth which were habitually used in her culture.

After six years in Carmel, Thérèse, in a letter to Céline, confides that she is not following the most basic pattern of advice adhered to by other religious (and laity) in her day. As late as the

1950s this pattern was a common method of spiritual formation. Thérèse says,

> . . . directors have others advance in perfection by having them perform a great number of acts of virtue, and they are right; but my director who is Jesus, teaches me not to count up my acts. . . . to do *all* through love . . . in peace, in *abandonment*, . . . [24]

This affirmation of Jesus as her director is Thérèse's way of saying that she trusts her own religious experience. Her departure from the common practice of "counting one's acts of virtue," was a personal choice for spiritual freedom.

Another ubiquitous presentation of the spiritual life assumed that religious perfection automatically meant a search for the "more difficult." Thérèse breaks with this perspective, also. She conveys this in a letter to her sister, Léonie, whose worries and scruples were generated, in part, by the commonly accepted image of God as being fully satisfied only when humans suffer.[25] Thérèse not only affirms a maternal God, unusual in her time, but also maintains that we can share Jesus' redemptive mission by offering the *joys* of life as well as the sacrifices.

Another original insight into the nature of spiritual development is presented in summary form in this same letter to Léonie. Later on (in Manuscript B) Thérèse will explain her own style of spiritual life to her sister, Marie, as a "Little Way" of love and confidence which differs from the common assumption that one must please God by manifesting "works," that is, by making many acts of virtue. Marie, embedded in the latter assumptions, persists in interpretations of Thérèse's message as one of "works." Here, in this letter, one should note that Thérèse is communicating her "Little Way" for the first time to Léonie, who was considered by the Martin family, as backward and almost a misfit since she was in and out of the convent four different times.[26] For this sister, considered a "poor soul," Thérèse took the initiative to explain her central message, even before she gave it to her Carmelite sister, Marie. Thérèse declares that there are not two classes of souls: on the one side, the great souls capable of heroic abnegation and, on the other, the lesser souls who can do ordinary things. Rather, "the *smallest actions* done out of love are the ones which charm [God's] Heart . . . Jesus allows himself to be enchanted by the *smallest* things."[27]

Ironically, although Thérèse's canonization process was designed to prove that she practiced "heroic virtue" (as is every canonization), Thérèse rejected that ideal of holiness. She was never interested in the extraordinary, in what others could observe and testify about. Only once in Thérèse's autobiography does she use the word heroic.[28] There it refers to her burning desire to do every courageous, daring deed to make Jesus loved. Yet her thoughts move immediately to declare that she was not satisfied to identify herself with any visible organ of the mystical body of Christ (i.e., which did heroic deeds), but could only rest in identity with the heart (love) which is hidden. Thérèse always chooses what is hidden. This term (*caché*) appears forty-six times in her autobiography and represents her own ideal of holiness.

A common misunderstanding of Thérèse's hiddenness is the portrayal of her as practicing "little heroism" rather than great heroism; that is, she is imaged as being heroic in doing little things (e.g., picking up pins for the love of God, allowing dirty laundry water to splash in her face). This influences some people to imagine her as preoccupied with little things, as a typical product of the cloistered milieu where small things take on a disproportionately larger significance. On the contrary, in the context of her autobiography, Thérèse speaks of these small acts with ironic humor, genuinely seeing them as small and candidly admitting that she "often . . . allow(s) these little sacrifices . . . to slip by."[29] For example, she does not describe herself as standing heroically silent to receive the reprimand of a sister who was upset when Thérèse caused a racket which awoke the sick prioress. Rather, knowing that she could not take this reprimand in peace, Thérèse describes her own flight and the angry sister as one who delivered a "heroic oration."[30] For Thérèse, striving for heroism is a misplaced ideal. True holiness is hidden, even from oneself. Love is all that matters.

Lastly, Thérèse's final manuscript reveals that she clearly departs from the ascetic ideal of the nineteenth-century Carmel: "the rough stairway of perfection." Rather than use this classical metaphor, which some authors have associated with a Platonic hierarchy of being which has levels to which not everyone can aspire, Thérèse's central image is very modern (for 1897): an elevator. Trusting her own experience of desire for a straight, short way to God, Thérèse searches the Scripture and finds a reinforcing image of God as mother (Is. 66:12,13) which she immediately associates with Jesus. For her, the "elevator" is Jesus' maternal embrace into which she abandons herself and is content to be little and to be lifted up to God.[31]

I have examined some of the evidence which supports the conclusion that Thérèse was the author of her own vision of life, that she manifests genuine originality, and is, in that sense, autonomous. There is a final aspect of maturity that must be explored. What is characteristic of Thérèse's experience of relationship? Does it reflect a desire for mutuality and equality? More significantly, could Thérèse be said to reveal that the closer one comes to God the more one actually experiences equality with others and even with God?

A FEMINIST PERSPECTIVE CONTINUED: MATURE RELATIONSHIPS MANIFEST MUTUALITY, EQUALITY

As I continue to interpret and evaluate Thérèse's religious experience according to a feminist model of maturity, I look for feminist values in her relationships. In a saintly Carmelite nun I expect to find love and concern for others, but the issue here is what *kind* of loving relationship characterizes Thérèse's life? Does she desire and experience true mutuality and equality? Focusing my investigation on the final two years of her life, I see that Thérèse does desire and experience mutuality in four relationships: (1) with her companions in Carmel; (2) with those in the Church; (3) with sinners and unbelievers; (4) with Christ and with God.

Relationship with Her Companions in Carmel

The following examples from her autobiography and letters demonstrate how Thérèse, the youngest nun in the Carmel of Lisieux, relates to her companions in a way that is inclusive and reveals mutuality. She disagrees with others' standards of virtue without being patronizing. Her instinct for mutuality prompts her to approach even her prioress in this way.

In the last year of her life Thérèse summarized, in her autobiography, her experience of charity:

> This year . . . God has given me the grace to understand what charity is; I understood it before, it is true, but in an imperfect way. I had never fathomed the meaning of these words of Jesus: " . . . You shall love your neighbor as yourself." . . . How did Jesus love his disciples and why did he love them? Ah! it was not their natural qualities which could have attracted him since there was between him and them an infinite distance . . . And still Jesus called them his *friends, his brothers* . . . charity which must enlighten and rejoice not only those who are dearest to us but "ALL who are in the house" without distinction.[32]

Thérèse loved and honored all, not favoring her family who were in Carmel with her, but caring especially for the women who were very difficult and neurotic or compulsive. Her desires lead her to notice the way Jesus manifests a desire for mutuality with humanity, for friendship with all. This mutuality, this equality in friendship is her ideal of loving relationship.

Thérèse's instinct for egalitarian relations, in a situation that could foster a condescending attitude, emerges in the following narrative from her autobiography. She recalls the year she entered Carmel and the tension she felt in her relationship to another novice who was eight years her senior. Although these two young women had been given special permission to talk during times ordinarily restricted to silence, Thérèse was uneasy because the conversations were too worldly, the other novice was infatuated with the prioress, and she was doing things Thérèse "would have liked to see her change." This is how Thérèse communicated her disapproval:

> The hour we decided upon for coming together arrived; the poor little sister, casting a look at me, saw immediately that I was no longer the same; she sat down beside me, blushing, and I, placing her head upon my heart, told her with tears in my voice *everything I was thinking about her,* but I did this

with such tender expressions and showed her such a great
affection that very soon her tears were mingled with mine . . .
When the time came for us to separate . . . in us was realized
this passage from Scripture: "A brother who is helped by a
brother is like a strong city."[33]

There is no patronizing self-righteousness here; rather, Thérèse
creates an equality in tears and affection. Having no "sister helping sister" passage to quote from the Scripture, Thérèse's senti-
ment is clear, nevertheless.

A rare example of daring, even bold love is the letter Thérèse
wrote to her superior, Mother Marie de Gonzague, who was very
upset at the time of her re-election as prioress.[34] She was humiliated because she had been elected only on the the seventh ballot
when she finally gained more votes than Thérèse's sister, Pauline.
Marie de Gonzague confided her feelings to Thérèse who wrote
her a letter to console her. In this letter Thérèse creates a parable
of a "Shepherdess" (Marie de Gonzague) and a "lamb"
(Thérèse), and Thérèse places herself in the prioress' point of
view and tries to encourage the "Shepherdess" to be detached
from her self-esteem and be consoled at the good that could be
done through this humiliation. This tender letter gives us a
glimpse of Thérèse's intuition that mutuality, even between an
older prioress and a very young nun, was not only possible but
also preferable for the sake of genuine charity.

Relationship to the Church

Although living a secluded life in a cloistered convent,
Thérèse desired to be connected with the entire world and to be
effective for the good of the world. This desire for completely inclusive love is clearest in her identification with the symbolism of the
heart, an experience she recalled vividly in her autobiography.[35]

Considering the mystical body of the Church, I had not recognized myself in any of the members described by St Paul, or
rather I desired to see myself in them *all*. *Charity* gave me the
key to my *vocation* . . . O Jesus, my Love . . . my *vocation,* at
last I have found it . . . MY VOCATION IS LOVE!

Constance FitzGerald, commenting on this text out of her own experience as a Carmelite contemplative,[36] stresses that in order to situate this text, it is essential to remember Thérèse is near the end of her spiritual journey, five months after her first hemorrhage and only a year before her death and enshrouded in her dark night, the "trial of faith," she reaches out of a deep prayer presence to Christ, out of the genuine mystic's refusal to partialize awareness, the contemplative ability to become increasingly present and conscious at the deepest level. FitzGerald explains the inclusive maturity attained by Thérèse:

> Paradoxically, while experiencing and ultimately surrendering to her own fragility, brokenness, limitation and the death-dealing forces within her body . . . Thérèse, by awareness or empathy, does break through the barriers of human finitude to a presence in spirit, a presence of love and compassion, that is universal, all-embracing, personal and Christ-centered.[37]

Companionship with Sinners and Unbelievers

An unusual and unexpected experience of mutuality and equality emerges for Thérèse when she is plunged into a deep darkness and radical trial of faith. In one of the most moving pieces of spiritual literature, Thérèse describes her trial and interprets its meaning.[38] Whereas she once enjoyed a clear, living faith and the thought of heaven made up all her happiness, now, since the Easter season of 1896, her soul has been "invaded by the thickest darkness" and the thought of heaven is no longer anything but the cause of struggle and torment. Part one of this account concludes with Thérèse's cry that she experiences a "night of nothingness." Part two concludes with her interpretation of this night, her new feeling about the Lord, and her new appreciation of the implications of the Act of Oblation to God's Merciful Love which she made two years before writing this (June 9, 1895):

> Never have I felt before this . . . how sweet and merciful the Lord really is, for he did not send me this trial until the moment I was capable of bearing it . . . I no longer have any

great desires except that of loving to the point of dying of love.
June 9.[39]

By writing the date, June 9, at the end of this page of her
manuscript Thérèse shows that she interprets her "night of nothingness" to be the way Jesus is leading her to live out the unconditional surrender, the "dying of love" which she intended in her
declaration of June 9, 1895. Thérèse's contemplative reception
of this dark "nothingness" bears fruit in the paradoxical way of
all spiritual darkness; it generates the light of self-knowledge. In
this case, it is new insight into her relationship to unbelievers.

First, Thérèse's darkness gives her the capacity to accept the
fact of authentic unbelief. Before this time, she says, "I was unable
to believe there were really people who had no faith. I believed
they were actually speaking against their own inner convictions
when they denied the existence of heaven . . . " After being
plunged into darkness herself, she reverses her opinion: "Jesus
made me feel that there were really souls who have no faith . . . "[40]

Second, not only can she affirm the existence of unbelievers, but she can also rejoice in a relationship of sisterhood with
them. In contrast to her maternalistic attitude toward sinners
after the conversion of Christmas 1886, when she wanted to
convert them or to snatch them from the flames of purgatory,[41]
Thérèse now demonstrates a sisterly attitude. She now identifies
with them and participates in their experience. She does not
view sinners from some purified place above them but, instead,
accepts participation at their table. She speaks of her relationship to sinners in imagery that is an inverse analogue of the
Eucharistic table.[42]

> Your child . . . begs pardon for her brothers. She is resigned
> to eat the bread of sorrow as long as you desire it; she does not
> wish to rise up from this table . . . at which poor sinners are
> eating until the day set by you.[43]

Thérèse who, formerly, was afraid of soiling her baptismal robe,[44]
can now peacefully accept her role of solidarity with sinners and
be a sister to unbelievers.[45]

In a Relationship of Mutual Intimacy with God and with Jesus

Not only does Thérèse desire to be in full mutuality with her Carmelite sisters and the whole Church as well as with sinners and unbelievers, but she also is convinced that God and Jesus, the Son of God, in the Spirit, desire mutuality with her. She is amazed to realize that the one whom she most desires, desires her. Thérèse's experience of God is an experience of "having the ground of my being desire me," to use the vocabulary of Sebastian Moore.[46] Both her autobiography and her letters reveal this mutuality.

In her autobiography Thérèse speaks of God having "need" in relationship to us. God does not need our works, she maintains, but God does genuinely need us.

> See, then, all that Jesus lays claim to from us; he has no need of our works but only of our *love,* for the same God who declares he *has no need to tell us when he is hungry* did not fear to *beg* for a little water from the Samaritan woman. He was thirsty. But when he said: *"Give me to drink,"* it was *love* of his poor creatures the Creator of the universe was seeking. He was thirsty for love. Ah! I feel it more than ever before, Jesus is *parched . . .* [47]

Thérèse experiences that the One she loves above all is, actually, in need of her love.

In a letter to her sister Léonie, who is feeling powerless and insignificant, Thérèse declares that the God who approaches us is also fragile. God is begging.

> Ah! we who are living in the law of love, how can we not profit by the loving advances our Spouse is making to us . . . how can we fear him who allows himself to be enchained by *a hair* fluttering on our neck.
> . . . understand, then, how to hold him prisoner, this God who becomes the beggar of our love.[48]

Here the issue is not one of collapsing the difference between the status of God and of creatures; rather the focus of Thérèse's message is her experience of relationship. The more deeply she is related to God, the more Thérèse is amazed to discover that this relationship is an experience of genuine mutuality.

CONCLUSION

Having addressed my feminist concerns to Thérèse's texts, I believe that these texts reveal an adult, in a mature stage of faith, who understands the meaning of her trial of darkness as an experience of profound and mutual relationships. Thérèse's loving response in these relationships is far from immature conformity to role-expectations; indeed, it is the surrender of a mature adult who has struggled to be the author of her own vision of life: freely chosen, completely inclusive Love.

My feminist perspective also continues to make me uncomfortable with some aspects of Thérèse's life. Her preference for sentimental religious art and language are, at times, repugnant. Her literal interpretation of Scripture jars my theological nerves. Her confining bounds of social awareness are disappointing yet expected, given her culture.[49] For example, a primary source of suffering is her self and her family: her father's illness, her own dryness in prayer. There is no expression of concern for the suffering of the Vietnamese under French colonialism, even when she volunteers to go to the Carmelite monastery in Saigon. There is no awareness of oppression caused by the patriarchal church aligned with French monarchists. But these effects of Thérèse's physical and cultural enclosure do not cancel, for me, the benefits of Thérèse's life as a resource for Christian feminist spirituality.

One great benefit of Thérèse's spirituality is its confirmation of the truth that psychological enlargement results from the experience of mutuality, despite its cultural limitations in Thérèse's case. In other words, it is clear that mutuality increases her vitality; it enlarges her ability to act within relationships as well as beyond them; it increases her knowledge of herself and others; it strengthens her self-worth and deepens her desire for more connections beyond her immediate interaction.[50] This ability to make and sustain relationships characterized by mutuality is fundamental to Thérèse and to Christian feminist spirituality.

NOTES

1. This phrase is a theme in Elisabeth Schüssler Fiorenza, *In Memory of Her* (New York: Crossroad, 1983).
2. For a detailed account of Thérèse's life and culture see Guy Gaucher, *The Story of a Life*. For an original and provocative biography see Monica Furlong, *Thérèse of Lisieux* (New York: Virago/Pantheon Pioneers, 1987) and my review of Furlong in *Spiritual Life* 34 (Summer 1988):116–118.
3. Sandra Harding, "The Instability of the Analytical Categories of Feminist Theory," *Signs* 11 (Summer 1986):645–664.
4. Joann Wolski Conn, ed. *Women's Spirituality* (New York: Paulist, 1986).
5. Karl Rahner, *The Christian Commitment* (New York: Sheed and Ward, 1963). See also George Vandervelde, "The Grammar of Grace: Karl Rahner as a Watershed in Contemporary Theology." *Theological Studies* 49 (September 1988):445–459.
6. Joann Wolski Conn, "Spirituality and Human Maturity," in R. Wicks, R. Parsons, and D. Capps eds. *Clinical Handbook of Pastoral Counseling* (New York: Paulist, 1985).
7. Robert Kegan, *The Evolving Self* (Cambridge, MA: Harvard, 1982). My reasons for preferring Kegan to Carol Gilligan, *In a Different Voice* (Cambridge, MA: Harvard, 1982) are explained in Joann Wolski Conn, *Spirituality and Personal Maturity* (New York: Paulist, 1989).
8. Patricia O'Connor, *In Search of Thérèse* (Wilmington, DE: Michael Glazier, 1987).
9. See S. (*Story of a Soul*)
10. See L1 and L2. (*Letters*. Volumes 1 and 2.)
11. Joann Wolski Conn, "Review of *St Thérèse of Lisieux, Her Last Conversations*," *Horizons* 6 (Fall 1979):308–309.
12. *Thérèse de Lisieux: Dialogue entre René Laurentin et Jean-François Six* (Paris: Beauchesne, 1973).
13. Joann Wolski Conn, "Thérèse of Lisieux from a Feminist Perspective," *Spiritual Life* 28/4 (Winter 1982):233–239.
14. Bernard Lonergan, *Method in Theology* (New York: Herder & Herder, 1972).

15. Joann Wolski Conn, "Conversion in Thérèse of Lisieux," *Spiritual Life* 24 (Fall 1978):154–163.

16. S, 97–99.

17. Ibid., 97.

18. Ibid.

19. Jean-François Six, *La Véritable Enfance de Thérèse de Lisieux* (Paris: Éditions du Seuil, 1972), 218.

20. *Dialogue entre René Laurentin et Jean-François Six,* 85–86.

21. LT 201, Thérèse to P. Roulland, 1 Nov. 1896, L2:1016–17.

22. "Thérèse from a Feminist Perspective."

23. Ibid.

24. LT 142, Thérèse to Céline, 6 July 1893, L2:796. See note 17 to this letter for an example of Thérèse's mature self-sacrifice regarding this practice.

25. LT 191, Thérèse to Léonie, 12 July 1896, L2:965–67.

26. Jean-François Six, *Thérèse de Lisieux au Carmel* (Paris, Éditions du Seuil, 1973).

27. LT 191, Thérèse to Léonie, 12 July 1896, L2:966.

28. S, 192.

29. S, 250.

30. S, 224.

31. S, 208.

32. S, 219–220.

33. S, 236.

34. LT 90, Thérèse to Mo. Marie de Gonzague, 29 June 1896, L2:958–62.

35. S, 193–194.

36. Constance FitzGerald, O.C.D., "Contemplative Life as Charismatic Presence," *Spiritual Life* 29/1 (Spring 1983):25–26.

37. Ibid., 28.

38. S, 211–214.

39. S, 214.

40. S, 211.

41. S, 99.

42. Six, *Thérèse au Carmel,* 251. See also Jean-François Six, *Thérèse de Lisieux et les incroyants,* Les Nouvelles de l'Institut Catholique de Paris, Numéro Spécial-Mai, 1973: 156–59.

43. S, 212.

44. S, 150.

45. S, 212.

46. Sebastian Moore, *The Inner Loneliness* (New York: Crossroad, 1982).

47. S, 189.

48. LT 191, Thérèse to Léonie, 12 July 1896, L2:966.

49. On the cultural interpretation of Thérèse, see Barbara Corrado Pope, "A Heroine Without Heroics: The Little Flower of Jesus and Her Times," *Church History* 57 (March 1988):46–60.

50. These effects of mutuality are developed by Jean Baker Miller, "What Do We Mean By Relationships?" *Work in Progress, No. 22* (Wellesley, MA: Stone Center Working Paper Series, 1986).

Contributors

ANNE CARR, professor of theology at the University of Chicago Divinity School, is the author of *Transforming Grace: Christian Tradition and Women's Experience.*

JOANN WOLSKI CONN, professor of religious studies at the Neumann College Graduate Program in Pastoral Counseling and Spiritual Direction, is the author of *Spirituality and Personal Maturity.*

LUISE EICHENBAUM is co-director of The Women's Therapy Centre Institute in New York and co-founder of The Women's Therapy Centre in London.

ELISABETH SCHÜSSLER FIORENZA, Krister Stendahl Professor of Scripture and Interpretation at Harvard University Divinity School, is the author of *Jesus: Miriam's Child, Sophia's Prophet.*

KATHLEEN FISCHER, teacher and counselor, is the author of *Women at the Well: Feminist Perspectives on Spiritual Direction in Our Time.*

CONSTANCE FITZGERALD, contemplative nun in the Carmelite Monastery of Baltimore and author of many articles on contemporary spirituality, is a member of the Carmelite Forum: scholars who teach the texts of the Carmelite mystical tradition.

JAMES FOWLER, professor of theology and human development at Emory University, is the author of *Stages of Faith.*

CAROL GILLIGAN, professor at the Harvard Graduate School of Education, is the author of *In a Different Voice: Psychological Theory and Women's Development.*

ROSEMARY HAUGHTON, lecturer and author of many books on religious experience, presented the essay included here at the Catholic Theological Society of America seminar on spirituality.

IGNATIUS LOYOLA (1491–1556), mystic and religious reformer, founded the Society of Jesus.

JANE DE CHANTAL (1572–1641), wife, mother and contemplative nun, co-founded the Visitation of Holy Mary with her friend Francis de Sales.

JESUIT GENERAL CONGREGATION 34 is the highest lawmaking body in the Society of Jesus.

JOHN OF THE CROSS (1542–1591), mystic and one of the greatest Spanish poets, also wrote commentaries on his poetic texts such as *The Spiritual Canticle* and *Dark Night of the Soul.*

ELIZABETH A. JOHNSON, professor of theology at Fordham University, is the author of *She Who Is: The Mystery of God in Feminist Theological Discourse.*

ROBERT KEGAN, senior lecturer at the Harvard Graduate School of Education and senior faculty at the Massachusetts School of Professional Psychology, is the author of *In Over Our Heads: The Mental Demands of Modern Life.*

ELIZABETH LIEBERT, professor of spiritual life at San Francisco Theological Seminary, is the author of *Changing Life Patterns: Adult Development in Spiritual Direction.*

JOHN McDARGH, associate professor of theology at Boston College, is the author of *Psychoanalytic Object Relations Theory and the Study of Religion: On Faith and the Imaging of God.*

JEAN BAKER MILLER, psychiatrist and director of The Stone Center for Developmental Services and Studies, Wellesley College, is the author of *Toward a New Psychology of Women.*

SUSIE ORBACH is co-director of The Women's Therapy Centre Institute in New York and co-founder of The Women's Therapy Centre in London.

SANDRA M. SCHNEIDERS, professor of New Testament and spirituality at the Jesuit School of Theology and the Graduate Theological Union, Berkeley, California, is the author of *Beyond Patching: Faith and Feminism in the Catholic Church.*

TERESA OF AVILA (1515–1582), mystic and religious reformer, is a Doctor of the Church.

ELISABETH TETLOW, former teacher of biblical and women's studies at Loyola University and director of the *Spiritual Exercises* at several Jesuit Spirituality Centers, is the translator of *The Spiritual Exercises of St. Ignatius Loyola.*

MARY JO WEAVER, professor of religious studies at Indiana University, Bloomington, is the author of *New Catholic Women.*

ROWAN WILLIAMS, formerly Lady Margaret Professor of Divinity at Oxford and now Bishop of Monmouth, Wales, is the author of *The Wound of Knowledge: Christian Spirituality from the New Testament to John of the Cross.*

WENDY M. WRIGHT, professor of church history and spirituality at Creighton University, is the author of *Francis de Sales: A Contemporary Reading.*